Anti-Inflammatory
Diet Cookbook

1800+ Easy & Flavorful Everyday Recipes, 60-Day Meal Plans to Soothe Your Immune System and Balance Your Body

Veronica Smith

CONTENTS

INTRODUCTION 9

What Is the Anti-Inflammatory Diet? 10

Basic principals of the anti-inflammatory diet 11
How to Start an Anti-inflammatory Diet? 12
Anti-inflammatory diet tips 13
Five Types of Anti-Inflammatory Foods to Eat 14

Measurement Conversions 15

Breakfast and Brunch 17

Breakfast Pudding With Chia 18
Almond Yogurt With Berries & Walnuts 18
Cherry & Cashew Pudding 18
Scrambled Tofu With Bell Pepper 18
Tropical French Toasts 18
Egg Tart With Cheesy Yellow Sauce Or Cauliflower
Alfredo 19
Chocolate & Carrot Bread With Raisins 19
Nutritious Chia And Berry Breakfast 19
Sweet Potato, Tomato, & Onion Frittata 19
Banana & Pumpkin Smoothie 19
Ginger Banana Smoothie 20
Strawberry & Pecan Breakfast 20
Healthy And Tasty Vanilla Crepes 20
Vanilla & Chia Yogurt With Berries 20
Satisfying Eggs Benny 20
Spicy Quinoa Bowl With Black Beans 21
Coconut Oat Bread 21
Chocolate-blueberry Smoothie 21
Veggie Panini 21
Breakfast Ground Beef Skillet 21
Sweet Kiwi Oatmeal Bars 21
Hazelnut & Raspberry Quinoa 22
Sweet Potato-kale Egg Casserole 22
Smoked Salmon And Cucumber Wrap With Lettuce 22
Terrific Pancakes With Coconut And Banana 22
Morning Green Smoothie 22
Appetizing Crepes With Berries 23
Cherry & Coconut Oatmeal With Chia 23
Thyme Cremini Oats 23
Blackberry Waffles 23
Coconut Blueberry Muffins 23
Fiery Quinoa 24
Mushroom Crepes 24
Omelette With Smoky Shrimp 24
Giant Coconut Pancake 24
Baked Berry Millet With Applesauce 24
Blueberry Chia Pudding 25
Cherry Quinoa 25
Hearty Smoothie 25
Pecan & Pumpkin Seed Oat Jars 25
Orange-glazed Raspberry Muffins 25
Pumpkin Cake With Pistachios 25
Almond Oats With Cherries 26
Morning Pecan & Pear Farro 26
Berry, Walnut & Almond Yogurt Parfait 26
Cherry & Chocolate Oatmeal 26
Sautéed Cherry Tomatoes With Scrambled Herb 26
Cinnamon Apple Muesli 26
Cinnamon Buckwheat With Almonds 27
No-bread Avocado Sandwich 27
Matcha Smoothie With Berries 27
Maple Coconut Pancakes 27
Classic Walnut Waffles With Maple Syrup 27
Fantastic Fruit Cereal 27
Cold Oatmeal With Apple And Cinnamon 27
Granola Dish With Buckwheat, Berries, Apples,
Pumpkin Seeds And Sunflower Seeds 28
Coconut Fruit Smoothie 28
Cranberry Oat Cookies 28
Flaxseed & Fig Smoothie 28
Almond Waffles 28
Simple Apple Muffins 29
Cauliflower Bowl With Avocado And Kale 29
Breakfast Naan Bread 29
Coconut Porridge With Strawberries 29
Dilly Vegetable Quinoa 29
Choco-berry Smoothie 29
Sweet Orange Crepes 30
Scotch Eggs With Pork Sausage And Hemp Seeds 30
Orange-bran Cups With Dates 30
Green Banana Smoothie 30

Vegetarian Mains 31

Vegetarian Spaghetti Bolognese 32
Cheesy Cauliflower Casserole 32
Scrumptious Lentils With Tomatoes And Turmeric ... 32
Pressure Cooked Ratatouille................................. 32
Chickpea & Bean Patties...................................... 32
Full Of Flavour Braised Bok Choy With Shiitake
Mushrooms 33
Festive Pesto-mushroom Burgers 33
Hot Lentil Tacos With Guacamole 33
Balanced Sweet Potatoes And Buckwheat.............. 33
Bean & Spinach Casserole................................... 34
Sneaky Fiery Veggie Burgers 34
Versatile Zucchini Patties 34
Lovely Spring Roll Wraps With Vegetable 34
Zucchini & Chickpea Casserole............................. 34
Marinated Tempah And Spaghetti Squash 35
Veggie Burger Patties.. 35
Hot And Spicy Scrambled Tofu And Spinach............ 35
Stuffed Zucchini Rolls With Tempeh & Tofu.............. 35
Cucumber & Carrot Pizza With Pesto 35
Appetizing Casserole With Broccoli And Bean 36
Soft Zucchini With White Beans And Olives Stuffing 36
Grilled Tempeh With Green Beans 36
American-style Tempeh With Garden Peas.............. 36
Savoy Cabbage Rolls With Tofu 37
Spicy Moong Beans... 37
Quinoa & Chickpea Pot 37
Bean Gyros.. 37
Watercress & Mushroom Spaghetti....................... 37
Meatless Shepherd's Pie 38
Celery & Turmeric Lentils 38
Amazing Toasted Cumin Crunch 38
Black Olive & Chickpea Lunch 38
Bell Pepper & Tempeh Balls With Asparagus........... 39
Colourful Roasted Cauliflower 39
Oat & Chickpea Patties With Avocado Dip.............. 39

Luxurious Creamy Carrot Marinara With Brown Rice
Pasta 39
Teriyaki Vegetable Stir-fry.................................... 39
Seitan & Lentil Chili 40
Challenging Grain-free Fritters 40
Saucy Seitan With Sesame Seeds........................ 40
Baked Mustard Beans 40
Spicy Black Bean.. 40
Sweet Potato Chili 41
Frittata With Kale & Seeds 41
Delicious Creamy Polenta With Buckwheat And
Vegetable.. 41
Mushroom & Green Bean Biryani........................... 41
Pea & Basil Fettuccine 41
Quinoa A La Puttanesca 42
Hot Quinoa Florentine 42
Hot Coconut Beans With Vegetables 42
Vegan Sloppy Joes.. 42
Mediterranean Chickpeas With Vegetables............. 42
Hot Seitan With Rice 43
Tofu Caprese Casserole 43
Ultimate Burger With Hummus 43
Spinach & Cheese Sauté 43
Tempeh Garam Masala Bake................................ 43
Cashew & Chickpea Curry 44
Tofu Cabbage Stir-fry... 44
Habanero Pinto Bean & Bell Pepper Pot................. 44
Energy Boosting Bright Red Lentil Stew.................. 44
Health Supportive Vegetable Curry 44
Herby Quinoa With Walnuts 44
Soft Vegetarian Tacos... 45
Vegetarian Sloppy Joes....................................... 45
Baked Tofu With Roasted Peppers........................ 45
Chipotle Kidney Bean Chili................................... 45
Traditional Buckwheat Noodle Pad Thai.................. 46
Tomato & Alfredo Penne 46
Awesome Barley Jambalaya 46

Salads.. 47

Traditional Middle Eastern Chopped Salad 48
Light And Excellent Salad With Mango And Avocado 48
Impressive Super Salad With Beetroot And Mackerel
48
Bean & Roasted Parsnip Salad 48
Broccoli Salad With Tempeh & Cranberries 48
Radish & Fennel Salad With Eggs 49
Radish & Cabbage Ginger Salad 49
Carrot & Cabbage Salad With Avocado 49

Cucumber, Lettuce & Tomato Salad 49
Lettuce & Tomato Salad With Quinoa..................... 49
Effortless Half-sour Pickled Salad 49
Spinach Salad With Blackberries & Pecans............. 50
Mediterranean Pasta Salad 50
Refreshingly Spicy Chicken Salad With Cumin And
Mango.. 50
Out Of This World Salad With Basil And Tomato...... 50
Ready To Eat Taco Salad 50

Mushroom And Green Bean Salad 51
Hot Chickpea Salad 51
Tender Chicken Salad 51
Beetroot Salad With Mackerel 51
Chinese-style Cabbage Salad 51
High-spirited Salmon Salad 52
Porky Salad With Spinach 52
Gratifying Healthy Sweet Potato Salad With Mustard
And Tarragon 52
Apple & Arugula Salad With Walnuts 52
Tomato Bean & Bulgur Salad 52
Coleslaw & Spinach Salad With Grapefruit 52
Low In Calories Salad With Artichoke And Almond ..53
Cowboy Salad 53
Balanced Salad With Avocado And Grapefruit 53
Radish & Tomato Salad 53
Oily Salad With Celery And Kipper 53
Quick Insalata Caprese 54
Pantry Salad With White Bean And Tuna 54
Lemony Spinach Salad 54
Broccoli & Mango Rice Salad 54
Luscious Salad Niçoise 54
Sweet Potato & Kale Salad With Pine Nuts 55
Italian Vegetable Relish 55
Warm Cod & Zucchini Salad 55
Fruity Salad With Spinach, Orange, And Cranberry . 55
Spinach & Pomegranate Salad 55
Minty Eggplant Salad 55
Colorful Salad 56
Zucchini & Bell Pepper Salad With Beans 56

Tropical Salad 56
Ruby Salad With Avocado Dressing 56
Avocado Salad With Mango & Almonds 56
Beet Tofu Salad 56
Tempting Salad With Celery, Beet, And Sliced Apple 57
Cashew & Raisin Salad 57
Pleasant And Tender Salad With Kale 57
Hazelnut & Pear Salad 57
Maple Walnut & Pear Salad 57
Enticing Japanese Salad With Avocado And Shrimp 57
Arugula Salad With Salmon 58
Beet Slaw With Apples 58
Fragrant Coconut Fruit Salad 58
Radicchio & Cabbage Coleslaw 58
Carrot Salad With Cherries & Pecans 58
Marinated Chicken Salad With Turmeric 59
Summer Time Sizzling Green Salad With Salmon ...59
Summer Salad 59
African Zucchini Salad 59
Mango Rice Salad With Lime Dressing 59
Daikon Salad With Caramelized Onion 60
Asparagus & Pasta Salad 60
Irresistible Pear And Walnut Salad 60
Orange & Kale Salad 60
Quick Fresh Salad 60
Yummy Salad With Sweet Potato And Salmon 60
Mushroom & Wild Rice Salad 60
Diverse Salad With Shredded Root Vegetable 61
Bean & Farro Salad 61
Crunchylicious Colourful Asian Salad 61

Fish and Seafood 62

Tarragon Scallops 63
Wild Salmon With Toasted Coconut 63
Baked Tilapia With Chili Kale 63
Saucy Tropical Halibut 63
Baked Garlicky Halibut With Lemon 63
Sheet Pan Baked Salmon With Asparagus 64
Japanese Salmon Cakes 64
Golden, Crispy, Buttery Pan-seared Cod 64
Fresh, Delicate And Meaty Tuna Steak With Fennel
Salad 64
Smoky Boneless Haddock With Pea Risotto 64
Avocado & Tuna Toast 65
Pan-seared Salmon Au Pistou 65
Mushroom & Olive Cod Fillets 65
Pineapple Mahi-mahi 65
Seared Salmon With Gremolata 65
Extraordinary Scallops With Lime And Cilantro 66

Yummy Fish Curry 66
Gingery Swordfish Kabobs 66
Minimalist Chowder With Whitefish 66
Halibut Al Ajillo 66
Flavourful Shrimp And Grits..................................67
Old Bay Crab Cakes 67
Southern Trout With Crusty Pecan 67
Hawaiian Tuna 67
Battered Bite Size Shrimp With Gluten-free
Coconut 68
Glazed And Curried Salmon With Quinoa 68
Wonderful Baked Sea Bass With Tomatoes, Olives,
And Capers 68
Shrimp & Egg Risotto 68
Trout Fillets With Almond Crust 68
Cumin Salmon With Daikon Relish 69
Hot Shrimp Paella 69

Lime Salmon Burgers 69
Olive & Salmon Quinoa 69
Tasty Sardine Donburi 69
Love At First Bite Shrimp Linguine 70
Cod In Tomato Sauce 70
Beautifully Glazed Salmon With Honey Mustard 70
Elegant Sesame Tuna With Asparagus 70
Simple Tacos With Fish And Pineapple Salsa 71
Mediterranean Trout 71
Dense Oven Roasted Cod And Shiitake
Mushrooms 71
Seared Trout With Greek Yogurt Sauce 71
Salmon & Asparagus Parcels 71
Fried Haddock With Roasted Beets 72
Spicy Shrimp Scampi 72
Shanghai Cod With Udon Noodles 72
Unforgettable Tasty Calamari 72
Greek-style Sea Bass 73
Parsnip & Tilapia Bake 73
Fish Stew 73
Beneficial Baked Salmon Patties With Vegetables... 73
Creamy Crabmeat 74
Asian-inspired Salmon 74

Fancy Cod Stew With Cauliflower 74
Aromatic Curried Whitefish 74
A Must-try Spicy Sea Bass Fillets With Ginger 74
Sardine & Butter Bean Meal 75
Briny Flavoured Herbed Tuna Cakes 75
Rich Grandma's Salmon Chowder 75
Satisfying Peperonata With Seared Ahi Tuna 75
Fennel & Shallot Salmon Casserole 75
One-skillet Shrimp With Sriracha Pak Choy 75
Tuna & Pea Cheesy Noodles 76
Mango Halibut Curry 76
Mustardy Salmon Patties 76
Lemony Spanish Shrimp With Parsley 76
Autenthic Salmon Ceviche 76
Crispy Coconut Prawns 77
Lobster & Parmesan Pasta 77
Rosemary Salmon With Orange Glaze 77
Chipotle Trout With Spinach 77
Tropical-style Cod 77
Skinless Salmon And Arugula With Lime 77
Chard Trout Fillets 78
Baked Swordfish With Cilantro And Pineapple 78

Poultry and Meats 79

Classic And Minty Lamb Burgers 80
Pecan-dusted Pork Tenderloin Slices 80
Holiday Turkey 80
Remarkable Korean Beef Wrapped In Lettuce 80
Cumin Lamb Meatballs With Aioli 80
Baked Basil Chicken 81
Harissa Chicken Drumsticks 81
Mexican-style Chicken With Butternut Squash 81
Marvellous Chocolate Chili 81
Chicken A La Tuscana 81
Basic Poached Wrapped Chicken 82
Cherry Tomato & Basil Chicken Casserole 82
Korean Chicken Thighs 82
Fruity Chicken Breast With Cherry Sauce 82
Creamy Beef Tenderloin Marsala 82
A Fresh Lean Beef Burger That You Can Truly
Enjoy 83
Awesome Herbaceous Roasted Chuck And Scrummy
Vegetable 83
Hawaiian-style Turkey Burgers 83
Dairy Free Chicken Alfredo 83
Sunday Pork Tacos 84
Thyme Pork Loin Bake 84
Worcestershire Pork Chops 84

Lamb Shanks Braised Under Pressure 84
Korean Vegetable Salad With Smoky Crispy Kalua
Pork 84
Creamy Turkey With Mushrooms 85
Cute Tiny Chicken Burgers 85
Hot & Spicy Beef Chili 85
Homemade Chicken & Pepper Cacciatore 85
Chicken Stir-fry With Bell Pepper 86
Mexican-style Chicken 86
Sloppy Joes & Coleslaw 86
Mustardy Beef Steaks 86
Homemade Pizza With Lean Meat, Jalapeno, And
Tapioca Starch 86
Grilled Chicken Sandwiches 87
Italian Turkey Meatballs 87
Mustard Pork Chops With Collard Greens 87
Tempting And Tender Beef Brisket 87
Simple Cooked Whole Chicken 87
Appealing Hot Turkey 88
The Best General Tso's Chicken 88
Baked Turkey Meatballs 88
Tangy Beef Ribs 88
Spicy Lime Pork Tenderloins 88
Smoky Lamb Souvlaki 89

Chicken Piccata 89
Aromatic Turkey With Mushrooms 89
Delightful Stuffed Lamb With Peppers 89
Slow Cooker Chicken Curry 89
Chopped Lambs With Rosemary 90
Hot & Spicy Shredded Chicken 90
Paleo Turkey Thighs With Mushroom 90
Lemon & Caper Turkey Scaloppine 90
Cinnamon Pork Chops In Apple Sauce 90
Nutritious Apricot And Zucchini Mash With Lamb
Shoulder 91
Classic Pork Chops And Creamy Green Beans 91
Scallion & Broccoli Chicken Sauté 91
Spicy Beef Fajitas 91

Enjoyable Braised Turkey Legs And Wilted Greens .92
Italian Spinach Chicken 92
Lettuce-wrapped Beef Roast 92
Turkey Stuffed Bell Peppers 92
Authentic Chicken Curry With Coconut 92
Incredible Tacos With Pork 93
Rosemary Pork Loin 93
Miso Chicken With Sesame 93
Cheap Pork Sausage 93
Turmeric Chicken & Chickpea Stew 93
Magnificent Herbaceous Pork Meatballs 94
Herby Green Whole Chicken 94
Veggie & Beef Brisket 94

Soups and Stews 95

Spicy Beef & Sweet Potato Soup 96
Carrot & Mushroom Broth 96
Black-eyed Pea Soup 96
Brussels Sprouts & Tofu Soup 96
Kale & Cabbage Stew 96
Rosemary White Bean Soup 97
Indian Curried Stew With Lentil And Spinach 97
Tomato Lentil Dahl 97
Arugula Coconut Soup 97
Power Green Cream Soup 97
Distinctive Thai Soup With Potato 98
Beef-farro Stew 98
Healthy Soup With Turmeric And Broccoli 98
Soulful Roasted Vegetable Soup 98
Easy Thai Pork Stew 98
Basil Coconut Soup 99
Vegetable & Rice Soup 99
Shiitake Mushroom Soup 99
Coconut Butternut Squash Soup 99
Dairy-free Split Pea Soup 99
Creamy Soup With Broccoli 99
Broccoli Cream Soup With Peanuts 100
Shallot Lentil Soup With Walnuts 100
Chickpea & Vegetable Soup 100
Vegetable Bean Soup 100
Daikon & Sweet Potato Soup 101
Broccoli Fennel Soup 101
Spinach & Kale Soup With Fried Collards 101
Yummy Spiced Soup With Almond And Sweet Potato
101
Classy Soup With Carrot And Ginger 101
Spinach, Rice & Bean Soup 102
Dairy-free Rice Soup With Mushrooms 102

Vegetable & Black Bean Soup 102
Chicken & Ginger Soup 102
Spinach Soup With Gnocchi 102
Spinach & Mushroom Soup 103
Special Miso Soup 103
Celery & Sweet Potato Soup 103
Italian Bean Soup 103
Green Bean & Zucchini Velouté 103
Beef Stew With Sweet Potato Noodles 103
Mushroom & Bean Stew 104
Cold Cantaloupe Soup 104
Habanero Bean Soup With Brown Rice 104
Cannellini Bean Soup 104
Parsley Tomato Soup 104
Sweet French Onion Soup With White Bean 105
Gingery Soup With Carrots & Celery 105
Chili Gazpacho 105
Mixed Mushroom Soup 105
Fennel & Parsnip Bisque 105
Tofu Miso Soup 106
Homemade Succotash Stew 106
Mushroom & Tofu Soup 106
Vegetable Soup With Vermicelli 106
Green Chili Bean Stew 106
Gingered Broccoli Soup 106
Cauliflower Dill Soup 107
Hearty Stew With Kasha And Squash 107
Spanish Gazpacho 107
Tomato Lentil Stew 107
Vegetable Chili 107
Lime Pumpkin Soup 108
Chipotle Pumpkin Soup 108
Kabocha Squash Soup 108

Beef & Mushroom Rice Soup 108
One-pot Chunky Beef Stew 108
Super Simple Stew With Mango And Black Bean ... 108
Minestrone Soup With Quinoa................................ 109
Chili Cannellini Bean Stew 109
Lime Lentil Soup.. 109
Easy Sweet Potato Soup....................................... 100
Sharp-tasting Soup With Rice And Sweet Potato.... 110
Spicy Gazpacho 110
Beef & Tomato Chili 110
Cold Soup With Coconut And Avocado 110
Lentil Soup... 110
Cayenne Pumpkin Soup 111
Proteinaceous Noodle Bowl With Vegetable 111
Rotini & Tomato Soup.. 111
Soothing Broth With Mushrooms 111
Gluten-free Tortellini Minestrone Soup 111
Tomato Chicken Soup 112

Coconut Artichoke Soup With Almonds 112
Yellow Soup With Lentils 112
Low Maintenance Vegan Minestrone With Herb Oil 112
Classic Minestrone Soup.. 113
Turnip & Rutabaga Soup 113
Curry Soup With Butternut Squash And Coconut.... 113
Ruotic Lamb Stew.. 113
Sudanese Veggie Stew 113
Comfortable Chicken Soup..................................... 113
Veggie Thai Curry Soup 114
Ginger Squash Soup 114
Easy To Make Egg Drop Soup 114
Homemade Warm And Chunky Chicken Soup........ 114
Green Bean & Rice Soup 115
Native Asian Soup With Squash And Shitake......... 115
Spicy Thai Soup 115
Mediterranean Soup... 115

Sauces, Condiments, and Dressings 116

Buttery Slow Cooked Ghee 117
Verde Chimichurri With Parsley.............................. 117
Satisfying And Thick Dressing With Avocado 117
Fantastic On Hand Marinara Sauce 117
Excellent Tapenade With Green Olive..................... 117
Feels Like Summer Chutney With Mint 117
Decadent And Simple Alfredo With Cauliflower....... 118
Herbaceous Spread With Avocado......................... 118
Colourful And Sweet Spread With Carrot 118
Great On Everything Ginger Sauce........................ 118

Herbaceous Dressing With Creamy Coconut.......... 118
Vegan Sauce With Honey, Mustard, And Sesame .. 118
Lemony Honey With Ginger 119
Creamy Dressing With Sesame 119
Awesome Multi-purpose Cream Sauce 119
Goddess And Vibrant Green Dressing 119
To Die For Homemade Mayonnaise 119
French Pistou 119
Full Of Spice And Zesty Rub 120
Gluten Free Apple Chutney 120

Smoothies 121

Delicate Smoothie With Green Tea And Pear.......... 122
Combating Gingery Milkshake With Blackberry 122
Pain Reliever Smoothie 122
Cheery Cherry Smoothie 122
Nut-free Green Smoothie Bowl............................... 122
Tropical Strong Green Smoothie 122
Southern Smoothie With Sweet Potato 123
Delectable Multivitamin Smoothie 123
Stomach Soothing Smoothie With Green Apple...... 123
Smoothie That Can Soothe Inflammation................ 123
For Advanced Green Juice 123

For Beginners Juice With Granny Smith Apples...... 123
Fresh Berry Smoothie With Ginger......................... 123
Crunchy And Creamy Pistachio Smoothie.............. 124
Delicious Proteinaceous Smoothie......................... 124
Delightful Smoothie With Apple And Honey............ 124
Minty Juice With Pineapple And Cucumber............ 124
Vegetarian Mango Smoothie With Green Tea And
Turmeric 124
Distinctive Chai Smoothie...................................... 124
Great Watermelon Smoothie 124

Desserts 125

Coconut Chocolate Barks....................................... 126
Easiest Pressure-cooked Raspberry Curd 126
Great Pudding With Chocolate And Avocado 126
Vanilla Berry Tarts... 126
Peanut Chocolate Brownies 126

Almond & Chia Bites With Cherries 127
Cinnamon Pumpkin Pie 127
Lime Avocado Ic E Cream 127
Berry Macedonia With Mint 127
Apple & Cashew Quiche... 127

Apple & Berry Parfait 127
Delectable Honeyed Apple Cinnamon Compote 128
Wonderful Whipped Goat Cheese With Dark Berries. 128
Melon Chocolate Pudding 128
Vanilla Chocolate Pudding........................ 128
Compote With Blueberries & Lemon Juice.............. 128
Sweet And Special Spiced Pecans....................... 128
Apple-cinnamon Compote 129
Chocolate Fudge With Nuts........................ 129
Wound Healer Warm Almond Milk With Cinnamon And
Turmeric 129
Elegant Panna Cotta With Honey And Blackberry-lime
Sauce 129
Lemony Lavender With Strawberry Compote.......... 129
Mango Muffins With Chocolate Chips 130
Non-dairy Butter Mousse With Chocolate And
Almond 130
Delicious Nutmeg Muffins With Vanilla And
Blueberries 130
Oatmeal Cookies With Hazelnuts..................... 130
Cashew & Plum Cheesecake 130
Hazelnut Topped Caramelized Bananas 131
Walnut Pears With Maple Glaze....................... 131
Nutty Date Cake 131
Fruitylicious Hot Milk.................................. 131
Almond Berry Cream 131
Perfect Thickness Blueberry Ambrosia................. 131
Coconut & Chocolate Brownies........................ 131
A Different Pumpkin Pie.............................. 132
Pressure Cooker Apple Cupcakes..................... 132
Southern Apple Cobbler With Raspberries............. 132
Almond & Chocolate Cookies......................... 132
Pistachios & Chocolate Popsicles 132
Chocolate Peppermint Mousse 133
Walnut Chocolate Squares 133
Hearty Gelato With Chocolate And Cinnamon 133
Glazed Chili Chocolate Cake.......................... 133
Macedonia Salad With Coconut & Pecans............. 133
Healthy Brownies With Cacao 134
Raisin Oatmeal Biscuits............................... 134
Tangy Yogurt With Coconut And Vanilla 134

Mid Afternoon Grilled Banana And Homemade Nut
Butter 134
Pressure Cooked Cherry Pie......................... 134
Sherry-lime Mango Dessert.......................... 135
Spiced Supreme Orange 135
Caribbean Pudding.................................. 135
Special Brownies With Chocolate And Coconut 135
Mini Chocolate Fudge Squares 135
Stunning Lemon Cake With Almond, Pistachio, Citrus
Salad, And Coconut Whipped Cream.................... 135
Impressive Parfait With Yogurt, Berry, And Walnut .. 136
Oatmeal Chocolate Cookies.......................... 136
Mango & Coconut Rice Pudding 136
Blueberry Lime Granizado............................ 136
Flavourful Glazed Maple Pears And Hazelnuts 137
Savoury Spiced Pumpkin Pancakes................... 137
Comfort Cobbler With Blueberry And Peach 137
Interesting Snack Bars With Date And Pecan 137
Avocado-chocolate Mousse 137
Friendly Homemade Hot Cross Easter Buns.......... 137
Tasty Haystack Cookies From Missouri................ 138
Cinnamon Tropical Cobbler 138
Honey Pears With Pecans............................ 138
Nightshade Free Cinnamon Pecans................... 138
Blueberry & Almond Greek Yogurt.................... 138
Energy Boosting Thumbprint Cookies With Strawberry
Jam 139
Easy Maple Rice Pudding 139
Vanilla Cranberry & Almond Balls.................... 139
Mixed Berry Yogurt Ice Pops 139
Grain Free And Versatile Fruit Crisp.................. 139
Scrumptious Fruity Dark Chocolate Mousse 139
Balsamic-glazed Caramelized Quinces................ 140
Coconut Peach Tart 140
Summer Banana Pudding 140
Milk Dumplings In Cardamom Sauce 140
Coconut & Chocolate Macaroons..................... 140
Tropical Baked Fruit With Nut Pudding 140
Tofu & Almond Pancakes............................ 141
Poached Pears With Green Tea 141
Chocolate Campanelle With Hazelnuts................ 141

60 Day Meal Plan 142

APPENDIX : Recipes Index 146

I am very excited to announce the release of my third book, The Anti-Inflammatory Cookbook for Beginner, on the shelves. In this book of anti-inflammatory feature, we will explore the effectiveness of anti-inflammatory diet recipes and their potential benefits. It contains 1500+ family friendly and delicious recipes with easy 30 day of healthy meal plans.

It is now known that obesity is the number one risk factor for chronic inflammation, increasing the body's immune response. Other dietary influences include having an unhealthy gut microbiome, consuming excessive amounts of alcohol and eating improperly, especially a diet high in saturated fat. We all know that chronic inflammation is a serious health problem and may increase our risk of several age-related diseases, such as adult asthma, some cancers, heart disease and even Alzheimer's disease.

In fact, when I was young, my grandfather had Alzheimer's due to chronic inflammation. At that time, he had completely lost the ability to take care of himself and had to need the help of his family, and he often even forgot who I was. The good news is diet can play an important role in the management of autoimmune diseases and inflammation, by being a therapeutic tool to help soothe and reduce symptoms. The doctor suggested that we could prepare a more relevant anti-inflammatory diet for him.

In college I studied the applied science of nutrition, combined with a passion for nutrition, healthy eating and food, and also completed a graduate program in human nutrition. After graduating I became a certified nutritionist, health writer and recipe developer.

The recipes in this recipe book use whole, unprocessed foods to provide balanced nutrition and will guide you through understanding and following a simple and complete anti-inflammatory diet that will hopefully help you and your family develop healthy eating habits and make it a way of life. Now, enjoy the delicious recipes together!

What Is the Anti-Inflammatory Diet?

The Anti-inflammatory diet is a way of eating rather than a 'diet'. It aims to increase the foods which have an anti-inflammatory effect, such as omega-3 fatty acids, dietary fibre, polyphenols and antioxidants and reduce those with an inflammatory effect such as processed carbs, sugars and saturated fats.

The anti-inflammatory diet focuses on nutrient-rich foods, healthy fats and plenty of nutritious produce, such as those vegetables and fruits that reduce inflammation: cherries, pomegranates, berries and beets, while limiting processed foods, red meat, added sugars and refined grains (such as white bread and white flour).

Inflammation is part of your body's natural defenses—when a cut swells up and turns red, that's inflammation at work healing you. But when inflammation goes into overdrive, sparked by factors like poor diet and smoking, it can cause a host of health problems including cardiovascular disease, diabetes, arthritis, cancer and even depression. But how can you reduce inflammation in the body?

An anti-inflammatory diet follows some simple principles:

- Eat plenty of vegetables and fruits
- Minimize "bad" fats (saturated and trans fats)
- Include omega-3 fatty acids
- Sharply decrease or eliminate refined flours and sugars
- Increase consumption of whole grains
- Avoid processed foods
- Add spice to combat inflammation

Basic principals of the anti–inflammatory diet

Though the anti-inflammatory diet is not a calorie-restrictive diet, its emphasis on whole, unprocessed foods and reduced sugars and flours may result in weight loss.

The guidelines suggest consuming between 2,000 to 3,000 calories each day—depending on gender and activity level—with men and more active people needing more calories, and women and less active people needing less calories.

The anti-inflammatory diet recommends that 40 to 50 percent of daily calories come from carbohydrates, 30 percent from fat and 20 to 30 percent from protein; with an emphasis on including carbohydrates, fat, and protein in every meal.

- Carbohydrates

Vegetables and fruits should make up most of the carbohydrates consumed daily on the anti-inflammatory diet. Beans and whole grains (not whole wheat flour) can also be consumed to add bulk and satiety in this category.

- Fats

Monounsaturated fats like extra-virgin olive oil, nuts, avocados, and seeds are the healthy fats to be enjoyed on the anti-inflammatory diet.

- Proteins

An emphasis on plant-based and lean protein is recommended on the anti-inflammatory diet. Beans, particularly soybeans and whole soy products, and fish, especially fish high in omega-3 fatty acids, are recommended. Limit animal protein and avoid red meat.

In addition, the anti-inflammatory diet suggests that the timing of your meals is important. So I recommend that calories be consumed within an 11-hour window, leaving 13 hours overnight as a "fasting period." this fasting period provides time for the body to recalibrate immunity, repair cells, and replenish its capacity for antioxidants.

How to Start an Anti-inflammatory Diet?

The foods you eat (and the ones you avoid) can help soothe and even prevent inflammation by quashing your body's inflammatory responses. But because everyone's inflammatory triggers are different, there's no one-size-fits-all anti-inflammatory diet.

Primary goals for the anti-inflammatory diet kick start:

• Nourish your body and mind;

• Slow down and enjoy eating real food;

• Learn what foods help you feel your best;

• Find your favorite go-to recipes that can help reduce your inflammation;

Reset your mind and find your why –> Ask yourself… What are my intentions for my health?

The term 'anti-inflammatory diet' doesn't refer to a specific diet regimen but to an overall style of eating. There are, however, some guidelines to follow to eat in a way that reduces the likelihood of inflammation.

1. Scale way back on processed foods

The first key to minimizing inflammation is cutting foods that cause it. An anti-inflammatory diet is one that includes minimally processed foods, that typically means staying away from anything that comes in a box or a bag, or anything that has a laundry list of ingredients — especially if they start with sugar, salt or a processed oil and include ingredients you don't recognize.

Examples include:

• Sweets, like commercial baked goods, pre-packaged desserts.

• Processed meats, including bacon, sausage, hot dogs, bologna, pepperoni and salami.

• Processed cheeses, like nacho cheese dip and American cheese slices.

• Sugary beverages, including soda and sports drinks.

• Fried foods, like fried chicken and French fries.

2. Focus on whole foods and "GREEN"

Research suggests that people who eat a lot of vegetables, fruits, nuts, seeds, healthy oils, and fish have a reduced risk for inflammation-related diseases. Substances found in certain foods, especially antioxidants and omega-3 fatty acids, may also have anti-inflammatory effects.

Examples include:

• Apples, Artichokes, Avocados, Cherries, Berries (such as blue-berries, raspberries, and blackberries);

• Broccoli; Sweet potatoes; Dark green leafy vegetables (such as kale, spinach, and collard greens);

• Chicken/turkey breast, Fish (especially oily fish, such as salmon, tuna, herring or mackerel);

• Whole grains(Brown or wild rice); Beans (such as red beans, pinto beans, and black beans);

• Nuts and seeds(such as walnuts, almonds, pecans, and hazel-nuts)

• Dark chocolate (at least 70% cocoa);

and more...

Anti-inflammatory diet tips

It can be challenging to transition to a new way of eating, but the following tips may help:

• Pick up a variety of fruits, vegetables, and healthful snacks during the weekly shop.

• Gradually replace fast food meals with healthful, homemade lunches.

• Replace soda and other sugary beverages with still or sparkling mineral water.

Other tips include:

• Talking to a healthcare professional about supplements, such as cod liver oil or a multivitamin.

• Incorporating 30 minutes of moderate exercise into the daily routine.

• Practicing good sleep hygiene, as poor sleep can worsenTrusted Source inflammation.

Five Types of Anti-Inflammatory Foods to Eat

It is important to look at the overall diet you consume instead of focusing on individual foods. Research indicates that by consistently focusing on a healthy diet pattern, you can reduce inflammation.

- **Vegetables—especially cruciferous vegetables**

Veggies provide nutrients that are vital to fighting inflammation and maintaining proper body function.

These nutrient-rich veggies contain carotenoids, a type of antioxidant, vitamin C, E, K, folate, minerals, and fiber:Cabbage, cauliflower, broccoli, Brussels sprouts, kale, arugula, collard greens, and more.

- **Fibrous foods—especially legumes**

Fiber is key to reducing inflammation. A staple of the Mediterranean and the anti-inflammatory diet, legumes are a category of vegetables that includes beans, peas, and lentils. Legumes provide some of the highest natural sources of fiber found in any food and also provide an excellent source of plant-based protein.

- **Fruit—especially berries**

Fruit is nature's candy, which slows down the metabolic process and stabilizes blood sugar. Of all the beautiful fruits available to us, berries are the star of the show to reduce inflammation. Blueberries, strawberries, blackberries, and raspberries are high in antioxidants and are just a few of the many berries that are suggested as part of an anti-inflammatory diet.

- **Herbs and Spices—especially turmeric, ginger, cinnamon, and garlic**

Often overlooked as a source of nutrition, herbs and spices provide excellent anti-inflammatory properties. In addition to eating a wide variety of veggies and fruits, it is also important to incorporate herbs and spices such as turmeric, garlic, ginger, and cinnamon to help decrease inflammation.

- **Lean protein—especially fish**

In addition to being an excellent source of lean protein, fatty fish is also high in omega-3 fatty acids, which are essential to lowering inflammation. Fatty seafood like salmon, trout, albacore tuna, Atlantic herring, Atlantic mackerel, anchovies, sardines, and even mussels, provide an excellent dietary source of omega-threes and lean protein.

BASIC KITCHEN CONVERSIONS & EQUIVALENTS

DRY MEASUREMENTS CONVERSION CHART

3 TEASPOONS = 1 TABLESPOON = 1/16 CUP

6 TEASPOONS = 2 TABLESPOONS = 1/8 CUP

12 TEASPOONS = 4 TABLESPOONS = 1/4 CUP

24 TEASPOONS = 8 TABLESPOONS = 1/2 CUP

36 TEASPOONS = 12 TABLESPOONS = 3/4 CUP

48 TEASPOONS = 16 TABLESPOONS = 1 CUP

METRIC TO US COOKING CONVERSIONS

OVEN TEMPERATURES

120 °C = 250 °F

160 °C = 320 °F

180° C = 350 °F

205 °C = 400 °F

220 °C = 425 °F

LIQUID MEASUREMENTS CONVERSION CHART

8 FLUID OUNCES = 1 CUP = 1/2 PINT = 1/4 QUART

16 FLUID OUNCES = 2 CUPS = 1 PINT = 1/2 QUART

32 FLUID OUNCES = 4 CUPS = 2 PINTS = 1 QUART = 1/4 GALLON

128 FLUID OUNCES = 16 CUPS = 8 PINTS = 4 QUARTS = 1 GALLON

BAKING IN GRAMS

1 CUP FLOUR = 140 GRAMS

1 CUP SUGAR = 150 GRAMS

1 CUP POWDERED SUGAR = 160 GRAMS

1 CUP HEAVY CREAM = 235 GRAMS

VOLUME

1 MILLILITER = 1/5 TEASPOON

5 ML = 1 TEASPOON

15 ML = 1 TABLESPOON

240 ML = 1 CUP OR 8 FLUID OUNCES

1 LITER = 34 FL. OUNCES

WEIGHT

1 GRAM = .035 OUNCES

100 GRAMS = 3.5 OUNCES

500 GRAMS = 1.1 POUNDS

1 KILOGRAM = 35 OUNCES

US TO METRIC COOKING CONVERSIONS

1/5 TSP = 1 ML

1 TSP = 5 ML

1 TBSP = 15 ML

1 FL OUNCE = 30 ML

1 CUP = 237 ML

1 PINT (2 CUPS) = 473 ML

1 QUART (4 CUPS) = .95 LITER

1 GALLON (16 CUPS) = 3.8 LITERS

1 OZ = 28 GRAMS

1 POUND = 454 GRAMS

BUTTER

1 CUP BUTTER = 2 STICKS = 8 OUNCES = 230 GRAMS = 8 TABLESPOONS

WHAT DOES 1 CUP EQUAL

1 CUP = 8 FLUID OUNCES

1 CUP = 16 TABLESPOONS

1 CUP = 48 TEASPOONS

1 CUP = 1/2 PINT

1 CUP = 1/4 QUART

1 CUP = 1/16 GALLON

1 CUP = 240 ML

BAKING PAN CONVERSIONS

1 CUP ALL-PURPOSE FLOUR = 4.5 OZ

1 CUP ROLLED OATS = 3 OZ 1 LARGE EGG = 1.7 OZ

1 CUP BUTTER = 8 OZ 1 CUP MILK = 8 OZ

1 CUP HEAVY CREAM = 8.4 OZ

1 CUP GRANULATED SUGAR = 7.1 OZ

1 CUP PACKED BROWN SUGAR = 7.75 OZ

1 CUP VEGETABLE OIL = 7.7 OZ

1 CUP UNSIFTED POWDERED SUGAR = 4.4 OZ

BAKING PAN CONVERSIONS

9-INCH ROUND CAKE PAN = 12 CUPS

10-INCH TUBE PAN =16 CUPS

11-INCH BUNDT PAN = 12 CUPS

9-INCH SPRINGFORM PAN = 10 CUPS

9 X 5 INCH LOAF PAN = 8 CUPS

9-INCH SQUARE PAN = 8 CUPS

Breakfast and Brunch

Breakfast and Brunch

Breakfast Pudding With Chia

Servings: 4 | Cooking Time: 0 Minutes

Ingredients:
- ¾ cup chia seeds
- ½ cup hemp seeds
- 2 ¼ cups milk, coconut
- ½ cup cranberries, dried
- ¼ cup maple syrup

Directions:
1. Stir together the chia seeds, hemp seeds, coconut milk, cranberries, and maple syrup in a medium bowl. Ensure that the chia seeds is completely mixed with the milk.
2. Cover the bowl and refrigerate overnight.
3. Stir and serve in the morning.

Nutrition Info:
- Per Serving: Calories: 483 ;Fat: 41g ;Protein: 9g ;Carbs: 25g .

Almond Yogurt With Berries & Walnuts

Servings: 4 | Cooking Time: 10 Minutes

Ingredients:
- 4 cups almond milk
- 2 cups Greek yogurt
- 2 tbsp pure maple syrup
- 2 cups mixed berries
- ¼ cup chopped walnuts

Directions:
1. In a medium bowl, mix the yogurt and maple syrup until well-combined. Divide the mixture into 4 breakfast bowls. Top with the berries and walnuts. Enjoy immediately.

Nutrition Info:
- Per Serving: Calories: 703;Fat: 63g;Protein: 13g;Carbs: 32.1g.

Cherry & Cashew Pudding

Servings: 4 | Cooking Time: 10 Minutes

Ingredients:
- 1 cup fresh raspberries
- 1 cup fresh blueberries
- 2 cups almond milk
- ½ cup chia seeds
- 1 tsp vanilla extract
- ¼ cup pure maple syrup
- ½ cup chopped cashews
- 1 cup pitted cherries, chopped

Directions:
1. Place the almond milk, chia seeds, vanilla, and maple syrup in a mixing bowl. Stir well. Refrigerate overnight. Divide the almond milk mixture between four bowls, then serve with cashews and cherries on top.

Nutrition Info:
- Per Serving: Calories: 270;Fat: 15g;Protein: 6g;Carbs: 38g.

Scrambled Tofu With Bell Pepper

Servings: 4 | Cooking Time: 20 Minutes

Ingredients:
- 2 tbsp olive oil
- 1 firm tofu, crumbled
- 1 red bell pepper, chopped
- 1 green bell pepper, chopped
- 1 tomato, finely chopped
- 2 chopped green onions
- Sea salt and pepper to taste
- 1 tsp turmeric powder
- 1 tsp Creole seasoning
- ½ cup chopped baby kale
- ¼ cup grated Parmesan

Directions:
1. Warm the olive oil in a skillet over medium heat and add the tofu. Cook with occasional stirring until the tofu is light golden brown while making sure not to break the tofu into tiny bits but to have scrambled egg resemblance, 5 minutes. Stir in the bell peppers, tomato, green onions, salt, pepper, turmeric powder, and Creole seasoning. Sauté until the vegetables soften, 5 minutes. Mix in the kale to wilt, 3 minutes and then half of the Parmesan cheese. Allow melting for 1-2 minutes and then turn the heat off. Top with the remaining cheese and serve.

Nutrition Info:
- Per Serving: Calories: 159;Fat: 11g;Protein: 10g;Carbs: 7.1g.

Tropical French Toasts

Servings: 4 | Cooking Time: 55 Minutes

Ingredients:
- 2 eggs
- 1 ½ cups almond milk
- ½ cup almond flour
- 2 tbsp maple syrup
- 2 pinches of sea salt
- ½ tbsp cinnamon powder
- ½ tsp fresh lemon zest
- 1 tbsp fresh pineapple juice
- 8 whole-grain bread slices

Directions:
1. Preheat your oven to 400ºF. Lightly grease a roasting rack with olive oil. Set aside. In a medium bowl, whisk the eggs, then add the almond milk, almond flour, maple syrup, salt, cinnamon powder, lemon zest, and pineapple juice; stir well. Dip the bread in the almond milk mixture and allow sitting on a plate for 2-3 minutes.
2. Heat a large skillet over medium heat and grease with cooking oil. Place the bread in the pan. Cook until golden brown on the bottom side. Flip the bread and cook further until golden brown on the other side, 4 minutes in total. Transfer to a plate, drizzle some maple syrup on top and serve immediately.

Nutrition Info:
- Per Serving: Calories: 511;Fat: 33g;Protein: 14g;Carbs: 41g.

Egg Tart With Cheesy Yellow Sauce Or Cauliflower Alfredo

Servings: 4 | Cooking Time: 20 Minutes

Ingredients:
- 1 cup cheesy yellow sauce or cauliflower alfredo
- 1 baked pie crust
- 4 large eggs
- ¼ teaspoon Himalayan salt, fine
- ¼ teaspoon black pepper, ground
- 4 slices prosciutto di Parma

Directions:
1. On the bottom of the baked pie crust, spread the sauce evenly. Crack the eggs over the sauce and sprinkle with the salt and pepper. Around the eggs, distribute the prosciutto slices. Wrap the edges of the crust in aluminum foil to avoid burning.
2. For 20 minutes, bake until the egg whites are completely set. Gently shaking the pie to watch for a jiggle to test and when it doesn't move, it's done.
3. Remove from the oven and serve hot. Let cool and store in the refrigerator and cover it for 3 days. For 10 minutes, cut into four large slices, cover each slice with foil, and bake in a preheated 300°F oven to reheat.

Nutrition Info:
- Per Serving: Calories: 471 ;Fat: 40.6g ;Protein: 19.1g;Carbs: 9.2g .

Chocolate & Carrot Bread With Raisins

Servings: 4 | Cooking Time: 75 Minutes

Ingredients:
- 1 ½ cup whole-wheat flour
- ¼ cup almond flour
- ¼ tsp sea salt
- ¼ tsp clove powder
- ¼ tsp cayenne pepper
- 1 tbsp cinnamon powder
- ½ tsp nutmeg powder
- 1 ½ tsp baking powder
- 2 eggs
- ½ cup pure date sugar
- ¼ cup pure maple syrup
- ¾ tsp almond extract
- 1 tbsp grated lemon zest
- ½ cup sugar-free applesauce
- ¼ cup olive oil
- 4 carrots, shredded
- 3 tbsp dark chocolate chips
- 2/3 cup black raisins

Directions:
1. Preheat your oven to 375°F and line a loaf tin with baking paper. In a bowl, mix all the flour, salt, cloves powder, cayenne pepper, cinnamon powder, nutmeg powder, and baking powder.
2. In another bowl, whisk the eggs, date sugar, maple syrup, almond extract, lemon zest, applesauce, and olive oil. Combine both mixtures until smooth and fold in the carrots, chocolate chips, and raisins. Pour the mixture into a loaf pan and bake in the oven until golden brown on top or a toothpick inserted into the bread comes out clean, 45-50 minutes. Remove from the oven, transfer the bread onto a wire rack to cool, slice, and serve.

Nutrition Info:
- Per Serving: Calories: 598;Fat: 22g;Protein: 12g;Carbs: 86.8g.

Nutritious Chia And Berry Breakfast

Servings: 2 | Cooking Time: 0 Minute

Ingredients:
- 1 large green or red apple, peeled and sliced
- 1 tablespoon cacao powder
- 10 raisins, pitted
- 10 raspberries
- 2 cups blueberries, fresh and organic
- ½ cup almonds, raw and chopped
- 2 tablespoon chia seeds

Directions:
1. In a sealed container, add half the blueberries and apple.
2. Add the rest of the blueberries with raisins and raspberries separately. Then blend until smooth.
3. Add the blended mix to the apple and blueberries and pour in the chia seeds.
4. Serve the mix and top with the crushed almonds and a dusting of cacao powder. It can be kept in a sealed container in the fridge for up to 2-3 days.

Nutrition Info:
- Per Serving: Calories: 305 ;Fat: 1g ;Protein: 2g ;Carbs: 77g .

Sweet Potato, Tomato, & Onion Frittata

Servings: 4 | Cooking Time: 30 Minutes

Ingredients:
- 6 large eggs, beaten
- 1 tomato, chopped
- ¼ cup almond milk
- 1 tbsp tomato paste
- 1 tbsp olive oil
- 2 tbsp coconut flour
- 5 tbsp chopped onion
- 1 tsp minced garlic clove
- 2 shredded sweet potatoes

Directions:
1. Whisk the wet ingredients together in a bowl. Fold in the dry ingredients and stir to combine well. Place the mixture in a baking dish that will fit into the Instant Pot. Place a trivet in the pressure cooker and pour 1 cup of water inside. Place the baking dish in your pressure cooker on top of the trivet. Seal the lid and turn the sealing vent to "sealing". Cook for 18 minutes on "Manual" on High pressure. Once completed, let the pressure release naturally for 10 minutes and serve hot. Enjoy!

Nutrition Info:
- Per Serving: Calories: 190;Fat: 11g;Protein: 11g;Carbs: 12g.

Banana & Pumpkin Smoothie

Servings: 2 | Cooking Time: 5 Minutes

Ingredients:
- ½ cup canned pumpkin
- 1 banana, chopped
- 4 ice cubes
- 1 cup almond milk
- 2 tbsp almond butter
- 1 tsp ground nutmeg
- 1 tsp ground cinnamon
- 1 tsp vanilla extract
- 1 tsp maple syrup

Directions:
1. Place the pumpkin, banana, ice cubes, almond milk, almond butter, nutmeg, cinnamon, vanilla extract, and maple syrup in a blender and pulse until smooth. Serve.

Nutrition Info:
- Per Serving: Calories: 233;Fat: 10g;Protein: 6g;Carbs: 28g.

Ginger Banana Smoothie

Servings: 2 | Cooking Time: 5 Minutes

Ingredients:
- 1 banana, sliced
- 2 cups plain yogurt
- 1 tbsp lemon juice
- 2 tsp honey
- 1 tsp turmeric
- ½ tsp cinnamon
- ¼ tsp ginger

Directions:
1. Place the banana, yogurt, lemon juice, honey, turmeric, cinnamon, and ginger in a blender and pulse until smooth. Serve right away and enjoy!

Nutrition Info:
- Per Serving: Calories: 235;Fat: 8g;Protein: 9g;Carbs: 33g.

Strawberry & Pecan Breakfast

Servings: 2 | Cooking Time: 15 Minutes

Ingredients:
- 1 can coconut milk, refrigerated overnight
- 1 cup granola
- ½ cup pecans, chopped
- 1 cup sliced strawberries

Directions:
1. Drain the coconut milk liquid. Layer the coconut milk solids, granola, and strawberries in small glasses. Top with chopped pecans and serve right away.

Nutrition Info:
- Per Serving: Calories: 644;Fat: 79g;Protein: 23g;Carbs: 82g.

Healthy And Tasty Vanilla Crepes

Servings: 2 | Cooking Time: 10 Minutes

Ingredients:
- 2 free range eggs
- 1 teaspoon vanilla
- ½ cup nut milk
- ½ cup water
- 1 teaspoon maple syrup
- 1 cup all-purpose flour, gluten-free
- 3 tablespoons coconut oil

Directions:
1. Add the eggs, vanilla, nut milk, water, and syrup together until combined in a medium bowl. Add the flour to the mix and whisk to combine to a smooth paste.
2. Take 2 tablespoon of the coconut oil and melt in a pan over a medium heat.
3. Add ½ crepe mixture and tilt. To form a round crepe shape, swirl the pan.
4. For 2 minutes, cook until the bottom is light brown and comes away from the pan with the spatula.
5. Flip it and cook for 2 minutes more.
6. Serve and repeat with the rest of the mixture.

Nutrition Info:
- Per Serving: Calories: 556 ;Fat: 35g ;Protein: 8g ;Carbs: 54g .

Vanilla & Chia Yogurt With Berries

Servings: 4 | Cooking Time: 15 Minutes

Ingredients:
- ¼ tsp vanilla paste
- 4 cups almond yogurt
- 1 cup mixed berries
- 2 tbsp lemon juice
- 2 tbsp pure maple syrup
- 1 tbsp chia seeds

Directions:
1. Place the mixed berries, lemon juice, vanilla bean, and maple syrup in a saucepan over medium heat and stir well. Bring the mixture to a boil, stirring constantly. Reduce the heat to low and simmer for 3 minutes. Turn off the heat, then discard the vanilla bean. Mix in the chia seeds, then let sit for 10 minutes or until the seeds are thickened. Divide them into four serving bowls, then pour 1 cup of yogurt in each bowl. Serve immediately.

Nutrition Info:
- Per Serving: Calories: 245;Fat: 10g;Protein: 5g;Carbs: 35g.

Satisfying Eggs Benny

Servings: 4 | Cooking Time: 15 Minutes

Ingredients:
- 8 slices bacon
- 12 spears asparagus, trimmed
- 4 cups water
- 1 tablespoon white vinegar
- 4 large eggs
- 4 Savory Flax Waffles
- ¼ to ½ cup Hollandaise

Directions:
1. Spaced the bacon slices about 1 inch apart and place them on a sheet pan. Distribute the asparagus around the bacon. Place the sheet pan in the oven and set it to 400°F. Cook until the oven comes to temperature, then for 10 to 15 more minutes.
2. Once the asparagus tips are lightly browned and the bacon is toasty on the edges, turn off the oven and crack the door a bit so everything stays warm. I like to put my waffles in there, too.
3. Begin poaching the eggs by lining a plate with paper towels. Heat the water in a small saucepan over medium heat. Add the vinegar and bring to a steady simmer. Crack each of the eggs into its own small ramekin.
4. Stir the water in the saucepan with a slotted spoon to create a whirlpool, then slowly add an egg to the center of the whirlpool. Stir gently the water around the edge of the pot for another 10 seconds, until the swirling motion of the water wraps the egg white around the yolk to create a neat poached egg. For 3 minutes, cook undisturbed until the white is opaque and the egg looks like a teardrop.
5. Remove the egg from the water with a slotted spoon and place it on the lined plate. Repeat with the remaining eggs.
6. Assemble the eggs benny like a waffle on the bottom, a layer of asparagus, 2 slices of bacon, a poached egg, and then 1 to 2 tablespoons of hollandaise.
7. You can store the rest of the meal by packing each component separately in an airtight container. They will keep in the fridge for up to 5 days.

Nutrition Info:
- Per Serving: Calories: 410 ;Fat: 30g ;Protein: 23g ;Carbs: 12g .

Spicy Quinoa Bowl With Black Beans

Servings: 4 | Cooking Time: 25 Minutes

Ingredients:
- 1 cup brown quinoa, rinsed
- 3 tbsp Greek yogurt
- ½ lime, juiced
- 2 tbsp chopped cilantro
- 1 cup canned black beans
- 3 tbsp tomato salsa
- ¼ avocado, sliced
- 2 radishes, shredded
- 1 tbsp pepitas

Directions:
1. Cook the quinoa with 2 cups of salted water in a pot over medium heat or until the liquid absorbs, 15 minutes. Spoon the quinoa into serving bowls and fluff with a fork. In a small bowl, mix the yogurt, lime juice, cilantro, and salt. Divide this mixture on the quinoa and top with beans, salsa, avocado, radishes, and pepitas. Serve.

Nutrition Info:
- Per Serving: Calories: 340;Fat: 9g;Protein: 19.1g;Carbs: 49g.

Coconut Oat Bread

Servings: 4 | Cooking Time: 50 Minutes

Ingredients:
- 4 cups whole-wheat flour
- ¼ tsp sea salt
- ½ cup rolled oats
- 1 tsp baking soda
- 1 ¾ cups coconut milk, thick
- 2 tbsp pure maple syrup

Directions:
1. Preheat your oven to 450ºF. In a bowl, mix flour, salt, oats, and baking soda. Add in coconut milk and maple syrup and whisk until dough forms. Dust your hands with some flour and knead the dough into a ball. Shape the dough into a circle and place on a baking sheet.
2. Cut a deep cross on the dough and bake in the oven for 15 minutes. Reduce the heat to 400ºF and bake further for 20-25 minutes or until a hollow sound is made when the bottom of the bread is tapped. Slice and serve.

Nutrition Info:
- Per Serving: Calories: 761;Fat: 27g;Protein: 17g;Carbs: 115g.

Chocolate-blueberry Smoothie

Servings: 2 | Cooking Time: 5 Minutes

Ingredients:
- 2 cups plain rice milk
- 1 cup frozen wild blueberries
- 2 tbsp cocoa powder
- 1 packet stevia
- ¼ tsp turmeric
- 1 cup crushed ice

Directions:
1. Place the rice milk, blueberries, cocoa powder, stevia, turmeric, and ice in a food processor and pulse until smooth. Serve immediately.

Nutrition Info:
- Per Serving: Calories: 100;Fat: 6g;Protein: 2g;Carbs: 17g.

Veggie Panini

Servings: 4 | Cooking Time: 30 Minutes

Ingredients:
- 2 tbsp olive oil
- ½ lb sliced button mushrooms
- Sea salt and pepper to taste
- 1 ripe avocado, sliced
- 2 tbsp lemon juice
- ½ tsp pure maple syrup
- 8 whole-wheat bread slices
- 4 oz sliced Parmesan cheese

Directions:
1. Heat the olive oil in a medium skillet over medium heat and sauté the mushrooms until softened, 5 minutes. Season with salt and black pepper. Turn the heat off.
2. Preheat a panini press to medium heat, 3-5 minutes. Mash the avocado in a medium bowl and mix in the lemon juice, and maple syrup. Spread the mixture on 4 bread slices, divide the mushrooms and Parmesan cheese on top. Cover with the other bread slices and brush the top with olive oil. Grill the sandwiches one after another in the heated press until golden brown and the cheese is melted. Serve and enjoy!

Nutrition Info:
- Per Serving: Calories: 406;Fat: 25g;Protein: 19g;Carbs: 30.7g.

Breakfast Ground Beef Skillet

Servings: 4 | Cooking Time: 20 Minutes

Ingredients:
- 1 tablespoon olive oil
- 1 pound ground beef, lean
- 2 teaspoons bottled minced garlic
- 2 cups cauliflower, chopped
- 1 cup carrots, diced
- 1 zucchini, diced
- 2 scallions, white and green parts, chopped
- Sea salt
- Freshly ground black pepper
- 2 tablespoons fresh parsley, chopped

Directions:
1. Place a large skillet over medium-high heat and add the olive oil.
2. Add the ground beef and garlic. Sauté for about 8 minutes, or until cooked through.
3. Stir in the cauliflower, carrots, and zucchini. Sauté for about 10 minutes, or until tender.
4. Stir in the scallions and sauté for another minute.
5. Use sea salt and pepper to season the mixture. Serve topped with the parsley.

Nutrition Info:
- Per Serving: Calories: 214 ;Fat: 9g ;Protein: 26g;Carbs: 7g .

Sweet Kiwi Oatmeal Bars

Servings: 6 | Cooking Time: 50 Minutes

Ingredients:
- 2 cups rolled oats
- 2 cups whole-wheat flour
- 1 ½ cups pure date sugar
- 1 ½ tsp baking soda
- ½ tsp ground cinnamon
- 1 cup almond butter, melted
- 4 cups kiwi, chopped
- ¼ cup organic cane sugar

- 2 tbsp arrowroot

Directions:
1. Preheat your oven to 380ºF. In a bowl, mix the oats, flour, date sugar, baking soda, salt, and cinnamon. Put in almond butter and whisk to combine. In another bowl, combine the kiwis, cane sugar, and arrowroot until the kiwis are coated. Spread 3 cups of oatmeal mixture on a greased baking dish and top with kiwi mixture and finally put the remaining oatmeal mixture on top. Bake for 40 minutes. Allow cooling and slice into bars. Serve.

Nutrition Info:
- Per Serving: Calories: 482;Fat: 4g;Protein: 10.7g;Carbs: 101g.

Hazelnut & Raspberry Quinoa

Servings: 4 | Cooking Time: 30 Minutes

Ingredients:
- ½ cup shredded coconut
- 1 cup quinoa, rinsed well
- ¼ cup hemp seeds
- 1 tsp ground cinnamon
- 2 tbsp flaxseeds
- 1 tsp vanilla extract
- Sea salt to taste
- ¼ cup chopped hazelnuts
- 1 cup fresh raspberries

Directions:
1. Boil the quinoa with 2 cups of water in a saucepan over medium heat for 18-20 minutes. Mix in the hemp seeds, coconut, cinnamon, flaxseeds, vanilla, and salt. Serve the quinoa with hazelnuts and raspberries on top.

Nutrition Info:
- Per Serving: Calories: 290;Fat: 15g;Protein: 9g;Carbs: 32g.

Sweet Potato-kale Egg Casserole

Servings: 4 | Cooking Time: 30 Minutes

Ingredients:
- Olive oil
- 1 cup cooked sweet potato, diced
- 1 cup blanched cauliflower, chopped
- 1 cup kale, shredded
- 1 scallion, white and green parts, chopped
- 1 teaspoon fresh basil, chopped
- 8 eggs
- ¼ cup almond milk, unsweetened
- 1 teaspoon cumin, ground
- 1 teaspoon coriander, ground
- Pinch sea salt
- Pinch black pepper, freshly ground

Directions:
1. Preheat the oven to 375°F.
2. Lightly grease a 9-by-13-inch baking dish with olive oil.
3. The sweet potato, cauliflower, kale, scallion, and basil must be evenly spread in the prepared dish.
4. Whisk the eggs, almond milk, cumin, coriander, sea salt, and pepper in a medium bowl. Pour the egg mixture into the baking dish, lightly tap the dish on the counter to distribute the eggs among the vegetables.
5. Bake for 30 minutes, or until the eggs are set and the top is lightly golden.

Nutrition Info:
- Per Serving: Calories: 206 ;Fat: 10g ;Protein: 15g ;Carbs: 15g .

Smoked Salmon And Cucumber Wrap With Lettuce

Servings: 4 | Cooking Time: 0 Minute

Ingredients:
- 8 large butter lettuce leaves
- ½ English cucumber, sliced thin
- 8 ounces smoked salmon, divided
- 1 tablespoon fresh chives, chopped
- 4 tablespoons Almost Caesar Salad Dressing, divided

Directions:
1. Arrange the lettuce leaves in a single layer on a serving dish.
2. Evenly divide the cucumber slices among the lettuce leaves. Top each leaf with 2 ounces of smoked salmon.
3. Garnish with the chives and drizzle each wrap with 1 tablespoon of Almost Caesar Salad Dressing.

Nutrition Info:
- Per Serving: Calories: 107 ;Fat: 5g ;Protein: 11g ;Carbs: 6g .

Terrific Pancakes With Coconut And Banana

Servings: 4 | Cooking Time: 10 Minutes

Ingredients:
- ½ cup almond flour
- ¼ cup coconut flour
- 1 teaspoon baking soda
- 3 eggs, beaten
- 2 bananas, mashed
- 1 teaspoon pure vanilla extract
- 1 tablespoon coconut oil

Directions:
1. Stir the almond flour, coconut flour, and baking soda together in a medium bowl until well mixed.
2. Make a well in the center and add the eggs, bananas, and vanilla. Beat together until well blended.
3. Place a large skillet over medium-high heat and add the coconut oil.
4. Pour ¼ cup of batter into the skillet, four per batch for each pancake. Cook for about 3 minutes, or until the bottom is golden and the bubbles on the surface burst. Flip and cook for about 2 minutes more until golden and cooked through. Transfer to a plate and repeat with any remaining batter.
5. Serve the pancake.

Nutrition Info:
- Per Serving: Calories: 218 ;Fat: 15g ;Protein: 8g;Carbs: 17g .

Morning Green Smoothie

Servings: 2 | Cooking Time: 5 Minutes

Ingredients:
- ½-inch piece peeled fresh ginger
- 1 avocado, chopped
- 1 cup cucumber, chopped
- 2 cups curly endive
- 2 peeled apples, chopped
- 2 tbsp lime juice
- 2 cups soy milk
- 2 tbsp chia seeds
- 1 cup coconut yogurt

Directions:
1. Put in a food processor the avocado, cucumber, curly endive, apple, lime juice, soy milk, ginger, chia seeds, and coconut yogurt. Blend until smooth. Serve and enjoy!

Nutrition Info:
- Per Serving: Calories: 500;Fat: 34g;Protein: 13g;Carbs: 43.4g.

Appetizing Crepes With Berries

Servings: 4 To 6

Cooking Time: 5 Minutes

Ingredients:
- 1 cup buckwheat flour
- ½ teaspoon sea salt
- 2 tablespoons coconut oil (1 tablespoon melted)
- 1½ cups almond milk, or water
- 1 egg
- 1 teaspoon vanilla extract
- 3 cups fresh berries, divided
- 6 tablespoons Chia Jam, divided

Directions:

1. Whisk together the buckwheat flour, salt, 1 tablespoon of melted coconut oil, almond milk, egg, and vanilla in a small bowl until smooth.

2. Melt the remaining 1 tablespoon of coconut oil in a large (12-inch) nonstick skillet over medium-high heat. Tilt the pan, coating it evenly with the melted oil.

3. Into the skillet, ladle ¼ cup of batter. Tilt the skillet to coat it evenly with the batter.

4. Cook for 2 minutes, or until the edges begin to curl up. Flip the crêpe and cook for 1 minute on the second side using a spatula. Transfer the crêpe to a plate.

5. Continue to make crepes with the remaining batter. You should have 4 to 6 crêpes.

6. Place 1 crêpe on a plate, top with ½ cup of berries and 1 tablespoon of Chia Jam. Fold the crêpe over the filling. Repeat with the remaining crêpes and serve.

Nutrition Info:
- Per Serving: Calories: 242 ;Fat: 11g ;Protein: 7g ;Carbs: 33g .

Cherry & Coconut Oatmeal With Chia

Servings: 2 | Cooking Time: 15 Minutes

Ingredients:
- 3 cups coconut milk
- 2 cups wholemeal oats
- 1 tbsp milled chia seeds
- 3 tsp raw cacao
- ½ tsp stevia
- 1 tsp coconut shavings
- 6 fresh cherries

Directions:

1. Place a pan over medium heat. Add the oats, cacao, stevia, and coconut milk and simmer them until the oats are fully cooked through, 5-10 minutes. Pour into your favorite breakfast bowl and sprinkle the coconut shavings, cherries, and milled chia seeds on top.

Nutrition Info:
- Per Serving: Calories: 653;Fat: 21g;Protein: 29g;Carbs: 87g.

Thyme Cremini Oats

Servings: 4 | Cooking Time: 30 Minutes

Ingredients:
- 8 oz cremini mushrooms, sliced
- 14 oz chicken broth
- ½ onion, diced
- 2 tbsp olive oil
- 1 cup steel-cut oats
- 3 thyme sprigs
- 2 garlic cloves, minced
- Sea salt and pepper to taste

Directions:

1. Heat the olive oil in your pressure cooker on "Sauté". Add onion and mushrooms and sauté for 3 minutes. Add the garlic and sauté for one minute more. Stir in the oats and cook for an additional minute. Pour in ½ of water, broth, and add thyme sprigs. Season with some salt and pepper. Seal the lid and cook on "Manual" on High for 12 minutes. Once completed, let the pressure release naturally for 10 minutes, then perform a quick pressure release. Serve immediately and enjoy!

Nutrition Info:
- Per Serving: Calories: 270;Fat: 13g;Protein: 9g;Carbs: 30g.

Blackberry Waffles

Servings: 4 | Cooking Time: 15 Minutes

Ingredients:
- 1 ½ cups whole-wheat flour
- ½ cup old-fashioned oats
- ¼ cup date sugar
- 3 tsp baking powder
- ½ tsp sea salt
- 1 tsp ground cinnamon
- 2 cups soy milk
- 1 tbsp fresh lemon juice
- 1 tsp lemon zest
- ¼ cup coconut oil, melted
- ½ cup fresh blackberries

Directions:

1. Preheat your waffle iron. In a bowl, mix whole-wheat, oats, sugar, baking powder, salt, and cinnamon. Set aside. In another bowl, combine milk, lemon juice, lemon zest, and coconut oil. Pour into the wet ingredients and whisk to combine. Add the batter to the hot greased waffle iron, using approximately a ladleful for each waffle. Cook for 3-5 minutes, until golden brown. Repeat the process until no batter is left. Serve topped with blackberries.

Nutrition Info:
- Per Serving: Calories: 439;Fat: 17g;Protein: 10.6g;Carbs: 62g.

Coconut Blueberry Muffins

Servings: 6 | Cooking Time: 30 Minutes

Ingredients:
- 1 tbsp coconut oil, melted
- 1 cup quick-cooking oats
- 1 cup boiling water
- ½ cup almond milk
- ¼ cup ground flaxseed
- 1 tsp almond extract
- 1 tsp apple cider vinegar
- 1 ½ cups whole-wheat flour
- ½ cup pure date sugar
- 2 tsp baking soda
- A pinch of sea salt
- 1 cup blueberries

Directions:

1. Preheat your oven to 400ºF. In a bowl, stir oats with boiling water until they are softened. Pour in the coconut oil, milk, flaxseed, almond extract, and vinegar. Add the flour, date sugar, baking soda, and salt. Gently stir in blueberries. Divide the batter between greased muffins.

2. Bake for 20 minutes until lightly brown. Allow cooling for 10 minutes. Using a spatula, run the sides of the muffins to take out. Serve and enjoy!

Nutrition Info:
- Per Serving: Calories: 317;Fat: 10g;Protein: 7g;Carbs: 50.6g.

Fiery Quinoa

Servings: 4 | Cooking Time: 20 Minutes

Ingredients:
- 1 cup rinsed quinoa
- 2 cups water
- ½ cup coconut, shredded
- ¼ cup hemp seeds
- 2 tablespoons flaxseed
- 1 teaspoon cinnamon, ground
- 1 teaspoon vanilla extract
- Pinch sea salt
- 1 cup fresh berries of your choice, divided
- ¼ cup hazelnuts, chopped

Directions:
1. Combine the quinoa and water in a medium saucepan over high heat.
2. Bring to a boil, lower the heat to a simmer, and cook for 15 to 20 minutes, or until the quinoa is cooked through. It should double or triple in bulk to couscous, and be slightly translucent.
3. Stir in the coconut, hemp seeds, flaxseed, cinnamon, vanilla, and salt.
4. Divide the quinoa among four bowls and top each serving with ¼ cup of berries and 1 tablespoon of hazelnuts.

Nutrition Info:
- Per Serving: Calories: 286 ;Fat: 13g ;Protein: 10g ;Carbs: 32g .

Mushroom Crepes

Servings: 4 | Cooking Time: 25 Minutes

Ingredients:
- 1 cup whole-wheat flour
- 1 tsp onion powder
- ½ tsp baking soda
- ¼ tsp sea salt
- 1 cup crumbled tofu
- ⅓ cup almond milk
- ¼ cup lemon juice
- 2 tbsp extra-virgin olive oil
- ½ cup chopped mushrooms
- ½ cup finely chopped onion
- 2 cups collard greens

Directions:
1. Combine the flour, onion powder, baking soda, and salt in a bowl. Place the tofu, almond milk, lemon juice, and oil in your food processor. Blitz until everything is well combined. Add to the the flour mixture and mix to combine. Stir in mushrooms, onion, and collard greens.
2. Heat a skillet and grease with cooking spray. Lower the heat and spread a ladleful of the batter across the surface of the skillet. Cook for 4 minutes on both sides or until set. Remove to a plate. Repeat the process until no batter is left, greasing with a little more oil, if needed. Serve.

Nutrition Info:
- Per Serving: Calories: 282;Fat: 15g;Protein: 10g;Carbs: 30g.

Omelette With Smoky Shrimp

Servings: 2 | Cooking Time: 15 Minutes

Ingredients:
- 6 large eggs
- 1½ teaspoons fine Himalayan salt, divided
- 1 teaspoon black pepper, ground
- 1 teaspoon liquid smoke
- ¼ cup Garlic Confit with oil
- ¾ to 1-pound large shrimp, peeled and deveined
- 2 teaspoons avocado oil, divided
- 1 cup arugula

Directions:
1. In a large mixing bowl, place the eggs, ½ teaspoon of the salt, the pepper, and the liquid smoke. Whisk until frothy, then set aside.
2. Heat a 6-inch skillet over medium heat. Place the confit in the skillet when it's hot, quickly followed by the shrimp. Add the remaining teaspoon of salt and for 2 to 3 minutes sauté until the shrimp are pink and begins to coil. Transfer everything from the skillet to a plate. Don't clean the pan.
3. Quickly add 1 teaspoon of the avocado oil, swirl it, and pour in half of the whisked eggs in the same skillet. Add 6 shrimp and half of the garlic, once the bottom is no longer translucent. For 4 to 5 minutes, cover the skillet with a tight-fitting lid and cook.
4. Remove the lid and pick up the skillet to swirl the contents around for 30 seconds. There will be a thin layer of the egg still fluid on the top, and moving it around like this will spread that layer out over the top of the omelet so it will finish cooking while leaving the omelet slightly moist.
5. Run a spatula along the edge of the omelet and slide it onto a plate. Put the skillet back on the stove and use the remaining ingredients to make the second omelet in the same way by adding the remaining teaspoon of avocado oil.
6. Top each omelet with ½ cup arugula and serve right away.

Nutrition Info:
- Per Serving: Calories: 403 ;Fat: 21g ;Protein: 42g;Carbs: 5g .

Giant Coconut Pancake

Servings: 4 | Cooking Time: 55 Minutes

Ingredients:
- 1 cup coconut flour
- 1 tsp coconut extract
- 2 tbsp honey
- 2 eggs
- 1 ½ cups coconut milk
- 1 cup ground almonds
- ½ tsp baking soda
- 1 cup blackberries

Directions:
1. Whisk together the eggs and milk in a bowl. Gradually add the other ingredients, whisking constantly. Grease a large ramekin or a heatproof container that will fit into the Instant Pot. Pour the mixture into the greased ramekin. Pour 1 ½ cups of water into the Instant Pot and place the trivet inside. Place the ramekin with the mixture on top of the trivet. Seal the lid and turn the sealing vent to "sealing". Select "Manual" on High pressure and set the time to 45 minutes. Once completed, perform a quick pressure release by turning the valve to "venting". Carefully open the lid. Loosen the edges, then place the cooked pancake on a large plate. Serve with blackberries

Nutrition Info:
- Per Serving: Calories: 360;Fat: 15g;Protein: 16g;Carbs: 40g.

Baked Berry Millet With Applesauce

Servings: 6 | Cooking Time: 65 Minutes

Ingredients:
- 2 cups blueberries
- 1 cup millet
- 2 cups sugar-free applesauce
- ⅓ cup coconut oil, melted
- 2 tsp grated fresh ginger

• 1 ½ tsp ground cinnamon

Directions:

1. Place your oven to 350ºF. Mix the millet, blueberries, applesauce, coconut oil, ginger, and cinnamon in a large bowl. Pour the mixture into a casserole dish. Cover with aluminum foil. Bake for 40 minutes. Remove the foil and bake for 10-15 minutes more until lightly crisp on top.

Nutrition Info:

• Per Serving: Calories: 325;Fat: 14g;Protein: 6g;Carbs: 48g.

Blueberry Chia Pudding

Servings: 2 | Cooking Time: 5 Minutes + Chilling Time

Ingredients:

• ¾ cup coconut milk
• ½ tsp vanilla extract
• ½ cup blueberries
• 2 tbsp chia seeds
• Chopped walnuts to garnish

Directions:

1. In a blender, pour the coconut milk, vanilla, and half of the blueberries. Process the ingredients at high speed until the blueberries become incorporated into the liquid. Mix in the chia seeds. Share the mixture into two breakfast jars, cover, and refrigerate for 4 hours to allow the mixture to gel. Garnish the pudding with the remaining blueberries and walnuts. Serve immediately.

Nutrition Info:

• Per Serving: Calories: 459;Fat: 39g;Protein: 9g;Carbs: 24.3g.

Cherry Quinoa

Servings: 2 | Cooking Time: 25 Minutes

Ingredients:

• ½ cup fresh cherries
• ½ cup quinoa
• 1 cup water
• ¼ tsp ground nutmeg
• ½ tsp vanilla extract

Directions:

1. Place a pan over medium heat. Add all the ingredients and bring to a boil. Once boiling, cover and simmer for 15 minutes or until the quinoa is soft and the liquid has been absorbed. Pour into serving bowls and enjoy.

Nutrition Info:

• Per Serving: Calories: 180;Fat: 3g;Protein: 7g;Carbs: 32g.

Hearty Smoothie

Servings: 3 | Cooking Time: 5 Minutes

Ingredients:

• 1 banana
• ½ cup coconut milk
• 1 cup broccoli sprouts
• 2 cherries, pitted
• 1 tbsp hemp hearts
• ¼ tsp ground cinnamon
• ¼ tsp ground cardamom
• 1 tbsp grated fresh ginger

Directions:

1. In a food processor, place banana, coconut milk, 1 cup of water, broccoli, cherries, hemp hearts, cinnamon, cardamom, and ginger. Blitz until smooth. Divide the smoothie between glasses. Serve and enjoy!

Nutrition Info:

• Per Serving: Calories: 169;Fat: 11g;Protein: 3g;Carbs: 16.2g.

Pecan & Pumpkin Seed Oat Jars

Servings: 4 | Cooking Time: 10 Minutes + Chilling Time

Ingredients:

• 2 ½ cups old-fashioned rolled oats
• 5 tbsp pumpkin seeds
• 5 tbsp chopped pecans
• 5 cups soy milk
• 2 ½ tsp maple syrup
• Sea salt to taste
• 1 tsp ground cardamom
• 1 tsp ground ginger

Directions:

1. In a bowl, put oats, pumpkin seeds, pecans, soy milk, maple syrup, salt, cardamom, and ginger; toss to combine. Divide the mixture between mason jars. Seal the lids and place the jars in the fridge for about 10 hours. Serve.

Nutrition Info:

• Per Serving: Calories: 441;Fat: 16g;Protein: 18.4g;Carbs: 59g.

Orange-glazed Raspberry Muffins

Servings: 6 | Cooking Time: 40 Minutes

Ingredients:

• 2 eggs, beaten
• 2 cups whole-wheat flour
• 1 ½ tsp baking powder
• A pinch of sea salt
• 5 tbsp almond butter, softened
• 1 cup pure date sugar
• ½ cup oat milk
• 2 tsp vanilla extract
• 1 lemon, zested
• 1 cup dried raspberries
• 2 tbsp orange juice

Directions:

1. Preheat your oven to 400ºF. Grease 6 muffin cups with cooking spray. In a medium bowl, mix the flour, baking powder, and salt. In another bowl, cream the almond butter, half of the date sugar, and eggs. Mix in the oat milk, vanilla, and lemon zest. Combine both mixtures, fold in raspberries, and fill muffin cups two-thirds way up with the batter. Bake for 20-25 minutes. In a medium bowl, whisk orange juice and remaining date sugar until smooth. Remove the muffins when ready and transfer to them a wire rack to cool. Drizzle the glaze on top. Serve.

Nutrition Info:

• Per Serving: Calories: 370;Fat: 10g;Protein: 10.2g;Carbs: 62g.

Pumpkin Cake With Pistachios

Servings: 4 | Cooking Time: 70 Minutes

Ingredients:

• 2 eggs
• 3 tbsp avocado oil
• ¾ cup pumpkin, shredded
• ½ cup pure maple syrup
• 3 tbsp pure date sugar
• 1 ½ cups whole-wheat flour
• ½ tsp cinnamon powder
• ½ tsp baking powder
• ¼ tsp cloves powder
• ½ tsp allspice powder
• ½ tsp nutmeg powder
• 2 tbsp chopped pistachios

Directions:

1. Preheat your oven to 350°F. Lightly coat a loaf pan with cooking spray. In a bowl, whisk avocado oil, pumpkin, maple syrup, date sugar, and eggs. In another bowl, mix the flour, cinnamon powder, baking powder, cloves powder, allspice powder, and nutmeg powder. Add this mixture to the wet batter and mix until well combined. Pour the batter into the loaf pan, sprinkle the pistachios on top, and gently press the nuts onto the batter to stick.

2. Bake in the oven for 50-55 minutes or until a toothpick inserted into the cake comes out clean. Remove the cake onto a wire rack, allow cooling, slice, and serve.

Nutrition Info:
- Per Serving: Calories: 368;Fat: 5g;Protein: 8.8g;Carbs: 73.7g.

Almond Oats With Cherries

Servings: 2 | Cooking Time: 30 Minutes

Ingredients:
- 2 tbsp almond butter
- ¼ tsp vanilla extract
- 8 fresh pitted cherries, halved
- 1 cup quick cook oats
- 2 tbsp chia seeds
- ¼ cup whole milk yogurt
- 1 ¼ cups almond milk

Directions:
1. Combine the almond butter, vanilla extract, cherries, oats, chia seeds, whole yogurt, and almond milk in a bowl. Divide between two jars and let sit in the fridge for 25 minutes. Serve chilled. Enjoy!

Nutrition Info:
- Per Serving: Calories: 565;Fat: 33g;Protein: 21g;Carbs: 25g.

Morning Pecan & Pear Farro

Servings: 4 | Cooking Time: 20 Minutes

Ingredients:
- 1 cup farro
- 1 tbsp peanut butter
- 2 pears, peeled and chopped
- ¼ cup chopped pecans

Directions:
1. Bring salted water to a boil in a pot over high heat. Stir in farro. Lower the heat, cover, and simmer for 15 minutes until the farro is tender and the liquid has absorbed. Turn the heat off and add in the peanut butter, pears, and pecans. Cover and rest for 12-15 minutes. Serve.

Nutrition Info:
- Per Serving: Calories: 387;Fat: 28g;Protein: 8.6g;Carbs: 32g.

Berry, Walnut & Almond Yogurt Parfait

Servings: 2 | Cooking Time: 10 Minutes

Ingredients:
- 1 cup fresh raspberries
- 1 cup fresh blueberries
- 2 cups plain almond yogurt
- 2 tbsp honey
- ½ cup chopped walnuts

Directions:
1. Mix the yogurt and honey in a bowl. Stir to mix well, then divide half of the honey yogurt between 2 large glasses. Top with berries, then spoon the remaining honey yogurt on top. Sprinkle with walnut. Serve immediately.

Nutrition Info:
- Per Serving: Calories: 505;Fat: 22g;Protein: 22g;Carbs: 55g.

Cherry & Chocolate Oatmeal

Servings: 4 | Cooking Time: 15 Minutes

Ingredients:
- 3 ½ cups water
- ⅛ cup honey
- 1 cup oats
- 3 tbsp dark chocolate chips
- 1 cup frozen cherries, pitted

Directions:
1. Place all of the ingredients except the chocolate into your Instant Pot. Stir well to combine. Seal the lid. Choose the "Manual" option and cook on High pressure for 12 minutes. Once it goes off, perform a quick pressure release. Stir in the chocolate chips. Serve and enjoy!

Nutrition Info:
- Per Serving: Calories: 280;Fat: 6g;Protein: 5g;Carbs: 55g.

Sautéed Cherry Tomatoes With Scrambled Herb

Servings: 2 | Cooking Time: 10 Minutes

Ingredients:
- 4 eggs
- 2 teaspoons fresh oregano, chopped
- 1 tablespoon extra-virgin olive oil
- 1 cup cherry tomatoes, halved
- ½ garlic clove, sliced
- ½ avocado, sliced

Directions:
1. Beat the eggs until well combined and whisk in the oregano in a medium bowl.
2. Place a large skillet over medium heat. Add the olive oil once the pan is hot.
3. Pour the eggs into the skillet and use either a heat-resistant spatula or wooden spoon to scramble the eggs. Transfer the eggs to a serving dish.
4. For 2 minutes, add the cherry tomatoes and garlic to the pan and sauté. Spoon the tomatoes over the eggs and top the dish with the avocado slices.

Nutrition Info:
- Per Serving: Calories: 310 ;Fat: 26g ;Protein: 13g ;Carbs: 10g .

Cinnamon Apple Muesli

Servings: 4 | Cooking Time: 10 Minutes + Chilling Time

Ingredients:
- 1 apple, cored and chopped
- 2 cups rolled oats
- ¼ cup sugar-free apple juice
- 1 ¾ cups coconut milk
- 1 tbsp apple cider vinegar
- ¼ tsp ground cinnamon

Directions:
1. Add the oats, apple juice, coconut milk, and apple cider vinegar to a mixing bowl. Stir well. Wrap the bowl in plastic and refrigerate overnight. In the next morning, top with apple and sprinkle with cinnamon, then serve.

Nutrition Info:
- Per Serving: Calories: 212;Fat: 4g;Protein: 7g;Carbs: 39g.

Cinnamon Buckwheat With Almonds

Servings: 4 | Cooking Time: 20 Minutes

Ingredients:
- 1 cup almond milk
- 1 cup buckwheat groat
- 1 tsp cinnamon
- ¼ cup chopped almonds
- 2 tbsp pure date syrup

Directions:
1. Place almond milk, 1 cup of water, and buckwheat in a pot over medium heat and bring to a boil. Lower the heat and simmer covered for 15 minutes. Allow sitting covered for 5 minutes. Mix in the cinnamon, almonds, and date syrup. Serve warm.

Nutrition Info:
- Per Serving: Calories: 346;Fat: 18g;Protein: 7g;Carbs: 43.8g.

No-bread Avocado Sandwich

Servings: 2 | Cooking Time: 10 Minutes

Ingredients:
- 1 avocado, sliced
- 1 large red tomato, sliced
- 2 oz gem lettuce leaves
- 1 tsp almond butter, softened
- 1 oz tofu, sliced
- 1 tsp chopped parsley

Directions:
1. Put the avocado on a plate and place the tomato slices by the avocado. Arrange the lettuce on a flat plate to serve as the base of the sandwich.
2. To assemble the sandwich, smear each leaf of the lettuce with almond butter, and arrange some tofu slices in the leaves. Then, share the avocado and tomato slices on each cheese. Garnish with parsley and serve.

Nutrition Info:
- Per Serving: Calories: 273;Fat: 25g;Protein: 5g;Carbs: 12.6g.

Matcha Smoothie With Berries

Servings: 2 | Cooking Time: 5 Minutes

Ingredients:
- 2 cups almond milk
- 2 cups blueberries
- 1 banana, chopped
- ¼ tsp ground cinnamon
- 1 tbsp chia seeds
- 1 tbsp Matcha powder
- ¼ tsp ground ginger

Directions:
1. Place the almond milk, blueberries, banana, cinnamon, chia seeds, matcha powder, and ginger in a blender and pulse until smooth. Serve right away. Enjoy!

Nutrition Info:
- Per Serving: Calories: 210;Fat: 6g;Protein: 9g;Carbs: 30g.

Maple Coconut Pancakes

Servings: 4 | Cooking Time: 55 Minutes

Ingredients:
- ½ cup coconut flour
- 4 eggs
- 1 cup coconut milk
- 1 tbsp pure maple syrup
- 1 tsp vanilla extract

- 1 tbsp melted coconut oil
- 1 tsp baking soda
- ½ tsp sea salt

Directions:
1. Beat the eggs, coconut milk, maple syrup, vanilla, and coconut oil in a large bowl. Stir to combine. Put the coconut flour, baking soda, and salt in a separate bowl; mix well. Add the egg mixture and whisk the batter well until smooth and no lump.
2. Heat a greased nonstick skillet over medium heat and cook your pancakes until the edges begin to brown. Flip halfway through the cooking time. Serve immediately.

Nutrition Info:
- Per Serving: Calories: 190;Fat: 10g;Protein: 8g;Carbs: 15g.

Classic Walnut Waffles With Maple Syrup

Servings: 4 | Cooking Time: 15 Minutes

Ingredients:
- 1 ¾ cups whole-wheat flour
- ⅓ cup ground walnuts
- 1 tbsp baking powder
- 1 ½ cups soy milk
- 3 tbsp pure maple syrup
- 3 tbsp coconut oil, melted

Directions:
1. Preheat your waffle iron and grease with oil. Combine flour, walnuts, baking powder, and salt in a bowl. In another bowl, mix the milk and coconut oil. Pour into the walnut mixture and whisk until well combined. Spoon a ladleful of the batter onto the waffle iron. Cook for 3-5 minutes, until golden brown. Repeat the process until no batter is left. Top with maple syrup to serve.

Nutrition Info:
- Per Serving: Calories: 440;Fat: 18g;Protein: 11.4g;Carbs: 58g.

Fantastic Fruit Cereal

Servings: 2 | Cooking Time: 30 Minutes

Ingredients:
- 1 cup pineapple, dried and unsweetened
- ½ cup warm water
- 1 cup cashews
- 2½cup coconut flakes
- ½ teaspoon lemon zest
- 1 tablespoon honey

Directions:
1. Preheat oven to 375°F.
2. For 20 minutes, soak the pineapple slices in warm water until softened.
3. Combine with the rest of the ingredients and mix.
4. Spread onto a lined baking tray. Then bake for 20-30 minutes or until crispy.

Nutrition Info:
- Per Serving: Calories: 301 ;Fat: 12g ;Protein: 2g ;Carbs: 50g .

Cold Oatmeal With Apple And Cinnamon

Servings: 4 To 6

Cooking Time: 0 Minute

Ingredients:
- 2 cups rolled oats, gluten-free
- 1 ¾ cups coconut milk
- ¼ cup no-added-sugar apple juice
- 1 tablespoon apple cider vinegar
- 1 apple, cored and chopped

- Dash ground cinnamon

Directions:
1. Stir together the oats, coconut milk, apple juice, and vinegar in a medium bowl.
2. Cover and refrigerate overnight.
3. Stir in the chopped apple and season the cold oatmeal with cinnamon the next morning.

Nutrition Info:
- Per Serving: Calories: 213 ;Fat: 4g ;Protein: 6g ;Carbs: 39g .

Granola Dish With Buckwheat, Berries, Apples, Pumpkin Seeds And Sunflower Seeds

Servings: 2 | Cooking Time: 45 Minutes

Ingredients:
- 1 cup oats, whole meal or steel cut
- ⅓ cup buckwheat
- 2 cups water
- ⅓ cup sunflower seeds
- ⅓ cup pumpkin seeds
- ⅓ cup strawberries or raspberries, chopped
- ½ cup apples, peeled and finely chopped
- 5 tablespoon coconut oil
- 4 tablespoon cacao powder

Directions:
1. Preheat the oven to 350°F.
2. Into a bowl mix the oats, buckwheat, and seeds.
3. For 10 to 15 minutes, put the berries, apples, coconut oil and water in a pan. Then cover and simmer on a medium-high heat until the fruits are soft and stir in the ginger.
4. In a blender, add the fruit mixture with the cacao then blend until smooth. With the buckwheat, mix the fruits.
5. Use coconut oil to grease the baking tray and spread the granola mixture using a knife or spatula on top to create a thin layer. Bake for 45 minutes.
6. Every 15 minutes, stir the mixture so it doesn't burn. Remove the tray when crispy all over and allow to cool.

Nutrition Info:
- Per Serving: Calories: 780| Fat: 59g ;Protein: 22g ;Carbs: 69g .

Coconut Fruit Smoothie

Servings: 3 | Cooking Time: 5 Minutes

Ingredients:
- 1 cup strawberries
- 1 cup chopped watermelon
- 1 cup cranberries
- 1 tbsp chia seeds
- ½ cup coconut milk
- 1 cup water
- 1 tsp goji berries
- 2 tbsp fresh mint, chopped

Directions:
1. In a food processor, put the strawberries, watermelon, cranberries, chia seeds, coconut milk, water, goji berries, and mint. Pulse until smooth, adding more water or milk if needed. Divide the smoothie between 3 glasses. Serve.

Nutrition Info:
- Per Serving: Calories: 217;Fat: 13g;Protein: 3g;Carbs: 23.4g.

Cranberry Oat Cookies

Servings: 2 | Cooking Time: 20 Minutes

Ingredients:
- ½ cup rolled oats
- 1 tbsp whole-wheat flour
- ½ tsp baking powder
- 2 tbsp pure date sugar
- ¼ cup sugar-free applesauce
- 2 tbsp dried cranberries

Directions:
1. Combine the oats, flour, baking powder, and sugar in a bowl. Add in applesauce and cranberries. Stir until well combined. Form 2 cookies out of the mixture and microwave for 90 seconds. Allow cooling before serving.

Nutrition Info:
- Per Serving: Calories: 137;Fat: 1.8g;Protein: 3g;Carbs: 30.4g.

Flaxseed & Fig Smoothie

Servings: 2 | Cooking Time: 5 Minutes

Ingredients:
- 1 cup whole milk yogurt
- 7 figs, halved
- 1 banana
- 1 cup almond milk
- 1 tsp ground flax seeds
- 1 tbsp almond butter
- 1 tsp honey
- 4 ice cubes

Directions:
1. Place the whole yogurt, figs, banana, almond milk, flaxseed, almond butter, honey, and ice cubes in a blender and pulse until smooth. Serve right away and enjoy!

Nutrition Info:
- Per Serving: Calories: 360;Fat: 14g;Protein: 9g;Carbs: 62g.

Almond Waffles

Servings: 4 | Cooking Time: 65 Minutes

Ingredients:
- 1 ½ cups almond milk
- 1 ½ cups buckwheat flour
- ½ cup brown rice flour
- 2 tsp baking powder
- ½ tsp sea salt
- 1 egg
- 2 tsp vanilla extract
- 1 tbsp pure maple syrup

Directions:
1. Sift the flours, baking powder, and salt in a bowl; mix. Whisk together the egg, vanilla, maple syrup, almond milk, and 1 cup of water in a separate bowl. Pour the egg mixture into the flour mixture and keep stirring until a smooth batter forms. Let it stand for 10 minutes.
2. Preheat the waffle iron and grease with cooking oil. Pour the batter in the waffle iron to cover ¾ of the bottom. Cook for 10-12 minutes or until golden brown and crispy. Flip the waffle halfway through the cooking time. The cooking time will vary depending on the waffle iron you use. Serve the waffles immediately.

Nutrition Info:
- Per Serving: Calories: 280;Fat: 5g;Protein: 8g;Carbs: 55g.

Simple Apple Muffins

Servings: 6 | Cooking Time: 40 Minutes

Ingredients:
- 1 egg
- 2 cups whole-wheat flour
- 1 cup pure date sugar
- 2 tsp baking powder
- ¼ tsp sea salt
- 2 tsp cinnamon powder
- 1/3 cup melted coconut oil
- 1/3 cup almond milk
- 2 apples, chopped
- ½ cup almond butter, cubed

Directions:
1. Preheat your oven to 400ºF. Grease 6 muffin cups with cooking spray. In a bowl, mix 1 ½ cups of whole-wheat flour, ¾ cup of the date sugar, baking powder, salt, and 1 tsp of cinnamon powder. Whisk in the melted coconut oil, egg, and almond milk and fold in the apples. Fill the muffin cups two-thirds way up with the batter.
2. In a bowl, mix the remaining flour, remaining date sugar, and cold almond butter. Top the muffin batter with the mixture. Bake for 20 minutes. Remove the muffins onto a wire rack, allow cooling, and dust them with the remaining cinnamon powder. Serve and enjoy!

Nutrition Info:
- Per Serving: Calories: 463;Fat: 18g;Protein: 8.2g;Carbs: 71g.

Cauliflower Bowl With Avocado And Kale

Servings: 1 | Cooking Time: 5 Minutes

Ingredients:
- 4 thoroughly washed and chopped kale leaves
- 1 ½ cups cauliflower florets
- ½ chopped avocado
- 1 teaspoon lemon juice, freshly squeezed
- 1 teaspoon extra-virgin olive oil
- Pinch salt

Directions:
1. Fill 2 inches of water in a medium pot and insert a steamer basket. Bring to a boil over high heat.
2. In the basket, add the kale and cauliflower. For 5 minutes, cover and steam it.
3. Into a medium bowl, transfer the vegetables. Toss with the avocado, lemon juice, olive oil, and salt.

Nutrition Info:
- Per Serving: Calories: 317 ;Fat: 25g ;Protein: 7g ;Carbs: 24g .

Breakfast Naan Bread

Servings: 6 | Cooking Time: 25 Minutes

Ingredients:
- ¾ cup almond flour
- 2 tbsp psyllium husk powder
- ½ tsp sea salt
- ½ tsp baking powder
- 3 tbsp olive oil
- 4 oz peanut butter
- 2 garlic cloves, minced

Directions:
1. In a bowl, mix the almond flour, psyllium husk powder, salt, and baking powder. Mix in some olive oil and 2 cups of boiling water to combine the ingredients, like a thick porridge. Stir and allow the dough to rise for 5 minutes.

2. Divide the dough into 6 to 8 pieces and mold into balls. Place the balls on parchment paper and flatten them with your hands. Warm the peanut butter in a frying pan and fry the naan on both sides to have a beautiful, golden color. Transfer the naan to a plate and keep warm in the oven. For the garlic butter, add the remaining peanut butter to the frying pan and sauté the garlic until fragrant, about 3 minutes. Pour the garlic butter into a bowl and serve as a dip along with the naan.

Nutrition Info:
- Per Serving: Calories: 255;Fat: 23g;Protein: 7.5g;Carbs: 6.7g.

Coconut Porridge With Strawberries

Servings: 2 | Cooking Time: 15 Minutes

Ingredients:
- 1 egg
- 2 tsp olive oil
- 1 tbsp coconut flour
- 1 pinch ground chia seeds
- 5 tbsp coconut cream
- Thawed frozen strawberries

Directions:
1. Place a nonstick saucepan over low heat and pour in the olive oil, egg, coconut flour, chia seeds, and coconut cream. Cook the mixture while stirring continuously until your desired consistency is achieved. Turn the heat off and spoon the porridge into serving bowls. Top with 4 to 6 strawberries and serve immediately.

Nutrition Info:
- Per Serving: Calories: 210;Fat: 27g;Protein: 9g;Carbs: 20g.

Dilly Vegetable Quinoa

Servings: 1 | Cooking Time: 25 Minutes

Ingredients:
- ½ broccoli head, chopped
- ¼ cup quinoa
- 1 carrot, grated
- ¼ tsp sea salt
- 1 tbsp chopped fresh dill

Directions:
1. Stir the quinoa and ¾ cup water in a pot over high heat. Bring to a boil. Reduce the heat to low. Cover and cook for 5 minutes. Add the broccoli, carrot, and salt. Cook for 10-12 minutes more, or until the quinoa is fully cooked and tender. If the stew gets too dry, add more water. This should be on the liquid side, as opposed to the drier consistency of a pilaf. Fold in the dill and serve.

Nutrition Info:
- Per Serving: Calories: 220;Fat: 3g;Protein: 10g;Carbs: 42g.

Choco-berry Smoothie

Servings: 2 | Cooking Time: 10 Minutes

Ingredients:
- 1 tbsp poppy seeds
- 2 cups soy milk
- 2 cups blackberries
- 2 tbsp pure maple syrup
- 2 tbsp cocoa powder

Directions:
1. Submerge poppy seeds in soy milk and let sit for 5 minutes. Transfer to a food processor and add soy milk, blackberries, maple syrup, and cocoa powder. Blitz until smooth. Serve right away in glasses. Enjoy!

Nutrition Info:
- Per Serving: Calories: 288;Fat: 8g;Protein: 12g;Carbs: 47g.

Sweet Orange Crepes

Servings: 4 | Cooking Time: 30 Minutes

Ingredients:
- 2 eggs
- 1 tsp vanilla extract
- 1 tsp pure date sugar
- ¼ tsp sea salt
- 2 cups almond flour
- 1 ½ cups oat milk
- ½ cup melted coconut oil
- 3 tbsp fresh orange juice
- 3 tbsp olive oil

Directions:

1. In a medium bowl, whisk the eggs with vanilla, date sugar, and salt. Pour in a quarter cup of almond flour and whisk, then a quarter cup of oat milk, and mix until no lumps remain. Repeat the mixing process with the remaining almond flour and almond milk in the same quantities until exhausted. Mix in the coconut oil and orange juice until the mixture is runny, like pancakes.

2. Brush a nonstick skillet with some olive oil and place over medium heat. Pour 1 tablespoon of the batter into the pan and swirl the skillet quickly and all around to coat the pan with the batter. Cook until the batter is dry and golden brown beneath, about 30 seconds. Use a spatula to flip the crepe and cook the other side until golden brown too. Fold the crepe onto a plate and set aside. Repeat making more crepes with the remaining batter until exhausted. Serve and enjoy!

Nutrition Info:
- Per Serving: Calories: 677;Fat: 58g;Protein: 16.4g;Carbs: 23g.

Scotch Eggs With Pork Sausage And Hemp Seeds

Servings: 8 | Cooking Time: 35 Minutes

Ingredients:
- 6 cups water
- 8 large eggs
- 1 pork sausage, uncooked
- 2 tablespoons avocado oil
- 2 tablespoons hemp seeds, shelled
- 1 teaspoon Himalayan salt, fine

Directions:

1. Preheat the oven to 400°F.

2. In a large pot, bring the water to a rapid boil. Place the eggs in the water gently and cook for 8 minutes.

3. Form the sausage mix into eight ¼-inch-thick, 4-inch-diameter patties. Place them on a sheet of parchment paper or a cutting board and set aside.

4. Drain the hot water from the pot when the eggs are done, leaving the eggs in it and fill the pot with cold water and ice. For 2 minutes, let the eggs chill in the ice bath and immediately peel under the cold water.

5. Wrap the eggs. In one hand, place a pork patty and place an egg in the center of the patty using your other hand. Close your hand holding the pork around the egg and use your other hand to pinch the sausage closed. Shape the Scotch egg with both hands gently until smooth and even. Place the egg on a sheet pan, seam side down. Repeat with the remaining eggs and pork patties.

6. Use oil to brush or spray the egg. Sprinkle with the hemp seeds and salt. Bake for 25 minutes.

7. Remove from the oven and dig in. Let the eggs cool and store in an airtight container in the refrigerator for up to 5 days.

Nutrition Info:
- Per Serving: Calories: 260 ; Fat: 20.2g ;Protein: 17.1g;Carbs: 1.4g .

Orange-bran Cups With Dates

Servings: 6 | Cooking Time: 30 Minutes

Ingredients:
- 1 tsp avocado oil
- 3 cups bran flakes cereal
- 1 ½ cups whole-wheat flour
- ½ cup dates, chopped
- 3 tsp baking powder
- ½ tsp ground cinnamon
- ½ tsp sea salt
- ⅓ cup brown sugar
- ¾ cup fresh orange juice

Directions:

1. Preheat your oven to 400°F. Grease a 12-cup muffin tin with avocado oil. Mix the bran flakes, flour, dates, baking powder, cinnamon, and salt in a bowl. In another bowl, combine the sugar and orange juice until blended. Pour into the dry mixture and whisk. Divide the mixture between the cups of the muffin tin. Bake for 20 minutes or until golden brown and set. Cool for a few minutes before removing from the tin and serve.

Nutrition Info:
- Per Serving: Calories: 256;Fat: 1g;Protein: 5.8g;Carbs: 57g.

Green Banana Smoothie

Servings: 2 | Cooking Time: 5 Minutes

Ingredients:
- 2 cups flaxseed milk
- 2 cups spinach, chopped
- 2 bananas, peeled
- 1 packet stevia
- 1 tsp ground cinnamon
- 1 cup crushed ice

Directions:

1. Place the flaxseed milk, spinach, bananas, stevia, cinnamon, and ice in a food processor and pulse until smooth. Serve immediately.

Nutrition Info:
- Per Serving: Calories: 180;Fat: 5g;Protein: 4g;Carbs: 38g.

Vegetarian Mains

Vegetarian Mains

Vegetarian Spaghetti Bolognese

Servings: 6 | Cooking Time: 25 Minutes

Ingredients:
- 16 oz cooked whole-wheat spaghetti
- 1 cup cauliflower florets
- 2 cups shredded carrots
- 6 garlic cloves, minced
- 2 tbsp tomato paste
- 1 ½ tbsp dried oregano
- 28 oz canned diced tomatoes
- 2 tbsp balsamic vinegar
- 1 tbsp dried basil
- 10 oz mushrooms
- 2 cups chopped eggplants
- 1 cup water
- 1 ½ tsp dried rosemary
- Sea salt and pepper to taste

Directions:
1. Add the cauliflower, mushrooms, eggplant, and carrots to a food processor and process until finely ground. Add them to your Instant Pot. Stir in the rest of the ingredients. Seal the lid and cook for 8 minutes on "Manual" on high pressure. Once the cooking cycle has finished, release the pressure naturally for 10 minutes. Pour the sauce over the spaghetti. Serve and enjoy!

Nutrition Info:
- Per Serving: Calories: 360;Fat: 2g;Protein: 15g;Carbs: 75g.

Cheesy Cauliflower Casserole

Servings: 4 | Cooking Time: 35 Minutes

Ingredients:
- 1 white onion, chopped
- ½ celery stalk, chopped
- 1 green bell pepper, chopped
- Sea salt and pepper to taste
- 1 head cauliflower, chopped
- 1 cup paleo mayonnaise
- 4 oz grated Parmesan
- 1 tsp red chili flakes

Directions:
1. Preheat your oven to 400°F. Season onion, celery, and bell pepper with salt and black pepper. In a bowl, mix cauliflower, mayonnaise, Parmesan cheese, and red chili flakes. Pour the mixture into a greased baking dish and add the vegetables; mix to distribute. Bake for 20 minutes. Remove and serve warm.

Nutrition Info:
- Per Serving: Calories: 115;Fat: 4g;Protein: 17g;Carbs: 6g.

Scrumptious Lentils With Tomatoes And Turmeric

Servings: 4 | Cooking Time: 10 Minutes

Ingredients:
- 2 tablespoons extra-virgin olive oil, plus extra for garnish
- 1 onion, finely chopped
- 1 tablespoon turmeric, ground
- 1 teaspoon garlic powder
- One 14 ounces can lentils, drained
- One 14 ounces can chopped tomatoes, drained
- ½ teaspoon sea salt
- ¼ teaspoon black pepper, freshly ground

Directions:
1. Heat the olive oil in a large pot over medium-high heat until it shimmers.
2. Add the onion and turmeric and cook for 5 minutes while stirring occasionally until soft.
3. Add the garlic powder, lentils, tomatoes, salt, and pepper. Cook for 5 minutes and stir occasionally. Serve garnished with additional olive oil, if preferred,

Nutrition Info:
- Per Serving: Calories: 248 ;Fat: 8g ;Protein: 12g ;Carbs: 34g .

Pressure Cooked Ratatouille

Servings: 4 | Cooking Time: 20 Minutes

Ingredients:
- 1 zucchini, sliced
- 2 tomatoes, sliced
- 1 tbsp balsamic vinegar
- 1 eggplant, sliced
- 1 onion, sliced
- 1 tbsp dried thyme
- 2 tbsp olive oil
- 2 garlic cloves, minced

Directions:
1. Add the garlic to a springform pan. Arrange the veggies in a circle. Sprinkle them with thyme and drizzle with olive oil. Pour 1 cup of water in your Instant Pot. Place the pan inside. Close the lid and cook for 10 minutes on "Manual" on high pressure. Let the steam release naturally for about 10 minutes. Serve immediately.

Nutrition Info:
- Per Serving: Calories: 105;Fat: 7g;Protein: 2g;Carbs: 10g.

Chickpea & Bean Patties

Servings: 4 | Cooking Time: 30 Minutes

Ingredients:
- 4 whole-grain hamburger buns, split
- 1 can chickpeas
- 1 can pinto beans
- 1 can red kidney beans
- 2 tbsp whole-wheat flour
- ¼ cup dried mixed herbs
- ¼ tsp hot sauce
- ½ tsp garlic powder

- Sea salt and pepper to taste
- 4 lettuce leaves

Directions:

1. In a medium bowl, mash the chickpea, pinto beans, kidney beans and mix in the flour, mixed herbs, hot sauce, garlic powder, salt, and black pepper. Mold 4 patties out of the mixture and set aside.

2. Heat a grill pan to medium heat and grease with cooking spray. Cook the bean patties on both sides until light brown and cooked through, 10 minutes. Put the patties between the burger buns and top with lettuce. Serve.

Nutrition Info:

- Per Serving: Calories: 440;Fat: 5g;Protein: 15g;Carbs: 81g.

Full Of Flavour Braised Bok Choy With Shiita-ke Mushrooms

Servings: 4 | Cooking Time: 10 Minutes

Ingredients:

- 1 tablespoon coconut oil
- 8 baby bok choy, halved lengthwise
- ½ cup water
- 1 tablespoon coconut aminos
- 1 cup shiitake mushrooms, stemmed, sliced thin
- Salt
- Freshly ground black pepper
- 1 scallion, sliced thin
- 1 tablespoon sesame seeds, toasted

Directions:

1. Melt the coconut oil in a large pan over high heat. Add the bok choy in a single layer.

2. Add the water, coconut aminos, and mushrooms to the pan. Cover and braise the vegetables for 5 to 10 minutes, or until the bok choy is tender.

3. Remove the pan from the heat. Season the vegetables with salt and pepper.

4. Transfer the bok choy and mushrooms to a serving dish and garnish with scallions and sesame seeds.

Nutrition Info:

- Per Serving: Calories: 285 ;Fat: 8g ;Protein: 26g ;Carbs: 43g .

Festive Pesto-mushroom Burgers

Servings: 4 | Cooking Time: 25 Minutes

Ingredients:

- 4 whole-wheat hamburger buns
- 4 portobello mushroom caps
- ½ cup spinach-basil pesto
- 4 red onion slices
- 4 tomato slices
- 2 cups arugula

Directions:

1. Preheat your oven to 400°F. Rub each mushroom cap with pesto on all sides and place them on a baking sheet. Bake for 15-20 minutes until tender. To assemble, place the mushrooms on the buns and top with tomatoes, arugula, and onions. Serve right away.

Nutrition Info:

- Per Serving: Calories: 340;Fat: 24g;Protein: 6g;Carbs: 27g.

Hot Lentil Tacos With Guacamole

Servings: 4 | Cooking Time: 35 Minutes

Ingredients:

- ½ cup red lentils
- 2 tbsp olive oil
- ½ cup minced onion
- ½ cup roasted cashews
- ¼ cup chickpea flour
- 1 tbsp minced parsley
- 2 tsp hot powder
- Sea salt to taste
- 4 coconut flour tortillas
- Shredded romaine lettuce
- Guacamole

Directions:

1. Place the lentils in a pot and cover them with cold water. Bring to a boil and simmer for 15-20 minutes. Heat the oil in a skillet over medium heat. Add the onion cook for 5 minutes. Set aside. In a blender, mince cashews, add in cooked lentils and onion mixture. Pulse to blend. Transfer to a bowl and stir in flour, parsley, hot powder, and salt. Mix to combine. Mold patties out of the mixture. Heat the remaining oil in a skillet over medium heat. Brown the patties for 10 minutes on both sides. Put one patty in each tortilla, top with lettuce and guacamole.

Nutrition Info:

- Per Serving: Calories: 500;Fat: 25g;Protein: 15g;Carbs: 55g.

Balanced Sweet Potatoes And Buckwheat

Servings: 4 To 6

Cooking Time: 20 Minutes

Ingredients:

- 1 tablespoon coconut oil
- 2 cups sweet potatoes, cubed
- 1 yellow onion, chopped
- 2 garlic cloves, minced
- 2 teaspoons cumin, ground
- ½ cup buckwheat groats
- 1 cup lentils, rinsed
- 6 cups vegetable broth
- 1 teaspoon salt
- ½ teaspoon black pepper, freshly ground
- 2 cups chopped kale, thoroughly washed and stemmed

Directions:

1. Melt the coconut oil in a large pot over medium-high heat. Stir in the sweet potatoes, onion, garlic, and cumin. Sauté for 5 minutes.

2. Add the buckwheat groats, lentils, vegetable broth, salt, and pepper. Bring to a boil. Reduce the heat to simmer, and cover the pot. Cook for 15 minutes, or until the sweet potatoes, buckwheat, and lentils are tender.

3. Remove the pot from the heat. Add the kale and stir to combine. Cover the pot and let it sit for 5 minutes before serving.

Nutrition Info:

- Per Serving: Calories: 427 ;Fat: 7g ;Protein: 24g ;Carbs: 69g .

Bean & Spinach Casserole

Servings: 6 | Cooking Time: 35 Minutes

Ingredients:
- ½ cup whole-wheat breadcrumbs
- 1 can Great Northern beans
- 1 can Navy beans
- 3 tbsp olive oil
- 1 onion, chopped
- 2 carrots, chopped
- 1 celery stalk, chopped
- 2 garlic cloves, minced
- 1 cup baby spinach
- 3 tomatoes, chopped
- 1 cup vegetable broth
- 1 tbsp parsley, chopped
- 1 tsp dried thyme
- Sea salt and pepper to taste

Directions:
1. Preheat your oven to 380ºF. Heat the oil in a skillet over medium heat. Place in onion, carrots, celery, and garlic. Sauté for 5 minutes. Remove into a greased casserole. Add in beans, spinach, tomatoes, broth, parsley, thyme, salt, and pepper and stir to combine. Cover with foil and bake in the oven for 15 minutes. Take out the casserole from the oven, remove the foil, and spread the breadcrumbs all over. Bake for another 10 minutes until the top is crispy and golden. Serve warm.

Nutrition Info:
- Per Serving: Calories: 320;Fat: 8g;Protein: 16g;Carbs: 49g.

Sneaky Fiery Veggie Burgers

Servings: 2 | Cooking Time: 15 Minutes

Ingredients:
- extra firm Tempah, 1 pack
- 1 teaspoon red chili flakes
- ½ red onion, diced
- ½ cup baby spinach
- 1 tablespoon olive oil

Directions:
1. Heat the broiler on medium-high heat.
2. Marinate the Tempah in oil and red chili flakes.
3. Heat a little olive oil in a skillet on medium heat.
4. For 6 to 7 minutes, sauté the onion in the skillet until caramelized.
5. Stir in the pepper and baby spinach for 3 to 4 minutes more.
6. Broil the Tempah for 4 minutes on each side.
7. Lay down the Tempah in the buns and then add the caramelized onion, spinach, and diced peppers.
8. Serve immediately while hot with a side of arugula.

Nutrition Info:
- Per Serving: Calories: 82 ;Fat: 7g ;Protein: 1g ;Carbs: 5g .

Versatile Zucchini Patties

Servings: 2 | Cooking Time: 5 Minutes

Ingredients:
- 2 medium zucchinis, shredded
- 1 teaspoon salt, divided
- 2 eggs
- 2 tablespoons chickpea flour
- 1 scallion, chopped
- 1 tablespoon fresh mint, chopped
- ½ teaspoon salt
- 2 tablespoons extra-virgin olive oil

Directions:
1. In a fine-mesh strainer, place the shredded zucchini and sprinkle it with ½ teaspoon of salt. Set aside to drain while assembling the other ingredients.
2. Beat together the eggs, chickpea flour, scallion, mint, and the remaining ½ teaspoon of salt in a medium bowl.
3. Gently squeeze the zucchini to drain as much liquid as possible before adding it to the egg mixture. Stir to mix well.
4. Place a large skillet over medium-high heat.
5. Add the olive oil when the pan is hot. Drop the zucchini mixture by spoonful into the pan. Gently flatten the zucchini with the back of a spatula.
6. Cook for 2 to 3 minutes, or until golden brown. Flip and cook for about 2 minutes more on the other side.
7. Serve warm or at room temperature.

Nutrition Info:
- Per Serving: Calories: 263 ;Fat: 20g ;Protein: 10g ;Carbs: 16g .

Lovely Spring Roll Wraps With Vegetable

Servings: 4 To 6

Cooking Time: 0 Minutes

Ingredients:
- 10 rice paper wrappers
- 2 cups lightly packed baby spinach, divided
- 1 cup grated carrot, divided
- 1 cucumber, halved, seeded, and cut into thin, 4-inch-long strips, divided
- 1 avocado, halved, pitted, and cut into thin strips, divided

Directions:
1. Place a cutting board on a flat surface with the vegetables in front of you.
2. Fill a large, shallow bowl with warm water that is hot enough to cook the wrappers, but warm enough to touch it comfortably.
3. Soak 1 wrapper in the water and then place it on the cutting board.
4. Fill the middle of the wrapper with ¼ cup of spinach, 2 tablespoons of grated carrot, a few cucumber slices, and 1 or 2 slices of avocado.
5. Fold the sides over the middle, and then roll the wrapper tightly from the bottom like a burrito-style.
6. Repeat with the remaining wrappers and vegetables.
7. Serve immediately.

Nutrition Info:
- Per Serving: Calories: 246 ;Fat: 10g ;Protein: 4g ;Carbs: 36g.

Zucchini & Chickpea Casserole

Servings: 6 | Cooking Time: 45 Minutes

Ingredients:
- 2 tbsp olive oil
- 1 tsp dried oregano
- 15 oz canned chickpeas
- 2 garlic cloves, minced
- 1 zucchini, chopped
- 1 onion, chopped
- ½ tsp ground cumin
- 4 eggs, beaten lightly
- Sea salt and pepper to taste

Directions:
1. Preheat your oven to 350°F. Warm 2 tbsp of olive oil in a skillet over high heat and place the garlic, onion, and zucchini and cook for 5 minutes until the veggies are brown. Set aside in a bowl. Place the chickpeas in the bowl with the veggies and mash them. Stir in oregano, cumin, eggs, salt, and pepper, pour it in

a greased baking pan, and bake for 20 minutes. Let cool before serving.

Nutrition Info:
• Per Serving: Calories: 215;Fat: 10g;Protein: 10g;Carbs: 15g.

Marinated Tempah And Spaghetti Squash

Servings: 2 | Cooking Time: 50 Minutes

Ingredients:
• 1 pack of tempeh, drained and cubed
• 1 spaghetti squash or pumpkin, halved and deseeded
• 3 tablespoons tamari or reduced
• sodium soy sauce
• 1 can tomatoes, chopped
• 1 tablespoon extra-virgin olive oil
• 2 cloves of garlic, chopped finely
• 1 cup small broccoli florets
• ½ cup of baby spinach

Directions:
1. Preheat the oven to 375°F. Get a medium-sized bowl and toss together the tamari, tempeh, garlic.
2. Marinate and set aside for 30 minutes and overnight if possible. Grab a large baking dish and arrange the squash halves with the cut side down.
3. Pour half a cup of water into the dish. For 45 minutes, bake or until tender, and remove the dish out of the oven. Turn the squash over and allow it to slightly cool.
4. Get a large skillet and heat oil at medium heat.
5. Add tempeh and cook for 7 to 8 minutes until golden brown while occasionally stirring.
6. Remove the tempeh and keep warm on a plate.
7. Heat chopped tomatoes in a medium-sized pot at medium heat, and then add the broccoli and allow to cook until tender for 5 minutes. Stir the spinach in and remove it from heat.
8. Use a fork to scrape off spaghetti squash strands onto a platter. Spoon broccoli and hot chopped tomatoes over the dish.
9. Top with the tempeh to serve.

Nutrition Info:
• Per Serving: Calories: 193 ;Fat: 13g ;Protein: 9g ;Carbs: 15g.

Veggie Burger Patties

Servings: 4 | Cooking Time: 30 Minutes

Ingredients:
• 1 zucchini, grated
• 3 cups cauliflower florets
• 1 carrot, grated
• ½ cup veggie broth
• 2 cups broccoli florets
• ½ onion, diced
• ½ tsp turmeric powder
• 2 tbsp olive oil
• 2 cups sweet potato cubes
• ¼ tsp black pepper

Directions:
1. Heat 1 tablespoon of oil in your Instant Pot on "Sauté". Sauté the onions for about 3 minutes. Add carrots and cook for an additional minute. Add sweet potatoes and broth. Close the lid and cook on "Manual" for 10 minutes. Release the pressure quickly. Stir in the remaining veggies. Close the lid and cook for 3 more minutes on "Manual". Mash the veggies with a masher and stir in the seasonings. Let cool for a few minutes and make burger patties out of the mixture. Heat the rest of the oil. Cook the patties for about a minute on each side

Nutrition Info:

• Per Serving: Calories: 220;Fat: 7g;Protein: 3g;Carbs: 35g.

Hot And Spicy Scrambled Tofu And Spinach

Servings: 2 | Cooking Time: 10 Minutes

Ingredients:
• 1 pack extra firm tofu, pressed and crumbled
• 1 tablespoon of extra virgin olive oil
• 2 stems of spring onion, finely chopped
• 1 cup spinach leaves
• 1 clove of garlic, finely chopped
• 1 teaspoon lemon juice
• 1 teaspoon black pepper

Directions:
1. Heat olive oil in a skillet on medium heat.
2. Add the spring onion, tomatoes, and garlic and sauté for 3-4 minutes.
3. Lower the heat and add the tofu, lemon juice, and pepper.
4. Sauté for 3 to 5 minutes.
5. Turn the heat off and add the spinach then stir until spinach is wilted.
6. Transfer to a serving dish and enjoy.

Nutrition Info:
• Per Serving: Calories: 42 ;Fat: 3g ;Protein: 1g ;Carbs: 3g.

Stuffed Zucchini Rolls With Tempeh & Tofu

Servings: 4 | Cooking Time: 60 Minutes

Ingredients:
• 3 zucchinis, sliced lengthwise
• 1 tbsp olive oil
• ¾ lb crumbled tempeh
• 1 cup crumbled tofu
• 1 cup grated Parmesan
• ¼ cup chopped fresh basil
• 2 garlic cloves, minced
• 1 ½ cups marinara sauce

Directions:
1. Line a baking sheet with paper towels and lay the zucchini slices in a single layer. Sprinkle each side with salt and allow releasing of liquid for 15 minutes. Heat the olive oil in a skillet and cook tempeh for 10 minutes; set aside. In a bowl, mix tempeh, tofu, Parmesan, basil, and garlic.
2. Preheat your oven to 400ºF. Spread 1 cup of marinara sauce onto the bottom of a baking pan and set aside. Spread 1 tbsp of the cheese mixture evenly along with each zucchini slice. Roll up the zucchini slices over the filling and arrange in the baking pan. Top with the remaining marinara sauce. Bake for 25-30 minutes or until the cheese begins to brown. Serve immediately.

Nutrition Info:
• Per Serving: Calories: 415;Fat: 21g;Protein: 28g;Carbs: 27g.

Cucumber & Carrot Pizza With Pesto

Servings: 2 | Cooking Time: 30 Minutes

Ingredients:
• 1 prebaked pizza crust
• ½ cup pesto
• 1 tomato, sliced
• 1 carrot, grated
• 1 red onion, sliced
• 1 cucumber, sliced

Directions:
1. Preheat your oven to 390ºF. Spread half of the pesto over the pizza crust and top with tomato slices. Combine the grated carrot

with salt, toss to coat. Put the carrot over the tomato and top with onion. Transfer to a baking tray and put it in the oven. Bake for 15-20 minutes until golden. Serve topped with cucumber slices.

Nutrition Info:
• Per Serving: Calories: 890;Fat: 63g;Protein: 15g;Carbs: 73g.

Appetizing Casserole With Broccoli And Bean

Servings: 4 | Cooking Time: 35 To 45 Minutes

Ingredients:
• ¾ cup vegetable broth, or water
• 2 broccoli heads, crowns and stalks finely chopped
• 1 teaspoon salt
• 2 cups cooked pinto or navy beans, or One 14 ounces can
• 1 to 2 tablespoons brown rice flour, or arrowroot flour
• 1 cup walnuts, chopped

Directions:
1. Preheat the oven to 350°F.
2. Warm the broth in a large ovenproof pot set over medium heat.
3. Add the broccoli and salt. Cook for 6 to 8 minutes, or until the broccoli is bright green.
4. Stir in the pinto beans and brown rice flour. Cook for 5 minutes more, or until the liquid thickens slightly.
5. Sprinkle the walnuts over the top.

Nutrition Info:
• Per Serving: Calories: 410 ;Fat: 20g ;Protein: 22g ;Carbs: 43g.

Soft Zucchini With White Beans And Olives Stuffing

Servings: 4 | Cooking Time: 20 Minutes

Ingredients:
• 4 large zucchinis, halved lengthwise
• 2 tablespoons extra-virgin olive oil, plus additional for brushing
• ½ teaspoon salt, plus additional for seasoning
• Freshly ground black pepper
• Pinch ground rosemary
• One 15 ounces can white beans, drained and rinsed
• ½ cup pitted green olives, chopped
• 2 garlic cloves, minced
• 1 cup arugula, coarsely chopped
• ¼ cup fresh parsley, chopped
• 1 tablespoon apple cider vinegar

Directions:
1. Preheat the oven to 375°F.
2. Brush a rimmed baking sheet with olive oil.
3. Carefully scoop out using a small spoon or melon baller and discard the seeds from the zucchini halves.
4. Brush the scooped-out section of each zucchini boat with olive oil and lightly season the inside of each boat with salt, pepper, and rosemary.
5. Transfer the zucchini to the prepared baking sheet, cut-side up. Place the sheet in the preheated oven and roast for 15 to 20 minutes, or until the zucchini are tender and lightly browned.
6. Lightly mash in a medium bowl the white beans with a fork.
7. Add the olives, garlic, arugula, parsley, cider vinegar, the remaining ½ teaspoon of salt, and the remaining 2 tablespoons of olive oil. Season with pepper and mix well.
8. Spoon the bean mixture into the zucchini boats and serve.

Nutrition Info:
• Per Serving: Calories: 269| Fat: 12g ;Protein: 13g ;Carbs: 38g.

Grilled Tempeh With Green Beans

Servings: 4 | Cooking Time: 15 Minutes

Ingredients:
• 1 lb tempeh, sliced
• 1 lb green beans, trimmed
• Sea salt and pepper to taste
• 3 tbsp olive oil
• 1 tbsp maple syrup
• 1 lemon, juiced

Directions:
1. Preheat a grill pan over medium heat. Season the tempeh and green beans with salt and black pepper and brush them with some olive oil. Grill the tempeh and green beans on both sides until golden brown and tender, 10 minutes. Transfer to serving plates. In a small bowl, whisk the remaining olive oil, maple syrup, lemon juice, and drizzle all over the food. Serve warm.

Nutrition Info:
• Per Serving: Calories: 360;Fat: 23g;Protein: 23g;Carbs: 23g.

American-style Tempeh With Garden Peas

Servings: 4 | Cooking Time: 50 Minutes

Ingredients:
• 16 oz whole-wheat bow-tie pasta
• 3 tbsp whole-wheat breadcrumbs
• 2 tbsp olive oil, divided
• 2/3 lb tempeh, cubed
• Sea salt and pepper to taste
• 1 yellow onion, chopped
• ½ cup sliced mushrooms
• 2 tbsp whole-wheat flour
• ¼ cup white wine
• ¾ cup vegetable stock
• ¼ cup oats milk
• 2 tsp chopped fresh thyme
• ¼ cup chopped cauliflower
• ½ cup grated Parmesan

Directions:
1. Cook the pasta in slightly salted water for 10 minutes or until al dente. Drain and set aside. Preheat your oven to 375 F. Heat the 1 tbsp of olive oil in a skillet, season the tempeh with salt and pepper, and cook until golden brown all around. Mix in onion, mushrooms, and cook for 5 minutes. Stir in flour and cook for 1 more minute. Mix in wine and add two-thirds of the vegetable stock. Cook for 2 minutes while occasionally stirring. Add milk and continue cooking until the sauce thickens, 4 minutes.
2. Season with thyme, salt, pepper, and half of the Parmesan. Once the cheese melts, turn the heat off and allow cooling. Add the rest of the vegetable stock and cauliflower to a food processor and blend until smooth. Pour the mixture into a bowl, add in the sauce, and mix in pasta until combined. Grease a baking dish with cooking spray and spread in the mixture. Drizzle the remaining olive oil on top, breadcrumbs, some more thyme, and remaining cheese. Bake until the cheese melts and is golden brown on top, 30 minutes. Remove the dish from the oven, allow cooling for 3 minutes, and serve.

Nutrition Info:
• Per Serving: Calories: 445;Fat: 17g;Protein: 28g;Carbs: 53g.

Savoy Cabbage Rolls With Tofu

Servings: 4 | Cooking Time: 30 Minutes

Ingredients:
- 1 head Savoy cabbage, leaves separated (scraps kept)
- 2 tbsp olive oil
- 2 cups tofu, crumbled
- ½ onion, chopped
- 2 garlic cloves, minced
- Sea salt and pepper to taste
- 1 cup buckwheat groats
- 1 ¾ cups vegetable stock
- 1 bay leaf
- 2 tbsp chopped cilantro
- 23 oz canned diced tomatoes

Directions:
1. Warm the olive oil in a large bowl and cook the tofu until golden brown, 8 minutes. Stir in the onion and garlic until softened and fragrant, 3 minutes. Season with salt and black pepper and mix in the buckwheat, bay leaf, and vegetable stock. Close the lid, allow boiling, and then simmer until all the liquid is absorbed. Open the lid, remove the bay leaf, and adjust the taste with salt and pepper. Lay the cabbage leaves on a flat surface and add 3 to 4 tablespoons of the cooked buckwheat onto each leaf. Roll the leaves to secure the filling firmly. Pour the tomatoes with juices into a medium pot, season with a little salt, pepper, and lay the cabbage rolls in the sauce. Cook over medium heat until the cabbage softens, 5-8 minutes. Garnish with more cilantro and serve.

Nutrition Info:
- Per Serving: Calories: 330;Fat: 18g;Protein: 23g;Carbs: 24g.

Spicy Moong Beans

Servings: 4 | Cooking Time: 40 Minutes

Ingredients:
- 1 tsp paprika
- 2 tsp curry powder
- 2 cups moong beans, soaked
- 1 onion, diced
- 1 tsp turmeric
- Juice of 1 lime
- 1 jalapeno pepper, chopped
- 1 sprig curry leaves
- 4 garlic cloves, minced
- 2 tbsp olive oil
- 1 ½ tsp cumin seeds
- 2 tomatoes, chopped
- 1-inch piece ginger, grated

Directions:
1. Heat the oil in the pressure cooker on "Sauté". Add the cumin seeds and sauté for about a minute and a half. Add the onion and cook until translucent, about 2 minutes. Add the garlic, curry, turmeric, ginger, and salt. Cook for one more minute. Stir in the jalapeño and tomatoes and cook for 5 minutes, or until soft. Add the beans and pour water to cover the ingredients. Cover by at least 2 inches. Add the lime juice and curry leaves and close the lid. Select "Manual" and cook for 15 minutes on high pressure. Do a quick pressure release. Serve.

Nutrition Info:
- Per Serving: Calories: 330;Fat: 5g;Protein: 10g;Carbs: 63g.

Quinoa & Chickpea Pot

Servings: 2 | Cooking Time: 15 Minutes

Ingredients:
- 2 tsp extra-virgin olive oil
- 1 cup cooked quinoa
- 1 can chickpeas
- 1 bunch arugula chopped
- 1 tbsp soy
- Sea salt and pepper to taste

Directions:
1. Heat the oil in a skillet over medium heat. Stir in quinoa, chickpeas, and arugula and cook for 3-5 minutes until the arugula wilts. Pour in soy sauce, salt, and pepper. Toss to coat. Serve immediately.

Nutrition Info:
- Per Serving: Calories: 340;Fat: 10g;Protein: 14g;Carbs: 50g.

Bean Gyros

Servings: 6 | Cooking Time: 60 Minutes

Ingredients:
- 1 can white beans
- 2 scallions, minced
- ¼ cup parsley, chopped
- 8 Kalamata olives, chopped
- 1 tbsp tahini
- 1 tbsp lemon juice
- ½ tsp ground cumin
- ¼ tsp paprika
- 4 tsp olive oil
- 6 whole-grain wraps
- 1 cup hummus
- 1 cup arugula, chopped
- 2 tomatoes, chopped
- 1 cucumber, chopped
- ¼ cup chopped avocado

Directions:
1. In a blender, place the white beans, scallions, parsley, and olives. Pulse until finely chopped. In a bowl, beat the tahini with lemon juice. Add in cumin, paprika, and salt. Transfer into beans mixture and mix well to combine. Shape the mixture into balls; flatten to make 6 patties.
2. In a skillet over medium heat, warm the oil and cook the patties for 8-10 minutes on both sides; reserve. Spread each wrap with hummus and top with patties, tomatoes, cucumber, and avocado. Roll the wraps up to serve.

Nutrition Info:
- Per Serving: Calories: 540;Fat: 17g;Protein: 4g;Carbs: 82g.

Watercress & Mushroom Spaghetti

Servings: 4 | Cooking Time: 30 Minutes

Ingredients:
- ½ lb chopped button mushrooms
- 1 lb whole-wheat spaghetti
- 2 tbsp olive oil
- 2 shallots, chopped
- 2 garlic cloves, minced
- 4 tsp low-sodium soy sauce
- 1 tsp hot sauce
- A handful of watercress
- ¼ cup chopped parsley
- Sea salt and pepper to taste

Directions:

1. Cook spaghetti in lightly salted water in a large pot over medium heat until al dente, 10 minutes. Drain and set aside. Heat the olive oil in a skillet and sauté shallots, garlic, and mushrooms for 5 minutes. Stir in soy sauce, and hot sauce. Cook for 1 minute. Toss spaghetti in the sauce along with watercress and parsley. Season with black pepper. Dish the food and serve warm.

Nutrition Info:
- Per Serving: Calories: 485;Fat: 9g;Protein: 13g;Carbs: 90g.

Meatless Shepherd's Pie

Servings: 4 | Cooking Time: 20 Minutes

Ingredients:
- 2 cups steamed and mashed cauliflower
- 1 diced celery stalk
- 1 cup diced onion
- 1 tbsp olive oil
- ½ cup diced turnip
- 1 ¾ cup veggie broth
- 1 cup diced tomatoes
- 1 cup grated sweet potatoes
- ½ cup diced carrots

Directions:
1. Heat the olive oil in your Instant Pot on "Sauté". Add the onion, carrots, and celery, and cook for 3 minutes. Stir in turnips, sweet potatoes, and veggie broth. Seal the lid and cook for 10 minutes on "Manual" on high pressure. Once it goes off, do a quick pressure release and open the lid Stir in tomatoes. Transfer the mixture to 4 ramekins. Top each ramekin with ½ cup of mashed cauliflower. Place the trivet inside the Instant Pot and pour 1 cup of water. Seal the lid and cook for 5 minutes on "Manual" on high pressure. When the timer goes off, allow for a natural pressure release for 10 minutes, then release the remaining pressure. Serve.

Nutrition Info:
- Per Serving: Calories: 225;Fat: 15g;Protein: 16g;Carbs: 6g.

Celery & Turmeric Lentils

Servings: 4 | Cooking Time: 20 Minutes

Ingredients:
- 2 tbsp olive oil
- 1 celery stalk, chopped
- 1 onion, chopped
- 1 tbsp ground turmeric
- 1 tsp garlic powder
- 1 can lentils, drained
- 1 can diced tomatoes
- Sea salt and pepper to taste

Directions:
1. Warm the olive oil in a pot over medium heat and place the onion, celery, and turmeric. Cook for 5 minutes until tender. Stir in garlic powder, lentils, tomatoes, salt, and pepper and cook for 5 more minutes. Serve immediately.

Nutrition Info:
- Per Serving: Calories: 250;Fat: 9g;Protein: 16g;Carbs: 35g.

Amazing Toasted Cumin Crunch

Servings: 1 | Cooking Time: 5 Minutes

Ingredients:
- 1 tablespoon cumin seeds, ground
- 2 tablespoons extra virgin olive oil
- 1 teaspoon black peppercorns, cracked
- ½ teaspoon cumin seeds, whole
- 1 teaspoon cilantro, finely chopped
- ½ jalapeno, finely chopped
- 2 cups of green cabbage, sliced
- 2 cups of carrots, grated
- ½ cup of cilantro, chopped
- 3 tablespoons lime juice

Directions:
1. Get a large saucepan, and then heat the oil over medium heat.
2. Cook the peppercorns, coriander, and the whole cumin seeds for a minute until browned.
3. Add in the jalapeno and then cook for 45 seconds more until tender.
4. Add in then the carrots and the cabbage, cooking for 5 minutes or until the cabbage starts to soften.
5. Add in the crushed cumin seeds and cook for 30 seconds before taking off the heat and then stirring in the lime juice and the cilantro.
6. Serve warm.

Nutrition Info:
- Per Serving: Calories: 307 ;Fat: 15g ;Protein: 7g ;Carbs: 44g .

Black Olive & Chickpea Lunch

Servings: 4 | Cooking Time: 15 Minutes

Ingredients:
- 2 tbsp olive oil
- 2 cups chopped onion
- 2 garlic cloves, minced
- 2 carrots, sliced thick
- 1/3 cup white wine
- 3 cups cherry tomatoes
- 2/3 cup vegetable stock
- 1 1/3 cups canned chickpeas
- ½ cup pitted black olives
- 1 tbsp chopped oregano
- Sea salt and pepper to taste

Directions:
1. Heat the olive oil in a medium pot and sauté the onion, garlic, and carrots until softened, 5 minutes. Mix in the white wine, reduce one-third, and mix in the tomatoes and vegetable stock. Cover the lid and cook until the tomatoes break, soften, and the liquid reduces by half. Stir in the chickpeas, olives, oregano, and season with salt and pepper. Cook for 3 minutes to warm the chickpeas.

Nutrition Info:
- Per Serving: Calories: 380;Fat: 13g;Protein: 16g;Carbs: 55g.

Bell Pepper & Tempeh Balls With Asparagus

Servings: 4 | Cooking Time: 40 Minutes

Ingredients:
- 1 egg, beaten
- 1 lb tempeh, crumbled
- 1 chopped red bell pepper
- Sea salt and pepper to taste
- 1 tbsp almond flour
- 1 tsp garlic powder
- 1 tsp onion powder
- 1 tsp paleo mayonnaise
- 2 tbsp olive oil
- 1 lb asparagus, trimmed
- 2 tbsp pure maple syrup
- 1 tbsp lemon juice

Directions:
1. Preheat your oven to 400ºF. Line a baking sheet with parchment paper. In a bowl, mix the egg, tempeh, bell pepper, salt, pepper, almond flour, garlic powder, onion powder, and mayonnaise. Mix and form 1-inch balls from the mixture. Arrange on the baking sheet, brush with cooking spray, and bake for 15-20 minutes; set aside.
2. Warm the olive oil in a skillet and sauté asparagus until softened with some crunch, 7 minutes. Mix in maple syrup and lemon juice. Cook for 2 minutes and plate the asparagus. Serve warm with the tempeh balls.

Nutrition Info:
- Per Serving: Calories: 360;Fat: 21g;Protein: 26g;Carbs: 25g.

Colourful Roasted Cauliflower

Servings: 4 To 6

Cooking Time: 20 Minutes

Ingredients:
- 1½ cups white cauliflower florets
- 1½ cups purple cauliflower florets
- 1½ cups yellow cauliflower florets
- 3 tablespoons extra-virgin olive oil
- ¼ cup lemon juice, fresh
- 1 teaspoon salt
- ¼ teaspoon black pepper, freshly ground

Directions:
1. Preheat the oven to 400°F.
2. Combine the cauliflower, olive oil, and lemon juice in a large bowl. Toss to coat well.
3. Spread the cauliflower on a rimmed baking sheet and add the salt and pepper.
4. Cover with aluminum foil and bake for 15 minutes. Remove the foil and continue to bake until the cauliflower starts the edges appear brown for 5 minutes more.
5. Serve warm or at room temperature.

Nutrition Info:
- Per Serving: Calories: 120 ;Fat: 10g ;Protein: 2g ;Carbs: 7g .

Oat & Chickpea Patties With Avocado Dip

Servings: 4 | Cooking Time: 20 Minutes

Ingredients:
- 4 whole-grain hamburger buns, split
- 1 avocado, pitted and peeled
- 1 tomato, chopped
- 1 small red onion, chopped
- 3 cans chickpeas
- 2 tbsp almond flour

- 2 tbsp quick-cooking oats
- ¼ cup chopped parsley
- 1 tbsp hot sauce
- 1 garlic clove, minced
- Sea salt and pepper to taste

Directions:
1. In a medium bowl, mash avocados and mix in the tomato and onion. Set aside the dip. In another bowl, mash the chickpeas and add the almond flour, oats, parsley, hot sauce, garlic, garlic salt, and black pepper. Mix well. Mold 4 patties out of the mixture and set aside.
2. Heat a grill pan to medium heat and grease with cooking spray. Cook the bean patties on both sides until light brown and cooked through, 10 minutes. Place each patty between each burger bun and top with avocado dip.

Nutrition Info:
- Per Serving: Calories: 545;Fat: 15g;Protein: 16g;Carbs: 89g.

Luxurious Creamy Carrot Marinara With Brown Rice Pasta

Servings: 6 | Cooking Time: 20 Minutes

Ingredients:
- 1¼ cups cashews, soaked in water for 4 hours
- 5 large carrots, peeled and roughly chopped
- 1½ to 2 cups water
- 1 tablespoon fresh basil, finely chopped
- 1 teaspoon salt
- 1 package brown rice spaghetti, 12 ounces
- 1 bunch kale, thoroughly washed, stemmed, and chopped into 1 inch pieces

Directions:
1. Drain and rinse the cashews.
2. Combine the carrots with 1½ cups of water in a medium pot set over high heat. Bring to a boil. Reduce the heat to low and simmer for 5 to 8 minutes, or until tender. Drain the carrots and reserve the cooking water.
3. Combine the cashews, basil, and salt in a blender. Add the cooked carrots and reserved cooking water. Blend until smooth, taking care of the hot liquid. Thin with more water if the sauce is too thick.
4. Bring a large pot of water to a boil over high heat. Add the pasta and cook according to the package directions.
5. Toss in the kale during the last minute of cook time and let it wilt. Drain the pasta and return it to the pot. Toss with the carrot marinara. Do not use all of the sauce. Leftover sauce will keep refrigerated for 3 to 4 days and freezes well.

Nutrition Info:
- Per Serving: Calories: 408 ;Fat: 14g ;Protein: 10g ;Carbs: 65g .

Teriyaki Vegetable Stir-fry

Servings: 4 | Cooking Time: 25 Minutes

Ingredients:
- 2 tbsp olive oil
- 2 red bell peppers, chopped
- 1 onion, chopped
- 1 carrot, chopped
- 2 tbsp teriyaki sauce

Directions:
1. Warm the olive oil in a skillet over medium heat and place in bell peppers, onion, and carrot and cook for 5-7 minutes until the veggies are soft and golden brown. Mix the teriyaki sauce, pour it over the veggies, and cook for 3-4 minutes until the sauce thick-

ens. Serve immediately.
Nutrition Info:
- Per Serving: Calories: 170;Fat: 11g;Protein: 3g;Carbs: 18g.

Seitan & Lentil Chili

Servings: 4 | Cooking Time: 35 Minutes

Ingredients:
- 2 tbsp olive oil
- 1 onion, chopped
- 8 oz seitan, chopped
- 1 cup lentils
- 1 can diced tomatoes
- 1 tsp low-sodium soy sauce
- 1 tbsp chili powder
- 1 tsp ground cumin
- 1 tsp ground allspice
- ½ tsp ground oregano
- ¼ tsp ground cayenne
- Sea salt and pepper to taste

Directions:
1. Heat the oil in a pot over medium heat. Place in onion and seitan and cook for 10 minutes. Add in lentils, diced tomatoes, 2 cups of water, soy sauce, chili powder, cumin, allspice, sugar, oregano, cayenne pepper, salt, and pepper. Simmer for 20 minutes. Serve and enjoy!

Nutrition Info:
- Per Serving: Calories: 230;Fat: 14g;Protein: 18g;Carbs: 18g.

Challenging Grain-free Fritters

Servings: 12 | Cooking Time: 20 Minutes

Ingredients:
- 2 cups chickpea flour
- 1½ cups water
- 2 tablespoons chia seeds, ground
- ½ teaspoon salt
- 3 cups lightly packed spinach leaves, finely chopped
- 1 tablespoon coconut oil, or extra-virgin olive oil

Directions:
1. Whisk together the chickpea flour, water, chia seeds, and salt in a medium bowl. Ensure that there are no lumps by mixing it well.
2. Fold in the spinach.
3. Melt the coconut oil in a nonstick skillet set over medium-low heat.
4. Working in batches, use a ¼-cup measure to drop the batter into the pan. Flatten the fritters to about ½ inch thick. Don't crowd the pan.
5. Cook for 5 to 6 minutes. Flip the fritters and cook for 5 minutes more.
6. Transfer to a serving plate.

Nutrition Info:
- Per Serving: Calories: 318 ;Fat: 10g ;Protein: 15g ;Carbs: 45g .

Saucy Seitan With Sesame Seeds

Servings: 4 | Cooking Time: 20 Minutes

Ingredients:
- 1 lb seitan, cut into 1-inch pieces
- 4 tsp olive oil
- ½ tsp freshly grated ginger
- 3 garlic cloves, minced
- 1/3 tsp red chili flakes
- 1/3 tsp allspice
- ½ cup low-sodium soy sauce
- ½ cup + 2 tbsp date sugar
- 2 tsp arrowroot
- 1 ½ tbsp olive oil
- 1 tbsp toasted sesame seeds
- 1 tbsp sliced scallions

Directions:
1. Heat half of the olive oil in a wok and sauté ginger and garlic until fragrant, 30 seconds. Mix in red chili flakes, allspice, soy sauce, and date sugar. Allow the sugar to melt and set aside. In a small bowl, mix arrowroot and 2 tbsp of water. Stir the arrowroot mixture into the sauce and allow thickening for 1 minute. Heat the remaining olive oil in a medium skillet over medium heat and fry the seitan on both sides until crispy, 10 minutes. Mix the seitan into the sauce and warm over low heat. Dish the food, garnish with sesame seeds and scallions. Serve.

Nutrition Info:
- Per Serving: Calories: 390;Fat: 23g;Protein: 25g;Carbs: 28g.

Baked Mustard Beans

Servings: 4 | Cooking Time: 25 Minutes

Ingredients:
- 2 cans Great Northern beans
- 2 tbsp olive oil
- 1 onion, minced
- 2 garlic cloves, minced
- 1 can diced tomatoes
- ½ cup pure date syrup
- 1 ½ tsp dry mustard
- ¼ tsp cayenne pepper
- Sea salt and pepper to taste

Directions:
1. Preheat your oven to 350ºF. Heat the oil in a pot over medium heat. Place in onion and garlic and sauté for 3 minutes. Add in tomatoes, date syrup, mustard, cayenne pepper, salt, and pepper. Cook for 5 minutes. Pour the beans into a baking dish and stir in the sauce to coat. Bake for 10 minutes. Serve warm.

Nutrition Info:
- Per Serving: Calories: 815;Fat: 9g;Protein: 40g;Carbs: 148.6g.

Spicy Black Bean

Servings: 6 | Cooking Time: 1 Hour

Ingredients:
- 2 onions, chopped
- 2 tablespoons water
- 4 cups cooked black beans, 2 cups dried, or 2 14 ounces cans
- 28 ounces can crush tomatoes
- 4 teaspoons chili powder
- 1½ teaspoons salt, plus additional as needed

Directions:
1. Sauté the onions in the water in a large pot set over medium heat for 5 minutes, or until soft.
2. Add the black beans, tomatoes, chili powder, and salt. Bring to a boil. Reduce the heat to low. Simmer for 1 hour while stirring occasionally
3. Taste, and adjust the seasoning if necessary.

Nutrition Info:
- Per Serving: Calories: 294| Fat: 1g ;Protein: 18g ;Carbs: 55g ,

Sweet Potato Chili

Servings: 4 | Cooking Time: 30 Minutes

Ingredients:
- 15 oz canned black beans
- 2 cups veggie broth
- 28 oz canned diced tomatoes
- 15 oz canned kidney beans
- 2 sweet potatoes, chopped
- 1 red onion, chopped
- 1 red bell pepper, chopped
- 1 green bell pepper, chopped
- 1 tbsp olive oil
- 1 tbsp chili powder
- ¼ tsp cinnamon
- 1 tsp cumin
- 2 tsp cocoa powder
- 1 tsp cayenne pepper
- Sea salt to taste

Directions:
1. Heat the olive oil in your Instant Pot on "Sauté". Add the onions, peppers, and sweet potatoes. Cook until the onions become translucent. Stir in the rest of the ingredients. Seal the lid and cook on "Manual" for 12 minutes. Once the cooking is complete, let the pressure release naturally for 5 minutes. Serve hot.

Nutrition Info:
- Per Serving: Calories: 300;Fat: 4g;Protein: 16g;Carbs: 55g.

Frittata With Kale & Seeds

Servings: 4 | Cooking Time: 30 Minutes

Ingredients:
- 2 tbsp sour cream
- 2 tbsp olive oil
- 4 cups chopped kale
- 3 garlic cloves, minced
- 8 eggs
- Sea salt and pepper to taste
- 2 tbsp sunflower seeds

Directions:
1. Preheat your oven to 390°F. Warm the olive oil in a skillet over medium heat and place in kale. Cook for 5 minutes until soft. Add in garlic and cook for another 30 seconds. Beat the eggs, sour cream, salt, and pepper in a bowl and pour it over the kale. Cook for 3 minutes over low heat until set. Pull the eggs away from the edges of the pan and move the pan to allow the uncooked egg to spread into the pan. Cook for 3 minutes until set. Top with sunflower seeds and bake in the oven for 3-5 minutes until browns. Slice into wedges. Serve warm.

Nutrition Info:
- Per Serving: Calories: 230;Fat: 18g;Protein: 2g;Carbs: 10g.

Delicious Creamy Polenta With Buckwheat And Vegetable

Servings: 6 | Cooking Time: 20 Minutes

Ingredients:
- 3 cups buckwheat
- ¼ cup extra-virgin olive oil
- 6 garlic cloves, minced
- 7 to 8 cups warm vegetable broth, divided
- 2 cups zucchini, shredded
- 6 cups spinach, finely chopped
- 1 teaspoon salt, plus additional as needed

Directions:
1. Grind the buckwheat until fine in a spice grinder, high-speed blender, or food processor.
2. Heat the olive oil in a large pot set over medium-low heat. Add the garlic and sauté for 3 minutes.
3. Add the ground buckwheat and stir to coat with the garlic and oil.
4. Stir in 1 cup of vegetable broth. Add another 1 cup of broth when all the liquid is absorbed, along with the zucchini and spinach. Repeat with the remaining 4 cups of broth, 1 cup at a time, until the buckwheat is tender and has the consistency of a thick polenta. You may not need to use all the broth.
5. Add the salt. Stir, taste, and adjust the seasoning if necessary.

Nutrition Info:
- Per Serving: Calories: 426 ;Fat: 13g ;Protein: 18g ;Carbs: 65g .

Mushroom & Green Bean Biryani

Servings: 4 | Cooking Time: 50 Minutes

Ingredients:
- 1 cup chopped mushrooms
- 1 cup brown rice
- 3 tbsp olive oil
- 3 white onions, chopped
- 6 garlic cloves, minced
- 1 tsp ginger puree
- 1 tbsp turmeric powder
- ¼ tsp cinnamon powder
- 2 tsp garam masala
- ½ tsp cardamom powder
- ½ tsp cayenne powder
- ½ tsp cumin powder
- 1 tsp smoked paprika
- 3 large tomatoes, diced
- 2 green chilies, minced
- 1 tbsp tomato puree
- 1 cup chopped mustard greens
- 1 cup Greek yogurt

Directions:
1. Warm the olive oil in a large pot over medium heat. Sauté the onions until softened, 3 minutes. Mix in the garlic, ginger, turmeric, cardamom, garam masala, cayenne pepper, cumin, paprika, and salt. Stir-fry for 1-2 minutes. Pour in the tomatoes, green chili, tomato puree, and mushrooms. Once boiling, mix in the rice and cover it with water. Cover the pot and cook until the liquid absorbs and the rice is tender, 15-20 minutes. Open the lid and fluff in the mustard greens and parsley. Top with coconut yogurt and serve.

Nutrition Info:
- Per Serving: Calories: 395;Fat: 13g;Protein: 6g;Carbs: 59g.

Pea & Basil Fettuccine

Servings: 4 | Cooking Time: 25 Minutes

Ingredients:
- 16 oz whole-wheat fettuccine
- Sea salt and pepper to taste
- ¾ cup flax milk
- ½ cup almond butter
- 1 tbsp olive oil
- 2 garlic cloves, minced
- 1 cup green peas
- ½ cup chopped fresh basil

Directions:
1. Add the fettuccine and 10 cups of water to a large pot, and

cook over medium heat until al dente, 8-10 minutes. Drain the pasta through a colander and set aside. In a bowl, whisk the flax milk, almond butter, and salt until smooth. Set aside. Heat the olive oil in a large skillet and sauté the garlic until fragrant, 30 seconds. Mix in the peas, fettuccine, and basil. Toss well until the pasta is well-coated in the sauce and season with some black pepper. Dish the food and serve warm.

Nutrition Info:
- Per Serving: Calories: 675;Fat: 23g;Protein: 21g;Carbs: 99g.

Quinoa A La Puttanesca

Servings: 4 | Cooking Time: 30 Minutes

Ingredients:
- 1 cup brown quinoa
- 2 cups water
- Sea salt to taste
- 4 cups tomatoes, diced
- 4 pitted green olives, sliced
- 4 Kalamata olives, sliced
- 1 ½ tbsp capers
- 2 garlic cloves, minced
- 1 tbsp olive oil
- 1 tbsp chopped parsley
- ¼ cup chopped basil
- 1/8 tsp red chili flakes

Directions:
1. Add quinoa, water, and salt to a medium pot and cook for 15 minutes. In a bowl, mix tomatoes, green olives, olives, capers, garlic, olive oil, parsley, basil, and red chili flakes. Allow sitting for 5 minutes. Serve with quinoa.

Nutrition Info:
- Per Serving: Calories: 230;Fat: 7g;Protein: 7g;Carbs: 35g.

Hot Quinoa Florentine

Servings: 4 | Cooking Time: 30 Minutes

Ingredients:
- ½ tsp crushed red pepper
- 2 tbsp olive oil
- 1 onion, chopped
- 3 cups fresh baby spinach
- 3 garlic cloves, minced
- 2 cups quinoa well
- 4 cups vegetable broth
- Sea salt and pepper to taste

Directions:
1. Warm the olive oil in a pot over medium heat, place the onion and spinach, and cook for 3 minutes. Stir in garlic and crushed red pepper and cook for another 30 seconds. Mix in quinoa, vegetable broth, salt, and pepper, bring to a boil, low the heat, and simmer for 15-20 minutes until the liquid is absorbed. Fluff the quinoa and serve.

Nutrition Info:
- Per Serving: Calories: 410;Fat: 13g;Protein: 8g;Carbs: 63g.

Hot Coconut Beans With Vegetables

Servings: 4 | Cooking Time: 20 Minutes

Ingredients:
- 2 tbsp olive oil
- 1 onion, chopped
- 1 red bell pepper, chopped
- 2 garlic cloves, minced
- 1 tbsp hot powder
- 1 can coconut milk
- 2 cans white beans
- 1 can diced tomatoes
- 3 cups fresh baby spinach
- Sea salt and pepper to taste
- Chopped toasted walnuts

Directions:
1. Heat the oil in a pot over medium heat. Place in onion, garlic, hot powder, and bell pepper and sauté for 5 minutes, stirring occasionally. Put in the coconut milk and whisk until well mixed. Add in white beans, tomatoes, spinach, salt, and pepper and cook for 5 minutes until the spinach wilts. Garnish with walnuts and serve.

Nutrition Info:
- Per Serving: Calories: 690;Fat: 52g;Protein: 9g;Carbs: 48g.

Vegan Sloppy Joes

Servings: 4 | Cooking Time: 25 Minutes

Ingredients:
- 2 cans diced tomatoes, 1 drained and 1 undrained
- 1 tbsp olive oil
- 1 shallot, chopped
- 1 Italian pepper, chopped
- 10 oz tofu, chopped
- ¼ cup apple cider vinegar
- 1 tbsp chili powder
- 1 tsp garlic powder
- Sea salt and pepper to taste

Directions:
1. Warm the olive oil in a skillet over medium heat and place the shallot and Italian pepper. Cook for 5 minutes until the veggies are tender. Mix in tomatoes, apple cider vinegar, chili powder, garlic powder, salt, and pepper and simmer for 10 minutes. Serve right away.

Nutrition Info:
- Per Serving: Calories: 210;Fat: 11g;Protein: 9g;Carbs: 20g.

Mediterranean Chickpeas With Vegetables

Servings: 6 | Cooking Time: 40 Minutes

Ingredients:
- 3 tbsp olive oil
- 1 red onion, chopped
- 2 carrots, chopped
- 1 celery stalk, chopped
- 2 garlic cloves, minced
- 1 tsp grated fresh ginger
- 1 tsp ground cumin
- ½ tsp turmeric
- 2 parsnips, chopped
- 8 oz green beans, chopped
- 1 can chickpeas
- 1 can diced tomatoes
- 1 ½ cups vegetable broth
- 1 tsp fresh lemon juice

Directions:
1. Heat the oil in a pot over medium heat. Place in onion, carrots, celery, garlic, and ginger. Sauté for 5 minutes. Add cumin, turmeric, parsnips, green beans, chickpeas, tomatoes and juices, and broth. Bring to a boil, then lower the heat and sprinkle with salt and pepper. Simmer for 30 minutes. Sprinkle with lemon juice and cilantro.

Nutrition Info:
- Per Serving: Calories: 205;Fat: 9g;Protein: 5g;Carbs: 29g.

Hot Seitan With Rice

Servings: 4 | Cooking Time: 50 Minutes

Ingredients:
- 2 tbsp olive oil
- 1 lb seitan, cut into cubes
- Sea salt and pepper to taste
- 1 tsp chili powder
- 1 tsp onion powder
- 1 tsp cumin powder
- 1 tsp garlic powder
- 1 yellow onion, chopped
- 2 celery stalks, chopped
- 2 carrots diced
- 4 cloves garlic
- 1 cup vegetable broth
- 1 tsp oregano
- 1 cup diced tomatoes
- 3 green chilies, chopped
- 1 lime, juiced
- 1 cup brown rice

Directions:
1. Add brown rice, 2 cups of water, and salt to a pot. Cook for 15-20 minutes. Heat the olive oil in a large pot, season the seitan with salt, pepper, and cook in the oil until brown, 10 minutes. Stir in chili powder, onion powder, cumin powder, garlic powder, and cook until fragrant, 1 minute. Mix in the onion, celery, carrots, garlic, and cook until softened. Pour in broth, 1 cup of water, oregano, tomatoes, and green chilies. Cover the pot and cook until the tomatoes soften and the liquid reduces by half, 10-15 minutes. Open the lid, adjust the taste with salt, black pepper, and mix in the lime juice. Serve with brown rice.

Nutrition Info:
- Per Serving: Calories: 535;Fat: 23g;Protein: 24g;Carbs: 61g.

Tofu Caprese Casserole

Servings: 4 | Cooking Time: 25 Minutes

Ingredients:
- 1 cup tofu cubes
- 16 cherry tomatoes, halved
- 2 tbsp basil pesto
- 1 cup paleo mayonnaise
- 2 oz grated Parmesan
- 1 cup arugula
- 4 tbsp olive oil

Directions:
1. Preheat your oven to 350ºF. In a baking dish, mix the cherry tomatoes, tofu, basil pesto, mayonnaise, half of the Parmesan cheese, salt, and black pepper. Level the ingredients with a spatula and sprinkle the remaining Parmesan cheese on top. Bake for 20 minutes or until the top of the casserole is golden brown. Remove and allow cooling for a few minutes. Slice and dish into plates, top with some arugula and drizzle with olive oil.

Nutrition Info:
- Per Serving: Calories: 475;Fat: 42g;Protein: 8g;Carbs: 8g.

Ultimate Burger With Hummus

Servings: 4 | Cooking Time: 30 Minutes

Ingredients:
- 1 tablespoon extra-virgin olive oil, plus additional for brushing
- Two 15 ounces cans garbanzo beans, drained and rinsed
- ¼ cup tahini
- 1 tablespoon lemon juice, freshly squeezed

- 2 teaspoons lemon zest
- 2 garlic cloves, minced
- 2 tablespoons chickpea flour
- 4 scallions, minced
- 1 teaspoon salt

Directions:
1. Preheat the oven to 375°F.
2. Brush a baking sheet with olive oil.
3. Combine the garbanzo beans, tahini, lemon juice, lemon zest, garlic, and the remaining 1 tablespoon of olive oil in a food processor. Pulse until smooth.
4. Add the chickpea flour, scallions, and salt. Pulse to combine.
5. Form the mixture into four patties and place them on the prepared baking sheet. Place the sheet in the preheated oven and bake for 30 minutes.

Nutrition Info:
- Per Serving: Calories: 408 ;Fat: 18g ;Protein: 19g ;Carbs: 43g .

Spinach & Cheese Sauté

Servings: 4 | Cooking Time: 20 Minutes

Ingredients:
- 1 cup cottage cheese, crumbled
- 2 tbsp olive oil
- 1 onion, chopped
- 4 cups fresh baby spinach
- 3 garlic cloves, minced
- 1 orange, juiced
- 1 orange, zested
- Sea salt and pepper to taste

Directions:
1. Warm the olive oil in a skillet over medium heat and place in onion, spinach, and cottage cheese and cook for 5 minutes until the onion is soft. Stir in garlic and sauté for another 30 seconds. Mix in orange juice, orange zest, salt, and pepper and cook for 3 minutes. Serve warm.

Nutrition Info:
- Per Serving: Calories: 130;Fat: 11g;Protein: 3g;Carbs: 8g.

Tempeh Garam Masala Bake

Servings: 4 | Cooking Time: 30 Minutes

Ingredients:
- 3 tbsp olive oil
- 3 cups tempeh slices
- 2 tbsp garam masala
- 1 red bell pepper, diced
- 1 ¼ cups coconut cream
- 1 tbsp cilantro, chopped

Directions:
1. Preheat your oven to 400ºF. Warm the olive oil in a skillet over medium heat. Season the tempeh with some salt. Fry the tempeh until browned on both sides, about 4 minutes. Stir half of the garam masala into the tempeh until evenly mixed; turn the heat off. Transfer the tempeh with the spice into a baking dish. Then, mix the bell pepper, coconut cream, cilantro, and remaining garam masala in a small bowl. Pour the mixture over the tempeh and bake in the oven for 20 minutes or until golden brown on top. Garnish with cilantro and serve.

Nutrition Info:
- Per Serving: Calories: 595;Fat: 50g;Protein: 26g;Carbs: 20g.

Cashew & Chickpea Curry

Servings: 4 | Cooking Time: 30 Minutes

Ingredients:
- 1 apple, diced
- 2 yellow onions, diced
- 2 garlic cloves, minced
- 2 tbsp avocado oil
- ½ cup vegetable broth
- 1 red bell pepper, chopped
- ½ cup cashews, chopped
- ½ cup golden raisins
- ½ tsp sea salt
- 1 tbsp curry powder
- 2 cups cooked chickpeas
- ½ cup whole milk yogurt

Directions:
1. Warm the avocado oil in a skillet over medium heat. Place the garlic and onion and cook for 2-3 minutes. Add in bell pepper and cook for 5 minutes. Stir in salt, curry powder, and vegetable broth and bring to a simmer. Put in raisins, apple, and chickpeas and cook for another 5 minutes and add in cashews. Top with yogurt and serve.

Nutrition Info:
- Per Serving: Calories: 420;Fat: 19g;Protein: 11g;Carbs: 56g.

Tofu Cabbage Stir-fry

Servings: 4 | Cooking Time: 45 Minutes

Ingredients:
- 2 ½ cups bok choy, sliced
- 2 tbsp coconut oil
- 2 cups tofu, cubed
- 1 tsp garlic powder
- 1 tsp onion powder
- 1 tbsp plain vinegar
- 2 garlic cloves, minced
- 1 tsp chili flakes
- 1 tbsp grated ginger
- 3 green onions, sliced
- 1 tbsp olive oil
- 1 cup paleo mayonnaise

Directions:
1. Warm the coconut oil in a wok over medium heat. Add bok choy and stir-fry until softened. Season with salt, pepper, garlic powder, onion powder, and plain vinegar. Sauté for 2 minutes; set aside. To the wok, add the garlic, chili flakes, and ginger and sauté them until fragrant. Put the tofu in the wok and cook until browned on all sides. Add the green onions and bok choy, heat for 2 minutes, and add the olive oil. Stir in mayonnaise. Serve.

Nutrition Info:
- Per Serving: Calories: 200;Fat: 16g;Protein: 9g;Carbs: 6g.

Habanero Pinto Bean & Bell Pepper Pot

Servings: 6 | Cooking Time: 20 Minutes

Ingredients:
- 1 tsp olive oil
- 2 red bell peppers, diced
- 1 habanero pepper, minced
- 2 cans pinto beans
- ½ cup vegetable broth
- 1 tsp ground cumin
- 1 tsp chili powder
- Sea salt and pepper to taste

Directions:
1. Heat the oil in a pot over medium heat. Place in bell and habanero peppers. Sauté for 5 minutes until tender. Add beans, broth, cumin, chili powder, salt, and pepper. Bring to a boil, then lower the heat and simmer for 10 minutes.

Nutrition Info:
- Per Serving: Calories: 135;Fat: 2g;Protein: 7g;Carbs: 23g.

Energy Boosting Bright Red Lentil Stew

Servings: 6 | Cooking Time: 35 Minutes

Ingredients:
- 2 onions, peeled and finely diced
- 4 celery stalks, finely diced
- 6½ cups plus 2 tablespoons water, divided
- 3 cups red lentils
- 2 zucchini, finely diced
- 1 teaspoon oregano, dried
- 1 teaspoon salt, plus additional as needed

Directions:
1. Sauté the onions and celery in 2 tablespoons of water for about 5 minutes in a large pot set over medium heat until soft.
2. Add the lentils, zucchini, the remaining 6½ cups of water, the oregano, and salt. Bring to a boil. Reduce the heat to low. Cover and simmer for 30 minutes while stirring occasionally.
3. Taste, and adjust the seasoning if necessary.

Nutrition Info:
- Per Serving: Calories: 367 ;Fat: 1g ;Protein: 26g ;Carbs: 64 g .

Health Supportive Vegetable Curry

Servings: 4 To 6

Cooking Time: 15 Minutes

Ingredients:
- 1 tablespoon coconut oil
- 1 onion, chopped
- 2 cups (½-inch) butternut squash cubes
- 1 large sweet potato, peeled and cut into ½-inch cubes
- 2 garlic cloves, sliced
- One 13 ½ ounces can coconut milk
- 2 cups vegetable broth
- 2 teaspoons curry powder
- 1 teaspoon salt
- 2 tablespoons fresh cilantro, chopped

Directions:
1. Heat the oil over high heat in a Dutch oven.
2. Add the onion and sauté until softened for 3 minutes.
3. Add the butternut squash, sweet potato, and garlic and sauté for 3 minutes more.
4. Add the coconut milk, broth, curry powder, and salt and bring to a boil. Reduce to a simmer and cook until the vegetables are tender for 5 minutes.
5. Top with cilantro and serve.

Nutrition Info:
- Per Serving: Calories: 120 ;Fat: 5g ;Protein: 2g ;Carbs: 20g .

Herby Quinoa With Walnuts

Servings: 4 | Cooking Time: 20 Minutes

Ingredients:
- 2 minced sundried tomatoes
- 1 cup quinoa
- 2 cups vegetable broth
- 2 garlic cloves, minced
- ¼ cup chopped chives

- 2 tbsp chopped parsley
- 2 tbsp chopped basil
- 2 tbsp chopped mint
- 1 tbsp olive oil
- ½ tsp lemon zest
- 1 tbsp lemon juice
- 2 tbsp minced walnuts

Directions:

1. In a pot, combine quinoa, vegetable broth, and garlic. Boil until the quinoa is tender and the liquid absorbs, 10-15 minutes. Fuff with a fork and stir in chives, parsley, basil, mint, tomatoes, olive oil, zest, lemon juice, and walnuts. Warm for 5 minutes. Serve.

Nutrition Info:

- Per Serving: Calories: 225;Fat: 8g;Protein: 28g;Carbs: 31g.

Soft Vegetarian Tacos

Servings: 4 | Cooking Time: 10 Minutes

Ingredients:

- Extra-virgin olive oil, for brushing
- 8 gluten-free, corn-free tortillas
- 2 cups Mango and Black Bean Stew, warm
- 1 cup shredded red cabbage, coarsely chopped
- 1 avocado, pitted and chopped
- ½ cup pineapple, chopped
- 1 scallion, chopped
- 1 teaspoon apple cider vinegar
- ¼ cup fresh cilantro, chopped
- Salt
- Freshly ground black pepper
- Lime wedges

Directions:

1. Preheat the oven to 350°F.
2. Brush a baking sheet with olive oil.
3. Place the tortillas on a work surface. Top each tortilla with about ¼ cup of Mango and Black Bean Stew. Place the folded tortilla on the prepared baking sheet. Lightly brush the top side of the tortillas with olive oil.
4. Place the sheet in the preheated oven and warm them for 10 minutes.
5. In a medium bowl, mix together the cabbage, avocado, pineapple, scallion, vinegar, and cilantro while the tacos are warming. Season with salt and pepper.
6. Stuff a portion of the cabbage mixture into the warmed tacos and serve garnished with the lime wedges.

Nutrition Info:

- Per Serving: Calories: 577 ;Fat: 16g ;Protein: 13g ;Carbs: 93g .

Vegetarian Sloppy Joes

Servings: 4 | Cooking Time: 30 Minutes

Ingredients:

- 2 tbsp avocado oil
- 2 garlic cloves, minced
- 1 yellow onion, chopped
- 1 celery stalk, chopped
- 1 carrot, minced
- ½ red bell pepper, chopped
- 1 lb cooked lentils
- 7 tbsp tomato paste
- 2 tbsp apple cider vinegar
- 1 tbsp maple syrup
- 1 tsp chili powder
- 1 tsp Dijon mustard
- ½ tsp dried oregano

Directions:

1. Warm 1 tbsp of avocado oil in a skillet over medium heat and place the garlic, carrot, onion, and celery and cook for 3 minutes until the onion is translucent. Add lentils and remaining avocado oil and cook for 5 more minutes.
2. Put in bell peppers and cook for 2 more minutes. Stir in tomato paste, apple cider vinegar, maple syrup, chili powder, Dijon mustard, and oregano and cook for another 10 minutes. Serve over rice.

Nutrition Info:

- Per Serving: Calories: 275;Fat: 8g;Protein: 14g;Carbs: 30g.

Baked Tofu With Roasted Peppers

Servings: 4 | Cooking Time: 20 Minutes

Ingredients:

- 3 oz Greek yogurt
- ¾ cup paleo mayonnaise
- 2 oz cucumber, diced
- 1 large tomato, chopped
- 2 tsp dried parsley
- 4 orange bell peppers
- 2 ½ cups cubed tofu
- 1 tbsp olive oil
- 1 tsp dried basil

Directions:

1. Preheat your oven's broiler to 450°F. In a salad bowl, combine yogurt, mayonnaise, cucumber, tomato, salt, pepper, and parsley. Refrigerate. Arrange the bell peppers and tofu on a greased baking sheet, drizzle with olive oil and season with basil, salt, and pepper. Bake for 10-15 minutes or until the peppers have charred lightly and the tofu browned. Serve with the prepared yogurt salad.

Nutrition Info:

- Per Serving: Calories: 465;Fat: 32g;Protein: 12g;Carbs: 18g.

Chipotle Kidney Bean Chili

Servings: 4 | Cooking Time: 30 Minutes

Ingredients:

- 2 tbsp olive oil
- 1 onion, chopped
- 2 garlic cloves, minced
- 1 can tomato sauce
- 1 tbsp chili powder
- 1 chipotle chili, minced
- 1 tsp ground cumin
- ½ tsp dried marjoram
- 1 can kidney beans
- Sea salt and pepper to taste
- ½ tsp cayenne pepper

Directions:

1. Heat the oil in a pot over medium heat. Place in onion and garlic and sauté for 3 minutes. Put in tomato sauce, chipotle chili, chili powder, cumin, cayenne pepper, marjoram, salt, and pepper and cook for 5 minutes. Stir in kidney beans and 2 cups of water. Bring to a boil, then lower the heat and simmer for 15 minutes, stirring often.

Nutrition Info:

- Per Serving: Calories: 260;Fat: 11g;Protein: 6g;Carbs: 37g.

Traditional Buckwheat Noodle Pad Thai

Servings: 4 | Cooking Time: 15 Minutes

Ingredients:
- 1 package buckwheat soba noodles, 8 ounces
- 1 tablespoon coconut oil
- 1 red onion, chopped
- 2 garlic cloves, minced
- 2 teaspoons fresh ginger, minced
- 1 zucchini, chopped
- 2 bok choy, sliced thin
- 1 tablespoon coconut aminos
- 1 tablespoon apple cider vinegar
- 3 tablespoons almond butter or cashew butter
- 2 tablespoons sesame oil, toasted
- 1 tablespoon raw honey or coconut sugar
- ¼ cup vegetable broth, or water
- Salt
- 2 scallions, sliced thin
- ¼ cup fresh cilantro, chopped
- 2 tablespoons sesame seeds

Directions:
1. Cook the soba noodles according to the package directions, drain and set aside.
2. Melt the coconut oil in a large pan over high heat. Add the red onion, garlic, ginger, zucchini, and bok choy. Sauté for 5 minutes.
3. Add the coconut aminos, cider vinegar, almond butter, sesame oil, honey, and vegetable broth. Cook for 2 minutes while stirring constantly.
4. Add the soba noodles to the pan and sauté them, using a large spatula to scoop the mixture from the bottom of the pan to the top to combine the vegetables with the noodles. Season with salt, and transfer the Pad Thai to a serving dish. Garnish with scallions, cilantro, and sesame seeds.

Nutrition Info:
- Per Serving: Calories: 486 ;Fat: 21g ;Protein: 19g ;Carbs: 63g .

Tomato & Alfredo Penne

Servings: 4 | Cooking Time: 20 Minutes

Ingredients:
- 2 cups almond milk
- 1 ½ cups vegetable broth
- 3 tbsp olive oil
- 1 large garlic clove, minced
- 16 oz whole-wheat penne
- ½ cup coconut cream
- 18 halved cherry tomatoes
- ¾ cup grated Parmesan
- 2 tbsp chopped parsley

Directions:
1. Bring almond milk, vegetable broth, olive oil, and garlic to a boil in a large pot, 5 minutes. Mix in the fettuccine and cook until tender while frequently tossing for about 10 minutes. Mix in coconut cream, tomatoes, Parmesan cheese, salt, and pepper. Cook for 3 minutes or until the cheese melts. Garnish with some parsley and serve warm.

Nutrition Info:
- Per Serving: Calories: 720;Fat: 27g;Protein: 22g;Carbs: 100g.

Awesome Barley Jambalaya

Servings: 4 | Cooking Time: 25 Minutes

Ingredients:
- 2 tbsp olive oil
- 1 onion, chopped
- 2 celery stalks, chopped
- 1 green bell pepper, chopped
- 2 garlic cloves, minced
- 1 cup pearl barley
- 2 cans kidney beans
- 1 can diced tomatoes
- 1 tsp dried rosemary
- 2 ½ cups vegetable broth
- 1 tbsp chopped parsley
- Sriracha sauce

Directions:
1. Heat the oil in a pot over medium heat. Place in onion, celery, bell pepper, and garlic. Sauté for 5 minutes. Add in barley, beans, tomatoes, rosemary, salt, and pepper. Stir in broth and simmer for 15 minutes. Top with parsley and drizzle with sriracha sauce to serve.

Nutrition Info:
- Per Serving: Calories: 440;Fat: 9g;Protein: 11g;Carbs: 78g.

Salads

Salads

Traditional Middle Eastern Chopped Salad

Servings: 4 | Cooking Time: 0 Minutes

Ingredients:
- 2 cups packed spinach
- 3 large tomatoes, diced
- 1 bunch radishes, sliced thin
- 1 English cucumber, peeled and diced
- 2 scallions, sliced
- 2 garlic cloves, minced
- 1 tablespoon fresh mint, chopped
- 1 tablespoon fresh parsley, chopped
- 1 cup plain almond yogurt, unsweetened
- ¼ cup extra-virgin olive oil
- 3 tablespoons lemon juice, freshly squeezed
- 1 tablespoon apple cider vinegar
- 1 teaspoon sea salt
- ¼ teaspoon black pepper, freshly ground
- 1 tablespoon sumac

Directions:
1. Combine the spinach, tomatoes, radishes, cucumber, scallions, garlic, mint, parsley, yogurt, olive oil, lemon juice, cider vinegar, salt, pepper, and sumac in a large bowl. Toss to combine.
2. Serve and enjoy.

Nutrition Info:
- Per Serving: Calories: 194 ;Fat: 14g ;Protein: 4g ;Carbs: 15g .

Light And Excellent Salad With Mango And Avocado

Servings: 4 | Cooking Time: 0 Minutes

Ingredients:
- 2 romaine lettuce hearts, chopped
- 1 cucumber, peeled and cut into ¼-inch cubes
- 2 ripe mangos, cut into
- ½-inch cubes
- 2 scallions, sliced thin
- 1 large ripe avocado
- 1 cup Creamy Coconut-Herb Dressing

Directions:
1. Combine the romaine lettuce, cucumber, mangos, scallions, and avocado in a large serving bowl.
2. Pour the Creamy Coconut-Herb Dressing over the fruit and vegetables. Toss to combine.

Nutrition Info:
- Per Serving: Calories: 253 ;Fat: 13g ;Protein: 4g ;Carbs: 37g .

Impressive Super Salad With Beetroot And Mackerel

Servings: 2 | Cooking Time: 20 Minutes

Ingredients:
- 1 cup sweet potatoes, peeled
- 12 ounces smoked mackerel fillets, skin removed
- 2 green onions, finely sliced
- 1 cup cooked beetroot, sliced into wedges
- 2 tablespoons bunch dill, finely chopped
- 2 tablespoons olive oil
- juice 1 lemon, zest of half
- 1 teaspoon caraway seeds, crushed using pestle and mortar

Directions:
1. Place the potatoes in a small saucepan of boiling water and simmer for 15 minutes on medium-high heat or until fork-tender.
2. Cool and cut into thick slices.
3. Into a bowl, flake the mackerel and add the cooled potatoes, green onions, beetroot, and dill.
4. Whisk together in a separate bowl the olive oil, lemon juice, caraway seeds, and black pepper.
5. Pour over the salad and toss well to coat.
6. Scatter over the lemon zest.
7. Pack into plastic containers and chill for later, or enjoy it straight away.

Nutrition Info:
- Per Serving: Calories: 316 ;Fat: 16g ;Protein: 5g ;Carbs: 45g .

Bean & Roasted Parsnip Salad

Servings: 3 | Cooking Time: 40 Minutes

Ingredients:
- 1 can cannellini beans
- 4 parsnips, sliced
- 2 tsp olive oil
- ½ tsp ground cinnamon
- Sea salt to taste
- 3 cups chopped spinach
- 2 tsp pomegranate seeds
- 2 tsp sunflower seeds
- ¼ cup raspberry vinaigrette

Directions:
1. Preheat your oven to 390°F. In a bowl, combine parsnips, olive oil, cinnamon, and salt. Spread on a baking tray and roast for 15 minutes. Flip the parsnips and add the beans. Roast for another 15 minutes. Allow cooling. Divide the spinach among plates and place the pomegranate seeds, sunflower seeds, and roasted parsnips and beans. Sprinkle with raspberry vinaigrette and serve.

Nutrition Info:
- Per Serving: Calories: 300;Fat: 12g;Protein: 8g;Carbs: 45g.

Broccoli Salad With Tempeh & Cranberries

Servings: 4 | Cooking Time: 15 Minutes

Ingredients:
- 3 oz olive oil
- ¾ lb tempeh slices, cubed
- 1 lb broccoli florets
- Sea salt and pepper to taste
- 2 tbsp almonds, chopped
- ½ cup frozen cranberries

Directions:
1. In a skillet, warm the olive oil over medium heat until no longer foaming, and fry the tempeh cubes until brown on all sides. Add the broccoli and stir-fry for 6 minutes. Season with salt and pepper. Turn the heat off. Stir in the almonds and cranberries to warm through. Serve.

Nutrition Info:
- Per Serving: Calories: 390;Fat: 31g;Protein: 20g;Carbs: 13g.

Radish & Fennel Salad With Eggs

Servings: 4 | Cooking Time: 25 Minutes

Ingredients:
- 1 tsp Dijon mustard
- ¼ cup olive oil
- 3 tbsp lemon juice
- 2 tsp raw honey
- Sea salt to taste
- ½ cup chopped pecans
- 10 radishes, sliced
- 3 hard-boiled eggs, chopped
- ½ fennel bulb, sliced
- ½ cup sliced radishes

Directions:
1. Whisk the olive oil, lemon juice, honey, salt, and mustard in a bowl. Add the fennel, radishes, and pecans and toss to coat. Top with chopped eggs and serve.

Nutrition Info:
- Per Serving: Calories: 240;Fat: 20g;Protein: 6g;Carbs: 9g.

Radish & Cabbage Ginger Salad

Servings: 4 | Cooking Time: 15 Minutes

Ingredients:
- 8 oz napa cabbage, cut crosswise into strips
- 2 tbsp chopped roasted hazelnuts
- 1 cup grated carrots
- 1 cup sliced radishes
- 2 green onions, minced
- 2 tbsp chopped parsley
- 2 tbsp rice vinegar
- 2 tsp olive oil
- 1 tsp low-sodium soy sauce
- 1 tsp grated fresh ginger
- ½ tsp dry mustard
- Sea salt and pepper to taste

Directions:
1. Place the cabbage, carrot, radishes, green onions, and parsley in a bowl, stir to combine. In another bowl, mix vinegar, olive oil, soy sauce, ginger, mustard, salt, and pepper. Pour over the slaw and toss to coat. Place in the fridge for 2 hours. Serve topped with hazelnuts.

Nutrition Info:
- Per Serving: Calories: 80;Fat: 6g;Protein: 10g;Carbs: 6g.

Carrot & Cabbage Salad With Avocado

Servings: 4 | Cooking Time: 15 Minutes

Ingredients:
- 1 carrot, shredded
- 1 cup shredded red cabbage
- 16 cherry tomatoes, halved
- 1 red bell pepper, sliced
- 1 can chickpeas
- ¼ cup capers
- 1 avocado, sliced
- ¼ cup olive oil
- 1 ½ tbsp fresh lemon juice
- Sea salt and pepper to taste

Directions:
1. Mix the oil, lemon juice, salt, and pepper until combined in a bowl. Add carrot, cabbage, tomatoes, bell pepper, chickpeas, capers, and avocado and toss to coat. Serve.

Nutrition Info:

- Per Serving: Calories: 325;Fat: 23g;Protein: 7g;Carbs: 28g.

Cucumber, Lettuce & Tomato Salad

Servings: 4 | Cooking Time: 15 Minutes

Ingredients:
- ½ cup halved pitted Kalamata olives
- ¾ cup olive oil
- ¼ cup white wine vinegar
- 2 tsp Dijon mustard
- 1 garlic clove
- 1 tbsp minced green onions
- ½ head romaine lettuce, torn
- ½ head iceberg lettuce, torn
- 1 can lentils
- 2 ripe tomatoes, chopped
- 1 peeled cucumber, diced
- 1 carrot, chopped
- 3 red radishes, chopped
- 2 tbsp chopped parsley
- 1 ripe avocado, chopped
- Sea salt and pepper to taste

Directions:
1. Put the oil, vinegar, mustard, garlic, green onions, salt, and pepper in a food processor. Pulse until blended. Set aside. In a bowl, place the lettuces, lentils, tomatoes, cucumber, carrot, olives, radishes, parsley, and avocado. Pour enough dressing over the salad and toss to coat.

Nutrition Info:
- Per Serving: Calories: 560;Fat: 50g;Protein: 8g;Carbs: 27g.

Lettuce & Tomato Salad With Quinoa

Servings: 4 | Cooking Time: 25 Minutes

Ingredients:
- 1 cup quinoa, rinsed
- ⅓ cup white wine vinegar
- 2 tbsp extra-virgin olive oil
- 1 tbsp chopped fresh dill
- Sea salt and pepper to taste
- 2 cups sliced sweet onions
- 2 tomatoes, sliced
- 4 cups shredded lettuce

Directions:
1. Place the quinoa in a pot with 2 cups of salted water. Bring to a boil. Lower the heat and simmer covered for 15 minutes. Turn the heat off and let sit for 5 minutes. Using a fork, fluff the quinoa and set aside. In a small bowl, whisk the vinegar, olive oil, dill, salt, and pepper; set aside. In a serving plate, combine onions, tomatoes, quinoa, and lettuce. Pour in the dressing and toss to coat.

Nutrition Info:
- Per Serving: Calories: 380;Fat: 11g;Protein: 12g;Carbs: 58g.

Effortless Half-sour Pickled Salad

Servings: 2 | Cooking Time: 0 Minutes

Ingredients:
- 1 large cucumber, cut into 4-inch spears
- Brine:
- 2 cups water
- 1 cup apple cider vinegar
- ½ teaspoon Himalayan salt, fine
- 1 whole clove
- 1 bay leaf
- ½ medium Hass avocado, peeled, pitted, and sliced

- ¼ cup Pickled Red Onions
- 2 or 3 slices Genoa salami
- 2 or 3 slices soppressata or smoked turkey
- ¼ teaspoon fine Himalayan salt
- 1 tablespoon avocado oil

Directions:
1. Place the cucumber spears in a clean glass container.
2. Bring the water, vinegar, salt, and clove to a light simmer in a saucepan over medium heat. Add the bay leaf to the cucumbers and pour the brine over them.
3. Cover and refrigerate for 3 hours or up to overnight. Arrange the pickled cucumbers on a plate with the avocado slices and pickled onions to serve. Roll up the deli meats and place them around the spears. Sprinkle everything with the salt and drizzle with the avocado oil.
4. Store leftovers in an airtight container in the fridge for up to 2 days.

Nutrition Info:
- Per Serving: Calories: 236 ;Fat: 20g ;Protein: 6g;Carbs: 11g .

Spinach Salad With Blackberries & Pecans

Servings: 4 | Cooking Time: 10 Minutes

Ingredients:
- 10 oz baby spinach
- 1 cup raisins
- 1 cup fresh blackberries
- ¼ red onion, thinly sliced
- ½ cup chopped pecans
- ¼ cup balsamic vinegar
- ¾ cup olive oil
- Sea salt and pepper to taste

Directions:
1. Combine the spinach, raisins, blackberries, red onion, and pecans in a bowl. In another bowl, mix the vinegar, olive oil, salt, and pepper. Pour over the salad and toss to coat. Serve immediately.

Nutrition Info:
- Per Serving: Calories: 600;Fat: 50g;Protein: 4g;Carbs: 40g.

Mediterranean Pasta Salad

Servings: 4 | Cooking Time: 15 Minutes

Ingredients:
- ½ cup minced sun-dried tomatoes
- 2 roasted bell red peppers, chopped
- 8 oz whole-wheat pasta
- 1 can chickpeas
- ½ cup pitted black olives
- 1 jar dill pickles, sliced
- ½ cup frozen peas, thawed
- 1 tbsp capers
- 3 tsp dried chives
- ½ cup olive oil
- ¼ cup white wine vinegar
- ½ tsp dried basil
- 1 garlic clove, minced
- Sea salt and pepper to taste

Directions:
1. Cook the pasta in salted water for 8-10 minutes until al dente. Drain and remove to a bowl. Stir in chickpeas, black olives, sun-dried tomatoes, dill pickles, roasted peppers, peas, capers, and chives. In another bowl, whisk oil, white wine vinegar, basil, garlic, sugar, salt, and pepper. Pour over the pasta and toss to coat. Serve.

Nutrition Info:
- Per Serving: Calories: 590;Fat: 32g;Protein: 12g;Carbs: 67g.

Refreshingly Spicy Chicken Salad With Cumin And Mango

Servings: 2 | Cooking Time: 15 Minutes

Ingredients:
- 2 free range chicken breasts, skinless
- 1 teaspoon oregano, finely chopped
- 1 garlic clove, minced
- 1 teaspoon chili flakes
- 1 teaspoon cumin
- 1 teaspoon turmeric
- 1 tablespoon extra-virgin olive oil
- 1 lime, juiced
- 1 cup mango, cubed
- ½ iceberg/romaine lettuce or similar, sliced

Directions:
1. Mix oil, garlic, herbs, and spices with the lime juice in a bowl.
2. Add the chicken and marinate for at least 30 minutes up to overnight.
3. Preheat the broiler when ready to serve to medium-high heat.
4. Add the chicken to a lightly greased baking tray and broil for 10-12 minutes or until cooked through.
5. In a serving bowl, combine the lettuce with the mango.
6. Serve immediately once the chicken is cooked on top of the mango and lettuce.

Nutrition Info:
- Per Serving: Calories: 216 ;Fat: 9g ;Protein: 19g ;Carbs: 19g .

Out Of This World Salad With Basil And Tomato

Servings: 4 | Cooking Time: 0 Minutes

Ingredients:
- 4 large heirloom tomatoes, chopped
- ¼ cup fresh basil leaves, torn
- 2 garlic cloves, finely minced
- ¼ cup extra-virgin olive oil
- ½ teaspoon sea salt
- ¼ teaspoon black pepper, freshly ground

Directions:
1. Gently mix together the tomatoes, basil, garlic, olive oil, salt, and pepper in a medium bowl.
2. Serve and enjoy.

Nutrition Info:
- Per Serving: Calories: 140 ;Fat: 14g ;Protein: 1g ;Carbs: 4g .

Ready To Eat Taco Salad

Servings: 2 | Cooking Time: 30 Minutes

Ingredients:
- 1 tablespoon extra-virgin olive oil
- 2 skinless chicken breasts, chopped
- 2 carrots, sliced
- ½ large onion, chopped
- 2 teaspoons cumin seeds
- ½ avocado, chopped
- 1 juiced lime
- ½ cucumber, chopped
- ½ cup fresh spinach, washed
- 1 mason or Kilner jar

Directions:

1. Heat up the oil in a skillet on medium heat and then cook the chicken for 10 to 15 minutes until browned and cooked through.
2. Remove and place to one side to cool.
3. Add the carrots and onion and continue to cook for 5 to 10 minutes or until soft.
4. Add the cumin seeds in a separate pan on high heat and toast until they're brown before crushing them in a pestle and mortar or blender.
5. Put them into the pan with the veggies and turn off the heat.
6. Into a food processor, add the avocado and lime juice and blend until creamy.
7. Layer the jar with half of the avocado and lime mixture, then the cumin roasted veggies, and then the chicken, packing it all in.
8. Top with the tomatoes, cucumbers, and cilantro, and spinach, refrigerate for 20 minutes before serving.

Nutrition Info:
- Per Serving: Calories: 644 ;Fat: 38g ;Protein: 63g ;Carbs: 12g.

Mushroom And Green Bean Salad

Servings: 4 | Cooking Time: 25 Minutes

Ingredients:
- 1 lb cremini mushrooms, sliced
- ½ cup green beans
- 3 tbsp olive oil
- Sea salt and pepper to taste
- Juice of 1 lemon
- 4 tbsp toasted hazelnuts

Directions:
1. Preheat your oven to 450°F. Arrange the mushrooms and green beans in a baking dish, drizzle the olive oil over, and sprinkle with salt and black pepper. Use your hands to rub the vegetables with the seasoning and roast in the oven for 20 minutes or until they are soft. Transfer the vegetables into a salad bowl, drizzle with the lemon juice, and toss the salad with hazelnuts. Serve and enjoy!

Nutrition Info:
- Per Serving: Calories: 130;Fat: 11g;Protein: 11g;Carbs: 6g.

Hot Chickpea Salad

Servings: 4 | Cooking Time: 30 Minutes

Ingredients:
- 1 tsp chili pepper flakes
- 1 avocado, chopped
- 1 bunch of kale, sliced
- 2 tsp lemon juice
- 2 tbsp extra-virgin olive oil
- Sea salt to taste
- 1 can chickpeas

Directions:
1. Add the kale to a large bowl. Sprinkle with salt, 1 tablespoon of olive oil, and lemon juice. Gently knead the kale leaves in the bowl for 5 minutes or until wilted and bright. Rip the leafy part of the kale off the stem, then discard the stem.
2. Warm the remaining olive oil in a nonstick skillet over medium heat. Add the chickpeas, chili pepper flakes, and salt and cook for 15 minutes or until the chickpeas are crispy. Transfer the kale to a large serving bowl, then top with chickpeas and avocado. Toss to combine and serve.

Nutrition Info:
- Per Serving: Calories: 360;Fat: 20g;Protein: 12g;Carbs: 35g.

Tender Chicken Salad

Servings: 2 | Cooking Time: 10 To 15 Minutes

Ingredients:
- ½ cup low-fat Greek yogurt
- 1 tablespoon turmeric
- ¼ teaspoon cumin
- ½ teaspoon ginger, grated
- ½ onion, chopped
- 2 tablespoon lemon juice, freshly squeezed
- ½ teaspoon paprika
- a sprinkle of ground pepper
- 2 boneless, skinless chicken breast halves
- 1 teaspoon extra virgin olive oil
- ¼ cup water
- ½ cucumber, diced
- 1 cup watercress or raw spinach
- pinch of cilantro, freshly chopped

Directions:
1. In a mixing bowl, add the spices to the yogurt before adding the chicken and cover.
2. Allow marinating for at least an hour up to overnight.
3. Preheat the broilComplementary Spinach Salad er to medium heat and grease a baking tray with olive oil. Shake off the excess marinade from the chicken and then grill for 10 minutes by turning once halfway. Check the meat is cooked and piping hot in the middle before removing it from the broiler and placing it to one side.
4. Slice carefully the chicken.
5. Layer the salad onto serving plates and squeeze over the juice of your lemon.
6. Add a pinch of fresh finely chopped cilantro to serve.

Nutrition Info:
- Per Serving: Calories: 96 ;Fat: 2g ;Protein: 5g ;Carbs: 15g .

Beetroot Salad With Mackerel

Servings: 2 | Cooking Time: 30 Minutes

Ingredients:
- 12 oz smoked mackerel
- 1 lime, zested and juiced
- 1 cup peeled sweet potatoes
- 2 spring onions, sliced
- 4 cooked beetroot wedges
- 2 tbsp chopped dill
- 2 tbsp olive oil
- 1 tsp crushed caraway seeds

Directions:
1. Boil the potatoes in a small saucepan for 15 minutes over medium heat. Drain, cool and slice. Flake the mackerel into a bowl and add the cooled potatoes, green onions, beetroot and dill. Pour in the olive oil, lime juice, caraway seeds, lime zest, and black pepper and toss to coat. Serve.

Nutrition Info:
- Per Serving: Calories: 535;Fat: 38g;Protein: 33g;Carbs: 15g.

Chinese-style Cabbage Salad

Servings: 6 | Cooking Time: 15 Minutes

Ingredients:
- 4 cups shredded red cabbage
- 2 cups sliced white cabbage
- 1 cup red radishes, sliced
- ¼ cup fresh orange juice
- 2 tbsp Chinese black vinegar

- 1 tsp low-sodium soy sauce
- 2 tbsp olive oil
- 1 tsp grated fresh ginger
- 1 tbsp black sesame seeds

Directions:
1. Mix the red cabbage, white cabbage, and radishes in a bowl. In another bowl, whisk the orange juice, vinegar, soy sauce, olive oil, and ginger. Pour over the slaw and toss to coat. Marinate covered in the fridge for 2 hours. Serve topped with sesame seeds.

Nutrition Info:
- Per Serving: Calories: 80;Fat: 6g;Protein: 2g;Carbs: 7g.

High-spirited Salmon Salad

Servings: 2 | Cooking Time: 0 Minutes

Ingredients:
- 3 cups baby spinach
- ½ cucumber, thinly sliced
- 1 small fennel bulb, trimmed and thinly sliced
- 2 leftover Basic Baked Salmon fillets, flaked
- 1 small ripe avocado, peeled, pitted, and sliced
- ¼ cup extra-virgin olive oil
- 2 tablespoons lemon juice, fresh
- 1 teaspoon salt
- ¼ teaspoon black pepper, freshly ground
- 1 teaspoon fresh dill, chopped

Directions:
1. Arrange the spinach on a serving platter or in a bowl.
2. Top with the cucumber, fennel, salmon, and avocado.
3. Whisk together the olive oil, lemon juice, salt, pepper, and dill in a small bowl or shake in a small jar with a tight-fitting lid.
4. Pour the dressing over the salad, and serve.

Nutrition Info:
- Per Serving: Calories: 590 ;Fat: 48g ;Protein: 23g ;Carbs: 20g .

Porky Salad With Spinach

Servings: 2 | Cooking Time: 0 Minutes

Ingredients:
- 2 cups baby spinach
- 8 (½-inch-thick) slices leftover Pan-Seared Pork Loin
- 4 leftover Roasted Fingerling Potatoes, cut in half lengthwise
- 1 green apple, cored and thinly sliced
- ½ red bell pepper, thinly sliced
- ¼ cup Ginger-Turmeric Dressing

Directions:
1. Toss together the spinach, pork loin, potatoes, green apple, and red bell pepper in a medium bowl.
2. Pour the dressing over and toss to combine.
3. Divide between two bowls and serve.

Nutrition Info:
- Per Serving: Calories: 590 ;Fat: 39g ;Protein: 42g ;Carbs: 19g .

Gratifying Healthy Sweet Potato Salad With Mustard And Tarragon

Servings: 2 | Cooking Time: 30 Minutes

Ingredients:
- 2 medium-sized sweet potatoes, peeled and cubed
- 2½cup of low-fat Greek yogurt
- 2 tablespoons Dijon mustard
- 1 tablespoon tarragon, dried
- 1 beef tomato, finely chopped
- 2½ yellow pepper, finely chopped

- ½ red onion, finely chopped
- pinch of black pepper

Directions:
1. Boil water in a large pot on high heat.
2. Cook the potatoes in the pot for 20 minutes or until tender.
3. After draining, set aside to cool down.
4. In a serving bowl, combine Dijon mustard, plain yogurt, tarragon, peppers, tomatoes, and red onion.
5. Add the cooled potatoes and mix well then serve.

Nutrition Info:
- Per Serving: Calories: 260 ;Fat: 3g ;Protein: 12g ;Carbs: 50g.

Apple & Arugula Salad With Walnuts

Servings: 4 | Cooking Time: 20 Minutes

Ingredients:
- ¼ cup chopped walnuts
- 10 oz arugula
- 1 apple, thinly sliced
- 1 tbsp finely minced shallot
- 2 tbsp champagne vinegar
- 2 tbsp olive oil
- Sea salt and pepper to taste
- ¼ tsp English mustard

Directions:
1. Preheat your oven to 360°F. In a baking sheet, spread the walnuts and toast for 6 minutes. Let cool. In a bowl, combine the walnuts, arugula, and apple. In another bowl, mix the shallot, vinegar, olive oil, salt, pepper, and mustard. Pour over the salad and toss to coat. Serve.

Nutrition Info:
- Per Serving: Calories: 140;Fat: 11g;Protein: 3g;Carbs: 10g.

Tomato Bean & Bulgur Salad

Servings: 4 | Cooking Time: 25 Minutes

Ingredients:
- 3 cups water
- 1 ½ cups bulgur, rinsed
- Sea salt and pepper to taste
- 1 can black beans
- 4 ripe plum tomatoes, sliced
- 1 red onion, sliced
- ¼ cup chopped parsley
- ¼ cup olive oil
- 2 tbsp sherry vinegar

Directions:
1. Place the bulgur in a pot with boiling salted water. Lower the heat and simmer for 20 minutes. Remove to a bowl. Stir in black beans, tomatoes, onion, and parsley. In another bowl, mix the olive oil, vinegar, salt, and pepper. Pour over the bulgur mixture and toss to coat. Let sit covered for 20 minutes. Serve and enjoy!

Nutrition Info:
- Per Serving: Calories: 280;Fat: 15g;Protein: 4g;Carbs: 32g.

Coleslaw & Spinach Salad With Grapefruit

Servings: 4 | Cooking Time: 10 Minutes

Ingredients:
- 1 large grapefruit
- 2 cups coleslaw mix
- 2 cups green leaf lettuce, torn
- 2 cups baby spinach
- 1 bunch watercress

- 6 radishes, sliced
- Juice of 1 lemon
- 2 tsp date syrup
- 1 tsp white wine vinegar
- Sea salt and black pepper
- ¼ cup extra-virgin olive oil

Directions:

1. Slice the grapefruit by cutting the ends, peeling all the white pith, and making an incise in the membrane to take out each segment. Transfer to a bowl. Stir in coleslaw, lettuce, spinach, watercress, and radishes. In a bowl, mix the lemon juice, date syrup, vinegar, salt, and pepper. Gently beat the olive oil until emulsified. Pour over the salad and toss to coats. Serve and enjoy!

Nutrition Info:

- Per Serving: Calories: 205;Fat: 14g;Protein: 1g;Carbs: 21g.

Low In Calories Salad With Artichoke And Almond

Servings: 4 | Cooking Time: 0 Minutes

Ingredients:

- 2 cups cooked quinoa
- Two 15 ounces cans water-packed artichoke hearts, drained
- 1 cup kale, chopped
- ½ cup red onion, chopped
- ½ cup almonds, chopped
- 3 tablespoons fresh parsley, finely chopped
- Juice of 1 lemon or 3 tablespoons
- 2 tablespoons olive oil
- 1 tablespoon balsamic vinegar
- 1 teaspoon bottled minced garlic
- Sea salt

Directions:

1. Toss together the quinoa, artichoke hearts, kale, red onion, almonds, parsley, lemon juice, olive oil, balsamic vinegar, and garlic in a large bowl until well mixed.
2. Season with sea salt and serve.

Nutrition Info:

- Per Serving: Calories: 402 ;Fat: 16g ;Protein: 16g;Carbs: 56g .

Cowboy Salad

Servings: 4 | Cooking Time: 15 Minutes

Ingredients:

- 2 heads romaine lettuce, torn
- 16 cherry tomatoes, halved
- 1 peeled avocado, diced
- 1 peeled cucumber, diced
- 4 oz smoked salmon, flaked
- 4 scallions, thinly sliced
- 2 tbsp ranch dressing

Directions:

1. Place a bed of romaine lettuce in a serving bowl. Layer tomatoes, avocado, cucumber, and smoked salmon. Serve topped with scallions and ranch dressing.

Nutrition Info:

- Per Serving: Calories: 235;Fat: 14g;Protein: 12g;Carbs: 20g.

Balanced Salad With Avocado And Grapefruit

Servings: 4 | Cooking Time: 0 Minutes

Ingredients:

- Dressing:
- ½ avocado, peeled and pitted
- ¼ cup lemon juice, freshly squeezed
- 2 tablespoons raw honey
- Pinch sea salt
- Water, for thinning the dressing
- Salad:
- 4 cups spinach, fresh
- 1 Ruby Red grapefruit, peeled, sectioned, and cut into chunks
- ¼ cup radishes, sliced
- ¼ cup sunflower seeds, roasted
- ¼ cup cranberries, dried

Directions:

1. Combine the avocado, lemon juice, honey, and sea salt in a blender. Pulse until very smooth.
2. Add enough water to reach your desired consistency and set the dressing aside.
3. In a large bowl toss the spinach with half the dressing. Divide the dressed spinach among four plates.
4. Top each with grapefruit, radishes, sunflower seeds, and cranberries.
5. Drizzle the remaining half of the dressing over the salads and serve.

Nutrition Info:

- Per Serving: Calories: 126 ;Fat: 7g ;Protein: 2g;Carbs: 16g .

Radish & Tomato Salad

Servings: 4 | Cooking Time: 15 Minutes

Ingredients:

- 2 tomatoes, sliced
- 6 small red radishes, sliced
- 2 ½ tbsp white wine vinegar
- ½ tsp chopped chervil
- Sea salt and pepper to taste
- ¼ cup olive oil

Directions:

1. Mix the tomatoes and radishes in a bowl. Set aside. In another bowl, whisk the vinegar, chervil, salt, and pepper until mixed. Pour over the salad and toss to coat. Serve.

Nutrition Info:

- Per Serving: Calories: 140;Fat: 14g;Protein: 1g;Carbs: 4g.

Oily Salad With Celery And Kipper

Servings: 2 | Cooking Time: 0 Minutes

Ingredients:

- 1 can kippers, cooked
- 1 celery stalk, chopped
- 1 tablespoon fresh parsley, chopped
- ½ cup low fat Greek yogurt
- 1 lemon, juiced
- 1 clove garlic, minced
- 1 onion, minced

Directions:

1. All of the ingredients must be combined apart from the kippers into a salad bowl.
2. Drain the kippers and then toss in the dressing mix.
3. Chill before serving for at least 20 minutes in the fridge.

Nutrition Info:

- Per Serving: Calories: 140 ;Fat: 2g ;Protein: 8g ;Carbs: 24g ;Sugar: 15g .

Quick Insalata Caprese

Servings: 4 | Cooking Time: 10 Minutes

Ingredients:
- 16 oz fresh mozzarella cheese, sliced
- 4 large tomatoes, sliced
- ¼ cup fresh basil leaves
- ¼ cup extra-virgin olive oil
- Sea salt and pepper to taste

Directions:
1. On a salad platter, layer alternating slices of tomatoes and mozzarella. Add a basil leaf between each slice. Season with olive oil, salt, and pepper. Serve right away.

Nutrition Info:
- Per Serving: Calories: 150;Fat: 15g;Protein: 1g;Carbs: 5g.

Pantry Salad With White Bean And Tuna

Servings: 4 | Cooking Time: 0 Minutes

Ingredients:
- 4 cups arugula
- Two 5 ounces cans flaked white tuna, drained
- One 15 ounces can white beans, drained and rinsed
- ½ pint cherry tomatoes, halved lengthwise
- ½ red onion, finely chopped
- ½ cup pitted Kalamata olives
- ¼ cup extra-virgin olive oil
- 2 tablespoons freshly squeezed lemon juice
- Salt
- Freshly ground black pepper
- 2 ounces crumbled sheep's milk or goat's milk feta cheese

Directions:
1. Mix together the arugula, tuna, white beans, tomatoes, onion, olives, olive oil, and lemon juice in a large bowl. Season with salt and pepper.
2. Top the salad with the feta cheese before serving.

Nutrition Info:
- Per Serving: Calories: 373 ; Fat: 19g ; Protein: 29g;Carbs: 28g.

Lemony Spinach Salad

Servings: 4 | Cooking Time: 10 Minutes

Ingredients:
- 2 tbsp pine nuts, toasted
- 6 cups baby spinach
- 2 tbsp lemon juice
- ¼ cup Dijon mustard
- 1 ½ tbsp maple syrup
- 2 tbsp extra-virgin olive oil
- Sea salt to taste

Directions:
1. Combine all the ingredients, except for the spinach and pine nuts, in a small bowl. Mix well. Put the spinach in a large serving bowl, drizzle with the lemon dressing, toss to combine well. Top with pine nuts and serve.

Nutrition Info:
- Per Serving: Calories: 155;Fat: 15g;Protein: 2g;Carbs: 8g.

Broccoli & Mango Rice Salad

Servings: 4 | Cooking Time: 25 Minutes

Ingredients:
- 3 cups broccoli florets, blanched
- 1/3 cup roasted almonds, chopped
- ½ cup brown rice, rinsed
- 1 mango, chopped
- 1 red bell pepper, chopped
- 1 jalapeño, minced
- 1 tsp grated fresh ginger
- 2 tbsp fresh lemon juice
- 3 tbsp grapeseed oil

Directions:
1. Place the rice in a bowl with salted water and cook for 18-20 minutes. Remove to a bowl. Stir in broccoli, mango, bell pepper, and chili. In another bowl, mix the ginger, lemon juice, and oil. Pour over the rice and toss to combine. Top with almonds. Serve and enjoy!

Nutrition Info:
- Per Serving: Calories: 290;Fat: 15g;Protein: 1g;Carbs: 35g.

Luscious Salad Niçoise

Servings: 4 | Cooking Time: 20 Minutes

Ingredients:
- 2 baby beets, peeled and cut into large dice
- 2 tablespoons extra-virgin olive oil
- 8 ounces green beans, trimmed
- Four 4 ounces skin-on salmon fillets, pin bones removed
- Kosher salt
- French Vinaigrette
- Freshly ground black pepper
- 1 cup halved cherry tomatoes, 6 ½ ounces
- 3 hard-boiled eggs, quartered
- ½ cup (2 ½ ounces) oil-cured Niçoise olives, pitted
- 1 tablespoon minced chives

Directions:
1. Preheat the oven to 400°F.
2. Toss the beets in a small roasting pan with 1 tablespoon of the olive oil. Roast, stirring every 10 to 15 minutes, until the beets are soft and caramelized, for 40 minutes. Set aside to cool.
3. Bring a pot of salted water to a boil and fill a medium bowl with ice water. Add the green beans to the boiling water and cook for 2 minutes. , Transfer the beans with a slotted spoon to the ice-water bath to stop the cooking. Be careful not to overcook the beans. Dry the beans.
4. Rinse the salmon and pat dry with a paper towel. Sprinkle each side with a small pinch of salt.
5. Place a medium nonstick sauté pan over medium-high heat. Add the remaining 1 tablespoon olive oil when the pan is hot. Place the salmon fillets skin-side down in the pan and cook until the skin is crispy for 2 minutes. For medium-rare salmon, Turn the fillets and cook for 1 minute more. For medium salmon, also turn the salmon on its sides, cooking each side for 1 minute. Remove and place on a wire rack so the skin doesn't get soggy.
6. In a medium bowl, place the green beans then add 1 tablespoon of the vinaigrette, and toss to coat. Taste and add a pinch of salt and pepper if needed. Arrange the beans in a pile on a serving platter. Repeat with the beets and cherry tomatoes. Add the hard-boiled eggs and olives to the platter, then top with the salmon fillets. Drizzle with a little vinaigrette, then sprinkle with the chives. Serve family style.

Nutrition Info:
- Per Serving: Calories: 460 ;Fat: 41g ;Protein: 16g ;Carbs: 9g .

Sweet Potato & Kale Salad With Pine Nuts

Servings: 6 | Cooking Time: 30 Minutes

Ingredients:
- 2 sweet potatoes, peeled
- 1 leek
- 1 apple, peeled
- 2 tbsp apple cider vinegar
- Sea salt and pepper to taste
- ½ tsp red pepper flakes
- ¼ cup pine nuts
- 1 tbsp avocado oil
- 3 tbsp olive oil
- 15 oz kale, chopped

Directions:
1. Preheat your oven to 350°F. Line a baking sheet with parchment paper. Place the kale, olive oil, red pepper flakes, pepper, and vinegar in a bowl and toss to coat. Transfer 3/4 of this mixture to the sheet and bake for 20 minutes, turning once. Put in the remaining mixture.
2. Cut the leek, sweet potatoes, and apple into bite-size pieces. Warm the avocado oil in a skillet over medium heat and add the veggie pieces. Cook for 10 minutes until the sweet potatoes are soft. Transfer the kale mixture to a plate and stir in sweet potato mix and pine nuts. Serve.

Nutrition Info:
- Per Serving: Calories: 215;Fat: 15g;Protein: 5g;Carbs: 23g.

Italian Vegetable Relish

Servings: 6 | Cooking Time: 15 Minutes

Ingredients:
- ¼ cup sliced pimiento-stuffed green olives
- 1 carrot, sliced
- 1 red bell pepper, sliced
- 1 cup cauliflower florets
- 2 celery stalks, chopped
- ½ cup chopped red onion
- 1 garlic clove, minced
- 1 jalapeño pepper, chopped
- 3 tbsp white wine vinegar
- 1/3 cup olive oil
- Sea salt to taste

Directions:
1. Combine the carrot, bell pepper, cauliflower, celery, and onion in a bowl. Add in salt and cold water. Cover and transfer to the fridge for 4-6 hours. Strain and wash the veggies. Remove to a bowl and mix in olives. Set aside. In another bowl, mix the garlic, jalapeño pepper, vinegar, and olive oil. Pour over the veggies and toss to coat. Let chill in the fridge for at least 2 hours. Serve and enjoy!

Nutrition Info:
- Per Serving: Calories: 135;Fat: 13g;Protein: 1g;Carbs: 4g.

Warm Cod & Zucchini Salad

Servings: 2 | Cooking Time: 25 Minutes

Ingredients:
- 2 cups mustard greens
- 1 skinless cod fillets
- ½ zucchini, sliced
- 1 tbsp balsamic vinegar
- 2 tbsp extra-virgin olive oil
- 2 thyme sprigs, torn
- 1 lemon, juiced

Directions:
1. Brush the cod fillet with olive oil and fry it in a pan over medium heat until browned. Remove and flake it. Sauté the zucchini and mustard greens in the same pan for 4-5 minutes. Transfer to a plate and top with cod. Drizzle with lemon and sprinkle with thyme.

Nutrition Info:
- Per Serving: Calories: 530;Fat: 26g;Protein: 68g;Carbs: 5g.

Fruity Salad With Spinach, Orange, And Cranberry

Servings: 1 | Cooking Time: 2 Minutes

Ingredients:
- 1 cup fresh spinach with trimmed leaves and coarsely chopped
- 1 orange, peeled and sliced
- 1 cup fresh cranberries, chopped
- 2 tablespoons red wine vinegar
- 4 teaspoons olive oil
- 2 teaspoons ginger, peeled and grated
- a pinch of black pepper

Directions:
1. Grab a salad bowl and mix the vinegar and olive oil until it blends. Then add in the cranberries and ginger, adding pepper to taste.
2. Add the spinach and orange slices to the dressing, and then toss to coat.
3. Chill before serving.

Nutrition Info:
- Per Serving: Calories: 368 ;Fat: 19g Protein: 7g ;;Carbs: 46g.

Spinach & Pomegranate Salad

Servings: 4 | Cooking Time: 10 Minutes

Ingredients:
- 2 tbsp extra-virgin olive oil
- 4 cups fresh baby spinach
- ¼ cup pomegranate seeds
- ¼ cup raspberry vinaigrette

Directions:
1. Mix the spinach and walnuts in a bowl. Sprinkle with olive oil and raspberry vinaigrette and toss to combine.

Nutrition Info:
- Per Serving: Calories: 500;Fat: 49g;Protein: 12g;Carbs: 10g.

Minty Eggplant Salad

Servings: 2 | Cooking Time: 45 Minutes

Ingredients:
- 1 lemon, half zested and juiced, half cut into wedges
- 1 tsp olive oil
- 1 eggplant, chopped
- ½ tsp ground cumin
- ½ tsp ground ginger
- ¼ tsp turmeric
- ¼ tsp ground nutmeg
- Sea salt to taste
- 2 tbsp capers
- 1 tbsp chopped green olives
- 1 garlic clove, pressed
- 2 tbsp fresh mint, chopped
- 2 cups watercress, chopped

Directions:
1. In a skillet over medium heat, warm the oil. Place the eggplant

and cook for 5 minutes. Add in cumin, ginger, turmeric, nutmeg, and salt. Cook for another 10 minutes. Stir in lemon zest, lemon juice, capers, olives, garlic, and mint. Cook for 1-2 minutes more. Place some watercress on each plate and top with the eggplant mixture. Serve.

Nutrition Info:
• Per Serving: Calories: 110;Fat: 3g;Protein: 44g;Carbs: 20g.

Colorful Salad

Servings: 6 | Cooking Time: 5 Minutes

Ingredients:
• 1 cup English peas, shelled
• 3 Chioggia beets, sliced
• 6 cups mixed greens
• 1 red onion, sliced
• 1 avocado, sliced
• 5 tsp lemon-mustard dressing

Directions:
1. Combine peas, beets, mixed greens, onion, and avocado in a bowl. Toos in the lemon-mustard dressing. Serve.

Nutrition Info:
• Per Serving: Calories: 110;Fat: 7g;Protein: 12g;Carbs: 16g.

Zucchini & Bell Pepper Salad With Beans

Servings: 2 | Cooking Time: 40 Minutes

Ingredients:
• 1 can cannellini beans
• 1 tbsp olive oil
• 2 tbsp balsamic vinegar
• 1 tsp minced fresh chives
• 1 garlic clove, minced
• 1 tbsp rosemary, chopped
• 1 tbsp oregano, chopped
• A pinch of sea salt
• 1 green bell pepper, sliced
• 1 zucchini, diced
• 2 carrots, diced

Directions:
1. In a bowl, mix the olive oil, balsamic vinegar, chives, garlic, rosemary, oregano, and salt. Stir in the beans, bell pepper, zucchini, and carrots. Serve and enjoy!

Nutrition Info:
• Per Serving: Calories: 150;Fat: 8g;Protein: 1g;Carbs: 1g.

Tropical Salad

Servings: 4 | Cooking Time: 15 Minutes

Ingredients:
• 2 cups blanched snow peas, sliced
• ½ cup chopped roasted almonds
• ½ tsp minced garlic
• ½ tsp grated fresh ginger
• ¼ cup olive oil
• ¼ tsp crushed red pepper
• 3 tbsp rice vinegar
• 3 tbsp water
• 1 tsp low-sodium soy sauce
• ½ papaya, chopped
• 1 large carrot, shredded
• 1 peeled cucumber, sliced
• 1 shredded romaine lettuce
• Sea salt to taste

Directions:
1. Combine garlic, ginger, olive oil, red pepper, vinegar, water, salt, and soy sauce in a bowl. Add papaya, snow peas, cucumber slices, and carrot and toss to coat. Spread the lettuce on a plate. Top with salad and almonds.

Nutrition Info:
• Per Serving: Calories: 280;Fat: 20g;Protein: 1g;Carbs: 23g.

Ruby Salad With Avocado Dressing

Servings: 4 | Cooking Time: 20 Minutes

Ingredients:
• 1 peeled grapefruit, cut into chunks
• ¼ cup roasted sunflower seeds
• ¼ cup extra-virgin olive oil
• ¼ cup lime juice
• ½ peeled avocado, pitted
• 2 tbsp raw honey
• Sea salt to taste
• ¼ cup dried cranberries
• 4 cups fresh spinach
• ¼ cup sliced radishes

Directions:
1. Combine the olive oil, avocado, lime juice, honey, ¼ cup of water, and sea salt in your food processor and pulse until your desired consistency is reached. In a large bowl, toss the spinach with half of the dressing. Divide the dressed spinach among 4 plates. Top each with grapefruit, radishes, sunflower seeds, and cranberries. Drizzle the remaining dressing over the salads and serve.

Nutrition Info:
• Per Serving: Calories: 125;Fat: 9g;Protein: 3g;Carbs: 15g.

Avocado Salad With Mango & Almonds

Servings: 2 | Cooking Time: 10 Minutes

Ingredients:
• 1 avocado, sliced
• 1 Romaine lettuce, torn
• ¼ cup dressing
• ¼ cup almonds, toasted
• 1 tbsp chives, chopped
• 1 mango, sliced

Directions:
1. Share the avocado and lettuce between bowls and top each with mango and chives. Sprinkle with dressing and almonds. Serve immediately.

Nutrition Info:
• Per Serving: Calories: 505;Fat: 40g;Protein: 8g;Carbs: 42g.

Beet Tofu Salad

Servings: 4 | Cooking Time: 50 Minutes

Ingredients:
• 8 oz red beets
• 2 oz tofu, cubed
• 2 tbsp olive oil
• ½ red onion
• 1 cup paleo mayonnaise
• 1 romaine lettuce, torn
• 2 tbsp chopped chives
• Sea salt and pepper to taste

Directions:
1. Put beets in a pot, cover with water, and cook for 40 minutes. Warm the olive oil in a pan over medium heat and fry tofu until

browned. Set aside to cool. When the bits are ready, drain through a colander and allow cooling. Slip the skin off after and slice them. In a salad bowl, combine beets, tofu, red onions, lettuce, salt, pepper, and mayonnaise and mix until the vegetables are adequately coated with the mayonnaise. Top with chives and serve.

Nutrition Info:
• Per Serving: Calories: 330;Fat: 28g;Protein: 7g;Carbs: 15g.

Tempting Salad With Celery, Beet, And Sliced Apple

Servings: 4 | Cooking Time: 0 Minutes

Ingredients:
• 2 green apples, cored and quartered
• 2 small beets, peeled and quartered
• 4 cups spinach
• 2 celery stalks, sliced thin
• ½ red onion, sliced thin
• ½ cup shredded carrots
• 1 tablespoon apple cider vinegar
• 1 tablespoon raw honey or maple syrup
• 3 tablespoons extra-virgin olive oil
• Sea salt
• Freshly ground black pepper
• ¼ cup pumpkin seeds

Directions:
1. Slice the apples and the beets using a mandoline or the slicing disk of a food processor.
2. Place the spinach on a large platter. Arrange the apples and beets over the spinach. Top with the celery, red onion, and carrots.
3. Whisk together the cider vinegar, honey, and olive oil in a small bowl. Season with salt and pepper.
4. Drizzle the dressing over the salad and garnish with the pumpkin seeds.

Nutrition Info:
• Per Serving: Calories: 239 ;Fat: 15g ;Protein: 4g ;Carbs: 27g.

Cashew & Raisin Salad

Servings: 4 | Cooking Time: 15 Minutes

Ingredients:
• 3 cups haricots verts, trimmed and chopped
• 2 carrots, sliced
• 3 cups shredded cabbage
• 1/3 cup golden raisins
• ¼ cup roasted cashew
• 1 garlic clove, minced
• 1 medium shallot, chopped
• 1 ½ tsp grated fresh ginger
• 1/3 cup creamy peanut butter
• 2 tsp low-sodium soy sauce
• 2 tbsp fresh lemon juice
• Sea salt to taste
• ⅛ tsp ground cayenne
• ¾ cup coconut milk

Directions:
1. Place the haricots verts, carrots, and cabbage in a pot with water and steam for 5 minutes. Drain and transfer to a bowl. Add in raisins and cashew. Let cool. In a food processor, put the garlic, shallot, and ginger. Pulse until puréed. Add in peanut butter, soy sauce, lemon juice, salt, cayenne pepper. Blitz until smooth. Stir in coconut milk. Sprinkle the salad with the dressing and toss to coat.

Nutrition Info:
• Per Serving: Calories: 410;Fat: 31g;Protein: 40g;Carbs: 30g.

Pleasant And Tender Salad With Kale

Servings: 4 | Cooking Time: 0 Minutes

Ingredients:
• 1 pound dinosaur or curly kale
• 1 teaspoon fine Himalayan salt
• ¼ cup ripe green olives, pitted
• 2 tablespoons Garlic Confit
• 2 tablespoons Toum or Homemade Mayo
• Juice of 1 lemon

Directions:
1. Tear the kale leaves into 1- to 2-inch pieces and place in a bowl with the salt. Massage with your hands the salt into the kale for 2 minutes, or until the kale begins to release some liquid and has become very tender.
2. Add the olives, garlic confit, toum, and lemon juice. Toss to combine and serve, or store in a quart-sized jar in the fridge for up to 4 days.

Nutrition Info:
• Per Serving: Calories: 87 ;Fat: 2g ;Protein: 3g;Carbs: 13g .

Hazelnut & Pear Salad

Servings: 4 | Cooking Time: 10 Minutes

Ingredients:
• ¼ cup chopped hazelnuts
• 4 pears, peeled and chopped
• 2 tbsp honey
• 2 tbsp balsamic vinegar
• 2 tbsp extra-virgin olive oil

Directions:
1. Combine the pears and hazelnuts in a salad bowl. Drizzle with honey, balsamic vinegar, and olive oil. Serve.

Nutrition Info:
• Per Serving: Calories: 265;Fat: 12g;Protein: 4g;Carbs: 40g.

Maple Walnut & Pear Salad

Servings: 4 | Cooking Time: 10 Minutes

Ingredients:
• 4 cored pears, chopped
• ¼ cup walnuts, chopped
• 2 tbsp maple syrup
• 2 tbsp balsamic vinegar
• 2 tbsp extra-virgin olive oil

Directions:
1. Mix the pears and walnuts in a bowl. In another bowl, combine the maple syrup, balsamic vinegar, and olive oil, pour it over pears, and toss to coat. Serve immediately.

Nutrition Info:
• Per Serving: Calories: 280;Fat: 14g;Protein: 4g;Carbs: 43g.

Enticing Japanese Salad With Avocado And Shrimp

Servings: 2 | Cooking Time: 4 Minutes

Ingredients:
• 1 garlic clove, minced
• 2 cups of raw shrimp, with the tails removed
• ½ tablespoon extra-virgin olive oil
• ½ teaspoon chili powder
• ¼ teaspoon cayenne
• 1 avocado, sliced
• ½ cucumber, chopped

- 2 cups spinach or baby kale, washed and chopped
- Miso Dressing:
- 1 thumb-sized piece of fresh ginger, finely chopped
- 2 tablespoons extra virgin olive oil
- 3 tablespoons lime juice
- 2 tablespoons agave nectar/honey
- 1 tablespoon white miso
- ½ teaspoon minced garlic

Directions:
1. Heat the oil in a skillet over medium heat, adding in the garlic and shrimp, and then sprinkle with chili powder and cayenne. Sauté for 8 to 10 minutes or until shrimp cooked through.
2. Cut the avocadoes in half and scoop out the flesh.
3. Dice the cucumber, and chop the baby spinach and kale into small spices.
4. Arrange in a bowl with the cooked shrimp.
5. Into a food processor, put all of the ingredients for the dressing and process until smooth.
6. Pour over the salad and serve immediately, topping with cilantro and peanuts for an extra crunch.

Nutrition Info:
- Per Serving: Calories: 725 ;Fat: 41g ;Protein: 57g ;Carbs: 34g .

Arugula Salad With Salmon

Servings: 2 | Cooking Time: 15 Minutes

Ingredients:
- 1 tbsp lemon juice
- 1 skinless salmon fillet
- 3 tbsp extra-virgin olive oil
- Black pepper to taste
- 1 cup cherry tomatoes, halved
- 4 cups arugula leaves
- ½ cup sliced red onion
- 1 tbsp balsamic vinegar

Directions:
1. Rub the salmon with some olive oil, lemon juice, and pepper. Heat 1 tbsp of olive oil in a skillet over medium heat and cook the salmon, skin-side down, for 6-8 minutes or until cooked through, turning once. Remove and let it cool, then flake it. Place the arugula, onion, and cherry tomatoes in a salad bowl. Add the remaining olive oil and balsamic vinegar and toss to coat. Top the salad with fish and serve.

Nutrition Info:
- Per Serving: Calories: 570;Fat: 29g;Protein: 66g;Carbs: 9g.

Beet Slaw With Apples

Servings: 4 | Cooking Time: 10 Minutes

Ingredients:
- 2 tbsp olive oil
- Juice of 1 lemon
- ½ beet, shredded
- Sea salt to taste
- 2 peeled apples, julienned
- 4 cups shredded red cabbage

Directions:
1. Mix the olive oil, lemon juice, beet, and salt in a bowl. In another bowl, combine the apples and cabbage. Pour over the vinaigrette and toss to coat. Serve right away.

Nutrition Info:
- Per Serving: Calories: 145;Fat: 7g;Protein: 2g;Carbs: 21g.

Fragrant Coconut Fruit Salad

Servings: 4 | Cooking Time:0 Minutes

Ingredients:
- Dressing:
- ¾ cup canned lite coconut milk
- 2 tablespoons almond butter
- 2 tablespoons lime juice, freshly squeezed
- Salad:
- 6 cups mixed greens
- ½ pineapple, peeled, cored, and diced, or 3 cups precut packaged pineapple
- 1 mango, peeled, pitted, and diced, or 2 cups frozen chunks, thawed
- 1 cup quartered strawberries, fresh
- 1 cup (1 inch) green bean pieces
- ½ cup shredded coconut, unsweetened
- 1 tablespoon fresh basil, chopped

Directions:
1. Whisk the coconut milk, almond butter, and lime juice in a small bowl until smooth. Set it aside.
2. Toss the mixed greens with three-fourths of the dressing in a large bowl. Arrange the salad on four plates.
3. Toss the pineapple, mango, strawberries, and green beans in the same bowl with the remaining fourth of the dressing.
4. Top each salad with the fruit and vegetable mixture and serve garnished with the coconut and basil.

Nutrition Info:
- Per Serving: Calories: 311| Fat: 19g ;Protein: 5g;Carbs: 36g .

Radicchio & Cabbage Coleslaw

Servings: 2 | Cooking Time: 10 Minutes

Ingredients:
- ½ head cabbage, shredded
- ¼ head radicchio, shredded
- 1 large carrot, shredded
- ¾ cup paleo mayonnaise
- ¼ cup soy milk
- 1 tbsp cider vinegar
- ½ tsp dry mustard
- ¼ tsp celery seeds
- Sea salt and pepper to taste

Directions:
1. Combine cabbage, radicchio, and carrot in a bowl. In another bowl, whisk mayonnaise, soy milk, mustard, vinegar, celery seeds, salt, and pepper. Pour over the slaw and toss to coat. Serve immediately.

Nutrition Info:
- Per Serving: Calories: 370;Fat: 30g;Protein: 9g;Carbs: 19g.

Carrot Salad With Cherries & Pecans

Servings: 4 | Cooking Time: 15 Minutes

Ingredients:
- 1 lb carrots, shredded
- 1 cup dried cherries, sliced
- 2 ½ cups toasted pecans
- 3 tbsp fresh lemon juice
- 3 tbsp avocado oil
- Sea salt and pepper to taste

Directions:
1. Combine the carrots, cherries, and pecans in a bowl. In another bowl, mix the lemon juice, avocado oil, salt, and pepper. Pour over the salad and toss to coat. Serve.

Marinated Chicken Salad With Turmeric

Servings: 4 | Cooking Time: 20 Minutes

Ingredients:
- 4 chicken breasts, boneless and skinless
- 1 tablespoon extra-virgin olive oil
- 1 tablespoon fresh cilantro, chopped
- 1 garlic clove, minced
- 1 teaspoon salt
- ¼ teaspoon turmeric, ground
- ¼ teaspoon black pepper, freshly ground
- ½ cup plain almond yogurt, unsweetened
- 1 tablespoon lemon juice, freshly squeezed
- 1 teaspoon lemon zest
- ½ cup almonds, chopped
- 6 cups romaine lettuce, chopped

Directions:
1. Place the chicken breast in a shallow baking dish.
2. Whisk together the olive oil, cilantro, garlic, salt, turmeric, and pepper in a small bowl. Rub the mixture all over the chicken. Cover the chicken and marinate, refrigerated for 30 minutes, or overnight.
3. Preheat the oven to 375°F. Place the baking dish in the pre-heated oven when it's hot and bake the chicken for 20 minutes. Remove from the oven and set aside.
4. Whisk together the yogurt, lemon juice, and lemon zest in a large bowl. Add the almonds and romaine lettuce and toss to coat the lettuce with the dressing.
5. Transfer the salad to a serving platter. Slice the chicken breasts into strips and arrange them over lettuce.

Nutrition Info:
- Per Serving: Calories: 418 ;Fat: 21g ;Protein: 46g ;Carbs: 10g .

Summer Time Sizzling Green Salad With Salm-on

Servings: 2 | Cooking Time: 10 Minutes

Ingredients:
- 2 salmon fillets, skinless
- 2 cups of seasonal greens
- ½ cup zucchini, sliced
- 1 tablespoon balsamic vinegar
- 2 tablespoons extra virgin olive oil
- 2 sprigs thyme, torn from the stem
- 1 lemon, juiced

Directions:
1. Preheat the broiler to a medium-high heat.
2. For 10 minutes, broil the salmon in parchment paper with some oil, lemon, and pepper.
3. Slice the zucchini and sauté for 4-5 minutes with the oil in a pan on medium heat.
4. Build the salad by creating a bed of zucchini and topping it with flaked salmon.
5. Drizzle with balsamic vinegar and sprinkle with thyme.

Nutrition Info:
- Per Serving: Calories: 67 ;Fat: 6g ;Protein: 7g;Carbs: 3g .

Summer Salad

Servings: 4 | Cooking Time: 25 Minutes

Ingredients:
- 1 Lebanese cucumber, cubed
- 4 cups watermelon cubes
- 1 cup snow peasp halved
- 1 scallion, chopped
- 2 cups shredded kale
- 1 tbsp chopped cilantro
- ½ lime, zested and juiced
- ½ cup olive oil
- 2 tbsp honey
- Sea salt to taste

Directions:
1. Whisk the olive oil, lime zest, lime juice, honey, and salt in a bowl. Add the watermelon, cucumber, snow peas, scallion, and toss to coat. Top with the watermelon mixture. Serve garnished with cilantro.

Nutrition Info:
- Per Serving: Calories: 350;Fat: 25g;Protein: 3g;Carbs: 30g.

African Zucchini Salad

Servings: 2 | Cooking Time: 20 Minutes

Ingredients:
- 1 lemon, half zested and juiced, half cut into wedges
- 1 tsp olive oil
- 1 zucchini, chopped
- ½ tsp ground cumin
- ½ tsp ground ginger
- ¼ tsp turmeric
- ¼ tsp ground nutmeg
- A pinch of sea salt
- 2 tbsp capers
- 1 tbsp chopped green olives
- 1 garlic clove, pressed
- 2 tbsp fresh mint, chopped
- 2 cups spinach, chopped

Directions:
1. Warm the olive oil in a skillet over medium heat. Place the zucchini and sauté for 10 minutes. Stir in cumin, ginger, turmeric, nutmeg, and salt. Pour in lemon zest, lemon juice, capers, garlic, and mint and cook for 2 minutes more. Divide the spinach between serving plates and top with zucchini mixture. Garnish with lemon and olives.

Nutrition Info:
- Per Serving: Calories: 50;Fat: 3g;Protein: 41g;Carbs: 5g.

Mango Rice Salad With Lime Dressing

Servings: 4 | Cooking Time: 15 Minutes

Ingredients:
- ½ cup chopped roasted peanuts
- 3 ½ cups cooked brown rice
- 1 mango, sliced
- 4 green onions, chopped
- 3 tbsp fresh lime juice
- 2 tsp agave nectar
- 1 tsp grated fresh ginger
- 1/3 cup grapeseed oil
- Sea salt and pepper to taste

Directions:
1. In a bowl, mix the rice, peanuts, mango, and green onions. Set aside. In another bowl, whisk the lime juice, agave nectar, and

ginger. Add oil, salt, and pepper and stir to combine. Pour over the rice and toss to coat. Serve.

Nutrition Info:
• Per Serving: Calories: 490;Fat: 29g;Protein: 10g;Carbs: 50g.

Daikon Salad With Caramelized Onion

Servings: 4 | Cooking Time: 50 Minutes

Ingredients:
• 1 lb daikon, peeled
• 2 cups sliced sweet onions
• 2 tsp olive oil
• Sea salt to taste
• 1 tbsp rice vinegar

Directions:
1. Place the daikon in a pot with salted water and cook 25 minutes, until tender. Drain and let cool. In a skillet over low heat, warm olive oil and add the onion. Sauté for 10-15 minutes until caramelized. Sprinkle with salt. Remove to a bowl. Chop the daikon into wedges and add to the onion bowl. Stir in the vinegar. Serve.

Nutrition Info:
• Per Serving: Calories: 90;Fat: 3g;Protein: 2g;Carbs: 15g.

Asparagus & Pasta Salad

Servings: 4 | Cooking Time: 30 Minutes

Ingredients:
• 1 lb asparagus, sliced
• 2 cups arugula
• 1 cup basil sauce
• 1 tbsp olive oil
• 12 oz whole-wheat penne
• 2 scallions, sliced
• Sea salt and pepper to taste

Directions:
1. Cook the pasta according to the package´s instructions, then before cooking ends, about 2 minutes add the asparagus. Strain them and place them back in the pot. Mix in basil sauce and olive oil. Let cool before combining the scallions, salt, and pepper. Serve right away.

Nutrition Info:
• Per Serving: Calories: 455;Fat: 4g;Protein: 13g;Carbs: 70g.

Irresistible Pear And Walnut Salad

Servings: 4 | Cooking Time: 0 Minutes

Ingredients:
• 4 pears, peeled, cored, and chopped
• ¼ cup walnuts, chopped
• 2 tablespoons honey
• 2 tablespoons balsamic vinegar
• 2 tablespoons extra-virgin olive oil

Directions:
1. Combine the pears and walnuts in a medium bowl.
2. Whisk the honey, balsamic vinegar, and olive oil in a small bowl. Toss with the pears and walnuts.

Nutrition Info:
• Per Serving: Calories: 263 ;Fat: 12g ;Protein: 3g ;Carbs: 41g.

Orange & Kale Salad

Servings: 4 | Cooking Time: 10 Minutes

Ingredients:
• 2 tbsp Dijon mustard
• 2 tbsp olive oil
• ¼ cup fresh orange juice
• 1 tsp honey
• 2 tbsp minced fresh parsley
• 1 tbsp minced green onions
• 4 cups fresh kale, chopped
• 1 peeled orange, segmented
• ½ red onion, sliced thin
• Sea salt and pepper to taste

Directions:
1. Blend the mustard, oil, orange juice, honey, salt, pepper, parsley, and green onions in your food processor until smooth. Set aside. In a bowl, combine the kale, orange, and onion. Pour over the dressing and toss to coat. Serve.

Nutrition Info:
• Per Serving: Calories: 105;Fat: 7g;Protein: 1g;Carbs: 10g.

Quick Fresh Salad

Servings: 4 | Cooking Time: 15 Minutes

Ingredients:
• 1 lb carrots, shredded
• 2 oranges, chopped
• ½ cup roasted walnuts
• ¼ cup chopped parsley
• 2 tbsp fresh orange juice
• 2 tbsp fresh lime juice
• 2 tsp pure date sugar
• Sea salt and pepper to taste
• ¼ cup olive oil

Directions:
1. In a bowl, mix the carrots, oranges, walnuts, and parsley. Set aside. Blend the orange juice, lime juice, sugar, salt, pepper, and oil in another bowl. Pour over the carrots mixture and toss to coat. Adjust the seasonings. Serve.

Nutrition Info:
• Per Serving: Calories: 280;Fat: 20g;Protein: 3g;Carbs: 24g.

Yummy Salad With Sweet Potato And Salmon

Servings: 2 | Cooking Time: 0 Minutes

Ingredients:
• 2 cups arugula or other greens
• 2 leftover Fennel Baked Salmon fillets, flaked
• 1 leftover Roasted Sweet Potato, cut in wedges
• 1 cup leftover Zucchini and Red Onion Salad with Olives
• ¼ cup Lemony Mustard Dressing

Directions:
1. In a medium bowl, combine the arugula, salmon, sweet potato wedges, and zucchini salad.
2. Pour the dressing over and toss to mix, then serve.

Nutrition Info:
• Per Serving: Calories: 570 ;Fat: 42g ;Protein: 22g ;Carbs: 22g .

Mushroom & Wild Rice Salad

Servings: 6 | Cooking Time: 25 Minutes

Ingredients:
• 2 cups cremini mushrooms, sliced
• 2 garlic cloves, minced

- 1 sweet onion, diced
- 3 cups wild rice, cooked
- 2 tbsp avocado oil
- ½ tsp dried thyme
- ½ cup vegetable broth
- ½ tsp sea salt

Directions:
1. Place the wild rice in a bowl and set aside. Warm the avocado oil in a saucepan over medium heat. Place the garlic and onion and cook for 5 minutes, stirring often. Mix in vegetable broth, thyme, salt, and mushrooms and cook for 10 minutes until the mushrooms are tender and the broth reduces by half. Stir in wild rice. Serve.

Nutrition Info:
- Per Serving: Calories: 145;Fat: 1g;Protein: 20g;Carbs: 5g.

Diverse Salad With Shredded Root Vegetable

Servings: 4 | Cooking Time: 0 Minutes

Ingredients:
- Dressing:
- ¼ cup olive oil
- 3 tablespoons pure maple syrup
- 2 tablespoons apple cider vinegar
- 1 teaspoon fresh ginger, grated
- Sea salt
- Slaw:
- 1 jicama, or 2 parsnips, peeled and shredded
- 2 carrots, shredded, or 1 cup pre-shredded packaged carrots
- ½ celeriac, peeled and shredded
- ¼ fennel bulb, shredded
- 5 radishes, shredded
- 2 scallions, white and green parts, peeled and thinly sliced
- ½ cup pumpkin seeds, roasted

Directions:
1. Whisk the olive oil, maple syrup, cider vinegar, and ginger in a small bowl until well blended. Season with sea salt and set it aside.
2. Toss together the jicama, carrots, celeriac, fennel, radishes, and scallions in a large bowl.
3. Add the dressing and toss to coat.
4. Top the slaw with the pumpkin seeds and serve.

Nutrition Info:
- Per Serving: Calories: 343 ;Fat: 21g ;Protein: 7g;Carbs: 36g .

Bean & Farro Salad

Servings: 4 | Cooking Time: 20 Minutes

Ingredients:
- 4 cups watercress and arugula mix
- 1 can black beans
- ¼ cup cilantro, chopped
- Zest and juice of 1 lime
- 3 tsp chili powder
- Sea salt and pepper to taste
- 12 cherry tomatoes, halved
- 1 red bell pepper, chopped
- 2 scallions, chopped
- 4 large whole-grain tortillas
- 2 tsp olive oil
- 1 tbsp oregano
- 1 tsp cayenne pepper
- ¾ cup cooked faro
- ¼ cup chopped avocado
- ¼ cup mango salsa

Directions:
1. Combine black beans, cilantro, lime juice, lime zest, chili powder, salt, pepper, cherry tomatoes, bell peppers, and scallions in a bowl. Set aside. Brush the tortillas with olive oil and season with salt, pepper, oregano, and cayenne pepper. Slice into 8 pieces. Line with parchment paper a baking sheet. Arrange tortilla pieces and bake for 3-5 minutes until browned. Put the watercress and arugula mix on a serving platter, top with faro, bean mixture, avocado, and sprinkle with mango salsa all over to serve.

Nutrition Info:
- Per Serving: Calories: 270;Fat: 8g;Protein: 3g;Carbs: 45g.

Crunchylicious Colourful Asian Salad

Servings: 6 | Cooking Time: 0 Minutes

Ingredients:
- ¼ medium head red cabbage
- ¼ medium head green cabbage
- 2 green onions, minced
- Leaves from 2 sprigs fresh basil, minced
- Leaves from 4 sprigs fresh cilantro, minced
- 1 teaspoon fine Himalayan salt
- Dressing:
- Juice of 4 limes
- 3 tablespoons avocado oil
- 2 tablespoons coconut aminos
- 4 cloves garlic, minced
- One 1 inch piece ginger, peeled and minced

Directions:
1. Lay one of the cabbage wedges on the cutting board and to trim off the core on the diagonal use a sharp knife. Then slice the cabbage as thinly as possible. Repeat with the second wedge. In a large bowl, combine the shredded red and green cabbage.
2. Add the green onions, basil, and cilantro and toss with the cabbage. Sprinkle in the salt and toss to combine.
3. Make the dressing by placing the lime juice, avocado oil, and coconut aminos in a small bowl. Add the garlic and ginger and whisk to combine.
4. Pour the dressing over the cabbage and toss to thoroughly distribute the dressing if you're serving the salad right away.
5. Store the salad in an airtight container in the fridge with a folded paper towel to absorb moisture if you're not serving the salad right away. Store the dressing in a separate airtight container in the fridge. Both the salad and the dressing will keep for up to 5 days.

Nutrition Info:
- Per Serving: Calories: 103 ;Fat: 7g ;Protein: 1g ;Carbs: 7g .

Anti-Inflammatory Cookbook

Fish and Seafood

Fish and Seafood

Tarragon Scallops

Servings: 1 | Cooking Time: 10 Minutes

Ingredients:
- 2 garlic cloves, minced
- 1 red chili, minced
- 8 king scallops
- 1 tbsp olive oil
- Juice of ½ lime
- 2 tbsp chopped tarragon

Directions:
1. Warm the olive oil in a skillet over medium heat and fry scallops for about 1 minute per side until lightly golden. Add the chopped chili and garlic cloves to the pan and squeeze the lime juice over the scallops. Saute for 2-3 minutes. Sprinkle the tarragon over the top and serve.

Nutrition Info:
- Per Serving: Calories: 235;Fat: 15g;Protein: 15g;Carbs: 13g.

Wild Salmon With Toasted Coconut

Servings: 4 To 6

Cooking Time: 8 Minutes

Ingredients:
- 1 1½-pound salmon fillet
- 1 teaspoon Himalayan salt, fine
- 1 tablespoon nutritional yeast
- ¼ cup coconut butter
- 1 teaspoon lemon zest, grated
- 1 teaspoon thyme leaves, dried
- 1 green onion, sliced

Directions:
1. Preheat the oven to 400°F.
2. Lay the salmon skin side down on a sheet pan. To check for pin bones, run your fingers along the length of the fish. Use kitchen tweezers or pliers to pull them out.
3. Sprinkle the fillet evenly with the salt. Let it sit at room temperature while the oven preheats.
4. Sprinkle the nutritional yeast evenly over the fillet, then spread the coconut butter over it when the oven is ready. It will leave clumps of it. Sprinkle the lemon zest and then the thyme over the fillet, as evenly as possible.
5. Roast the salmon on the middle rack of the oven for 5 minutes then set the oven to broil. Broil for 2 to 3 minutes until the clumps of coconut butter are browned and the fish is cooked through. A good indicator that the salmon is ready is when the meat flakes easily. Test this for a minute interval until the thickest part of the fish easily flakes when pierced with a fork.
6. Remove the salmon from the oven. Garnish the fillet with the green onion slices but let it rest first for a few minutes. Slice the fillet into as many portions as you need and lift the pieces off of the skin with a spatula to serve.
7. Store leftovers in an airtight container in the fridge for up to 4 days. Flake and sauté the salmon in a skillet over medium heat for 4 minutes to reheat.

Nutrition Info:
- Per Serving: Calories: 238 ;Fat: 14g ;Protein: 23g;Carbs: 3g .

Baked Tilapia With Chili Kale

Servings: 2 | Cooking Time: 20 Minutes

Ingredients:
- ½ cup whole-grain breadcrumbs
- ½ cup ground hazelnuts
- 2 tilapia fillets, skinless
- 2 tsp extra-virgin olive oil
- 2 tsp whole-grain mustard
- 5 oz kale, chopped
- 1 red chili, sliced
- 1 clove garlic, mashed

Directions:
1. Preheat your oven to 350ºF. Combine the hazelnuts and breadcrumbs in a bowl. Spread a thin layer of mustard over the fish and then dip into the breadcrumb mixture. Transfer to a greased baking dish. Bake for 12 minutes or until cooked through. Warm the olive oil in a skillet over medium heat and sauté the garlic for 30 seconds. Add the kale and red chili and cook for 5 more minutes. Serve fish with the kale on the side.

Nutrition Info:
- Per Serving: Calories: 540;Fat: 32g;Protein: 35g;Carbs: 29g.

Saucy Tropical Halibut

Servings: 4 | Cooking Time: 35 Minutes

Ingredients:
- ½ mango, diced
- 1 avocado, diced
- ½ cup chopped strawberries
- 1 tsp chopped fresh mint
- 1 lemon, juiced and zested
- 1 tbsp olive oil
- 4 boneless, skinless halibut fillets
- Sea salt and pepper to taste

Directions:
1. Mix avocado, mango, strawberries, mint, lemon juice, and lemon zest in a bowl; stir well. Set the sauce aside.
2. Warm the olive oil in a pan over medium heat. Lightly season the halibut with salt and pepper. Add the fish and fry for 3-4 minutes per side, turning once or until it is just cooked through. Top with avocado salsa and serve.

Nutrition Info:
- Per Serving: Calories: 355;Fat: 15g;Protein: 42g;Carbs: 12g.

Baked Garlicky Halibut With Lemon

Servings: 2 | Cooking Time: 15 Minutes

Ingredients:
- 2 halibut fillets
- a pinch of black pepper
- 2 garlic cloves, pressed
- 2 tablespoons olive oil
- 2 tablespoons low fat Greek yogurt
- 4 lemon wedges

Directions:
1. Preheat the oven to 400°F.
2. Season with pepper and add to a parchment paper-lined baking dish.

3. Scatter the garlic cloves around the fish and drizzle with the oil.
4. Squeeze the lemon juice over the fish.
5. Bake for 15 minutes until the fish is firm and well cooked.
6. Serve and pour over the juices for a delicious garlic feast.

Nutrition Info:
- Per Serving: Calories: 410 ;Fat: 29g ;Protein: 21g ;Carbs: 18g ;.

Sheet Pan Baked Salmon With Asparagus

Servings: 4 | Cooking Time: 20 Minutes

Ingredients:
- 1 red bell pepper, sliced
- 1 lb asparagus, trimmed
- 2 tbsp olive oil
- Sea salt and pepper to taste
- 4 salmon fillets
- 1 lemon, zested and sliced

Directions:
1. Preheat your oven to 425°F. Season the asparagus and red pepper slices with salt and drizzle with olive oil. Arrange them on a sheet pan. Sprinkle salmon fillets with pepper and salt and put them skin-side down on top of the vegetables. Garnish with lemon zest and lemon slices. Place in the oven and roast for 12-15 minutes until the salmon is cooked through. Serve warm.

Nutrition Info:
- Per Serving: Calories: 310;Fat: 19g;Protein: 3g;Carbs: 6g.

Japanese Salmon Cakes

Servings: 2 | Cooking Time: 15 Minutes

Ingredients:
- 1 beaten egg
- 1 cup canned wild salmon,
- 2 spring onions, chopped
- ½ tsp honey
- 1 lime, zested
- 2 tsp reduced-salt soy sauce
- 1 tsp wasabi powder
- 2 tbsp coconut oil
- 1 tbsp ginger, minced

Directions:
1. Combine the salmon, egg, ginger, and lime zest, spring onions in a bowl and mix with your hands. Shape the mixture into 4 patties. In a separate bowl, add wasabi powder, soy sauce, and honey and whisk until blended.
2. Warm the coconut oil over medium heat in a skillet and cook the patties for 4 minutes until firm and browned on each side. Glaze the top of each patty with the wasabi mixture and cook for another 15 seconds. Serve.

Nutrition Info:
- Per Serving: Calories: 550;Fat: 30g;Protein: 67g;Carbs: 4g.

Golden, Crispy, Buttery Pan-seared Cod

Servings: 4 | Cooking Time: 10 Minutes

Ingredients:
- 4 to 6 ounces boneless, skinless cod fillets
- 1 teaspoon Himalayan salt. fine
- 3 tablespoons ghee or bacon fat
- 2 sprigs parsley, fresh
- 1 green onion, sliced
- 1 tablespoon Garlic Confit
- Lime or lemon halves

Directions:
1. Pat the fish fillets dry and rub the salt all over them.
2. Heat a large cast-iron skillet over medium heat until it's very hot by rotating the pan halfway every few minutes. Drip water on it for temperature check, if the droplets dance then it's ready.
3. Melt the ghee in the skillet. Add the fish fillets. Be careful not to crowd the pan by cooking two fillets at a time. Sear the fish for 4 to 6 minutes. If the edges of the fish begin to appear opaque white and you can see that it is golden at the bottom by using a thin spatula to flip the fish.
4. Place the parsley, green onion slices, and garlic confit around the fish. Cook for 3 to 4 minutes until the fish is tender and flakes easily with a fork.
5. Transfer the fish to a serving platter. Spoon the ghee mixture over the fish. Garnish with lime halves, if preferred. Let it rest for 3 to 5 minutes before serving.
6. Cook as many fillets to avoid having leftovers. Store leftovers in an airtight container in the fridge for up to 3 days.

Nutrition Info:
- Per Serving: Calories: 223 ;Fat: 11g ;Protein: 28g;Carbs: 3g .

Fresh, Delicate And Meaty Tuna Steak With Fennel Salad

Servings: 2 | Cooking Time: 25 Minutes

Ingredients:
- 2 tuna steaks, each 1 inch thick
- 2 tablespoons olive oil
- 1 tablespoon olive oil for brushing
- 1 teaspoon black peppercorns, crushed
- 1 teaspoon crushed fennel seeds
- 1 fennel bulb, trimmed and sliced
- ½ cup water
- 1 lemon, juiced
- 1 teaspoon fresh parsley, chopped

Directions:
1. Coat the fish with oil and then season with peppercorns and fennel seeds.
2. Heat the oil on a medium heat and sauté the fennel bulb slices for 5 minutes or until light brown. Stir in the garlic and cook for a minute.
3. Add the water to the pan and cook for 10 minutes until the fennel is tender.
4. Stir in the lemon juice and lower heat to a simmer.
5. Heat another skillet and sauté the tuna steaks for 2 to 3 minutes each side for medium-rare.
6. Serve the fennel mix with the tuna steaks on top and garnish with the fresh parsley.

Nutrition Info:
- Per Serving: Calories: 232 ;Fat: 21g ;Protein: 2g ;Carbs: 12g .

Smoky Boneless Haddock With Pea Risotto

Servings: 2 | Cooking Time: 40 Minutes

Ingredients:
- 2 smoked haddock fillets, boneless and skinless
- 1 tablespoon extra-virgin olive oil
- 1 white onion, finely diced
- 2 cups brown rice
- 4 cups vegetable stock
- 1 cup spinach leaves, fresh
- 1 cup peas, frozen
- 3 tablespoons low fat Greek yogurt
- a pinch of black pepper
- 4 lemon wedges

• 1 cup of arugula

Directions:
1. Heat the oil in a large pan on a medium heat.
2. For 5 minutes, sauté the chopped onion until soft before adding in the rice and stirring for 1 to 2 minutes.
3. Add half of the stock and stir slowly.
4. Slowly add the rest of the stock whilst continuously stirring for up to 20 to 30 minutes.
5. Stir in the spinach and peas fish to the risotto.
6. Place the fish on top of the rice, cover and steam for 10 minutes.
7. To break up the fish fillets, use your fork and stir into the rice with the yogurt.
8. Sprinkle with freshly ground pepper to serve and a squeeze of fresh lemon.
9. Garnish with the lemon wedges and serve with the arugula.

Nutrition Info:
• Per Serving: Calories: 4023 ;Fat: 441g ;Protein: 35g ;Carbs: 22
.

Avocado & Tuna Toast

Servings: 4 | Cooking Time: 15 Minutes

Ingredients:
• 2 cans wild-caught albacore tuna
• 1 shallot, minced
• 4 sourdough bread slices
• ¼ cup paleo mayonnaise
• 1 tsp lemon juice
• ¼ tsp paprika
• 1 avocado, cut into 8 slices
• 1 tomato, cut into 8 slices
• 3 tsp grated Parmesan cheese

Directions:
1. Preheat your broiler to high. Line a baking sheet with foil. Place the bread slices on the sheet. Combine the mayonnaise, tuna, lemon juice, shallot, and paprika in a bowl and put it on top of each slice. Add in 2 tomato slices and 2 avocado slices on each bread and scatter with 1 tbsp of Parmesan cheese. Place the sheet in the broil and cook for 3-4 minutes. Serve immediately.

Nutrition Info:
• Per Serving: Calories: 470;Fat: 28g;Protein: 27g;Carbs: 30g.

Pan-seared Salmon Au Pistou

Servings: 3 | Cooking Time: 30 Minutes

Ingredients:
• 2 garlic cloves
• 1 cup fresh oregano leaves
• ¼ cup almonds
• 1 lime, juiced and zested
• Zest of 1 lime
• 2 tbsp extra-virgin olive oil
• 1 tsp turmeric
• 4 salmon fillets
• Sea salt and pepper to taste

Directions:
1. Spritz oregano, almonds, garlic, lime juice, lime zest, 1 tbsp of oil, salt, and pepper in your blender until finely chopped. Transfer the pistou to a bowl and set it aside.
2. Preheat your oven to 400ºF. Lightly season the salmon with salt and pepper. Warm the remaining olive oil in a skillet over medium heat and add the salmon. Sear for 4 minutes per side. Place the skillet in the oven and bake the fish for about 10 minutes, or until it is just cooked through. Serve the salmon topped with pis-

tou.

Nutrition Info:
• Per Serving: Calories: 460;Fat: 25g;Protein: 48g;Carbs: 8g.

Mushroom & Olive Cod Fillets

Servings: 4 | Cooking Time: 35 Minutes

Ingredients:
• 4 cod fillets
• 1 garlic clove, minced
• 1 leek, thinly sliced
• 1 tsp minced fresh ginger
• 8 stoned black olives, sliced
• 1 tbsp olive oil
• ½ cup dry white wine
• ½ cup sliced mushrooms
• Sea salt and pepper to taste

Directions:
1. Preheat your oven to 375ºF. Combine the garlic, leek, ginger root, wine, olive oil, olives, and mushrooms in a baking pan, and toss until the mushrooms are evenly coated. Bake in the preheated oven for 10 minutes until lightly browned. Remove the baking pan from the oven. Spread the cod fillets on top and season with salt and pepper. Cover with aluminum foil and add back to the oven. Bake for 5-8 more minutes, or until the fish is flaky. Remove the foil and cool for 5 minutes before serving.

Nutrition Info:
• Per Serving: Calories: 165;Fat: 8g;Protein: 20g;Carbs: 5g.

Pineapple Mahi-mahi

Servings: 2 | Cooking Time: 25 Minutes

Ingredients:
• 1 red onion, chopped
• 1 cup cubed pineapple
• 1 lime, juiced
• 2 tsp cilantro, chopped
• 2 tsp coconut oil
• 2 mahi-mahi fillets

Directions:
1. Mix the red onion, pineapple, lime, and cilantro in a bowl and set aside to macerate. Warm the coconut oil in a skillet over medium heat and add the fillets. Fry for about 8 minutes on both sides or until the flesh flakes away. Top with pineapple salsa and serve.

Nutrition Info:
• Per Serving: Calories: 735;Fat: 21g;Protein: 82g;Carbs: 55g.

Seared Salmon With Gremolata

Servings: 4 | Cooking Time: 30 Minutes

Ingredients:
• 1 bag mixed greens
• 1 cucumber, sliced thin
• 1 cup watercress
• 4 salmon fillets
• 3 tsp extra-virgin olive oil
• 1 lemon, juiced and zested
• Sea salt and pepper to taste
• 1 bunch basil
• 1 garlic clove

Directions:
1. Preheat your oven to 375ºF. Brush the salmon fillets with some olive oil and season with salt and pepper. Place in a baking dish. Add the lemon juice. Bake the fillets for about 20 minutes, or un-

til firm and cooked through.

2. Blend the basil, garlic, and lemon zest in your food processor until everything is coarsely chopped. Arrange the greens, cucumber, and watercress on a serving platter. Drizzle them with the remaining olive oil and season with salt and pepper. Place the salmon fillets on top of the greens and spread the gremolata over the salmon.

Nutrition Info:
• Per Serving: Calories: 275;Fat: 12g;Protein: 33g;Carbs: 10g.

Extraordinary Scallops With Lime And Cilantro

Servings: 1 | Cooking Time: 5 Minutes

Ingredients:
• 8 queen or king scallops
• 1 tablespoon extra sesame oil
• 2 large garlic cloves, finely chopped
• 1 red chili, finely chopped
• ½ lime juice
• 2 tablespoons cilantro, chopped
• a pinch of black pepper

Directions:
1. Heat oil in a skillet on a medium to high heat and fry scallops for a minute on each side until lightly golden.
2. Add the chopped chili and garlic cloves to the pan and squeeze the lime juice over the scallops. Sauté for 2-3 minutes.
3. Remove the scallops and sprinkle the cilantro over the top to serve.

Nutrition Info:
• Per Serving: Calories: 153 ;Fat: 14g ;Protein: 1g ;Carbs: 8g .

Yummy Fish Curry

Servings: 4 | Cooking Time: 30 Minutes

Ingredients:
• 2 shallots, chopped
• 2 garlic cloves, minced
• 2 tbsp coconut oil
• 1 tbsp minced fresh ginger
• 2 tsp curry powder
• Sea salt and pepper to taste
• 2 cups cubed butternut squash
• 2 cups chopped broccoli
• 1 can coconut milk
• 1 cup vegetable broth
• 1 lb firm white fish fillets
• ¼ cup chopped cilantro
• 1 scallion, sliced thin
• Lemon wedges, for garnish

Directions:
1. Melt the coconut oil in a large pot over medium heat. Add the shallots, garlic, ginger, curry powder, salt, and pepper. Sauté for 5 minutes. Add the butternut squash and broccoli. Sauté for 2 minutes more. Stir in the coconut milk and vegetable broth and bring to a boil. Reduce the heat to simmer and add the fish. Cover the pot and simmer for 5 minutes, or until the fish is cooked through. Remove and discard the lemongrass. Ladle the curry into a serving bowl. Garnish with the cilantro and scallion and serve with lemon wedges.

Nutrition Info:
• Per Serving: Calories: 550;Fat: 39g;Protein: 33g;Carbs: 22g.

Gingery Swordfish Kabobs

Servings: 4 | Cooking Time: 35 Minutes

Ingredients:
• 4 thick swordfish steaks, cubed
• ¾ cup sesame seeds
• Sea salt and pepper to taste
• ½ tsp ground ginger
• 2 tbsp extra-virgin olive oil

Directions:
1. Preheat your oven to 400ºF. In a shallow dish, combine the sesame seeds, salt, ground ginger, and pepper. In a medium bowl, toss the swordfish with the olive oil to coat. Press the oiled cubes into the sesame seed mixture. Thread the cubes onto bamboo skewers. Place the skewers on a greased baking sheet. Bake them for 10-12 minutes, turning once halfway through. Serve and enjoy!

Nutrition Info:
• Per Serving: Calories: 390;Fat: 20g;Protein: 44g;Carbs: 7g.

Minimalist Chowder With Whitefish

Servings: 6 To 8

Cooking Time: 35 Minutes
Ingredients:
• 4 carrots, peeled and cut into ½-inch pieces
• 3 sweet potatoes, peeled and cut into ½-inch pieces
• 3 cups coconut milk, full-fat
• 2 cups water
• 1 teaspoon thyme, dried
• ½ teaspoon salt
• 10½ ounces white fish, skinless and firm, such as cod or halibut, cut into chunks

Directions:
1. Combine the carrots, sweet potatoes, coconut milk, water, thyme, and salt in a large pot. Bring to a boil over high heat. Reduce the heat to low. Cover and simmer for 20 minutes.
2. Purée half of the soup in a blender. Return the purée to the pot. Add the fish chunks.
3. Cook for 12 to 15 minutes more or until the fish is tender and hot.

Nutrition Info:
• Per Serving: Calories: 451 ;Fat: 29g ;Protein: 14g ;Carbs: 39g .

Halibut Al Ajillo

Servings: 2 | Cooking Time: 20 Minutes

Ingredients:
• 4 lemon wedges
• 2 halibut fillets
• Black pepper to taste
• 2 garlic cloves, pressed
• 2 tbsp olive oil
• 1 tbsp dill, chopped

Directions:
1. Preheat your oven to 400ºF. Place the fish in a foil-lined baking dish. Sprinkle with black pepper and garlic. Drizzle with oil. Bake for 15 minutes until the fish is firm and well cooked. Top with dill. Serve with lemon wedges.

Nutrition Info:
• Per Serving: Calories: 490;Fat: 19g;Protein: 55g;Carbs: 3g.

Flavourful Shrimp And Grits

Servings: 4 | Cooking Time: 20 Minutes

Ingredients:
- Grits:
- 3 tablespoons coconut butter
- 2 tablespoons ghee, unsalted butter, or lard
- 3 cloves garlic, minced
- 1 piece lemon peel, 1 inch
- 5 cups riced cauliflower
- 1 cup bone broth
- 1 teaspoon Himalayan salt, fine
- Shrimp:
- 1 teaspoon Himalayan salt, fine
- 1 teaspoon black pepper, ground
- 1 teaspoon cumin, ground
- 1 teaspoon fresh rosemary, minced
- ½ teaspoon ginger powder
- 1-pound fresh shrimp, peeled and deveined
- 5 slices bacon, diced
- Juice of 1 lemon
- 2 tablespoons coconut aminos
- Fresh arugula or parsley

Directions:
1. Make the grits by heating a large skillet over medium heat. Add the coconut butter, ghee, garlic, and lemon peel when it's hot. Let the fats melt and come to a simmer. Cook and stir occasionally for 2 to 3 minutes until the coconut butter becomes brown. It will be light brown and smell like toasted coconut.
2. Add the cauliflower and stir to combine. Cook the cauliflower if frozen while stirring often, until it's thawed. Then add the broth and salt. Bring to a simmer and cook undisturbed until the liquid is reduced by half, about 10 minutes.
3. Prepare the shrimp by heating a second large skillet over high heat. Combine the salt, pepper, cumin, rosemary, and ginger powder while it heats in a large bowl. Add the shrimp and toss to coat the shrimp thoroughly.
4. Place the bacon in the skillet when it's hot and cook while stirring often for 8 minutes or until well browned and almost crispy. Add the shrimp and sauté, then stir it often for 2 to 3 minutes until the shrimp have curled and turned pink. Add the lemon juice and coconut aminos and quickly stir to deglaze the skillet and coat the shrimp in the sauce. It should appear browned and caramelized with sticky chunks and lots of crispy bacon.
5. Remove the skillet from the heat. Give the cauliflower grits a stir. It should be creamy without too much pooling liquid. Spoon the grits into four shallow bowls and fish out the lemon peel. To each bowl, add four or five shrimp by making sure to get some chunks of bacon in there, too. Garnish with arugula or parsley.
6. Store leftovers in an airtight container in the fridge for up to 3 days. Sauté in a hot skillet for 3 to 4 minutes to reheat.

Nutrition Info:
- Per Serving: Calories: 363 ;Fat: 21g ;Protein: 26g;Carbs: 13g .

Old Bay Crab Cakes

Servings: 4 | Cooking Time: 30 Minutes

Ingredients:
- ½ cup shredded carrots
- 2 scallions, chopped
- 2 lb cooked lump crabmeat
- ½ cup shredded coconut
- ½ cup coconut flour
- 2 eggs
- 1 tsp Old Bay spice mix

- 1 tsp lemon zest
- 2 tbsp olive oil

Directions:
1. Mix together the crab, coconut, coconut flour, carrot, scallions, eggs, Old Bay spice mix, and lemon zest in a large bowl. Shape the mixture into 8 patties and flatten them until they are about 1 inch thick. Warm the olive oil in a skillet over medium heat. Add the crab cakes and sear for about 6 minutes per side until cooked through and golden on both sides, turning once. Serve.

Nutrition Info:
- Per Serving: Calories: 405;Fat: 20g;Protein: 49g;Carbs: 5g.

Southern Trout With Crusty Pecan

Servings: 4 | Cooking Time: 15 Minutes

Ingredients:
- Extra-virgin olive oil, for brushing
- 4 large trout fillets, boneless
- Salt
- Freshly ground black pepper
- 1 cup pecans, finely ground, divided
- 1 tablespoon coconut oil, melted, divided
- 2 tablespoon fresh thyme leaves, chopped
- Lemon wedges

Directions:
1. Preheat the oven to 375°F.
2. Brush a rimmed baking sheet with olive oil.
3. Place the trout fillets on the baking sheet skin-side down. Season with salt and pepper.
4. Into the flesh of each fillet, press gently ¼ cup of ground pecans.
5. Drizzle the melted coconut oil over the nuts and then sprinkle the thyme over the fillets.
6. Give each fillet another sprinkle of salt and pepper.
7. Place the sheet in the preheated oven and bake for 15 minutes, or until the fish is cooked through.

Nutrition Info:
- Per Serving: Calories: 672 ;Fat: 59g ;Protein: 30g ;Carbs: 13g .

Hawaiian Tuna

Servings: 4 | Cooking Time: 35 Minutes

Ingredients:
- 2 lb tuna, cubed
- 1 cup pineapple chunks
- ¼ cup chopped cilantro
- 2 tbsp chopped parsley
- 2 garlic cloves, minced
- 1 tbsp coconut oil
- 1 tbsp coconut aminos
- Sea salt and pepper to taste

Directions:
1. Preheat your oven to 400ºF. Add the tuna, pineapple, cilantro, parsley, garlic, coconut aminos, salt, and pepper to a baking dish and stir to coat. Bake for 15-20 minutes, or until the fish feels firm to the touch. Serve warm.

Nutrition Info:
- Per Serving: Calories: 410;Fat: 15g;Protein: 59g;Carbs: 7g.

Battered Bite Size Shrimp With Gluten-free Coconut

Servings: 2 | Cooking Time: 15 Minutes

Ingredients:
- 2 cups shrimp, peeled and deveined
- ¼ cup coconut flour
- ½ teaspoon cayenne pepper
- 1 teaspoon garlic powder
- 2 free range eggs, beaten
- ½ cup coconut, shredded
- ¼ cup almond flour
- a pinch of black pepper
- 1 cup arugula or watercress

Directions:
1. Preheat oven to 400°F.
2. Line a baking sheet with parchment paper.
3. In a bowl, mix the coconut flour, cayenne pepper, and garlic powder.
4. Whisk the eggs in another bowl.
5. Add the shredded coconut, almond flour and pepper in a separate bowl.
6. Dip the shrimp into each dish in consecutive order then place on the baking sheet. Bake for 10 to 15 minutes or until cooked through.
7. Serve piping hot and straight from the oven with a side salad of arugula or watercress.

Nutrition Info:
- Per Serving: Calories: 166 ;Fat: 10g ;Protein: 11g ;Carbs: 8g.

Glazed And Curried Salmon With Quinoa

Servings: 6 | Cooking Time: 30 To 35 Minutes

Ingredients:
- ¼ cup liquid honey
- 1 teaspoon curry powder, plus additional as needed
- 6 wild salmon fillets, 4 ounces
- 2 cups quinoa, rinsed well
- 4 cups water
- ½ teaspoon salt

Directions:
1. Preheat the oven to 350°F.
2. Line a baking sheet with parchment paper.
3. Mix together the honey and curry powder in a small bowl. Taste, and add more curry powder if needed.
4. Pat the fillets dry with a clean kitchen towel and place them on the prepared sheet.
5. Brush the fillets with the curry and honey mixture.
6. Combine the quinoa, water, and salt in a medium pot. Bring to a boil over high heat. Reduce the heat to low. Cover and cook for 15 minutes.
7. Put the salmon into the preheated oven and bake for 15 to 20 minutes, or until the flesh is opaque and flakes easily with a fork.
8. Fluff the quinoa and serve alongside the salmon.

Nutrition Info:
- Per Serving: Calories: 445 ;Fat: 13g ;Protein: 32g ;Sodium-Carbs: 48g.

Wonderful Baked Sea Bass With Tomatoes, Olives, And Capers

Servings: 4 | Cooking Time: 15 Minutes

Ingredients:
- 2 tablespoons extra-virgin olive oil
- 4 sea bass fillets, 5 ounces
- 1 small onion, diced
- ½ cup vegetable or chicken broth
- 1 cup diced tomatoes, canned
- ½ cup Kalamata olives, pitted and chopped
- 2 tablespoons capers, drained
- 2 cups spinach, packed
- 1 teaspoon salt
- ¼ teaspoon black pepper, freshly ground

Directions:
1. Preheat the oven to 375°F.
2. Add the olive oil in a baking dish. Place the fish fillets in the dish, turning to coat both sides with the oil.
3. Top the fish with the onion, vegetable broth, tomatoes, olives, capers, spinach, salt, and pepper.
4. Cover the baking dish with aluminum foil and place it in the preheated oven. Bake for 15 minutes, or until the fish is cooked through.

Nutrition Info:
- Per Serving: Calories: 273 ;Fat: 12g ;Protein: 35g ;Carbs: 5g .

Shrimp & Egg Risotto

Servings: 6 | Cooking Time: 40 Minutes

Ingredients:
- 4 cups water
- 4 garlic cloves, minced
- 2 eggs, beaten
- ½ tsp grated ginger
- 3 tbsp olive oil
- ¼ tsp cayenne pepper
- 1 ½ cups frozen peas
- 2 cups brown rice
- ¼ cup soy sauce
- 1 cup chopped onion
- 12 oz peeled shrimp, thawed

Directions:
1. Heat the olive oil in your Instant Pot on "Sauté". Add the onion and garlic and cook for 2 minutes. Stir in the remaining ingredients except for the shrimp and eggs.
2. Close the lid and cook on "Manual" for 20 minutes. Wait about 10 minutes before doing a quick release. Stir in the shrimp and eggs. And let them heat for a couple of seconds with the lid off. Serve and enjoy!

Nutrition Info:
- Per Serving: Calories: 220;Fat: 10g;Protein: 13g;Carbs: 20g.

Trout Fillets With Almond Crust

Servings: 4 | Cooking Time: 20 Minutes

Ingredients:
- ½ cup whole-wheat breadcrumbs
- 2 trout fillets
- 1 tbsp extra-virgin olive oil
- 1 tsp Italian seasoning
- 1 lemon, juiced and zested
- ½ cup chopped almonds

Directions:

1. Preheat your oven to 375°F. Mix breadcrumbs, Italian seasoning, lemon zest, lemon juice, and half of the almonds in a shallow dish. Lay the fillets skin side down onto the oiled baking tray and then flip over so that both sides of your fish are coated in the oil. Roll the fillets into the nut mixture on both sides to coat. Return to the baking tray. Bake for 6-7 minutes on each side and serve.
Nutrition Info:
• Per Serving: Calories: 870;Fat: 50g;Protein: 51g;Carbs: 56g.

Cumin Salmon With Daikon Relish
Servings: 4 | Cooking Time: 35 Minutes
Ingredients:
• 1 scallion, chopped
• 4 tangerines, chopped
• ½ cup chopped daikon
• 2 tbsp chopped cilantro
• 1 tsp lemon zest
• A pinch of sea salt
• 1 tsp ground cumin
• 1 tsp ground coriander
• 4 skin-on salmon fillets
• 1 tsp olive oil
Directions:
1. Stir together tangerines, daikon, scallion, cilantro, salt, and lemon zest in a mixing bowl. Set the relish aside. Preheat your oven to 425°F. In a small bowl, stir together the cumin and coriander. Rub the flesh side of the fillets with the spice mixture. Arrange the salmon in a baking dish in a single layer, skin-side up. Brush with olive oil. Bake for 15 minutes, or until just cooked through, and lightly golden. Spoon the relish over the fish. Serve.
Nutrition Info:
• Per Serving: Calories: 295;Fat: 11g;Protein: 33g;Carbs: 14g.

Hot Shrimp Paella
Servings: 4 | Cooking Time: 30 Minutes
Ingredients:
• 12 whole shrimp, peeled, deveined and the tails still intact
• 2 garlic cloves, crushed
• 1 red bell pepper, chopped
• 1 onion, diced
• 1 cup wild rice
• 2 tbsp extra-virgin olive oil
• ½ tsp red pepper flakes
• 1 tbsp parsley, chopped
• 1 lemon, juiced and zested
• 1 lemon, cut into quarters
Directions:
1. Warm the oil in a skillet over medium heat. Sauté the onion, bell pepper, and garlic for 5 minutes until softened. Add the rice and 2 cups of water. Season with black pepper and cook for 15 minutes. Add the shrimp and simmer for 5-8 minutes or until the shrimp is opaque. Add parsley, zest and juice of 1 lemon and mix well. Serve paella topped with lemon wedges.
Nutrition Info:
• Per Serving: Calories: 760;Fat: 15g;Protein: 29g;Carbs: 132g.

Lime Salmon Burgers
Servings: 4 | Cooking Time: 30 Minutes + Chilling Time
Ingredients:
• 2 tbsp olive oil
• 1 lime, cut into wedges
• 1 tsp garlic powder
• 1 scallion, chopped
• 1 lb cooked salmon fillet, flaked
• 2 eggs
• ¾ cup almond flour
• 1 lime, juiced and zested
• 1 tbsp chopped dill
• A pinch of sea salt
Directions:
1. Combine the salmon, eggs, almond flour, garlic powder, scallion, lime juice, lime zest, dill, and salt in a large bowl and mix until the mixture holds together when pressed. Divide the salmon mixture into 4 equal portions, and press them into patties about ½ inch thick. Refrigerate them for about 30 minutes to firm up.
2. Warm the olive oil in a skillet over medium heat. Add the salmon patties and brown for about 5 minutes per side, turning once. Serve the patties with lime wedges.
Nutrition Info:
• Per Serving: Calories: 245;Fat: 17g;Protein: 19g;Carbs: 5g.

Olive & Salmon Quinoa
Servings: 4 | Cooking Time: 30 Minutes
Ingredients:
• 1 lb salmon fillets
• 1 red onion, diced
• 2 cups cooked quinoa
• 16 cherry tomatoes, halved
• ½ cup chopped fresh dill
• ¼ cup chopped green olives
• 1 tbsp extra-virgin olive oil
• Sea salt and pepper to taste
• 1 tbsp lemon juice
Directions:
1. Preheat your oven to 375°F. Put the salmon fillets on a greased baking sheet and brush the tops with olive oil. Season with salt and pepper. Bake for 20 minutes.
2. Warm 1 tbsp of olive oil in a large pan over medium heat. Add the onion and sauté for 3 minutes. Stir in the quinoa, cherry tomatoes, dill, olives, and lemon juice. Cook for 1-2 minutes, or until the tomatoes and quinoa are warmed through. Transfer the tomatoes, quinoa, and salmon to a serving platter and serve.
Nutrition Info:
• Per Serving: Calories: 395;Fat: 15g;Protein: 29g;Carbs: 36g.

Tasty Sardine Donburi
Servings: 4 To 6
Cooking Time: 45 To 50 Minutes
Ingredients:
• 2 cups brown rice, rinsed well
• 4 cups water
• ½ teaspoon salt
• Three 4 ounces cans sardines packed in water, drained
• 3 scallions, sliced thin
• 1 inch piece fresh ginger, grated
• 4 tablespoons sesame oil, or extra-virgin olive oil, divided
Directions:
1. Combine the rice, water, and salt in a large pot. Bring to a boil

over high heat. Reduce the heat to low. Cover and cook for 45 to 50 minutes until tender.
2. Roughly mash the sardines in a medium bowl.
3. Add the sardines, scallions, and ginger to the pot when the rice is done. Mix thoroughly.
4. Divide the rice among four bowls. Drizzle each bowl with 1 teaspoon to 1 tablespoon of sesame oil.

Nutrition Info:
• Per Serving: Calories: 604 ;Fat: 24g ;Protein: 25g ;Carbs: 74g .

Love At First Bite Shrimp Linguine

Servings: 2 | Cooking Time: 10 Minutes

Ingredients:
• 1 package kelp noodles, 12 ounces
• 2 tablespoons unsalted butter, ghee, or lard
• 5 cloves garlic, smashed and minced
• 8 jumbo shrimp, peeled and deveined
• 1 teaspoon dried thyme leaves
• 1 teaspoon Himalayan salt, fine
• 1 teaspoon black pepper, ground
• 1 cup Cauliflower Alfredo

Directions:
1. Heat a large cast-iron skillet over medium heat. Submerge the kelp noodles in a bowl of warm water and set aside.
2. Place the butter in the hot skillet and heat until it bubbles for 2 minutes. It will turn golden brown and smell slightly toasted when it's ready. Add the garlic to the butter. With a kitchen towel, wrapped around the skillet's handle, tilt the skillet with one hand so the garlic and butter pool at one end. Use a spoon to keep pouring the butter over the garlic for 1 to 2 minutes until it turns golden brown.
3. Add the shrimp to the skillet, then sprinkle in the thyme, salt, and pepper. Use a spatula to keep moving the shrimp and garlic around for 4 to 5 minutes. Once the shrimp have turned pink and most of them have just coiled, drain the kelp noodles and add them to the skillet. Use tongs to toss and combine the noodles with the shrimp. Add the Alfredo and continue to cook, stirring occasionally for 2 to 3 minutes until the noodles have softened.
4. Serve immediately in large bowls with forks and spoons. Store leftovers in an airtight container in the fridge for up to 3 days. Simmer in a hot skillet for 5 to 6 minutes to reheat.

Nutrition Info:
• Per Serving: Calories: 413 ;Fat: 37g ;Protein: 19g;Carbs: 14g.

Cod In Tomato Sauce

Servings: 4 | Cooking Time: 15 Minutes

Ingredients:
• 4 cod fillets
• 2 cups chopped tomatoes
• 1 tbsp olive oil
• Sea salt and pepper to taste
• ¼ tsp garlic powder

Directions:
1. Place the tomatoes in a baking dish and crush them with a fork. Season with some salt, pepper, and garlic powder. Season the cod with salt and pepper and place it over the tomatoes. Drizzle the olive oil over the fish and tomatoes. Add 1 cup of water and a trivet in your Instant Pot. Place the baking dish on the trivet. Close the lid and cook on "Manual" for 10 minutes. Once the timer goes off, let the steam release naturally for about 10 minutes before releasing the remaining pressure manually. Serve.

Nutrition Info:
• Per Serving: Calories: 250;Fat: 5g;Protein: 45g;Carbs: 3g.

Beautifully Glazed Salmon With Honey Mustard

Servings: 4 | Cooking Time: 8 Minutes

Ingredients:
• 4 tablespoons honey, 90g
• 2 tablespoons Dijon mustard
• Four 4 ounces skin-on salmon fillets, 1 inch thick, pin bones removed
• Olive oil
• Kosher salt
• Freshly ground black pepper

Directions:
1. Whisk together the honey and mustard in a small bowl. Set aside.
2. Use a paper towel to rinse the salmon and pat dry. Brush all sides of each fillet with olive oil and season with a pinch each of salt and pepper.
3. Prepare a grill for direct cooking over medium-high heat to grill the salmon. Fold a 24-by-12-inch piece of aluminum foil to form a square. Crimp the edges upward to form a rim. Prick the foil several times with a fork then brush with olive oil.
4. Place the foil on the grill grate then set the salmon, skin-side down, on the foil, leaving 1 inch between each piece. For 4 minutes, close the lid and grill. Lift the lid and generously brush the fish with the honey mustard. Close the lid and grill for 2 to 3 minutes more for medium, or until the salmon is cooked to the desired doneness. Remove the salmon from the grill.
5. Place a rack in the top third of the oven and preheat the oven to broil to cook the salmon in the oven. Line a baking sheet with aluminum foil and brush with olive oil. Place the salmon, skin-side down, on the foil, leaving 1 inch between each piece. Broil for 2 minutes, then brush each fillet with the honey mustard. Continue broiling for 3 to 4 minutes more, or until the salmon is cooked to the desired doneness. Remove the salmon from the oven.
6. Brush the salmon with more honey mustard and let rest for 3 to 5 minutes before serving.

Nutrition Info:
• Per Serving: Calories: 131 ;Fat: 4g ;Protein: 8g ;Carbs: 18g .

Elegant Sesame Tuna With Asparagus

Servings: 4 | Cooking Time: 15 Minutes

Ingredients:
• 2 asparagus bunches, washed and trimmed
• 3 tablespoons toasted sesame oil, divided
• ½ teaspoon salt
• 4 tuna steaks, 4-ounce
• 2 tablespoons sesame seeds

Directions:
1. Preheat the oven to 375°F.
2. Line a baking sheet with parchment paper.
3. Combine the asparagus, 1½ tablespoons of sesame oil, and the salt in a large bowl. Spread the asparagus onto the prepared sheet.
4. Place the sheet in the preheated oven and bake for 15 minutes.
5. Brush the tuna with the remaining 1½ tablespoons of sesame oil while the asparagus cooks.
6. Place a sauté pan over medium heat. Add the tuna when the pan is hot. Cook the tuna steaks one or two at a time.
7. Sear the tuna for 3 to 4 minutes on each side, or longer if you like your tuna more well done.
8. Plate the tuna and the asparagus on four plates. Sprinkle 1½ teaspoons of sesame seeds over each serving.

• Per Serving: Calories: 349 ;Fat: 20g ;Protein: 37g ;Carbs: 6g .

Simple Tacos With Fish And Pineapple Salsa

Servings: 6 | Cooking Time: 12 Minutes

Ingredients:
• Salsa:
• 1½ cups fresh, or canned, pineapple chunks, cut into small dice
• 1 small red onion, minced
• Juice of 1 lime
• Zest of 1 lime
• Tacos:
• 1 head romaine lettuce
• 3 tablespoons coconut oil
• 14 ounces white fish, skinless and firm, such as cod or halibut
• Juice of 1 lime
• Zest of 1 lime
• ½ teaspoon salt

Directions:
1. Stir together the pineapple and onion in a medium bowl. Add the lime juice and lime zest. Stir well and set aside.
2. Separate the lettuce leaves, choosing the 6 to 12 largest and most suitable to hold the filling. Wash the leaves and pat them dry.
3. Heat the coconut oil in a large pan set over medium-low heat.
4. Brush the fish with lime juice and lime zest. Sprinkle with salt.
5. Place the fish in the pan. Cook for 8 minutes.
6. Flip the fish over and break it up into small pieces. Cook for 3 to 4 minutes more. The flesh should be opaque and flake easily with a fork.
7. Fill the lettuce leaves with the cooked fish and spoon the salsa over the top.

Nutrition Info:
• Per Serving: Calories: 198 ;Fat: 9g ;Protein: 19g ;Carbs: 12g.

Mediterranean Trout

Servings: 2 | Cooking Time: 30 Minutes

Ingredients:
• 2 trout fillets
• ¼ cup juice
• 2 tsp olive oil
• 3 tbsp capers
• Sea salt and pepper to taste
• 1 lemon, juiced and zested

Directions:
1. Warm the olive oil in a skillet over medium heat. Add the trout fillets and cook for 3 minutes per side, or until the center is flaky. Set aside. Add the lemon juice, zest, capers, salt, and pepper to the skillet and cook for 2-3 more minutes. Spoon the sauce over the fish. Serve.

Nutrition Info:
• Per Serving: Calories: 300;Fat: 21g;Protein: 22g;Carbs: 9g.

Dense Oven Roasted Cod And Shiitake Mushrooms

Servings: 4 To 6

Cooking Time: 20 Minutes

Ingredients:
• 1½ pounds cod fillets
• ½ teaspoon salt, plus additional for seasoning
• Freshly ground black pepper
• 1 tablespoon extra-virgin olive oil
• 1 leek, white part only, sliced thin
• 8 ounces shiitake mushrooms, stemmed, sliced
• 1 tablespoon coconut aminos
• 1 teaspoon sweet paprika
• ½ cup vegetable broth, or chicken broth

Directions:
1. Preheat the oven to 375°F.
2. Season the cod with salt and pepper. Set aside.
3. Combine in a shallow baking dish the olive oil, leek, mushrooms, coconut aminos, paprika, and ½ teaspoon of salt. Season with pepper, and give everything a gentle toss to coat with the oil and spices.
4. For 10 minutes, place the dish in the preheated oven and bake the vegetables.
5. Stir the vegetables and place the cod fillets on top in a single layer.
6. Pour in the vegetable broth. Return the dish to the oven and bake for 10 to 15 minutes more, or until the cod is firm but cooked through.

Nutrition Info:
• Per Serving: Calories: 221 ;Fat: 6g ;Protein: 32g ;Carbs: 12g.

Seared Trout With Greek Yogurt Sauce

Servings: 4 | Cooking Time: 30 Minutes

Ingredients:
• 1 garlic clove, minced
• 2 dill pickles, cubed
• ¼ cup Greek yogurt
• 3 tbsp olive oil
• 4 trout fillets, patted dry
• 1 tbsp olive oil
• Sea salt and pepper to taste

Directions:
1. Whisk yogurt, pickles, garlic, 1 tbsp of olive oil, and salt in a small bowl. Set the sauce aside. Season the trout fillets lightly with salt and pepper.
2. Heat the remaining olive oil in a skillet over medium heat. Add the trout fillets to the hot skillet and panfry for about 10 minutes, flipping the fish halfway through or until the fish is cooked to your liking. Spread the salsa on top of the fish and serve.

Nutrition Info:
• Per Serving: Calories: 325;Fat: 15g;Protein: 38g;Carbs: 5g.

Salmon & Asparagus Parcels

Servings: 4 | Cooking Time: 30 Minutes

Ingredients:
• 16 asparagus spears, sliced
• 4 salmon fillets
• 2 lemons, sliced
• 1 cup cherry tomatoes
• Sea salt and pepper to taste
• 2 tsp extra-virgin olive oil
• ½ cup hollandaise sauce

Directions:

1. Preheat your oven to 400ºF. Cut 4 squares of nonstick baking paper. Divide the fish fillets between the sheets. Season with salt and pepper, then drizzle with olive oil. Place three lemon slices on each fillet, overlapping them slightly to cover the fish. Sprinkle one-fourth each of the asparagus and tomatoes evenly around the fish and season again with salt and pepper. Drizzle with a little olive oil and wrap up the paper around the fish and asparagus to create parcels. Place on a baking sheet and bake for 15-20 minutes or until the salmon is cooked through and the asparagus are tender. Drizzle with hollandaise sauce and serve immediately.

Nutrition Info:
- Per Serving: Calories: 165;Fat: 5g;Protein: 23g;Carbs: 12g.

Fried Haddock With Roasted Beets

Servings: 4 | Cooking Time: 50 Minutes

Ingredients:
- 4 peeled beets, cut into wedges
- 4 haddock fillets
- 2 shallots, thinly sliced
- 2 tbsp apple cider vinegar
- 2 tbsp olive oil, divided
- 1 tsp minced garlic
- 1 tsp chopped mint
- Sea salt to taste

Directions:

1. Preheat your oven to 400ºF. Place the beets, shallots, vinegar, 1 tablespoon of olive oil, garlic, thyme, and sea salt in a medium bowl and toss to coat well. Spread out the beet mixture on a baking dish. Roast in the preheated oven for about 30 minutes, turning once or twice with a spatula, or until the beets are tender.
2. Warm the remaining olive oil in a skillet over medium heat. Add the haddock and sear each side for 4-5 minutes, or until the flesh is opaque and it flakes apart easily. Top with roasted beets.

Nutrition Info:
- Per Serving: Calories: 340;Fat: 9g;Protein: 37g;Carbs: 20g.

Spicy Shrimp Scampi

Servings: 4 | Cooking Time: 25 Minutes

Ingredients:
- 1 ½ lb shrimp, peeled and tails removed
- 1 tsp ancho chili powder
- ¼ cup coconut oil
- 1 tsp paprika
- 1 onion, finely chopped
- 1 red bell pepper, chopped
- 2 garlic cloves, minced
- 1 lemon, zested and juiced
- Sea salt and pepper to taste

Directions:

1. Warm the coconut oil in a skillet over medium heat. Add the onion and red bell pepper and cook for 6 minutes until tender. Put in shrimp and cook for 5 minutes until it's pink. Mix in garlic and cook for another 30 seconds. Add lemon juice, lemon zest, ancho chili powder, paprika, salt, and pepper and simmer for 3 minutes. Serve warm.

Nutrition Info:
- Per Serving: Calories: 350;Fat: 17g;Protein: 1g;Carbs: 11g.

Shanghai Cod With Udon Noodles

Servings: 2 | Cooking Time:10 Minutes

Ingredients:
- 3 heads bok choy
- 2 black cod fillets
- 2 cups chicken broth
- 2 cups udon noodles
- 1 carrot, sliced
- 1 green onion, thinly sliced
- 1 tsp coconut oil
- 1 tsp five-spice powder
- 1 tbsp olive oil
- 1 tbsp ginger, minced
- Black pepper to taste
- 1 tbsp rice wine
- 1 tsp low-sodium soy sauce
- 2 tsp cilantro, chopped
- 1 tsp sesame seeds

Directions:

1. Place soy sauce, rice wine, pepper, 1 cup of chicken broth, coconut oil, and spice blend in a bowl and stir to combine. Warm the olive oil in a large saucepan over medium heat and cook the bok choy, ginger, and carrot for about 2 minutes until the bok choy is green. Add the rest of the reserved chicken stock and heat through.
2. Add the udon noodles and stir, bringing to a simmer. Add the green onion and the fish and cook for 10-15 minutes until the fish is tender. Add the fish, noodles, and vegetables into serving bowls. Pour the broth over the top.Garnish with cilantro and sesame seeds. Serve.

Nutrition Info:
- Per Serving: Calories: 485;Fat: 15g;Protein: 36g;Carbs: 43g.

Unforgettable Tasty Calamari

Servings: 4 | Cooking Time: 20 Minutes

Ingredients:
- 1 cup coconut oil, or more if needed
- ½ cup coconut flour
- 1 teaspoon Himalayan salt, fine
- 1 teaspoon black pepper, ground
- 3 large eggs
- 1 tablespoon red wine vinegar
- 1 cup shredded coconut, unsweetened
- 1 pound cleaned calamari tubes, sliced into ½-inch rings
- Serving:
- 2 limes, cut into wedges
- ½ cup Ginger Sauce
- ½ cup Roasted Beet Marinara

Directions:

1. Set a cooling rack on a sheet pan or line a plate with paper towels.
2. Heat an 8-inch heavy-bottomed pot or skillet over medium heat. Add the coconut oil, it should be 1 inch deep, Heat the oil until it sizzles around the end of a wooden spoon handle when it's inserted in the oil.
3. Bread the calamari while the oil heats. Combine the coconut flour, salt, and pepper in a large bowl. Whisk the eggs with the vinegar in a separate bowl. Place the shredded coconut in another bowl.
4. Add the calamari to the bowl with the flour mixture and toss to coat. Remove half of the calamari and place in a colander then shake to remove the excess flour.
5. Dredge the calamari from the colander by working with three

or four rings at a time in the egg mixture and in the shredded co-conut. Place it in the skillet with the hot oil. Fry until golden all over, turning once, for 4 minutes. To remove the crispy rings from the oil, use tongs then place on the cooling rack or paper towel–lined plate.

6. Repeat until the breaded calamari are all done. The eggs and shredded coconut should be done by no. Remove the rest of the calamari from the coconut flour and shake to remove the excess flour.

7. Fry all the coconut flour–coated rings together for 5 to 6 minutes, turning and stirring occasionally until they're golden around the edges and all of it are rounded. Remove from the oil and set to drain next to the twice-breaded batch.

8. Serve right away with lime wedges and dipping sauces.

9. Place the calamari on a cooling rack over a sheet pan and store in the oven for up to an hour. Gently heat right before serving at 300°F for 8 to 10 minutes.

Nutrition Info:
• Per Serving: Calories: 422 ;Fat: 19g ;Protein: 36g ;Carbs: 12g .

Greek-style Sea Bass

Servings: 4 | Cooking Time: 25 Minutes

Ingredients:
• 4 sea bass fillets
• 1 small onion, diced
• ½ cup vegetable broth
• 1 cup canned diced tomatoes
• ½ cup chopped black olives
• 2 tbsp capers, drained
• 2 cups packed spinach
• 2 tbsp extra-virgin olive oil
• Sea salt and pepper to taste
• 1 tsp Greek oregano

Directions:
1. Preheat your oven to 375ºF. Coat the fish with olive oil in a baking dish Season with Greek oregano, salt, and pepper. Top the fish with the onion, broth, tomatoes, olives, capers, spinach, salt, and pepper. Cover the baking dish with aluminum foil and place it in the oven. Bake for 15 minutes, or until the fish is cooked through. Serve.

Nutrition Info:
• Per Serving: Calories: 275;Fat: 12g;Protein: 34g;Carbs: 5g.

Parsnip & Tilapia Bake

Servings: 4 | Cooking Time: 55 Minutes

Ingredients:
• 2 cups diced parsnip
• 4 onion wedges
• 2 cups diced carrot
• 1 cup asparagus pieces
• 2 tsp cayenne pepper
• 1 tsp minced garlic
• ¼ tsp sea salt
• 2 tbsp olive oil
• 4 skinless tilapia fillets
• Juice of 1 lemon

Directions:
1. Preheat your oven to 350ºF. Take 4 pieces of aluminum foil and fold each piece in half to make four pieces. In a mixing bowl, toss together the sweet potato wedges, carrot, parsnip, onion, asparagus, cayenne pepper, garlic, salt, and olive oil. Place one-fourth of the vegetables in the center of each foil piece. Top each vegetable mound with one tilapia fillet. Sprinkle the fish with

lemon juice.
2. Fold the foil to create sealed packages with a bit of space at the top, and arrange the packets on a baking sheet. Bake for about 30 minutes, or until the fish begins to flake and the vegetables are tender. Serve and enjoy!

Nutrition Info:
• Per Serving: Calories: 350;Fat: 5g;Protein: 35g;Carbs: 45g.

Fish Stew

Servings: 4 | Cooking Time: 30 Minutes

Ingredients:
• 2 lb white fish fillets, cut into 2-inch pieces
• 1 white onion, sliced thin
• 1 fennel bulb, sliced thin
• 2 garlic cloves, minced
• 1 can diced tomatoes
• 2 tbsp extra-virgin olive oil
• ¼ tsp turmeric
• 1 tsp ground cumin
• 1 tsp ground oregano
• Sea salt and pepper to taste
• 2 tbsp chopped parsley
• ½ lemon, juiced

Directions:
1. Warm the olive oil in a large pot over medium heat. Add the onion, fennel, and garlic. Sauté for 5 minutes. Stir in the crushed tomatoes, turmeric, cumin, oregano, salt, and pepper. Bring the mixture to a simmer.
2. Lay the fish fillets in a single layer over the vegetables, cover the pan, and simmer for 10 minutes. Garnish with parsley and lemon juice. Serve and enjoy!

Nutrition Info:
• Per Serving: Calories: 530;Fat: 20g;Protein: 61g;Carbs: 24g.

Beneficial Baked Salmon Patties With Vegetables

Servings: 4 | Cooking Time: 35 To 38 Minutes

Ingredients:
• 2 cups cooked, mashed sweet potatoes (2 large sweet potatoes)
• Two 6 ounces cans wild salmon, drained
• ¼ cup almond flour
• ¼ teaspoon turmeric, ground
• 2 tablespoons coconut oil
• 2 kale bunches, thoroughly washed, stemmed, and cut into ribbons
• ¼ teaspoon salt

Directions:
1. Preheat the oven to 350°F.
2. Line a baking sheet with parchment paper.
3. Stir together the mashed sweet potatoes and salmon in a large bowl.
4. Blend in the almond flour and turmeric.
5. Scoop the salmon mixture onto the baking sheet using a □?cup measure. Flatten slightly with the bottom of the measuring cup. Repeat with the remaining mixture.
6. Place the sheet in the preheated oven and bake for 30 minutes, flipping the patties halfway through.
7. Heat the coconut oil in a large pan set over medium heat.
8. Add the kale. Sauté for 5 to 8 minutes, or until the kale is bright and wilted. Sprinkle with the salt and serve with the salmon patties.

Nutrition Info:
• Per Serving: Calories: 320 ;Fat: 13g ;Protein: 21g ;Carbs: 32g .

Creamy Crabmeat

Servings: 4 | Cooking Time: 15 Minutes

Ingredients:
- ¼ cup olive oil
- 1 small red onion, chopped
- 1 lb lump crabmeat
- ½ celery stalk, chopped
- ½ cup plain yogurt
- ¼ cup chicken broth

Directions:
1. Season the crabmeat with some salt and pepper. Heat the oil in your Instant Pot on "Sauté". Add celery and onion and cook for 3 minutes, or until soft. Add the crabmeat and stir in the broth. Seal and lock the lid and set to "Steam" for 5 minutes on high pressure. Once the cooking is complete, do a quick release and carefully open the lid. Stir in the yogurt and serve.

Nutrition Info:
- Per Serving: Calories: 450;Fat: 10g;Protein: 40g;Carbs: 12g.

Asian-inspired Salmon

Servings: 4 | Cooking Time: 15 Minutes

Ingredients:
- 3 tbsp miso paste
- 1 tsp coconut aminos
- 4 salmon fillets
- 2 tbsp honey
- 1 tsp rice vinegar

Directions:
1. Preheat your broiler. Line a baking dish with foil. Place the salmon fillets on the baking dish. In a bowl, combine miso paste, honey, coconut aminos, and rice vinegar. Rub each fillet with this mixture and broil for 5 minutes. Turn the fillets and rub with the remaining glaze and broil for 5 more minutes. Serve immediately.

Nutrition Info:
- Per Serving: Calories: 265;Fat: 11g;Protein: 30g;Carbs: 15g.

Fancy Cod Stew With Cauliflower

Servings: 4 | Cooking Time: 30 Minutes

Ingredients:
- 3 cups water
- 1 large cauliflower head, broken into large florets (about 4 cups)
- 1 cup cashews, soaked in water for at least 4 hours
- 1 teaspoon salt
- 1 pound cod, cut into chunks
- 2 cups kale, thoroughly washed and sliced

Directions:
1. Bring the water to a boil in a large pot set over high heat. Reduce the heat to medium.
2. Add the cauliflower. For 12 minutes, cook until tender.
3. Drain and rinse the cashews and place them in a blender.
4. Add the cooked cauliflower and its cooking water to the blender.
5. Add the salt.
6. Blend until smooth. Add more water if you prefer a thinner consistency.
7. Return the blended cauliflower-cashew mixture to the pot. Place the pot over medium heat.
8. Add the cod. Cook for about 15 minutes, or until cooked through.
9. Add the kale. Let it wilt for 3 minutes.

Nutrition Info:
- Per Serving: Calories: 385 ;Fat: 17g ;Protein: 36g ;Carbs: 26g.

Aromatic Curried Whitefish

Servings: 4 To 6

Cooking Time: 15 Minutes

Ingredients:
- 2 tablespoons coconut oil
- 1 onion, chopped
- 2 garlic cloves, minced
- 1 tablespoon fresh ginger, minced
- 2 teaspoons curry powder
- 1 teaspoon salt
- ¼ teaspoon black pepper, freshly ground
- 1 piece lemongrass, bruised, 4 inch, and white part only
- 2 cups butternut squash, cubed
- 2 cups broccoli, chopped
- 1 can coconut milk, 13 ½ ounces
- 1 cup vegetable broth, or chicken broth
- 1 pound whitefish fillets, firm
- ¼ cup fresh cilantro, chopped
- 1 scallion, sliced thin
- Lemon wedges

Directions:
1. Melt the coconut oil in a large pot over medium-high heat. Add the onion, garlic, ginger, curry powder, salt, and pepper. Sauté for 5 minutes.
2. Add the lemongrass, butternut squash, and broccoli. Sauté for 2 minutes more.
3. Stir in the coconut milk and vegetable broth and bring to a boil. Reduce the heat to simmer and add the fish. Cover the pot and simmer for 5 minutes, or until the fish is cooked through. Remove the lemongrass.
4. Into a serving bowl, ladle the curry. Garnish with the cilantro and scallion and serve with the lemon wedges.

Nutrition Info:
- Per Serving: Calories: 553 ;Fat: 39g ;Protein: 34g ;Carbs: 22g .

A Must-try Spicy Sea Bass Fillets With Ginger

Servings: 2 | Cooking Time: 10 Minutes

Ingredients:
- 2 sea bass fillets
- 1 teaspoon black pepper
- 1 tablespoon extra-virgin olive oil
- 1 teaspoon ginger, peeled and chopped
- 1 garlic clove, thinly sliced
- 1 red chili, deseeded and thinly sliced
- 2 green onion stems, sliced

Directions:
1. Get a skillet and heat the oil on a medium to high heat.
2. Sprinkle black pepper over the Sea Bass and score the skin of the fish a few times with a sharp knife.
3. Add the sea bass fillet to the very hot pan with the skin side down.
4. For 5 minutes, cook and turn over.
5. Cook for 2 minutes more.
6. Remove seabass from the pan and rest.
7. Add the chili, garlic and ginger and cook for 2 minutes or until golden.
8. Remove from the heat and add the green onions.
9. Scatter the vegetables over your sea bass to serve.
10. Try with a steamed sweet potato or side salad.

Nutrition Info:
- Per Serving: Calories: 159 ;Fat: 6g ;Protein: 24g ;Carbs: 2g .

Sardine & Butter Bean Meal

Servings: 2 | Cooking Time: 20 Minutes

Ingredients:
- ½ cup cooked butter beans
- 1 red chili, sliced
- 10 sardines, scaled and cleaned
- 2 lemons, zested
- 2 tbsp parsley, chopped
- 2 garlic cloves, chopped
- ½ cup black olives
- 3 tbsp olive oil
- 2 diced tomatoes

Directions:
1. Mix the lemon zest, red chili, and parsley in a bowl; reserve. Warm the olive oil in a skillet over medium heat and lay the sardines flat on the pan. Saute for 3 minutes until golden underneath and turn over to fry for another 3 minutes. Remove to a plate. Sauté the garlic in the same skillet for 1 minute until softened. Pour in the diced tomatoes and olives and simmer for 4-5 minutes. Tip in the butter beans and tomatoes and stir until heated through. Add the sardines and continue cooking for a further 3- 4 minutes. Top with chili dressing and serve.

Nutrition Info:
- Per Serving: Calories: 455;Fat: 31g;Protein: 22g;Carbs: 23g.

Briny Flavoured Herbed Tuna Cakes

Servings: 4 | Cooking Time: 30 Minutes

Ingredients:
- 2 cups cooked and mashed parsnips
- Two 6 ounces cans wild tuna, drained
- ¼ cup almond flour, or brown rice flour
- 2 tablespoons ground flaxseed, or ground chia seed
- 1 bunch fresh parsley, stemmed and finely chopped

Directions:
1. Preheat the oven to 350°F.
2. Line a baking sheet with parchment paper.
3. Combine the mashed parsnips and tuna in a medium bowl. Flake the tuna with a fork.
4. Stir in the almond flour, flaxseed, and parsley. Mix well.
5. Scoop the patty mixture onto the prepared sheet using a ⬜?cup measure. Flatten slightly with the bottom of the measuring cup. Repeat with the remaining mixture.
6. Place the sheet in the preheated oven and bake for 30 minutes, flipping the patties halfway through.

Nutrition Info:
- Per Serving: Calories: 273 ;Fat: 9g ;Protein: 25g ;Carbs: 23g .

Rich Grandma's Salmon Chowder

Servings: 4 | Cooking Time: 25 Minutes

Ingredients:
- 2 cans diced tomatoes, 1 drained and 1 undrained
- 2 tbsp fresh chives, chopped
- ¼ cup olive oil
- 1 red bell pepper, chopped
- 1 lb skinless salmon, cubed
- 4 cups fish stock
- 2 cups diced sweet potatoes
- 1 tsp onion powder
- Sea salt and pepper to taste

Directions:
1. Warm the olive oil in a pot over medium heat and place the red bell pepper and salmon. Cook for 5 minutes until the salmon is opaque and the bell pepper is tender. Mix in tomatoes, fish stock, sweet potatoes, onion powder, salt, and pepper and bring to a simmer. Then low the heat and cook for 10 minutes until the potatoes are soft. Divide the chowder between bowls and scatter over the chopped chives. Serve immediately.

Nutrition Info:
- Per Serving: Calories: 580;Fat: 43g;Protein: 17g;Carbs: 56g.

Satisfying Peperonata With Seared Ahi Tuna

Servings: 4 | Cooking Time: 60 Minutes

Ingredients:
- One 1 pound ahi tuna fillet, about 1 inch thick
- Extra-virgin olive oil
- Kosher salt
- Freshly ground black pepper
- 1 cup Peperonata, 210 g
- Prepare a grill for direct cooking over high heat.

Directions:
1. Brush the tuna fillet with olive oil and season with salt and pepper. For 1 to 2 minutes, sear the tuna per side for rare, or longer to reach the desired doneness. Transfer to a carving board and let rest for 2 minutes.
2. Slice the tuna against the grain and divide among four plates. Spoon one-fourth of the peperonata over each piece of fish then serve.

Nutrition Info:
- Per Serving: Calories: 124 ;Fat: 1g ;Protein: 28g ;Carbs: 4g.

Fennel & Shallot Salmon Casserole

Servings: 4 | Cooking Time: 30 Minutes

Ingredients:
- 2 shallots, sliced thin
- 1 fennel bulb, sliced
- 4 salmon fillets
- Sea salt and pepper to taste
- 1 tbsp extra-virgin olive oil
- ½ cup vegetable broth
- 1 fresh rosemary sprig

Directions:
1. Preheat your oven to 375ºF. Brush the shallots and fennel with olive oil in a shallow roasting pan. Place the salmon fillets over the vegetables and sprinkle with salt and pepper. Pour in the vegetable broth and add the rosemary sprig to the pan. Cover tightly with aluminum foil. Bake for 20 minutes, or until the salmon is cooked through. Remove and discard the rosemary sprig. Serve.

Nutrition Info:
- Per Serving: Calories: 290;Fat: 15g;Protein: 32g;Carbs: 8g.

One-skillet Shrimp With Sriracha Pak Choy

Servings: 4 | Cooking Time: 25 Minutes

Ingredients:
- ¼ cup olive oil
- 1 ½ lb peeled shrimp
- Sea salt and pepper to taste
- 4 cups pak choi, chopped
- 2 garlic cloves, minced
- ½ cup orange juice
- 1 tbsp sriracha sauce

Directions:
1. Warm 2 tbsp of olive oil in a skillet over medium heat and place the shrimp and salt. Cook for 4 minutes until the shrimp is

pink. Set aside covered with aluminum foil. Warm 2 tbsp of olive oil in the skillet, add the pak choy, and cook for 3 minutes. Stir in garlic and cook for another 30 seconds. Mix the orange juice, Sriracha sauce, salt, and pepper in a bowl, pour it over the spinach, and cook for 3 more minutes. Top shrimp and serve.

Nutrition Info:
• Per Serving: Calories: 320;Fat: 17g;Protein: 1g;Carbs: 8g.

Tuna & Pea Cheesy Noodles
Servings: 4 | Cooking Time: 20 Minutes

Ingredients:
• ¼ cup whole-wheat breadcrumbs
• 28 oz canned mushroom soup
• 1 can tuna, drained
• 4 oz grated Parmesan cheese
• 16 oz egg noodles
• 1 cup frozen peas

Directions:
1. Pour 3 cups of water and noodles into your Instant Pot. Stir in soup, tuna, and frozen peas. Close the lid and cook for 5 minutes on "Manual". Release the pressure quickly. Stir in the Parmesan cheese. Transfer to a baking dish that can fit in your Instant Pot. Sprinkle with breadcrumbs on top. Place the baking dish in your Instant Pot. Seal the lid and cook on "Manual" on high pressure for another 2 minutes. Perform a quick pressure release. Serve.

Nutrition Info:
• Per Serving: Calories: 430;Fat: 20g;Protein: 18g;Carbs: 40g.

Mango Halibut Curry
Servings: 4 | Cooking Time: 20 Minutes

Ingredients:
• 1 tbsp olive oil
• 2 tbsp mango chutney
• 2 tsp ground turmeric
• 2 tsp curry powder
• 1 ½ lb halibut, cubed
• 4 cups chicken broth
• 1 can coconut milk
• Sea salt and pepper to taste
• 2 tbsp cilantro, chopped
• 1 red chili pepper, sliced

Directions:
1. Warm the olive oil in a skillet over medium heat and place in the turmeric and curry powder and cook for 2 minutes. Stir in halibut, chicken broth, coconut milk, mango chutney, salt, and pepper. Bring to a simmer, then cook for 6-7 minutes over low heat until the halibut is opaque and cooked through. Spoon into bowls and top with finely chopped cilantro and chili slices. Enjoy!

Nutrition Info:
• Per Serving: Calories: 430;Fat: 48g;Protein: 1g;Carbs: 6g.

Mustardy Salmon Patties
Servings: 4 | Cooking Time: 25 Minutes

Ingredients:
• ½ tsp garlic powder
• 1 egg, beaten
• 1 lb ground salmon
• ¼ tsp onion powder
• ½ cup almond flour
• 1 tsp Dijon mustard
• 1 tbsp lemon juice
• ¼ tsp chili pepper, chopped

• Sea salt and pepper to taste
• 1 tbsp avocado oil

Directions:
1. Mix the garlic powder, minced salmon, onion powder, almond flour, eggs, mustard, lemon juice, chili pepper, salt, and pepper in a bowl and stir until well incorporated. Shape the mixture into four ½-inch-thick patties.
2. Heat the avocado oil in a large skillet over medium heat. Add the patties to the hot skillet and cook each side for 4-5 minutes until lightly browned and cooked through.

Nutrition Info:
• Per Serving: Calories: 250;Fat: 12g;Protein: 27g;Carbs: 4g.

Lemony Spanish Shrimp With Parsley
Servings: 2 | Cooking Time: 20 Minutes

Ingredients:
• 2 cups wild or basmati rice
• 4 cups of water
• 12 whole shrimp, peeled, deveined and the tails still intact
• 2 garlic cloves, crushed
• 1 white onion, diced
• 2 tablespoons extra virgin olive oil
• ½ teaspoon red pepper flakes
• 1 tablespoon parsley, crushed
• 1 lemon, juice and zest
• 1 lemon, cut into quarters

Directions:
1. Add the rice and 4 cups of water to a saucepan and boil on a high heat.
2. Lower the heat, cover and simmer for 15 minutes once boiling.
3. Heat the oil in a skillet on a medium heat and then sauté the onion, garlic and red pepper flakes for 5 minutes until soft and add the shrimp.
4. Sauté for 5 to 8 minutes or until shrimp is opaque.
5. Drain the rice and return to the heat for 3 minutes more with the lid on.
6. Add the rice to the shrimps.
7. Add in the parsley, zest and juice of 1 lemon and mix well.
8. Serve in a wide paella dish or a large serving dish. Scatter the lemon wedges around the edge and sprinkle with a little fresher parsley.
9. Season with black pepper to taste.

Nutrition Info:
• Per Serving: Calories: 668 ;Fat: 8g ;Protein: 25g ;Carbs: 130g .

Autenthic Salmon Ceviche
Servings: 4 | Cooking Time: 30 Minutes

Ingredients:
• 1 lb salmon, cubed
• 1 lime, juiced
• 1 Spanish onion, chopped
• 2 tomatoes, diced
• ¼ cup cilantro, chopped
• 1 jalapeño pepper, diced
• 2 tbsp olive oil
• ½ tsp sea salt

Directions:
1. Mix the salmon and lemon juice and let marinate for 20 minutes. Stir in onion, tomatoes, cilantro, jalapeño, olive oil, and salt. Serve and enjoy!

Nutrition Info:
• Per Serving: Calories: 230;Fat: 15g;Protein: 1g;Carbs: 4g.

Crispy Coconut Prawns

Servings: 2 | Cooking Time: 25 Minutes

Ingredients:
- 1 lb prawns, peeled and deveined
- ¼ cup coconut flour
- ½ tsp cayenne pepper
- 1 tsp garlic powder
- 2 beaten eggs
- ½ cup shredded coconut
- ¼ cup almond flour
- Black pepper to taste

Directions:
1. Preheat your oven to 400ºF. Blend the coconut flour, cayenne pepper, and garlic powder in a bowl. In a separate bowl, whisk the eggs. In a third bowl, add the shredded coconut, almond flour and black pepper. Dip the prawns into each dish in consecutive order, and then place a parchment-lined baking sheet. Bake for 10-15 minutes or until cooked through. Serve and enjoy!

Nutrition Info:
- Per Serving: Calories: 475;Fat: 15g;Protein: 54g;Carbs: 30g.

Lobster & Parmesan Pasta

Servings: 4 | Cooking Time: 25 Minutes

Ingredients:
- 1 tbsp whole-wheat flour
- 8 oz whole-wheat ziti
- 1 cup plain yogurt
- 1 tbsp chopped tarragon
- ¾ cup Parmesan cheese
- 3 lobster tails
- ½ cup white wine
- ½ tsp pepper
- 1 tbsp Worcestershire sauce

Directions:
1. Add 6 cups of water to the Instant Pot. Add the lobster tails and ziti. Close the lid and cook for 10 minutes on "Manual". Do a quick pressure release. Drain the pasta and set aside. Remove the meat from the tails, chop it, and stir into the bowl with pasta. Stir in the rest of the ingredients in the Instant Pot. When the sauce thickens, add the pasta and lobster. Cook for another 1-2 minutes.

Nutrition Info:
- Per Serving: Calories: 440;Fat: 15g;Protein: 28g;Carbs: 45g.

Rosemary Salmon With Orange Glaze

Servings: 4 | Cooking Time: 30 Minutes

Ingredients:
- 2 tsp chopped rosemary
- 2 oranges, juiced
- 1 orange, zested
- ¼ cup pure maple syrup
- 2 tsp low-sodium soy sauce
- 1 tsp garlic powder
- 4 salmon fillets

Directions:
1. Preheat your oven to 400°F. Mix the orange juice, orange zest, maple syrup, soy sauce, and garlic powder in a bowl. Add in salmon pieces, flesh-side down, and let marinate for 10 minutes. Transfer each piece skin-side up to a lined baking sheet and bake for 15 minutes until the salmon is lightly browned. Garnish with rosemary and serve.

Nutrition Info:
- Per Serving: Calories: 300;Fat: 12g;Protein: 1g;Carbs: 19g.

Chipotle Trout With Spinach

Servings: 4 | Cooking Time: 25 Minutes

Ingredients:
- 2 tbsp olive oil
- 10 oz spinach
- ½ red onion, sliced
- 4 trout fillets, boneless
- 2 tbsp lemon juice
- ¼ tsp garlic powder
- ¼ tsp chipotle powder
- 1 tsp sea salt

Directions:
1. Preheat your oven to 375°F. Grease a baking pan with olive oil and place the spinach and red onion on the bottom. Add in trout fillets, chipotle powder, garlic, and salt and bake covered with foil for 15 minutes. Sprinkle with lemon juice and serve.

Nutrition Info:
- Per Serving: Calories: 162;Fat: 8g;Protein: 19g;Carbs: 6g.

Tropical-style Cod

Servings: 4 | Cooking Time: 25 Minutes

Ingredients:
- ½ pineapple, diced
- ½ avocado, diced
- 1 cup mango, diced
- 1 lime, juiced
- ¼ tsp chili powder
- 2 tbsp avocado oil
- 1 cup shredded coconut
- 1 egg, beaten
- 4 cod fillets
- Sea salt to taste

Directions:
1. Combine the pineapple, avocado, mango, lime juice, salt, and chili powder in a bowl. Dip each cod fillet in the beaten egg first, then in the shredded coconut. Warm the avocado oil in a skillet over medium heat. Place a fillet and cook for 4-5 minutes on both sides. Repeat the process until all the fillets are cook. Top with the salsa.

Nutrition Info:
- Per Serving: Calories: 370;Fat: 25g;Protein: 5g;Carbs: 20g.

Skinless Salmon And Arugula With Lime

Servings: 2 | Cooking Time: 10 Minutes

Ingredients:
- Fish:
- 2 salmon fillets, skinless
- 1 tablespoon extra-virgin olive oil
- ½ fresh lime, juiced
- a pinch of black pepper
- Salad:
- 4 cups baby arugula leaves
- 1 cup grapes or cherry tomatoes, cut into halves
- ½ cup slivered red onion
- 1 tablespoon olive oil
- 1 tablespoon balsamic vinegar

Directions:
1. Coat the salmon with the olive oil, lime juice and pepper in a bowl.
2. In a skillet, heat the oil over a medium heat and cook the salmon skin-side for 4 to 5 minutes each side or until completely cooked.

3. In a separate bowl, add and toss the arugula, onion and tomatoes with oil and vinegar.
4. Serve the fish on the bed of salad.

Nutrition Info:
• Per Serving: Calories: 130 ;Fat: 10g ;Protein: 2g ;Carbs: 9g.

Chard Trout Fillets

Servings: 4 | Cooking Time: 25 Minutes

Ingredients:
• 2 garlic cloves, minced
• 2 bunches chard, sliced
• 4 boneless trout fillets
• Sea salt and pepper to taste
• 1 tbsp extra-virgin olive oil
• 1 onion, chopped
• 2 oz capers
• 1 tbsp apple cider vinegar
• ½ cup vegetable broth

Directions:
1. Preheat your oven to 375ºF. Warm the olive oil in a large pan over medium heat. Sauté the onion and garlic for 3 minutes. Add the chard and cook for 2 more minutes. Add the chard, capers, cider vinegar, and broth to the pan. Season the trout fillets with salt and pepper and place them in the pan. Cover and place it in the oven for about 10 minutes, or until the trout is cooked through.

Nutrition Info:
• Per Serving: Calories: 230;Fat: 10g;Protein: 23g;Carbs: 15g.

Baked Swordfish With Cilantro And Pineapple

Servings: 4 | Cooking Time: 20 Minutes

Ingredients:
• 1 tablespoon coconut oil
• 2 pounds swordfish, or other firm white fish, cut into 2-inch pieces
• 1 cup pineapple chunks, fresh
• ¼ cup fresh cilantro, chopped
• 2 tablespoons fresh parsley, chopped
• 2 garlic cloves, minced
• 1 tablespoon coconut aminos
• 1 teaspoon salt
• ¼ teaspoon black pepper, freshly ground

Directions:
1. Preheat the oven to 400°F.
2. Grease a baking dish with the coconut oil.
3. Add the swordfish, pineapple, cilantro, parsley, garlic, coconut aminos, salt, and pepper to the dish and mix gently the ingredients together.
4. In the preheated oven, place the dish and bake for 15 to 20 minutes, or until the fish feels firm to the touch. Serve warm.

Nutrition Info:
• Per Serving: Calories: 408 ;Fat: 16g ;Protein: 60g ;Carbs: 7g.

Poultry and Meats

Poultry and Meats

Classic And Minty Lamb Burgers

Servings: 2 | Cooking Time: 20 Minutes

Ingredients:
- 8 oz ground lamb, lean
- 1 tablespoon fresh rosemary, finely chopped
- ½ cup extra virgin olive oil
- 1 lemon, juiced
- 1 clove of garlic, minced
- ½ cup of low-fat Greek yogurt
- ¼ cucumber, chopped
- ½ bunch fresh mint
- ½ cup arugula

Directions:
1. Mix together the ground lamb, garlic, and rosemary and a drizzle of the olive oil until combined, and then shape 1-inch-thick patties with your hands.
2. Heat the rest of the oil in a skillet over medium-high heat, and then cook the patties for 16 minutes, flipping once halfway through and ensuring they are cooked throughout.
3. Mix the yogurt, lemon juice, mint, and cucumber and serve on top of the lamb burger with a side salad of arugula.
4. Serve warm.

Nutrition Info:
- Per Serving: Calories: 1050 ;Fat: 79g ;Protein: 54g ;Carbs: 31g .

Pecan-dusted Pork Tenderloin Slices

Servings: 4 | Cooking Time: 20 Minutes

Ingredients:
- 1 lb pork tenderloin, sliced
- Sea salt and pepper to taste
- ½ cup pecans
- 1 cup full-fat coconut milk
- 2 tbsp olive oil

Directions:
1. Preheat your oven to 400°F. Pulse the pecans in your blender until a powder consistency is reached. Remove to a bowl and mix with salt and pepper. In another bowl, combine the coconut milk and olive oil. Dip the pork chops first in the coconut mixture, then in the pecan mix, and transfer to a parchment-lined baking sheet. Bake for 10 minutes until the meat reaches an internal temperature of 160°F. Serve immediately.

Nutrition Info:
- Per Serving: Calories: 440;Fat: 35g;Protein: 4g;Carbs: 7g.

Holiday Turkey

Servings: 4 | Cooking Time: 6 Hours 15 Minutes

Ingredients:
- 1 lb turkey breast strips
- 1 celery stalk, minced
- 1 carrot, minced
- 1 shallot, diced
- ½ red bell pepper, chopped
- 1 tbsp extra-virgin olive oil
- 6 tbsp tomato paste
- 2 tbsp apple cider vinegar
- 1 tbsp pure maple syrup
- 1 tsp Dijon mustard
- 1 tsp chili powder
- ½ tsp garlic powder
- ½ tsp sea salt
- ½ tsp dried oregano

Directions:
1. Blend the olive oil, turkey, celery, carrot, shallot, red bell pepper, tomato paste, vinegar, maple syrup, mustard, chili powder, garlic powder, salt, and oregano in your slow cooker. Using a large spoon, break up the turkey into smaller chunks as it combines with the other ingredients. Cover the cooker and set to "Low". Cook for 6 hours.

Nutrition Info:
- Per Serving: Calories: 250;Fat: 12g;Protein: 23g;Carbs: 13g.

Remarkable Korean Beef Wrapped In Lettuce

Servings: 4 To 6

Cooking Time: 6 To 7 Hours

Ingredients:
- 2 pounds beef chuck roast
- 1 small white onion, diced
- 1 cup broth of choice
- 3 tablespoons coconut aminos
- 2 tablespoons coconut sugar
- 1 tablespoon rice vinegar
- 1 teaspoon garlic powder
- 1 teaspoon sesame oil
- ½ teaspoon ginger, ground
- ¼ teaspoon red pepper flakes
- 8 romaine lettuce leaves
- 1 tablespoon sesame seeds
- 2 scallions, white and green parts

Directions:
1. Combine in your slow cooker the beef, onion, broth, coconut aminos, coconut sugar, vinegar, garlic powder, sesame oil, ginger, and red pepper flakes.
2. Cover the cooker and set to low. Cook for 7 to 8 hours.
3. Scoop spoonful of the beef mixture into each lettuce leaf. Garnish with sesame seeds and diced scallion then serve.

Nutrition Info:
- Per Serving: Calories: 428 ;Fat: 23g ;Protein: 46g ;Carbs: 12g .

Cumin Lamb Meatballs With Aioli

Servings: 4 | Cooking Time: 30 Minutes

Ingredients:
- 1 tsp ground cumin
- 2 tbsp chopped cilantro
- 1 ½ lb ground lamb
- 1 tbsp dried oregano
- 1 tsp onion powder
- 1 tsp garlic powder
- Sea salt and pepper to taste
- ½ cup garlic aioli

Directions:
1. Preheat your oven to 400°F. Combine the ground lamb, cumin, cilantro, rosemary, oregano, onion powder, garlic powder, salt,

and pepper in a bowl. Shape 20 meatballs out of the mixture and transfer to a parchment-lined baking sheet. Bake for 15 minutes until the meat reaches an internal temperature of 140°F. Serve warm with aioli.

Nutrition Info:
• Per Serving: Calories: 450;Fat: 24g;Protein: 2g;Carbs: 11g.

Baked Basil Chicken

Servings: 4 | Cooking Time: 45 Minutes

Ingredients:
• 2 garlic cloves, sliced
• 1 white onion, chopped
• 14 oz tomatoes, chopped
• 2 tbsp chopped rosemary
• Sea salt and pepper to taste
• 4 skinless chicken thighs
• 1 lb peeled pumpkin, cubed
• 1 tbsp extra virgin olive oil
• 2 tbsp basil leaves

Directions:
1. Preheat your oven to 375°F. Warm the olive oil in a skillet over medium heat. Add the garlic and onion and sauté for 5 minutes or until fragrant. Add the tomatoes, rosemary, salt, and pepper and cook for 15 minutes or until slightly thickened. Arrange the chicken thighs and pumpkin cubes on a baking sheet, then pour the mixture in the skillet over the chicken and sweet potatoes. Stir to coat well. Pour in enough water to cover the chicken and sweet potatoes. Bake in for 20 minutes. Top with basil.

Nutrition Info:
• Per Serving: Calories: 295;Fat: 9g;Protein: 21g;Carbs: 32g.

Harissa Chicken Drumsticks

Servings: 4 | Cooking Time: 60 Minutes + Marinating Time

Ingredients:
• 2 garlic cloves, minced
• 1 ½ chicken drumsticks
• 1 cup coconut yogurt
• ½ cup extra-virgin olive oil
• Juice of 2 limes
• 1 tbsp raw honey
• Sea salt and pepper to taste
• 1 tsp ground cumin
• ½ tsp harissa seasoning
• ½ tsp turmeric

Directions:
1. In a mixing bowl, whisk together the yogurt, olive oil, lime juice, garlic, honey, salt, cumin, harissa, turmeric, and pepper until smooth. Add the chicken and toss to coat. Cover with plastic wrap and chill for 30 minutes.
2. Preheat your oven to 375ºF. Remove the drumsticks from the marinade and place them on a greased baking sheet. Discard the marinade. Place the sheet in the oven and bake the drumsticks for 25-35 minutes, or until they brown and are cooked through. Serve and enjoy!

Nutrition Info:
• Per Serving: Calories: 375;Fat: 30g;Protein: 20g;Carbs: 9g.

Mexican-style Chicken With Butternut Squash

Servings: 4 | Cooking Time: 40 Minutes

Ingredients:
• 1 lb butternut squash, cubed
• 4 chicken breasts
• 1 onion, chopped
• 1 cup brown basmati rice
• 2 cups chicken broth
• 1 cup cooked black beans
• 1 lime, cut into wedges
• ½ tsp Mexican seasoning
• ½ tsp ground cumin
• 2 tbsp extra-virgin olive oil

Directions:
1. Warm the olive oil in a large saucepan over medium heat. Rub the chicken breasts with Mexican seasoning. Add the chicken and brown it for 3 minutes per side. Remove it to a plate. Add the onion to the saucepan. Sauté for about 3 minutes, or until just softened. Stir in the rice, butternut squash, and chicken broth. Return the chicken to the saucepan and cover it. Bring to a boil, reduce the heat to simmer, and cook for 20 minutes. Stir in cumin and black beans. Serve with lime wedges.

Nutrition Info:
• Per Serving: Calories: 620;Fat: 19g;Protein: 52g;Carbs: 60g.

Marvellous Chocolate Chili

Servings: 4 To 6

Cooking Time: 45 Minutes

Ingredients:
• 1 tablespoon extra-virgin olive oil
• 1 pound lean ground beef
• 1 large onion, chopped
• 2 garlic cloves, minced
• 1 tablespoon cocoa, unsweetened
• 1½ teaspoons chili powder
• 1 teaspoon salt
• ½ teaspoon cumin, ground
• 2 cups chicken broth
• 1 cup tomato sauce

Directions:
1. Heat the oil over high heat in a Dutch oven. Add the ground beef and brown well for 5 minutes.
2. Add the onion, garlic, cocoa, chili powder, salt, and cumin and cook while stirring for a minute.
3. Add the chicken broth and tomato sauce and bring to a boil. Reduce the heat to a simmer, cover, and cook, stirring occasionally for 30 to 40 minutes. Add more chicken broth or water if the sauce becomes too thick as it cooks to thin it.
4. Ladle into bowls and serve.

Nutrition Info:
• Per Serving: Calories: 370 ;Fat: 27g ;Protein: 23g ;Carbs: 9g.

Chicken A La Tuscana

Servings: 4 | Cooking Time: 25 Minutes

Ingredients:
• 2 cups cherry tomatoes
• 4 chicken breast halves
• 1 tsp garlic powder
• Sea salt and pepper to taste
• 2 tbsp extra-virgin olive oil
• ½ cup sliced green olives
• 1 eggplant, chopped
• ¼ cup dry white wine

Directions:
1. Pound the chicken breasts with a meat tenderizer until half an inch thick. Rub them with garlic powder, salt, and ground black pepper. Warm the olive oil in a skillet over medium heat. Add the chicken and cook for 14-16 minutes, flipping halfway through the

cooking time. Transfer to a plate and cover with aluminum foil. Add the tomatoes, olives, and eggplant to the skillet and sauté for 4 minutes or until the vegetables are soft. Add the white wine to the skillet and simmer for 1 minute. Remove the aluminum foil and top the chicken with the vegetables and their juices, then serve warm.

Nutrition Info:
• Per Serving: Calories: 170;Fat: 10g;Protein: 7g;Carbs: 8g.

Basic Poached Wrapped Chicken

Servings: 4 To 6

Cooking Time: 15 Minutes

Ingredients:
• 2 cups water, plus additional for soaking the wrappers
• 2 boneless skinless chicken breasts, 4 ounces
• 10 rice paper wrappers
• 1 small head romaine lettuce, sliced thin
• 2 cups lightly packed spinach, sliced thin
• ½ cup fresh dill, minced

Directions:
1. Bring the water to a boil in a shallow pan set over high heat. Reduce the heat to medium. Add the chicken breasts. Cover and cook for 15 minutes or until the chicken is cooked through and the internal temperature is at least 165°F. Remove the chicken from the pot. Let it cool and slice it thinly.
2. Place a cutting board on a flat surface with the fillings near you.
3. Fill a large, shallow bowl with warm water. The water should be hot enough to cook the wrappers but warm enough so you can comfortably touch it.
4. Soak one rice paper wrapper in the water, and place it on the cutting board.
5. Place ½ cup of romaine, ¼ cup of spinach, 1 teaspoon of dill, and a few chicken slices in the middle of the wrapper.
6. Fold the sides in over the fillings. Starting at the bottom, tightly roll up the wrapper burrito-style.
7. Repeat with the remaining wrappers, chicken, and vegetables.

Nutrition Info:
• Per Serving: Calories: 255 ;Fat: 5g ;Protein: 20g ;Carbs: 32g .

Cherry Tomato & Basil Chicken Casserole

Servings: 4 | Cooking Time: 30 Minutes

Ingredients:
• 8 small chicken thighs
• ½ cup green olives
• 1 lb cherry tomatoes
• A handful of basil leaves
• 1 ½ tsp minced garlic
• 1 tsp dried oregano
• 1 tbsp olive oil

Directions:
1. Heat the olive oil in your Instant Pot on "Sauté". Cook the chicken for about 2 minutes per side. Place the tomatoes in a plastic bag and smash them with a meat pounder. Remove the chicken from the cooker. Combine tomatoes, garlic, 1 cup of water, and oregano in the pot. Top with the browned chicken. Close the lid and cook for 15 minutes on "Manual" on high pressure. Let the pressure release naturally for at least 10 minutes, then release the rest of the pressure and take the lid off. Stir in the basil and olives. Stir and serve immediately.

Nutrition Info:
• Per Serving: Calories: 337;Fat: 21g;Protein: 27g;Carbs: 12g.

Korean Chicken Thighs

Servings: 4 | Cooking Time: 4 Hours 10 Minutes

Ingredients:
• 8 boneless, skinless chicken thighs
• ¼ cup miso paste
• 2 tbsp coconut oil, melted
• 1 tbsp honey
• 1 tbsp rice wine vinegar
• 2 garlic cloves, sliced
• 1 tsp minced ginger root
• 2 red chilies, sliced
• 1 cup chicken broth
• 2 scallions, sliced
• 1 tbsp sesame seeds

Directions:
1. Place the miso, coconut oil, honey, rice wine vinegar, garlic, chilies, and ginger root in your slow cooker and mix well. Add the chicken. Cover and cook on "High" for 4 hours. Top with scallions and sesame seeds. Serve.

Nutrition Info:
• Per Serving: Calories: 315;Fat: 14g;Protein: 31g;Carbs: 17g.

Fruity Chicken Breast With Cherry Sauce

Servings: 4 | Cooking Time: 30 Minutes

Ingredients:
• 1 tablespoon coconut oil
• 4 boneless chicken breasts, skinless
• Salt
• Freshly ground black pepper
• 2 scallions, sliced
• ¾ cup chicken broth
• 1 tablespoon balsamic vinegar
• ½ cup cherries, dried

Directions:
1. Preheat the oven to 375°F.
2. Melt the coconut oil in a large ovenproof skillet over medium-high heat.
3. Season the chicken with salt and pepper. In the pan, place the chicken and brown it on both sides for 3 minutes each side.
4. Add the scallions, chicken broth, balsamic vinegar, and dried cherries. Cover with an oven proof lid or aluminum foil and place the pan in the preheated oven. Bake for 20 minutes or until the chicken is cooked through.

Nutrition Info:
• Per Serving: Calories: 379 ;Fat: 14g ;Protein: 43g ;Carbs: 17g .

Creamy Beef Tenderloin Marsala

Servings: 4 | Cooking Time: 25 Minutes

Ingredients:
• 4 beef tenderloin fillets
• Sea salt and pepper to taste
• 2 tbsp olive oil
• 1 shallot, finely minced
• ½ cup Marsala wine
• 2 cups fresh blueberries
• 3 tbsp cold butter, cubed

Directions:
1. Pound the beef with a rolling pin to ¾-inch thickness. Sprinkle with salt and pepper. Warm the olive oil in a skillet over medium heat. Add the beef and brown for 10 minutes on both sides. Set aside covered with foil.
2. Place the shallot, Marsala wine, blueberries, salt, and pepper in

the skillet, and using a wide spatula, scrape any brown bits from the bottom. Bring to a simmer, then low the heat, and simmer for 4 minutes, until blueberries break down and the liquid has reduced by half. Add in butter cubed, one piece at time, and put the beef back to the skillet; toss to coat. Serve and enjoy!

Nutrition Info:
• Per Serving: Calories: 550;Fat: 33g;Protein: 2g;Carbs: 15g.

A Fresh Lean Beef Burger That You Can Truly Enjoy

Servings: 2 | Cooking Time: 25 Minutes

Ingredients:
• 8 ounces lean ground beef, 100% grass-fed
• 1 teaspoon black pepper
• 1 teaspoon garlic powder
• 1 teaspoon coconut oil
• 1 onion, sliced
• 1 avocado, sliced
• 2 tablespoons balsamic vinegar
• 1 large tomato, cut into 6 slices

Directions:
1. Mix the ground beef with pepper and garlic powder.
2. Heat a skillet on medium to high heat and add the coconut oil.
3. Sauté the onions for 5 to 10 minutes until it appears brown.
4. Add in the balsamic vinegar and sauté for 5 minutes more.
5. Using the palms of your hands, form burger shapes with the ground beef and add to the skillet. Sauté on each side for about 5 to 6 minutes then remove.
6. Let them sit on a tray to cool slightly and then assemble your burger on your serving plate by adding your sliced tomato, avocado, and onions on the top.
7. You can serve a bunless burger with salad or with a 100% whole grain burger bun as you preferred.

Nutrition Info:
• Per Serving: Calories: 583 ;Fat: 51g ;Protein: 19g ;Carbs: 14g .

Awesome Herbaceous Roasted Chuck And Scrummy Vegetable

Servings: 4 | Cooking Time: 7 Hours

Ingredients:
• 16 ounces chuck roast, lean
• 1 teaspoon pepper
• 2 onions cut, peeled and quartered
• 8 baby carrots, peeled and quartered
• 1 stalk of celery, sliced
• 1 bay leaf
• 10 cups water
• 1 cauliflower, cut into florets
• 5 cherry tomatoes
• Seasoning:
• 1 tablespoon cayenne pepper
• 2 tablespoons rosemary, dried or fresh

Directions:
1. Use a sharp knife to trim any fat from the chuck roast.
2. Season with herbs and spices.
3. Put the onions, carrots, and celery into the crockpot or slow cooker, then the meat, and finally add the bay leaf and water.
4. Cook on low for 5 to 7 hours or until the meat is tender.
5. You can add the cauliflower and cherry tomatoes for the last 15 minutes or until cooked through.
6. Serve hot.

Nutrition Info:

• Per Serving: Calories: 170 ;Fat: 5g ;Protein: 22g ;Carbs: 10g.

Hawaiian-style Turkey Burgers

Servings: 4 | Cooking Time: 20 Minutes

Ingredients:
• 2 tbsp reduced-sodium teriyaki sauce
• 2 tbsp cilantro, chopped
• 1 lb ground turkey
• Sea salt and pepper to taste
• 2 tbsp olive oil
• ½ tsp ginger powder
• 4 pineapple rings

Directions:
1. Season the turkey with salt and pepper and mix with your hands. Shape the mixture into 4 patties. Warm the olive oil in a skillet over medium heat. Fry the burgers for 6-8 minutes on both sides until browned.
2. In the meantime, place the teriyaki sauce in a pot over medium heat and bring to a simmer. Cook for 1-2 minutes until it thickens. Drizzle each patty with teriyaki sauce and top with pineapple rings and cilantro. Serve.

Nutrition Info:
• Per Serving: Calories: 370;Fat: 17g;Protein: 1g;Carbs: 24g.

Dairy Free Chicken Alfredo

Servings: 6 | Cooking Time: 4 To 8 Hours

Ingredients:
• Sauce:
• 1 large cauliflower head, broken or cut into florets
• Heaping ½ cup cashews, soaked in water for 4 hours
• 1 teaspoon salt
• ¼ cup water, reserved from cooking the cauliflower
• Chicken:
• 6 bone-in skinless chicken thighs, 2 to 3 ounces
• 4 cups spinach

Directions:
1. Fill a large pot with 2 inches of water and insert a steamer basket. Bring to a boil over high heat.
2. Add the cauliflower to the steamer basket. Cover and steam for 10 to 12 minutes or until very tender. Reserve ¼ cup of the cooking liquid.
3. Drain and rinse the cashews in a colander.
4. Combine in a blender the cooked cauliflower, cashews, salt, and ¼ cup of the cauliflower cooking liquid. Blend until smooth and creamy.
5. Place the chicken thighs in a slow cooker.
6. Pour the sauce over the chicken.
7. Cook on high for 3 to 4 hours, or on low for 7 to 8 hours.
8. Transfer the chicken to a work surface. Remove and discard the bones and gristle. Shred the meat.
9. Return the chicken meat to the cooker.
10. Stir in the spinach. Cook for 5 minutes or until the spinach wilts.

Nutrition Info:
• Per Serving: Calories: 286 ;Fat: 18g ;Protein: 27g ;Carbs: 12g .

Sunday Pork Tacos

Servings: 4 | Cooking Time: 8 Hours 15 Minutes

Ingredients:
- 3 lb pork shoulder
- 2 cups chicken broth
- Juice of 1 orange
- 1 small onion, chopped
- 4 coconut taco shells
- Sea salt and pepper to taste
- 1 tsp ground cumin
- 1 tsp garlic powder
- ½ tsp dried coriander

Directions:
1. Rub the pork with salt, cumin, garlic powder, coriander, and pepper. Put it in your slow cooker. Pour the broth and orange juice around the pork. Scatter the onion around the pork. Cover the cooker and set on "Low". Cook for 8 hours. Transfer the pork to a work surface and shred it with a fork. Serve in taco shells and enjoy!

Nutrition Info:
- Per Serving: Calories: 1150;Fat: 85g;Protein: 82g;Carbs: 12g.

Thyme Pork Loin Bake

Servings: 4 | Cooking Time: 90 Minutes

Ingredients:
- 1 lb boned pork loin
- 1 fennel bulb, sliced
- ½ celeriac, diced
- 2 tbsp olive oil
- 1 tbsp pure maple syrup
- 1 lemon, zested
- A pinch of sea salt
- 1 tsp chopped thyme

Directions:
1. Preheat your oven to 375ºF. Toss the fennel, celeriac, 1 tablespoon of olive oil, maple syrup, lemon zest, and sea salt in a baking dish. Warm the remaining olive oil in a large skillet over medium heat and add the pork loin. Brown it on all sides, turning, for about 15 minutes total. Place the browned pork on top of the vegetables and sprinkle with thyme. Roast the pork for about 1 hour until cooked through, but still juicy. Transfer the roast and vegetables to a serving platter and pour any pan juices over the top. Serve and enjoy!

Nutrition Info:
- Per Serving: Calories: 405;Fat: 22g;Protein: 32g;Carbs: 15g.

Worcestershire Pork Chops

Servings: 6 | Cooking Time: 35 Minutes

Ingredients:
- 1 onion, diced
- 8 pork chops
- ¼ cup olive oil
- 3 tbsp Worcestershire sauce
- 4 sweet potatoes, diced

Directions:
1. Heat half of the oil in your pressure cooker on "Sauté". Brown the pork chops on all sides and season with salt and pepper. Set aside.
2. Add the rest of the oil to the Instant Pot. Add onions and sauté for 2 or 3 minutes. Add potatoes and add 1 cup of water and Worcestershire sauce. Return the pork chops to the cooker. Close the lid, press "Manual" and cook for 15 minutes. When cooking

is complete, select Cancel and perform a natural pressure release. This will take about 15 minutes.

Nutrition Info:
- Per Serving: Calories: 785;Fat: 40g;Protein: 73g;Carbs: 26g.

Lamb Shanks Braised Under Pressure

Servings: 4 | Cooking Time: 50 Minutes

Ingredients:
- 4-6 lamb shanks
- 3 carrots, sliced
- 2 tomatoes, quartered
- 1 garlic clove, crushed
- 1 tbsp chopped oregano
- ¾ cup whole-wheat flour
- 8 tsp olive oil
- 1 onion, chopped
- ¾ cup red wine
- ¼ cup beef broth

Directions:
1. Place ¼ cup of flour and lamb shanks in a plastic bag. Shake until you coat the shanks well. Discard the excess flour. Heat 4 tsp of the oil in your Instant Pot on "Sauté". Brown the shanks on both sides. Set aside.
2. Heat the remaining olive oil and sauté the onions, garlic, and carrots for a couple of minutes. Stir in tomatoes, wine, broth, and oregano. Return the shanks to the cooker. Seal the lid and cook for 25 minutes on "Manual". Once ready, perform a quick pressure release. Whisk together the remaining flour and 8 tsp of cold water. Stir this mixture into the lamb sauce and cook with the lid off until it thickens. Serve and enjoy!

Nutrition Info:
- Per Serving: Calories: 800;Fat: 43g;Protein: 73g;Carbs: 20g.

Korean Vegetable Salad With Smoky Crispy Kalua Pork

Servings: 6 | Cooking Time: 10 Hours And 10 Minutes

Ingredients:
- Kalua Pork:
- 3 pounds bone-in pork shoulder
- 1 tablespoon Himalayan salt, fine
- 2 tablespoons liquid smoke
- 1 sweet onion, quartered
- 1 cup water
- 1 banana peel
- Vegetable Salad:
- 4 cups water
- 4 cups chopped watercress, ong choy, or broccoli florets
- 1 tablespoon garlic, minced
- 1 teaspoon fresh ginger, peeled and minced
- 1 tablespoon coconut aminos
- 1 tablespoon coconut vinegar
- 1 tablespoon sesame oil
- 1 teaspoon Himalayan salt, fine
- 1 teaspoon black pepper, ground

Directions:
1. On a flat surface, pat the pork shoulder dry and stand it up with the layer of fat facing up. Score the fat with a very sharp knife, gently cut the slits into a diagonal pattern.
2. Sprinkle the salt all over the pork shoulder, then rub in the liquid smoke until the pork is well covered.
3. In the slow cooker, place the onion quarters. Add the water and banana peel. Place the pork shoulder fat side up on top of the

onions. Cook on low for 9 to 10 hours.

4. Transfer the pork to a large bowl when it's done. Remove the bone and use two forks to shred the meat. Spoon 2 to 3 tablespoons of the liquid from the slow cooker onto the shredded pork.

5. Crisp up the shredded pork. Heat a large cast-iron skillet over medium heat. Add the shredded pork in one even layer when it's hot. Let it cook undisturbed for 5 minutes. Stir well, flatten again, and cook undisturbed for 5 minutes more. Then scrape it up from the bottom of the skillet using a spatula and stir.

6. Blanch the vegetables for the salad while the pork is crisping. Bring the water to a simmer in a large pot over medium heat. Add the watercress, garlic, and ginger, cover, and cook for 3 minutes. Prepare a large bowl of ice water. Remove the vegetables from the steaming water and quickly place in the ice bath for 2 to 3 minutes. Drain and pat dry.

7. Place the coconut aminos, vinegar, sesame oil, salt, and pepper in a small bowl. Add the blanched vegetables and gently toss to combine. Serve the crispy pork with this delicious cold salad.

8. Store the pork in an airtight container in the fridge for up to 5 days. Store the salad in a separate airtight container in the fridge for no more than 2 days.

Nutrition Info:
- Per Serving: Calories: 536 ;Fat: 36g ;Protein: 44g;Carbs: 6g .

Creamy Turkey With Mushrooms

Servings: 4 | Cooking Time: 40 Minutes

Ingredients:
- 1 ½ lb turkey breasts, boneless and skinless
- 6 oz white button mushrooms, sliced
- 3 tbsp chopped shallots
- ½ tsp dried thyme
- ½ cup dry white wine
- 1 cup chicken stock
- 1 garlic clove, minced
- 2 tbsp olive oil
- 3 tbsp coconut cream
- 1 ½ tbsp arrowroot
- Sea salt and pepper to taste

Directions:
1. Tie the turkey breast with a kitchen string horizontally, leaving approximately 2 inches apart. Season with salt and pepper. Heat half of the olive oil in your Instant Pot on "Sauté". Add the turkey and brown it for 3 minutes on each side. Transfer to a plate. Add the remaining oil, followed by the shallots, thyme, garlic, and mushrooms and cook for 5 minutes or until translucent. Add white wine and scrape up the brown bits from the bottom.

2. When the alcohol evaporates, return the turkey to the pot. Add the broth. Close the lid and cook for 20 minutes on "Manual". Combine the coconut cream and arrowroot in a bowl. Stir in the pot. Bring the sauce to a boil, then turn the cooker off. Slice the turkey in half and serve topped with the creamy mushroom sauce.

Nutrition Info:
- Per Serving: Calories: 192;Fat: 5g;Protein: 15g;Carbs: 12g.

Cute Tiny Chicken Burgers

Servings: 4 | Cooking Time: 30 Minutes

Ingredients:
- ¼ cup quinoa flour, brown rice flour, or chickpea flour
- 1 pound chicken, ground
- 4 scallions, finely sliced
- ¾ teaspoon salt
- 2 to 4 tablespoons coconut oil, divided

Directions:

1. Cover a large plate with parchment paper.

2. Mix together in a medium bowl the quinoa flour and chicken. Fold in the scallions and add the salt.

3. Take about 2 tablespoons of the chicken mixture and roll into a ball with wet hands. Flatten into a patty and place it on the prepared plate. Repeat with the remaining mixture.

4. Heat 2 tablespoons of coconut oil in a large sauté pan set over medium heat.

5. Add the patties and work in batches. Cook for 8 to 10 minutes per side. Add more oil to the pan, if necessary, for additional batches. Fully cooked patties should register at least 165°F on a meat thermometer.

6. Serve hot.

Nutrition Info:
- Per Serving: Calories: 365 ;Fat: 23g ;Protein: 37g ;Carbs: 3g .

Hot & Spicy Beef Chili

Servings: 4 | Cooking Time: 25 Minutes

Ingredients:
- 2 tbsp olive oil
- 1 tsp dried Mexican oregano
- 1 lb ground beef
- 1 onion, chopped
- 2 cans diced tomatoes
- 2 cans kidney beans,
- 1 tbsp red chili powder
- 1 tsp garlic powder
- ½ tsp sea salt

Directions:
1. Warm the olive oil in a heavy-bottomed pot over medium heat. Then, brown the ground beef for 5 minutes, crumbling with a wide spatula. Mix in tomatoes, Mexican oregano, kidney beans, red chili powder, garlic powder, and salt and bring to a simmer. Let it cook, partially covered, for 10 minutes longer. Serve warm.

Nutrition Info:
- Per Serving: Calories: 900;Fat: 21g;Protein: 18g;Carbs: 64g.

Homemade Chicken & Pepper Cacciatore

Servings: 4 | Cooking Time: 30 Minutes

Ingredients:
- 1 ½ lb chicken breasts, cubed
- 3 mixed peppers, cut into strips
- 28 oz canned diced tomatoes
- ½ cup chopped black olives
- 2 tbsp extra-virgin olive oil
- 1 tsp onion powder
- 1 tsp garlic powder
- Sea salt and pepper to taste

Directions:
1. Warm the olive oil in a large saucepan over medium heat. Add the chicken and sauté for 8-10 minutes until evenly browned, stirring occasionally. Add the peppers, tomatoes, olives, onion powder, garlic powder, salt, and pepper and allow to simmer for 10 minutes, stirring occasionally, or until the chicken is cooked through.

Nutrition Info:
- Per Serving: Calories: 305;Fat: 11g;Protein: 18g;Carbs: 34g.

Chicken Stir-fry With Bell Pepper

Servings: 4 | Cooking Time: 30 Minutes

Ingredients:
- 3 tbsp avocado oil
- ½ tsp red pepper flakes
- 1 red bell pepper, chopped
- 1 onion, chopped
- 1 ½ lb chicken breasts, cubed
- 2 garlic cloves, minced
- Sea salt and pepper to taste

Directions:
1. Warm the avocado oil in a skillet over medium heat and place in bell pepper, onion, and chicken. Sauté for 10 minutes. Stir in garlic, salt, and pepper and cook for another 30 seconds. Sprinkle with red flakes and serve.

Nutrition Info:
- Per Serving: Calories: 180;Fat: 14g;Protein: 2g;Carbs: 7g.

Mexican-style Chicken

Servings: 4 | Cooking Time: 30 Minutes

Ingredients:
- 1 tsp dried Mexican oregano
- 1 tsp Mexican chili powder
- 1 ½ lb chicken breast tenders
- 2 tbsp olive oil
- 2 tbsp chopped rosemary
- Sea salt and pepper to taste

Directions:
1. Preheat your oven to 425°F. Rub the chicken with Mexican oregano, chili powder, salt, and pepper. Arrange them on a lined baking sheet and drizzle with olive oil. Bake for 15-20 minutes until the chicken tenders are well browned, and their juices run clear. Serve and enjoy!

Nutrition Info:
- Per Serving: Calories: 390;Fat: 21g;Protein: 1g;Carbs: 2g.

Sloppy Joes & Coleslaw

Servings: 6 | Cooking Time: 35 Minutes

Ingredients:
- 1 cup chopped tomatoes
- 1 onion, chopped
- 1 carrot, chopped
- 1 lb ground beef
- 1 bell pepper, chopped
- ½ cup rolled oats
- 4 tbsp apple cider vinegar
- 1 tbsp olive oil
- 4 tbsp tomato paste
- 2 tsp garlic powder
- 1 tbsp Worcestershire sauce
- 1 ½ tsp sea salt
- ½ chopped red onion
- 1 tbsp honey
- ½ head cabbage, sliced
- 2 carrots, grated
- 2 tbsp apple cider vinegar
- 1 tbsp Dijon mustard

Directions:
1. Heat the olive oil in your pressure cooker by setting "Sauté" and brown the meat. Add the onions, carrots, pepper, garlic powder, salt, and sauté until soft. Stir in tomatoes, vinegar, Worcestershire sauce, 1 cup of water, and tomato paste. When the mixture starts to boil, stir in the oats. Seal the lid and cook for 15 minutes on "Manual" on high pressure. Once ready, perform a quick pressure release and let simmer with the lid off until thickened to your liking. Mix all of the slaw ingredients in a large bowl. Serve them with the slaw.

Nutrition Info:
- Per Serving: Calories: 180;Fat: 25g;Protein: 4g;Carbs: 20g.

Mustardy Beef Steaks

Servings: 4 | Cooking Time: 60 Minutes

Ingredients:
- ½ cup olive oil
- 2 tbsp Dijon mustard
- ½ cup balsamic vinegar
- 2 garlic cloves, minced
- 1 tsp rosemary, chopped
- 4 (½-inch thick) beef steaks
- Sea salt and pepper to taste

Directions:
1. Combine the olive oil, mustard, vinegar, garlic, rosemary, salt, and pepper in a bowl. Add in steaks and toss to coat. Let marinate covered for 30 minutes. Remove any excess of the marinade from the steaks and transfer them to a warm skillet over high heat and cook for 4-6 minutes on both sides. Let sit for 5 minutes and serve.

Nutrition Info:
- Per Serving: Calories: 480;Fat: 3g;Protein: 48g;Carbs: 4g.

Homemade Pizza With Lean Meat, Jalapeno, And Tapioca Starch

Servings: 4 | Cooking Time: 40 Minutes

Ingredients:
- Base:
- 1 cup tapioca starch
- ½ cup coconut flour
- 2 free-range eggs
- 1 cup water
- Topping:
- ½ can chopped tomatoes
- 1 clove garlic, minced
- 1 sprig rosemary
- 1 sprig basil
- 2 beef tomatoes, sliced
- 1 jalapeno, sliced
- ½ cup watercress or spinach
- 1 onion, chopped
- ½ cup lean meat, cooked and sliced

Directions:
1. Heat oven to 375°F.
2. In a bowl, mix together all of the ingredients for the base until a smooth dough is formed. Add a little more water if necessary.
3. Roll the dough into a pizza base.
4. Sauté onions and garlic over medium heat and add chopped tomatoes and herbs then cook for 5 to 10 minutes.
5. On a slatted rack, layer the base with the tomato sauce, jalapeno, herbs, tomato slices, and meat pieces, and then bake in the oven for 30 minutes.
6. Ensure the base is cooked through and not soggy.
7. Cut into eights then serve immediately with the watercress or spinach scattered on top.

Nutrition Info:
- Per Serving: Calories: 227 ;Fat: 1g ;Protein: 13g ;Carbs: 40g .

Grilled Chicken Sandwiches

Servings: 4 | Cooking Time: 20 Minutes

Ingredients:
- 2 tbsp olive oil
- 4 chicken breast halves
- Sea salt and pepper to taste
- 6 roasted red pepper slices
- 1 tbsp Dijon mustard
- ¼ cup paleo mayonnaise
- 4 whole-wheat buns, halved

Directions:
1. Pound the chicken with a rolling pin to ½-inch thickness. Preheat your grill to medium-high heat. Sprinkle the chicken breasts with salt and pepper and brush them with olive oil. Place them on the hot grill and cook for 8 minutes on all sides until cooked through.
2. In the meantime, place the mustard, mayonnaise, and 2 red pepper slices in a food processor and pulse until smooth. To make the sandwiches, cover the bottom halves of the buns with the mayo mixture, followed by the remaining roasted pepper slices and chicken. Finish with the top bun halves. Serve immediately.

Nutrition Info:
- Per Serving: Calories: 320;Fat: 16g;Protein: 7g;Carbs: 37g.

Italian Turkey Meatballs

Servings: 4 | Cooking Time: 7 Hours 15 Minutes

Ingredients:
- 1 spaghetti squash, halved lengthwise, scoop out seeds
- 1 can diced tomatoes
- ½ tsp garlic powder
- ½ tsp dried oregano
- ½ tsp sea salt
- 1 large egg, whisked
- ½ white onion, minced
- 1 lb ground turkey
- Sea salt and pepper to taste
- ½ tsp dried basil
- 1 cup arugula

Directions:
1. Pour the diced tomatoes into your slow cooker. Sprinkle with garlic powder, oregano, and salt. Put in the squash halves, cut-side down. In a medium bowl, mix together the turkey, egg, onion, salt, pepper, and basil. Shape the turkey mixture into balls and place them in the slow cooker around the spaghetti squash. Cover the cooker and set to "Low". Cook for 7 hours. Transfer the squash to a work surface and use a fork to shred it into spaghetti-like strands. Combine the strands with the tomato sauce, top with the meatballs and arugula, and serve.

Nutrition Info:
- Per Serving: Calories: 250;Fat: 8g;Protein: 23g;Carbs: 21g.

Mustard Pork Chops With Collard Greens

Servings: 4 | Cooking Time: 25 Minutes

Ingredients:
- 4 thin-cut pork chops
- Sea salt and pepper to taste
- 4 tbsp Dijon mustard
- 3 tbsp olive oil
- ½ red onion, finely chopped
- 4 cups chopped collard greens
- 2 tbsp apple cider vinegar

Directions:
1. Preheat your oven to 425°F. Sprinkle pork chops with salt and pepper. Rub them with 2 tbsp of mustard and transfer to a parchment-lined baking sheet. Bake for 15 minutes until the pork is cooked through.
2. Warm the olive oil in a skillet over medium heat. Add red onion and collard greens and cook for 7 minutes until soft. Combine the remaining mustard, apple cider vinegar, salt, and pepper in a bowl. Pour in the skillet and cook for 2 minutes. Serve the pork chops with kale side.

Nutrition Info:
- Per Serving: Calories: 510;Fat: 40g;Protein: 2g;Carbs: 11g.

Tempting And Tender Beef Brisket

Servings: 4 | Cooking Time: 4 Hours

Ingredients:
- 16 oz beef brisket, 100% grass-fed and fat trimmed
- 2 cloves garlic, minced
- 1 sprig of thyme
- 1 sprig of rosemary
- 1 tablespoon mustard
- ¼ cup extra virgin olive oil
- ¼ teaspoon pepper, ground
- 1 onion, sliced
- 1 cup carrots, sliced
- 2 cups tomatoes, chopped

Directions:
1. Heat oven to 300°F.
2. Use a fork to mash the mustard, thyme, and rosemary with the garlic for the paste before mixing in the oil and pepper.
3. Pour the mixture over the brisket.
4. Onto the bottom of a baking dish, place half of the veggies.
5. Place the beef on top of the vegetables and cover with the rest of the vegetables and chopped tomatoes.
6. Bake in the oven or slow cooker for about 3 to 4 hours, or until tender, and serve with your favorite side.

Nutrition Info:
- Per Serving: Calories: 297 ;Fat: 23g ;Protein: 18g ;Carbs: 4g .

Simple Cooked Whole Chicken

Servings: 4 | Cooking Time: 40 Minutes

Ingredients:
- 1 whole chicken
- 2 tbsp olive oil
- Sea salt and pepper to taste

Directions:
1. Rinse the chicken and pat dry. Season with salt and pepper. Press "Sauté" and heat the oil in your Instant Pot and cook the chicken until browned on all sides.
2. Add 1 cup of water to the pot, then place the steam rack inside. Place the chicken on the rack and seal the lid. Select "Manual" and cook on high pressure for 25 minutes. When it's done, do a quick pressure release. Carefully take the chicken out of the pot and serve.

Nutrition Info:
- Per Serving: Calories: 706;Fat: 32g;Protein: 25g;Carbs: 0g.

Appealing Hot Turkey

Servings: 6 | Cooking Time: 60 Minutes

Ingredients:
- 2 onions, finely diced
- 8 garlic cloves, minced
- 2 tablespoons water
- 1½ pound turkeys, ground
- 6 cups tomatoes, crushed or diced
- 2 tablespoons chili powder, plus additional as needed
- 1 teaspoon salt, plus additional as needed

Directions:
1. Sauté in a large pot set over medium heat the onions and garlic with the water for 5 minutes or until soft.
2. Add the ground turkey and break it up with a spoon. Cook for 5 minutes more.
3. Stir in the tomatoes, chili powder, and salt. Bring to a boil. Reduce the heat to low. Cover and simmer for 45 minutes while stirring occasionally. Add more water if the chili gets too dry.
4. Taste and adjust the seasoning, if needed.

Nutrition Info:
- Per Serving: Calories: 350 ;Fat: 13g ;Protein: 38g ;Carbs: 26g .

The Best General Tso's Chicken

Servings: 4 | Cooking Time: 30 Minutes

Ingredients:
- 3 tbsp coconut aminos
- 1 tsp Shaoxing wine
- 1 tbsp arrowroot powder
- ½ tsp red pepper flakes
- 2 garlic cloves, minced
- 2 tbsp rice vinegar
- 3 tbsp coconut sugar
- ¼ tsp ground ginger
- 1 tbsp almond butter
- 1 lb chicken breasts, cubed
- 1 tbsp avocado oil
- 1 cup brown rice flour
- ¼ tsp garlic powder
- ¼ tsp sea salt

Directions:
1. Cook the ginger and almond butter in a saucepan over medium heat for 2 minutes. Add the coconut aminos, Shaoxing wine, arrowroot powder, red pepper flakes, garlic, vinegar, and coconut sugar to the saucepan. Stir to mix well. Bring to a boil. Reduce the heat t and simmer for 5 minutes or until the sauce is thickened.
2. Heat the avocado oil in a nonstick skillet over medium heat. Combine the rice flour, garlic powder, and sea salt in a small bowl. Mix well. Dip the chicken in the mixture, then place in the skillet and cook for 8 minutes or until golden brown and crispy. Flip the chicken halfway through the cooking time. Transfer the chicken thighs to a large plate and pour over it the sauce. Serve and enjoy!

Nutrition Info:
- Per Serving: Calories: 480;Fat: 20g;Protein: 32g;Carbs: 41g.

Baked Turkey Meatballs

Servings: 4 | Cooking Time: 35 Minutes

Ingredients:
- 2 green onions, chopped
- 1 ½ lb ground turkey
- ¼ cup almond flour
- 1 tbsp chopped fresh thyme
- 2 tsp minced garlic
- 1 egg
- ¼ tsp ground nutmeg
- Sea salt to taste

Directions:
1. Preheat your oven to 350ºF. In a mixing bowl, combine the green onions, ground turkey, almond flour, thyme, garlic, egg, nutmeg, and salt until well mixed. Roll the turkey mixture into meatballs. Arrange the meatballs on a parchment-lined baking sheet. Bake for about 15 minutes, or until browned and cooked through. Serve.

Nutrition Info:
- Per Serving: Calories: 300;Fat: 15g;Protein: 35g;Carbs: 4g.

Tangy Beef Ribs

Servings: 4 | Cooking Time: 2 Hours 10 Minutes

Ingredients:
- 1 cup red wine
- 1 ½ lb beef short ribs
- 1 tsp mustard powder
- ½ tsp garlic powder
- Sea salt and pepper to taste
- 2 tbsp olive oil
- 2 cups beef broth
- 4 sprigs rosemary

Directions:
1. Preheat your oven to 350ºF. Rub the short ribs with mustard powder, garlic powder, salt, and black pepper. Let stand for 10 minutes. Warm the olive oil in a skillet over medium heat. Add the short ribs and sear for 5 minutes or until well browned. Flip the ribs halfway through. Transfer the ribs onto a plate and set aside.
2. Pour the beef broth and red wine into the skillet. Stir to combine well and bring to a boil. Turn down the heat to low and simmer for 10 minutes until the mixture reduces to two-thirds. Put the ribs back to the skillet. Add the rosemary sprigs. Put the skillet lid on, then braise in the oven for 2 hours until the ribs are browned and sticky. Discard the rosemary sprigs. Pour the cooking liquid over and serve warm.

Nutrition Info:
- Per Serving: Calories: 730;Fat: 70g;Protein: 24g;Carbs: 2g.

Spicy Lime Pork Tenderloins

Servings: 4 | Cooking Time: 7 Hours 15 Minutes

Ingredients:
- 2 lb pork tenderloins
- 1 cup chicken broth
- ¼ cup lime juice
- 3 tsp chili powder
- 2 tsp garlic powder
- 1 tsp ginger powder
- ½ tsp sea salt

Directions:
1. Combine chili powder, garlic powder, ginger powder, and salt in a bowl. Rub the pork all over with the spice mixture and put it in your slow cooker. Pour in the broth and lime juice around the pork. Cover with the lid and cook for 7 hours on "Low". Remove the pork from the slow cooker and let rest for 5 minutes. Slice the pork against the grain into medallions before serving.

Nutrition Info:
- Per Serving: Calories: 260;Fat: 6g;Protein: 49g;Carbs: 5g.

Smoky Lamb Souvlaki

Servings: 4 | Cooking Time: 25 Minutes + Marinating Time

Ingredients:
- 1 lb lamb shoulder, cubed
- 2 tbsp olive oil
- 1 tbsp apple cider vinegar
- 2 tsp crushed fennel seeds
- 2 tsp smoked paprika
- Salt and garlic powder to taste

Directions:
1. Blend the olive oil, cider vinegar, crushed fennel seeds, smoked paprika, garlic powder, and sea salt in a large bowl. Stir in the lamb. Cover the bowl and refrigerate it for 1 hour to marinate. Preheat a frying pan over high heat. Thread 4-5 pieces of lamb each onto 8 skewers. Fry for 3-4 minutes per side until cooked through. Serve.

Nutrition Info:
- Per Serving: Calories: 275;Fat: 15g;Protein: 31g;Carbs: 1g.

Chicken Piccata

Servings: 6 | Cooking Time: 20 Minutes

Ingredients:
- 1 cup pimento olives, minced
- 6 chicken breast halves
- ¼ cup olive oil
- 2 tbsp lemon juice
- 1 tbsp sherry wine
- ½ cup whole-wheat flour
- 4 shallots, chopped
- 3 garlic cloves, crushed
- ¾ cup chicken broth
- 1 tsp dried basil
- 3 tsp grated Parmesan cheese
- ¼ cup plain yogurt
- ¼ tsp white pepper

Directions:
1. Heat the olive oil in your Instant Pot on "Sauté". Add the chicken and brown it on all sides. This will take 5 to 8 minutes. Remove the chicken from the cooker. Add the shallots and garlic, and stir-fry them for a couple of minutes. Add the sherry wine, broth, lemon juice, salt, olives, basil, and pepper. Return the chicken to the cooker. Seal the lid and cook on "Manual" on High Pressure for 10 minutes. Once ready, carefully open the lid. Stir in plain yogurt and Parmesan cheese. Close the lid again and cook for an additional minute. Serve hot.

Nutrition Info:
- Per Serving: Calories: 320;Fat: 20g;Protein: 19g;Carbs: 15g.

Aromatic Turkey With Mushrooms

Servings: 4 | Cooking Time: 4 Hours 15 Minutes

Ingredients:
- 2 cups button mushrooms, sliced
- 2 turkey thighs
- 1 red bell pepper, sliced
- 1 large onion, sliced
- 1 garlic clove, sliced
- 1 tbsp extra-virgin olive oil
- 1 rosemary sprig
- Sea salt and pepper to taste
- 2 cups chicken broth
- ½ cup dry red wine

Directions:

1. Grease your slow cooker with olive oil. Add the turkey thighs, bell pepper, mushrooms, onion, garlic, rosemary sprig, salt, and pepper. Pour in the chicken broth and wine. Cover and cook on "High" for 4 hours. Remove and discard the rosemary sprig. Use a slotted spoon to transfer the thighs to a plate and allow them to cool for several minutes for easier handling. Cut the meat from the bones, stir the meat into the mushrooms, and serve.

Nutrition Info:
- Per Serving: Calories: 275;Fat: 9g;Protein: 42g;Carbs: 3g.

Delightful Stuffed Lamb With Peppers

Servings: 6 | Cooking Time: 60 Minutes

Ingredients:
- 1 onion, finely diced
- 2 tablespoons water, plus additional for cooking
- 1½ pounds lamb, ground
- 1 cup grated zucchini
- ¼ cup fresh basil, minced
- 1 teaspoon salt
- 6 bell peppers, any color, seeded, ribbed, tops removed and reserved

Directions:
1. Preheat the oven to 350°F.
2. Sauté the onion in the water in a large pan set over medium heat for 5 minutes, or until soft.
3. Add the ground lamb and zucchini. Cook for 10 minutes by breaking up the meat with a spoon.
4. Stir in the basil and salt. Remove from the heat.
5. Fill a casserole dish with 1½ inches of water.
6. Stuff each pepper with an equal amount of the lamb mixture and place them into the dish. Cap each pepper with its reserved top.
7. Place the dish in the preheated oven and bake for 45 to 50 minutes.

Nutrition Info:
- Per Serving: Calories: 258 ;Fat: 9g Protein: 348g ;;Carbs: 10g.

Slow Cooker Chicken Curry

Servings: 4 | Cooking Time: 4 Hours 10 Minutes

Ingredients:
- 1 ½ lb chicken thighs
- 1 onion, sliced
- 2 garlic cloves, minced
- 1 tbsp coconut oil
- 1 tsp ground coriander
- 2 tsp ground cumin
- 1 tsp turmeric
- Sea salt and pepper to taste
- 1 can coconut milk
- 3 cups chicken broth
- ¼ cup chopped cilantro
- 2 scallions, sliced

Directions:
1. Coat the slow cooker with coconut oil. Rub the chicken ground coriander, cumin, turmeric, salt, and pepper and add it to the slow cooker along with onion, garlic, coconut milk, and chicken broth. Cover the slow cooker and cook on High for 4 hours. Garnish with the cilantro and scallions before serving.

Nutrition Info:
- Per Serving: Calories: 650;Fat: 55g;Protein: 31g;Carbs: 10g.

Chopped Lambs With Rosemary

Servings: 4 To 6

Cooking Time: 7 To 8 Hours

Ingredients:
- 1 medium onion, sliced
- 2 teaspoons garlic powder
- 2 teaspoons rosemary, dried
- 1 teaspoon sea salt
- ½ teaspoon thyme leaves, dried
- Freshly ground black pepper
- 8 bone-in lamb chops, 3 pounds
- 2 tablespoons balsamic vinegar

Directions:
1. Line the bottom of the slow cooker with the onion slices.
2. Stir together the garlic powder, rosemary, salt, thyme, and pepper in a small bowl. Rub the chops evenly with the spice mixture and place gently in the slow cooker.
3. Drizzle the vinegar over the top.
4. Cover the cooker and set to low. Cook for 7 to 8 hours and serve.

Nutrition Info:
- Per Serving: Calories: 327 ;Fat: 14g ;Protein: 43g ;Carbs: 4g.

Hot & Spicy Shredded Chicken

Servings: 4 | Cooking Time: 1 Hour

Ingredients:
- 1 ½ lb boneless and skinless chicken breast
- 2 cups diced tomatoes
- ½ tsp oregano
- 2 green chilies, chopped
- ½ tsp paprika
- 2 tbsp coconut sugar
- ½ cup salsa
- 1 tsp cumin
- 2 tbsp olive oil

Directions:
1. In a small bowl, combine the oil with all of the spices. Rub the chicken breast with the spicy marinade. Place the meat in your Instant Pot. Add the diced tomatoes.
2. Close the lid and cook for 25 minutes on "Manual". Transfer the chicken to a cutting board and shred it. Return the shredded meat to the Instant Pot. Choose the "Slow Cook" setting and cook for 30 more minutes.

Nutrition Info:
- Per Serving: Calories: 310;Fat: 10g;Protein: 38g;Carbs: 12g.

Paleo Turkey Thighs With Mushroom

Servings: 4 | Cooking Time: 4 Hours

Ingredients:
- 1 tablespoon extra-virgin olive oil
- 2 turkey thighs
- 2 cups button or cremini mushrooms, sliced
- 1 large onion, sliced
- 1 garlic clove, sliced
- 1 rosemary sprig
- 1 teaspoon salt
- ¼ teaspoon black pepper, freshly ground
- 2 cups chicken broth
- ½ cup dry red wine

Directions:
1. Into a slow cooker, drizzle the olive oil. Add the turkey thighs, mushrooms, onion, garlic, rosemary sprig, salt, and pepper. Pour in the chicken broth and wine. Cover and cook on high for 4 hours.
2. Remove and discard the rosemary sprig. Transfer the thighs to a plate using a slotted spoon and allow them to cool for several minutes for easier handling.
3. Cut the meat from the bones, stir the meat into the mushrooms, and serve.

Nutrition Info:
- Per Serving: Calories: 280 ;Fat: 9g ;Protein: 43g ;Carbs: 3g .

Lemon & Caper Turkey Scaloppine

Servings: 4 | Cooking Time: 25 Minutes

Ingredients:
- 1 tbsp capers
- ¼ cup whole-wheat flour
- Sea salt and pepper to taste
- 4 turkey breast cutlets
- 2 tbsp olive oil
- 3 lemons, juiced
- 1 lemon, zested
- 1 tbsp chopped parsley

Directions:
1. Pound the turkey with a rolling pin to ¼-inch thickness. Combine flour, salt, and pepper in a bowl. Roll each cutlet piece in the flour, shaking off the excess. Warm the olive oil in a skillet over medium heat. Sear the cutlets for 4 minutes on both sides. Transfer to a plate and cover with aluminium foil. Pour the lemon juice and lemon zest in the skillet to scrape up the browned bits that stick to the bottom of the skillet. Stir in capers and rosemary. Cook for 2 minutes until the sauce has thickened slightly. Drizzle the sauce over the cutlets. Serve.

Nutrition Info:
- Per Serving: Calories: 190;Fat: 14g;Protein: 2g;Carbs: 9g.

Cinnamon Pork Chops In Apple Sauce

Servings: 4 | Cooking Time: 45 Minutes

Ingredients:
- ¼ cup chopped onions
- ½ tsp grated fresh ginger
- 2 apples, peeled and diced
- 2 tbsp olive oil
- 4 boneless pork chops
- 1 tsp garlic powder
- 1 tsp ground cinnamon
- Sea salt and pepper to taste

Directions:
1. Warm 1 tbsp of olive oil in a skillet over medium heat. Add the onions and ginger and sauté for 2 minutes until softened. Stir in the apples. Sauté for about 5 minutes, or until the fruit is just tender. Season with salt; set it aside.
2. Sprinkle the pork chops with garlic powder, cinnamon, salt, and pepper. Warm the remaining olive oil in the skillet and add the chops. Sear them for 3-4 minutes per side until just cooked through and browned, turning once. Serve the chops drizzled with the apple sauce.

Nutrition Info:
- Per Serving: Calories: 430;Fat: 30g;Protein: 25g;Carbs: 10g.

Nutritious Apricot And Zucchini Mash With Lamb Shoulder

Servings: 4 | Cooking Time: 4 To 5 Hours

Ingredients:
- 1 lamb shoulders, lean
- 2 zucchinis, chopped
- 4 tablespoons extra virgin olive oil
- 5 sprigs rosemary
- 3 sprigs thyme
- 1 tablespoon black pepper
- ½ cup apricots
- handful arugula
- 2 garlic cloves, chopped
- 8 baby cherry tomatoes, halved
- handful chopped cilantro

Directions:
1. Preheat oven to its highest setting.
2. Trimming the fat layer off will prepare the meat.
3. Rub the lamb with 3 tablespoons olive oil, rosemary, and thyme as well as a little black pepper.
4. Line a baking tray with the apricots.
5. Cover the dish with aluminum foil or a baking lid.
6. Turn the oven down to 325°F and add the lamb.
7. Cook for 4 to 5 hours and remove and rest.
8. Add 1 tbsp oil to a pan and heat on medium heat.
9. Throw in the zucchinis, tomatoes, and garlic and sauté for 5 to 6 minutes until soft. Add the arugula and cilantro and stir in.
10. Serve the lamb on a bed of the vegetable, drizzling over the juices from the bottom of the pan for extra-deliciousness.

Nutrition Info:
- Per Serving: Calories: 111 ;Fat: 6g ;Protein: 1g ;Carbs: 15g .

Classic Pork Chops And Creamy Green Beans

Servings: 4 | Cooking Time: 40 Minutes

Ingredients:
- Creamy Green Beans:
- 1 medium head cauliflower, roughly chopped
- 1½ cups bone broth
- ¼ cup Garlic Confit or 4 cloves garlic, peeled
- 2 tablespoons cooking fat
- 2 cups fresh green beans, trimmed
- 1 red onion, sliced
- 2 teaspoons fine Himalayan salt, divided
- 2 large egg yolks
- Pork Chops:
- 2 teaspoons Himalayan salt, fine
- 1 teaspoon garlic powder
- 1 teaspoon black pepper, ground
- 1 teaspoon onion powder
- 5 sprigs thyme, fresh
- 4 thick-cut pork chops, boneless
- 2 tablespoons avocado oil
- ¼ cup bone broth
- 2 tablespoons coconut aminos
- 2 tablespoons red wine vinegar

Directions:
1. Make the creamy green beans. In a medium-sized pot, place the cauliflower, broth, and garlic confit and bring to a simmer over medium heat. Cover and cook until the cauliflower is fork-tender for 20 minutes.
2. Heat a large skillet over medium heat. Heat the cooking fat in the skillet when it's hot. Add the green beans, red onion slices, and 1 teaspoon of the salt. Sauté and stir occasionally for 10 min-

utes until the beans appear brown and the onions are tender and translucent. Reduce the heat to medium-low.
3. Transfer it and all of the broth to a blender, add the remaining teaspoon of salt, and blend until smooth. Open the lid vent while the blender is running and drop in the egg yolks one at a time.
4. Pour the cauliflower cream over the green beans and onions once well combined in the skillet. Stir, cover, and remove from the heat, but keep the pan on the stove or in the oven so it stays warm.
5. Prepare the pork chops. Heat a large skillet over medium heat. Combine the salt, garlic powder, pepper, onion powder, and thyme sprigs in a small bowl while the skillet heats. Rub the seasoning mixture all over the pork chops, making sure they are evenly coated.
6. Melt the oil in the hot skillet. Add the chops and space them. Cook undisturbed for 5 minutes then flip the chops over and cook for 3 minutes on the other side.
7. Add the broth, coconut aminos, and vinegar to the skillet with the pork chops. Cover and cook for 3 minutes. Gently press on the center of a chop by using your finger. It should be firm when it's done but with a little give and the internal temperature should be 165°F. Remove from the heat.
8. Let the pork chops rest for a few minutes then pour the pan sauce over the chops. Serve with the creamy green beans.
9. Store leftovers in an airtight container in the fridge for up to 5 days. Reheat in a large skillet, covered, over medium-low heat for 8 to 10 minutes.

Nutrition Info:
- Per Serving: Calories: 563 ;Fat: 28g ;Protein: 59g;Carbs: 18g .

Scallion & Broccoli Chicken Sauté

Servings: 4 | Cooking Time: 30 Minutes

Ingredients:
- 2 tsp chicken seasoning
- 3 tbsp olive oil
- 6 scallions, chopped
- 1 cup broccoli florets
- 1 lb chicken breasts, cubed
- ½ cup chicken broth
- 2 tbsp toasted sesame seeds

Directions:
1. Rub the chicken with chicken seasoning. Warm the olive oil in a skillet over medium heat. Add the scallions, broccoli, and chicken and cook for 5-7 minutes until the chicken is no longer pink and the veggies are tender. Mix in broth and cook for another 5 minutes until the sauce has reduced. Serve topped with sesame seeds.

Nutrition Info:
- Per Serving: Calories: 370;Fat: 23g;Protein: 2g;Carbs: 8g.

Spicy Beef Fajitas

Servings: 4 | Cooking Time: 15 Minutes

Ingredients:
- 1 ½ lb flank steak, cut into strips
- ½ tsp ancho chili powder
- 3 tbsp olive oil
- 2 green bell peppers, sliced
- 1 onion, sliced
- 1 cup store-bought salsa
- 1 tsp garlic powder
- ½ tsp Fajita seasoning

Directions:
1. Warm the olive oil in a skillet over medium heat. Stir-fry the

flank steak strips, bell peppers, and onion for 6 minutes until browned. Stir in ancho chili powder, salsa, garlic powder, and fajita seasoning and cook for 3 minutes, stirring often. Serve right away.

Nutrition Info:
- Per Serving: Calories: 480;Fat: 26g;Protein: 3g;Carbs: 13g.

Enjoyable Braised Turkey Legs And Wilted Greens

Servings: 6 | Cooking Time: 1 Hour And 20 Minutes

Ingredients:
- 3 turkey legs, 1½- to 2-pound
- ¾ teaspoon salt
- 3 tablespoons coconut oil
- 1 onion, minced
- 4 garlic cloves, minced
- 5 cups water
- 6 cups lightly packed kale, thoroughly washed and chopped

Directions:
1. Pat the turkey legs dry and sprinkle with the salt.
2. Add the coconut oil to a large pot set over medium-high heat.
3. Add the turkey legs and sear for 5 minutes per side. Do this in batches, depending on the size of the pot. Transfer the turkey to a plate and set aside.
4. Add the onion and garlic to the pot. Sauté for 5 minutes or until soft.
5. Return the turkey to the pot and add the water. Bring to a boil. Reduce the heat to low. Cover and simmer for 1 hour or until the meat is tender and starting to fall off the bone. Scatter the kale over the turkey. Stir and cook for about 5 minutes or until the kale wilts.

Nutrition Info:
- Per Serving: Calories: 731 ;Fat: 37g ;Protein: 87g ;Carbs: 9g .

Italian Spinach Chicken

Servings: 4 | Cooking Time: 15 Minutes

Ingredients:
- 1 cup chopped spinach
- 2 lb chicken breasts, halved
- ½ cup chicken broth
- 2 garlic cloves, minced
- 2 tbsp olive oil
- ¾ cup heavy cream
- ½ cup sun-dried tomatoes
- 2 tsp Italian seasoning
- ½ cup Parmesan, grated
- ½ tsp sea salt

Directions:
1. Rub the meat with oil, garlic, salt, and seasonings. Add the chicken in your Instant Pot, select "Sauté" and brown it on all sides. Pour the broth in, seal the lid and cook for 5 minutes on "Manual" on high pressure. When it is done, release the pressure quickly, open the lid and add the cream. Simmer for 5 minutes with the lid off, then stir in the Parmesan cheese. Stir in tomatoes and spinach and cook on "Sauté" just until the spinach wilts. Serve.

Nutrition Info:
- Per Serving: Calories: 460;Fat: 25g;Protein: 57g;Carbs: 3g.

Lettuce-wrapped Beef Roast

Servings: 4 | Cooking Time: 8 Hours 15 Minutes

Ingredients:
- 2 lb beef chuck roast
- 1 shallot, diced
- 1 cup beef broth
- 3 tbsp coconut aminos
- 1 tbsp rice vinegar
- 1 tsp garlic powder
- 1 tsp olive oil
- ½ tsp ground ginger
- ¼ tsp red pepper flakes
- 8 romaine lettuce leaves
- 1 tbsp sesame seeds
- 1 scallion, diced

Directions:
1. Place the beef, shallot, broth, coconut aminos, vinegar, garlic powder, olive oil, ginger, and red pepper flakes in your slow cooker. Cover the cooker and set to "Low". Cook for 8 hours. Scoop spoonfuls of the beef mixture into each lettuce leaf. Top with sesame seeds and scallion.

Nutrition Info:
- Per Serving: Calories: 425;Fat: 22g;Protein: 45g;Carbs: 12g.

Turkey Stuffed Bell Peppers

Servings: 6 | Cooking Time: 30 Minutes

Ingredients:
- 6 bell peppers, tops removed and deseeded
- 3 tbsp avocado oil
- 1 lb ground turkey
- 1 onion, diced
- 2 garlic cloves, minced
- 16 oz canned tomatoes
- ½ tsp paprika
- ½ tsp ground cumin
- ½ tsp dried oregano
- Sea salt and pepper to taste

Directions:
1. Preheat your oven to 400°F. Warm the avocado oil in a skillet over medium heat and brown the ground turkey for 5 minutes. Add garlic and onion and cook for 2 minutes, stirring often. Stir in tomatoes, paprika, cumin, oregano, salt, and pepper. Spoon the mixture into the bell peppers. Arrange them on a greased baking dish. Bake for 20-25 minutes or until softened. Serve warm.

Nutrition Info:
- Per Serving: Calories: 190;Fat: 9g;Protein: 15g;Carbs: 10g.

Authentic Chicken Curry With Coconut

Servings: 6 | Cooking Time: 35 Minutes

Ingredients:
- 3 cups coconut milk
- 2 cups water
- 1 to 2 tablespoons curry powder
- 2 pounds boneless skinless chicken thighs, cut into cubes
- 1 teaspoon salt
- 3 bunches Swiss chard, washed, stemmed, and roughly chopped

Directions:
1. Combine the coconut milk, water, curry powder, chicken, and salt in a large pot. Bring to a boil over high heat. Reduce the heat to low. Cover and simmer for 30 minutes.
2. Add the Swiss chard to the pot. Cook for 5 minutes or until the chard wilts.

- Per Serving: Calories: 581 ;Fat: 40g ;Protein: 48g ;Carbs: 10g .

Incredible Tacos With Pork

Servings: 4 To 6

Cooking Time: 7 To 8 Hours

Ingredients:
- 1 teaspoon sea salt
- 1 teaspoon cumin, ground
- 1 teaspoon garlic powder
- ½ teaspoon oregano, dried
- ½ teaspoon black pepper, freshly ground
- 3 to 4 pounds pork shoulder or butt
- 2 cups broth of choice
- Juice of 1 orange
- 1 small onion, chopped
- 4 to 6 corn taco shells
- Shredded cabbage, lime wedges, avocado, and hot sauce

Directions:
1. Stir together in a small bowl the salt, cumin, garlic powder, oregano, and pepper. Rub the pork with the spice mixture and put it in your slow cooker.
2. Pour the broth and orange juice around the pork. Scatter the onion around the pork.
3. Cover the cooker and set on low. Cook for 7 to 8 hours.
4. Transfer the pork to a work surface and shred it with a fork. Serve in taco shells with any optional toppings you like.

Nutrition Info:
- Per Serving: Calories: 1156 ;Fat: 84g ;Protein: 84g ;Carbs: 12g
.

Rosemary Pork Loin

Servings: 4 | Cooking Time: 60 Minutes

Ingredients:
- 2 tbsp olive oil
- 2 lb boneless pork loin
- 1 tsp dried rosemary
- Sea salt and pepper to taste

Directions:
1. Preheat your oven to 375°F. Pour 1 cup of water into a roasting pan. Rub the pork loin with olive oil and place it in a skillet over medium heat. Cook for 4-6 minutes on all sides until browned. Transfer to the roasting pan, sprinkle with rosemary, salt, and pepper, and bake for 40 minutes. Let sit and serve.

Nutrition Info:
- Per Serving: Calories: 492;Fat: 20g;Protein: 76g;Carbs: 0g.

Miso Chicken With Sesame

Servings: 4 To 6

Cooking Time: 4 Hours

Ingredients:
- ¼ cup white miso
- 2 tablespoons coconut oil, melted
- 2 tablespoons honey
- 1 tablespoon rice wine vinegar, unseasoned
- 2 garlic cloves, thinly sliced
- 1 teaspoon fresh ginger root, minced
- 1 cup chicken broth
- 8 boneless, skinless chicken thighs
- 2 scallions, sliced
- 1 tablespoon sesame seeds

Directions:

1. Combine the miso, coconut oil, honey, rice wine vinegar, garlic, and ginger root in a slow cooker. Mix it well.
2. Add the chicken and toss to combine. Cover and cook on high for 4 hours.
3. Transfer the chicken and sauce to a serving dish. Garnish with the scallions and sesame seeds and serve.

Nutrition Info:
- Per Serving: Calories: 320 ;Fat: 15g ;Protein: 32g Carbs: 17g.

Cheap Pork Sausage

Servings: 10 | Cooking Time: 15 Minutes

Ingredients:
- 2 pounds pork, ground
- 2 ribs celery, minced
- 4 cloves garlic, minced
- 2 teaspoons Dijon mustard
- 2 teaspoons Himalayan salt, fine
- 1 teaspoon thyme leaves, dried
- 1 teaspoon black pepper, ground
- ¼ teaspoon ginger powder
- ¼ teaspoon cinnamon, ground
- Pinch of nutmeg, ground

Directions:
1. In a large bowl, place all of the ingredients and mix thoroughly with your hands.
2. Heat a large cast-iron skillet over medium heat. Shape the pork mixture into patties, about ¼ cup per patty while it heats.
3. Place four or five patties in the pan when the skillet is hot without crowding the pan. Cook the patties for 6 minutes per side or until the internal temperature reaches 165°F. Repeat with the remaining patties.
4. This sausage stores well side by side in an airtight container in the refrigerator for up to 5 days or in the freezer for up to 30 days. Place in a preheated 350°F oven for 8 to 10 minutes to reheat.

Nutrition Info:
- Per Serving: Calories: 157 ;Fat: 12g ;Protein: 9g;Carbs: 2g .

Turmeric Chicken & Chickpea Stew

Servings: 4 | Cooking Time: 4 Hours 15 Minutes

Ingredients:
- 1 lb boneless, skinless chicken thighs
- 1 onion, thinly sliced
- 2 garlic cloves, thinly sliced
- 1 tbsp extra-virgin olive oil
- 1 tsp minced ginger root
- 2 tsp ground turmeric
- 1 tsp fennel seeds, crushed
- Sea salt and pepper to taste
- 2 cups chicken broth
- 1 cup coconut milk
- ¼ cup chopped cilantro

Directions:
1. Grease your slow cooker with olive oil. Add the chicken, onion, garlic, ginger root, turmeric, fennel seeds, salt, pepper, chicken broth, and coconut milk, and toss to combine. Cover and cook on "High" for 4 hours. Garnish with the chopped cilantro and serve.

Nutrition Info:
- Per Serving: Calories: 375;Fat: 18g;Protein: 45g;Carbs: 4g.

Magnificent Herbaceous Pork Meatballs

Servings: 2 | Cooking Time: 20 Minutes

Ingredients:
- 8 ounces lean pork, minced
- 1 garlic clove, crushed
- ¼ cup bread, 100% wholegrain crumbs
- 1 teaspoon thyme, dried
- 1 teaspoon basil, dried
- 2 tablespoons extra virgin olive oil
- 1 cup spaghetti, 100% wholegrain or gluten-free
- Sauce:
- 1 tablespoon extra-virgin olive oil
- 1 red onion, finely chopped
- 1 can tomatoes, chopped
- 1 red pepper, finely chopped
- ½ cup water
- 1 tablespoon fresh basil

Directions:
1. In a bowl, mix the pork mince, 1 tablespoon oil, garlic, breadcrumbs, and herbs. Season with a little black pepper and separate into 8 balls, rolling with the palms of your hands.
2. In a pan over medium heat, heat 1 tablespoon oil and add onions and peppers, sauté for a few minutes until soft.
3. Add the tomatoes and ½ cup water.
4. For 15 minutes, cover and lower heat to simmer.
5. Boil your water and cook spaghetti to recommended guidelines.
6. Heat 1 tablespoon oil and add the meatballs to a separate pan, turning carefully to brown the surface of each. Continue this for 5 to 7 minutes before adding to the sauce and simmering for 5 minutes more.
7. Drain spaghetti, portion up, and pour a generous portion of meatballs and sauce over the top to serve.
8. Sprinkle with a little freshly torn basil.

Nutrition Info:
- Per Serving: Calories: 435 ;Fat: 23g ;Protein: 37g ;Carbs: 19g .

Herby Green Whole Chicken

Servings: 6 | Cooking Time: 1 Hour 45 Minutes

Ingredients:
- 1 sweet onion, quartered
- 1 whole chicken
- 2 lemons, halved
- 4 garlic cloves, crushed
- 4 fresh thyme sprigs
- 4 fresh rosemary sprigs
- 4 fresh parsley sprigs
- 3 bay leaves
- 2 tbsp olive oil
- Sea salt and pepper to taste

Directions:
1. Preheat your oven to 400ºF. Put the chicken in a greased pan. Stuff it with lemons, onion, garlic, thyme, rosemary, parsley, and bay leaves into the cavity. Brush the chicken with olive oil, and season lightly with sea salt and pepper. Roast the chicken for about 1 ½ hours until golden brown and cooked through. Remove the chicken from the oven and let it sit for 10 minutes. Remove the lemons, onion, and herbs from the cavity and serve.

Nutrition Info:
- Per Serving: Calories: 260;Fat: 9g;Protein: 39g;Carbs: 6g.

Veggie & Beef Brisket

Servings: 4 | Cooking Time: 60 Minutes

Ingredients:
- 4 beef tenderloin fillets
- 4 sweet potatoes, chopped
- 1 onion, chopped
- 2 bay leaves
- 2 tbsp olive oil
- 2 cups chopped carrots
- 3 tbsp chopped garlic
- 3 tbsp Worcestershire sauce
- 2 celery stalks, chopped
- Black pepper to taste
- 1 tbsp Knorr demi-glace sauce

Directions:
1. Heat 1 tbsp oil in your pressure cooker on "Sauté". Sauté the onion until caramelized. Transfer to a bowl. Season the meat with pepper to taste. Heat the remaining oil and cook the meat until browned on all sides. Add the remaining ingredients and 2 cups of water. Close the lid and cook for 30 minutes on "Manual" on High pressure. When cooking is complete, release the pressure naturally for 10 minutes. Transfer the meat and veggies to a serving platter. Whisk the Knorr Demi-Glace sauce in the pot and simmer for 5 minutes until thickened on "Sauté". Pour the gravy over the meat and enjoy.

Nutrition Info:
- Per Serving: Calories: 400;Fat: 20g;Protein: 28g;Carbs: 10g.

Soups and Stews

Soups and Stews

Spicy Beef & Sweet Potato Soup

Servings: 6 | Cooking Time: 25 Minutes

Ingredients:
- 1 lb ground beef
- 1 tsp olive oil
- 4 cups water
- 24 oz tomato sauce
- Sea salt and pepper to taste
- 4 cups cubed sweet potatoes
- 1 onion, chopped
- ½ tsp hot pepper sauce

Directions:
1. Select the "Sauté"setting and add the olive oil and onion. Sauté until the onion until tender, about 2-3 minutes. Add the beef and cook until browned. Then, stir in the remaining ingredients. Seal the lid, select "Manual", and cook on High pressure for 10 minutes. Once completed, perform a quick pressure release. Serve.

Nutrition Info:
- Per Serving: Calories: 245;Fat: 9g;Protein: 15g;Carbs: 27g.

Carrot & Mushroom Broth

Servings: 6 | Cooking Time: 1 Hour 15 Minutes

Ingredients:
- 5 dried porcini mushrooms, soaked and liquid reserved
- 8 oz cremini mushrooms, chopped
- 1 tbsp extra-virgin olive oil
- 1 unpeeled onion, quartered
- 1 carrot, coarsely chopped
- 1 celery rib, diced
- 1 onion, chopped
- ½ cup chopped parsley
- Sea salt and pepper to taste

Directions:
1. Warm the oil in a pot over medium heat. Place in onion, carrot, celery, and cremini mushrooms. Cook for 5 minutes until softened. Add in the dried mushrooms and reserved liquid, onion, salt, and 5 cups of water. Bring to a boil and simmer for 1 hour. Let cool for a few minutes, then pour over a strainer into a pot. Divide between glass mason jars and allow cooling completely. Seal and store in the fridge for up to 5 days or 1 month in the freezer.

Nutrition Info:
- Per Serving: Calories: 185;Fat: 4g;Protein: 5g;Carbs: 38g.

Black-eyed Pea Soup

Servings: 6 | Cooking Time: 45 Minutes

Ingredients:
- 2 carrots, chopped
- 1 onion, chopped
- 15 oz canned black-eyed peas
- 1 tsp low-sodium soy sauce
- 1 tsp onion powder
- ½ tsp garlic powder
- Sea salt and pepper to taste
- ¼ cup chopped black olives

Directions:

1. Place carrots, onion, black-eyed peas, 6 cups of water, soy sauce, onion powder, garlic powder, and pepper in a pot. Simmer slowly for 20 minutes. Allow cooling for a few minutes. Transfer to a food processor and blend until smooth. Stir in black olives. Serve and enjoy!

Nutrition Info:
- Per Serving: Calories: 35;Fat: 1g;Protein: 1g;Carbs: 6g.

Brussels Sprouts & Tofu Soup

Servings: 4 | Cooking Time: 40 Minutes

Ingredients:
- 7 oz firm tofu, cubed
- 2 tsp olive oil
- 1 cup sliced mushrooms
- 1 lb Brussels sprouts, halved
- 1 garlic clove, minced
- ½-inch piece minced ginger
- Sea salt to taste
- 2 tbsp apple cider vinegar
- 2 tsp low-sodium soy sauce
- 1 tsp pure date sugar
- ¼ tsp red pepper flakes
- 1 scallion, chopped

Directions:
1. Heat the oil in a skillet over medium heat. Place mushrooms, Brussels sprouts, garlic, ginger, and salt. Sauté for 7-8 minutes until the veggies are soft. Pour in 4 cups of water, vinegar, soy sauce, sugar, pepper flakes, and tofu. Bring to a boil, then lower the heat and simmer for 5-10 minutes. Top with scallions and serve.

Nutrition Info:
- Per Serving: Calories: 135;Fat: 8g;Protein: 9g;Carbs: 8g.

Kale & Cabbage Stew

Servings: 4 | Cooking Time: 30 Minutes

Ingredients:
- 1 onion, diced
- 2 tbsp extra-virgin olive oil
- 1 lb cabbage, shredded
- ⅓ cup chunky almond butter
- 1 tsp paprika
- ¼ tsp red pepper flakes
- Sea salt and pepper to taste
- 2 cups kale, chopped

Directions:
1. Warm the olive oil in a saucepan over medium heat and cook the onion for 3 minutes. Add the cabbage, paprika, pepper flakes, 4 cups of water, and salt; stir. Bring to a boil and simmer for 20 minutes. Add in the kale and cook for 5 minutes until wilted. Serve and enjoy!

Nutrition Info:
- Per Serving: Calories: 240;Fat: 19g;Protein: 7g;Carbs: 16g.

Rosemary White Bean Soup

Servings: 4 | Cooking Time: 30 Minutes

Ingredients:
- 2 tsp olive oil
- 1 carrot, chopped
- 1 onion, chopped
- 2 garlic cloves, minced
- 1 tbsp rosemary, chopped
- 2 tbsp apple cider vinegar
- 1 cup dried white beans
- ¼ tsp sea salt
- 2 tbsp nutritional yeast

Directions:
1. Heat the oil in a pot over medium heat. Place carrots, onion, and garlic and cook for 5 minutes. Pour in vinegar to deglaze the pot. Stir in 5 cups water and beans and bring to a boil. Lower the heat and simmer for 45 minutes until the beans are soft. Add in salt and nutritional yeast and stir. Serve topped with chopped rosemary.

Nutrition Info:
- Per Serving: Calories: 225;Fat: 3g;Protein: 14g;Carbs: 37g.

Indian Curried Stew With Lentil And Spinach

Servings: 2 | Cooking Time: 30 Minutes

Ingredients:
- 1 tablespoon extra-virgin olive oil
- 1 tablespoon curry powder
- 1 cup homemade chicken or vegetable stock
- 1 cup red lentils, soaked
- 1 onion, chopped
- 2 cups butternut squash, cooked peeled, and chopped
- 1 cup spinach
- 2 garlic cloves, minced
- 1 tablespoon cilantro, finely chopped

Directions:
1. Add the oil, chopped onion, and minced garlic, sauté for 5 minutes on low heat in a large pot.
2. Add the curry powder and ginger to the onions and cook for 5 minutes.
3. Add the broth and bring to a boil on high heat.
4. Stir in the lentils, squash, and spinach, reduce heat and simmer for 20 minutes more.
5. Season with pepper to taste and serve with fresh cilantro.

Nutrition Info:
- Per Serving: Calories: 1022 ;Fat: 19g ;Protein: 123g ;Carbs: 91g.

Tomato Lentil Dahl

Servings: 6 | Cooking Time: 30 Minutes

Ingredients:
- 1 cup red lentils
- 1 bay leaf
- 1 white onion, diced
- 2 garlic cloves, minced
- 3 cups vegetable broth
- 1 tbsp coconut oil
- 1 medium tomato, diced
- 1 tsp sesame seeds
- 1 tsp ground ginger
- 1 tsp ground cumin
- 1 tsp ground turmeric
- 1 tsp mustard seeds
- Sea salt to taste
- ½ tsp ground cinnamon
- 1 can coconut milk
- 2 tbsp chopped cilantro

Directions:
1. Pour the broth, lentils, and bay leaf in a large pot over medium heat and bring to a boil. Reduce the heat to medium-low and simmer for 20 minutes.
2. Meanwhile, in a medium saucepan over medium heat, sauté the onion and garlic in the coconut oil for 2 minutes. Add the tomato, sesame seeds, ginger, cumin, turmeric, mustard seeds, salt, and cinnamon. Cook, stirring frequently, for 5 minutes. Stir in the coconut milk and bring to a simmer. Remove and discard the bay leaf. Add the coconut milk mixture to the lentils along with the cilantro and stir to combine. Serve and enjoy!

Nutrition Info:
- Per Serving: Calories: 285;Fat: 5g;Protein: 15g;Carbs: 32g.

Arugula Coconut Soup

Servings: 4 | Cooking Time: 30 Minutes

Ingredients:
- 1 tsp coconut oil
- 1 onion, diced
- 2 cups green beans
- 4 cups water
- 1 cup arugula, chopped
- 1 tbsp fresh mint, chopped
- Sea salt and pepper to taste
- ¾ cup coconut milk

Directions:
1. Place a pot over medium heat and heat the coconut oil. Add in the onion and sauté for 5 minutes. Pour in green beans and water. Bring to a boil, lower the heat and stir in arugula, mint, salt, and pepper. Simmer for 10 minutes. Stir in coconut milk. Transfer to a food processor and blitz the soup until smooth. Serve and enjoy!

Nutrition Info:
- Per Serving: Calories: 145;Fat: 12g;Protein: 5g;Carbs: 9g.

Power Green Cream Soup

Servings: 4 | Cooking Time: 30 Minutes

Ingredients:
- 4 cups no-salt-added vegetable broth
- 1 garlic clove, minced
- 2 tbsp extra-virgin olive oil
- 4 green onions, chopped
- 4 cups baby spinach
- 1 cup broccoli florets
- Sea salt and pepper to taste

Directions:
1. Warm the olive oil in a pot over medium heat. Sauté the onion and garlic for 5 minutes until softened. Add the baby spinach, broccoli, vegetable broth, salt, and pepper and bring to a boil. Simmer for 10-15 minutes over low heat until the veggies are tender. Pulse the mixture with an immersion blender until smooth. Serve warm.

Nutrition Info:
- Per Serving: Calories: 130;Fat: 8g;Protein: 4g;Carbs: 17g.

Distinctive Thai Soup With Potato

Servings: 4 To 6

Cooking Time: 20 To 25minutes

Ingredients:
- 3 large sweet potatoes, cubed
- 2 cups water
- One 14 ounces can coconut milk
- ½-inch piece fresh ginger, sliced
- ½ cup almond butter
- Zest of 1 lime
- Juice of 1 lime
- 1 teaspoon salt, plus additional as needed

Directions:
1. Combine the sweet potatoes, water, coconut milk, and ginger in a large pot set over high heat. Bring to a boil. Reduce the heat to low and cover.
2. For 20 to 25 minutes, simmer until the potatoes are tender. Transfer to a blender the potatoes, ginger, and cooking liquid.
3. Add the almond butter, lime zest, lime juice, and salt.
4. Blend until smooth.
5. Taste, and adjust the seasoning if necessary.

Nutrition Info:
- Per Serving: Calories: 653 ;Fat: 42g ;Protein: 12g ;Carbs: 64g .

Beef-farro Stew

Servings: 4 | Cooking Time: 50 Minutes

Ingredients:
- 1 can diced tomatoes
- 1 lb ground beef
- 1 medium onion, chopped
- 2 cups beef broth
- 2/3 cup farro
- 2 tbsp extra-virgin olive oil
- Sea salt and pepper to taste
- 1 cup chopped carrots
- 2 cups broccoli florets
- ½ tsp dried oregano leaves

Directions:
1. Warm the olive oil in a saucepan over medium heat. Add the beef and onion and stir-fry for 7-8 minutes until the beef is brown. Add the remaining ingredients except for the broccoli. Cover and cook for 20 minutes. Stir in broccoli and continue cooking for another 10-15 minutes or until barley is tender. Serve and enjoy!

Nutrition Info:
- Per Serving: Calories: 300;Fat: 13g;Protein: 3g;Carbs: 13g.

Healthy Soup With Turmeric And Broccoli

Servings: 4 To 6

Cooking Time: 3 To 4 Hours

Ingredients:
- 2 medium heads broccoli
- ½ medium onion, diced
- 1 tablespoon extra-virgin olive oil
- 1 tablespoon turmeric, ground
- ½ teaspoon garlic powder
- ½ teaspoon ginger, ground
- 1 teaspoon lemon juice, freshly squeezed
- ½ teaspoon sea salt
- 4 cups vegetable broth
- Freshly ground black pepper

Directions:
1. Combine the broccoli, onion, olive oil, turmeric, garlic pow-

der, ginger, lemon juice, salt, and broth in your slow cooker and season with pepper.
2. Cover the cooker and set it to low. Cook for 3 to 4 hours and serve.

Nutrition Info:
- Per Serving: Calories: 144 ;Fat: 5g ;Protein: 9g ;Carbs: 22g .

Soulful Roasted Vegetable Soup

Servings: 2 | Cooking Time: 30 Minutes

Ingredients:
- 2 medium carrots, peeled
- 1 cup baby Brussels sprouts
- 1 rib celery
- ¼ medium head cabbage
- 2 teaspoons fine Himalayan salt, divided
- 2 tablespoons coconut oil
- 2 cups bone broth
- ½ medium Hass avocado, peeled, pitted, and sliced
- 1 green onion, minced
- 4 sprigs fresh cilantro, minced

Directions:
1. Preheat the oven to 400°F.
2. Cut all of the vegetables into small pieces and spread them out on a sheet pan. Sprinkle with 1 teaspoon of the salt and toss with the coconut oil. For 30 minutes, roast.
3. Heat the broth in a saucepan while the vegetables are roasting over medium heat.
4. Divide the vegetables between two serving bowls when they are ready. Add the avocado, green onion, and cilantro, and sprinkle in the remaining teaspoon of salt. Divide the broth between the bowls.
5. Serve immediately. Store leftovers in an airtight container in the fridge for up to 4 days.

Nutrition Info:
- Per Serving: Calories: 276 ;Fat: 23g ;Protein: 6g;Carbs: 19g .s

Easy Thai Pork Stew

Servings: 4 | Cooking Time: 50 Minutes

Ingredients:
- 1/3 cup whole-wheat flour
- ½ tsp garlic powder
- 1 lb pork loin, cubes
- Sea salt and pepper to taste
- 2 tbsp extra-virgin olive oil
- 1 cup peanut sauce
- 1 cup chicken broth
- 1 tsp red pepper flakes
- ½ lb cubed butternut squash
- 1 red bell pepper, diced
- 4 oz okra, sliced
- 2 tbsp cilantro, chopped

Directions:
1. Mix the whole-wheat flour, garlic powder, salt, and pepper in a large-sized resealable bag. Add the pork and shake to coat. Warm the olive oil in a large pot over medium heat. Add the pork and brown it for 4-6 minutes, stirring often. Pour in peanut sauce and broth, scraping up any brown bits stuck to the bottom of the pot. Lower the heat and simmer for 15 minutes. Then, add the squash and cook for another 10 minutes or until pork and squash are tender. Add the bell pepper, okra, and red pepper flakes and continue to cook for 5-7 minutes. Garnish with cilantro and serve immediately.

Nutrition Info:
- Per Serving: Calories: 482;Fat: 29g;Protein: 35g;Carbs: 19g.

Basil Coconut Soup

Servings: 4 | Cooking Time: 15 Minutes

Ingredients:
- 2 tbsp coconut oil
- 1 ½ cups vegetable broth
- 2 garlic cloves, minced
- 1 onion, chopped
- 1 tbsp minced fresh ginger
- 2 green bell peppers, sliced
- 1 can coconut milk
- Juice of ½ lime
- 2 tbsp chopped basil
- 1 tbsp chopped cilantro

Directions:
1. Warm the coconut oil in a pot over medium heat. Place in onion, garlic, and ginger and sauté for 3 minutes. Add in bell peppers and broth. Bring to a boil and simmer. Stir in coconut milk, lime juice, and chopped cilantro. Simmer for 5 minutes. Serve garnished with basil.

Nutrition Info:
- Per Serving: Calories: 330;Fat: 31g;Protein: 2g;Carbs: 15g.

Vegetable & Rice Soup

Servings: 6 | Cooking Time: 40 Minutes

Ingredients:
- 3 tbsp extra-virgin olive oil
- 2 carrots, chopped
- 1 onion, chopped
- 1 celery stalk, chopped
- 2 garlic cloves, minced
- 2 cups chopped cabbage
- ½ red bell pepper, chopped
- 4 sweet potatoes, quartered
- 6 cups vegetable broth
- ½ cup brown rice, rinsed
- ½ cup frozen green peas
- 2 tbsp chopped parsley

Directions:
1. Heat the oil in a pot over medium heat. Place carrots, onion, celery, and garlic. Cook for 5 minutes. Add in cabbage, bell pepper, sweet potatoes, and broth. Bring to a boil, lower the heat, and add the brown rice, salt, and pepper. Simmer uncovered for 25 minutes until vegetables are tender. Stir in peas and cook for 5 minutes. Top with parsley and serve warm.

Nutrition Info:
- Per Serving: Calories: 245;Fat: 8g;Protein: 2g;Carbs: 41g.

Shiitake Mushroom Soup

Servings: 4 | Cooking Time: 25 Minutes

Ingredients:
- 8 oz shiitake mushrooms, sliced
- 2 tbsp extra-virgin olive oil
- 4 green onions, chopped
- 1 carrot, chopped
- 3 tbsp rice wine
- 2 tsp low-sodium soy sauce
- 4 cups vegetable broth
- Sea salt and pepper to taste
- 2 tbsp parsley, chopped

Directions:
1. Heat the oil in a pot over medium heat. Place the green onions and carrot and cook for 5 minutes. Stir in mushrooms, rice wine, soy sauce, broth, salt, and pepper. Bring to a boil, then lower the heat and simmer for 15 minutes. Top with parsley and serve warm.

Nutrition Info:
- Per Serving: Calories: 150;Fat: 7g;Protein: 2g;Carbs: 21g.

Coconut Butternut Squash Soup

Servings: 4 | Cooking Time: 30 Minutes

Ingredients:
- 2 tbsp extra-virgin olive oil
- 2 garlic cloves, minced
- 1 onion, chopped
- 1 tbsp grated ginger
- 1 tbsp green curry paste
- 4 cups vegetable broth
- 1 lb butternut squash, cubed
- Sea salt and pepper to taste
- ¼ cup coconut milk
- 2 tbsp cilantro, minced

Directions:
1. Warm the olive oil in a pot over medium heat. Place the onion, garlic, and ginger and soften for 5 minutes. Add vegetable broth, butternut squash, green curry paste, salt, and pepper and simmer for 10-15 minutes until the squash is soft. Add coconut milk and purée with a stick blender. Garnish with cilantro. Serve warm.

Nutrition Info:
- Per Serving: Calories: 100;Fat: 8g;Protein: 1g;Carbs: 10g.

Dairy-free Split Pea Soup

Servings: 8 | Cooking Time: 4 To 8 Hours

Ingredients:
- 6½ cups water
- 2½ cups green or yellow split peas, well rinsed
- 2 small sweet potatoes, cut into ½-inch dice
- 1 tablespoon thyme, dried
- 1½ teaspoons salt, plus additional as needed

Directions:
1. Combine the water, split peas, sweet potatoes, thyme, and salt in a slow cooker.
2. For 8 hours or on high for 4 hours, cover and cook on low.
3. Blend half or all of the soup using an immersion blender or in a regular blender, working in batches as needed, and taking care of the hot liquid.
4. Taste and adjust the seasoning, if needed.

Nutrition Info:
- Per Serving: Calories: 51 ;Fat: 3g;Protein: 1g ;Carbs: 12g .

Creamy Soup With Broccoli

Servings: 6 | Cooking Time: 25 Minutes

Ingredients:
- 1 onion, finely chopped
- 4 garlic cloves, finely chopped
- 5 cups plus 2 tablespoons water, divided
- 1½ teaspoons sea salt, plus additional as needed
- 4 broccoli heads with stalks, heads cut into florets, and stalks roughly chopped
- 1 cup cashews, soaked in water for 4 hours

Directions:
1. Sauté the onion and garlic in 2 tablespoons of water in a large pot set over medium heat for about 5 minutes, or until soft.
2. Add the remaining 5 cups of water, salt, and broccoli. Bring to

a boil. Cover and reduce the heat to low. Simmer for 20 minutes.
3. Drain and rinse the cashews. Transfer them to a blender.
4. Add the soup to the blender. Blend until smooth, working in batches if necessary, and taking care of the hot liquid. Taste, and adjust the seasoning if necessary.

Nutrition Info:
- Per Serving: Calories: 224 ;Fat: 11g ;Protein: 11g ;Carbs: 26g .

Broccoli Cream Soup With Peanuts

Servings: 6 | Cooking Time: 40 Minutes

Ingredients:
- 3 tbsp extra-virgin olive oil
- 10 oz broccoli florets
- 1 onion, finely chopped
- 4 garlic cloves, chopped
- 2 tsp ground coriander
- 2 tsp ground cumin
- ½ tsp cayenne pepper
- Sea salt to taste
- 4 oz baby spinach
- 2 tbsp peanuts, chopped

Directions:
1. Warm the olive oil in a large pot over medium heat and sauté the onion and garlic for 5 minutes or until the onion has started to soften. Add the broccoli, salt, and 6 cups of water. Bring to a boil, then reduce the heat to low. Simmer for 20 minutes. Stir in baby spinach, ground coriander, cumin, and cayenne pepper and simmer for 2 minutes until the spinach has wilted. Puree the soup with a stick blender until creamy and smooth. Top the soup with peanuts and serve immediately.

Nutrition Info:
- Per Serving: Calories: 225;Fat: 10g;Protein: 10g;Carbs: 25g.

Shallot Lentil Soup With Walnuts

Servings: 4 | Cooking Time: 30 Minutes

Ingredients:
- 2 tbsp extra-virgin olive oil
- 3 shallots, chopped
- 3 cups vegetable broth
- 1 cup apple juice
- 4 cups fresh spinach
- ½ cup lentils
- ¼ tsp ground allspice
- Sea salt and pepper to taste
- 1 cup soy milk
- ¼ cup walnuts, chopped

Directions:
1. Heat the oil in a pot over medium heat. Place in the shallots and sauté for 3 minutes. Add in vegetable, apple juice, spinach, allspice, salt, and pepper. Bring to a boil, lower the heat and simmer for 10 minutes. With an immersion blender, pulse the soup until purée. Mix in soy milk and heat until hot. Top with walnuts to serve.

Nutrition Info:
- Per Serving: Calories: 190;Fat: 12g;Protein: 5g;Carbs: 18g.

Chickpea & Vegetable Soup

Servings: 5 | Cooking Time: 35 Minutes

Ingredients:
- 2 tbsp extra-virgin olive oil
- 1 onion, chopped
- 1 carrot, chopped
- 1 celery stalk, chopped
- 1 eggplant, chopped
- 1 can diced tomatoes
- 2 tbsp tomato paste
- 1 can chickpeas
- 2 tsp smoked paprika
- 1 tsp ground cumin
- 1 tsp za'atar spice
- ¼ tsp cayenne pepper
- 6 cups vegetable broth
- 4 oz whole-wheat vermicelli

Directions:
1. Heat oil in a pot over medium heat. Sauté the onion, carrot, and celery for 5 minutes. Add the eggplant, tomatoes, tomato paste, chickpeas, paprika, cumin, za'atar spice, and cayenne pepper. Stir in broth and salt. Bring to a boil and simmer for 15 minutes. Add in vermicelli and cook for another 5 minutes. Serve warm.

Nutrition Info:
- Per Serving: Calories: 290;Fat: 8g;Protein: 9g;Carbs: 50g.

Vegetable Bean Soup

Servings: 6 | Cooking Time: 50 Minutes

Ingredients:
- 3 tbsp extra-virgin olive oil
- 1 onion, chopped
- 2 carrots, chopped
- 1 sweet potato, chopped
- 1 yellow bell pepper, diced
- 2 garlic cloves, minced
- 4 tomatoes, chopped
- 6 cups vegetable broth
- 1 bay leaf
- Sea salt to taste
- 1 tsp cayenne pepper
- 1 can white beans
- 4 oz whole-wheat pasta
- ¼ tsp turmeric

Directions:
1. Heat the oil in a pot over medium heat. Place onion, carrots, sweet potato, bell pepper, and garlic. Cook for 5 minutes. Add in tomatoes, broth, bay leaf, salt, and cayenne pepper. Stir and bring to a boil. Lower the heat and simmer for 10 minutes. Put in white beans and simmer for 15 more minutes. Cook the pasta in a pot with boiling salted water and turmeric for 8-10 minutes, until pasta is al dente. Strain and transfer to the soup. Discard the bay leaf. Spoon into a bowl and serve.

Nutrition Info:
- Per Serving: Calories: 165;Fat: 7g;Protein: 3g;Carbs: 23g.

Daikon & Sweet Potato Soup

Servings: 6 | Cooking Time: 40 Minutes

Ingredients:
- 6 cups water
- 2 tsp olive oil
- 1 chopped onion
- 3 garlic cloves, minced
- 1 tbsp thyme
- 2 tsp paprika
- 2 cups chopped daikon
- 2 cups diced sweet potatoes
- 2 cups chopped parsnips
- ½ tsp sea salt
- 1 cup fresh mint, chopped
- ½ avocado
- 2 tbsp balsamic vinegar
- 2 tbsp pumpkin seeds

Directions:
1. Heat the oil in a pot and place onion and garlic. Sauté for 3 minutes. Add in thyme, paprika, daikon, sweet potato, parsnips, water, and salt. Bring to a boil and cook for 30 minutes. Remove the soup to a food processor and add in balsamic vinegar; purée until smooth. Top with mint and pumpkin seeds to serve.

Nutrition Info:
- Per Serving: Calories: 150;Fat: 6g;Protein: 22g;Carbs: 24g.

Broccoli Fennel Soup

Servings: 4 | Cooking Time: 25 Minutes

Ingredients:
- 1 fennel bulb, chopped
- 10 oz broccoli florets
- 3 cups vegetable stock
- Sea salt and pepper to taste
- 1 garlic clove
- 1 cup coconut cream
- 2 tbsp extra-virgin olive oil
- 1 tbsp chopped oregano

Directions:
1. Put the fennel and broccoli into a pot, and cover with the vegetable stock. Bring the ingredients to a boil over medium heat until the vegetables are soft, about 10 minutes. Season the liquid with salt and black pepper, and drop in the garlic. Simmer the soup for 5 to 7 minutes and turn the heat off. Pour the coconut cream, olive oil, and oregano into the soup; puree the ingredients with an immersion blender until completely smooth. Adjust the taste with salt and black pepper. Serve immediately.

Nutrition Info:
- Per Serving: Calories: 305;Fat: 28g;Protein: 5g;Carbs: 14g.

Spinach & Kale Soup With Fried Collards

Servings: 4 | Cooking Time: 20 Minutes

Ingredients:
- 4 tbsp extra-virgin olive oil
- 1 cup spinach, chopped
- 1 cup fresh kale, chopped
- 1 large avocado
- 3 ½ cups coconut cream
- 4 cups vegetable broth
- 3 tbsp chopped mint leaves
- Sea salt and pepper to taste
- Juice from 1 lime
- 1 cup collard greens
- 2 garlic cloves, minced
- ¼ tsp cardamom powder

Directions:
1. Warm half of the olive oil in a saucepan over medium heat and sauté spinach and kale for 5 minutes. Turn the heat off. Add the avocado, coconut cream, vegetable broth, salt, and pepper. Puree the ingredients with an immersion blender until smooth. Pour the lime juice.
2. Melt the remaining olive oil in a pan and add the collard greens, garlic, and cardamom; sauté until the garlic is fragrant and has achieved a golden brown color, about 4 minutes. Fetch the soup into serving bowls and garnish with fried collards and mint. Serve warm.

Nutrition Info:
- Per Serving: Calories: 920;Fat: 94g;Protein: 10g;Carbs: 25g.

Yummy Spiced Soup With Almond And Sweet Potato

Servings: 4 To 6

Cooking Time: 6 To 8 Hours

Ingredients:
- 4 cups vegetable broth, plus more if needed
- 1 can tomatoes, 15 ounces and diced
- 2 medium sweet potatoes, peeled and diced
- 1 medium onion, diced
- 1 jalapeño pepper, seeded and diced
- ½ cup almond butter, unsalted
- ½ teaspoon sea salt
- ½ teaspoon garlic powder
- ½ teaspoon turmeric, ground
- ½ teaspoon ginger, ground
- ¼ teaspoon cinnamon, ground
- Pinch nutmeg, ground
- ½ cup coconut milk, full-fat

Directions:
1. Combine the broth, tomatoes, sweet potatoes, onion, jalapeño, almond butter, salt, garlic powder, turmeric, ginger, cinnamon, and nutmeg in your slow cooker.
2. Cover the cooker and set it to low. Cook for 6 to 8 hours.
3. After cooking, stir in the coconut milk.
4. Purée the soup using an immersion blender until smooth and serve.

Nutrition Info:
- Per Serving: Calories: 358 ;Fat: 23g ;Protein: 7g ;Carbs: 34g .

Classy Soup With Carrot And Ginger

Servings: 6 To 8

Cooking Time: 30 Minutes

Ingredients:
- 1 large onion, peeled and roughly chopped
- 4½ cups plus 2 tablespoons water, divided
- 8 carrots, peeled and roughly chopped
- 1½-inch piece thin fresh ginger, sliced
- 1¼ teaspoons sea salt
- 2 cups coconut milk, unsweetened

Directions:
1. Sauté the onion in 2 tablespoons of water for about 5 minutes, or until soft in a large pot set over medium heat.
2. Add the carrots, the remaining 4½ cups of water, the ginger, and salt. Bring to a boil. Reduce the heat to low and cover the pot. Simmer for 20 minutes.
3. Stir in the coconut milk and for 4 to 5 minutes, let it heat.

4. Blend the soup in a blender until creamy, working in batches if necessary and taking care of the hot liquid.

Nutrition Info:
- Per Serving: Calories: 228 ;Fat: 19g ;Protein: 3g ;Carbs: 15g .

Spinach, Rice & Bean Soup

Servings: 6 | Cooking Time: 45 Minutes

Ingredients:
- 6 cups baby spinach
- 2 tbsp extra-virgin olive oil
- 1 onion, chopped
- 2 garlic cloves, minced
- 15 oz canned black-eyed peas
- 6 cups vegetable broth
- Sea salt and pepper to taste
- ½ cup brown rice

Directions:
1. Heat oil in a pot over medium heat. Place the onion and garlic and sauté for 3 minutes. Pour in broth and season with salt and pepper. Bring to a boil, then lower the heat and stir in rice. Simmer for 15 minutes. Stir in peas and spinach and cook for another 5 minutes. Serve warm.

Nutrition Info:
- Per Serving: Calories: 200;Fat: 5g;Protein: 1g;Carbs: 32g.

Dairy-free Rice Soup With Mushrooms

Servings: 4 To 6

Cooking Time: 6 To 8 Hours

Ingredients:
- 1½ cups uncooked wild rice
- 6 cups vegetable broth
- 2 carrots, diced
- 1 celery stalk, diced
- ½ medium onion, diced
- ¼ cup porcini mushrooms, dried
- 1 tablespoon extra-virgin olive oil
- 1 teaspoon sea salt
- ½ teaspoon garlic powder
- ½ teaspoon thyme leaves, dried
- 1 bay leaf
- Freshly ground black pepper

Directions:
1. Combine the rice, broth, carrots, celery, onion, mushrooms, olive oil, salt, garlic powder, thyme, and bay leaf in your slow cooker and season with pepper.
2. Cover the cooker and set it to low. Cook for 6 to 8 hours.
3. Remove and discard the bay leaf before serving.

Nutrition Info:
- Per Serving: Calories: 425 ;Fat: 4g ;Protein: 16g ;Carbs: 78g.

Vegetable & Black Bean Soup

Servings: 4 | Cooking Time: 50 Minutes

Ingredients:
- 2 tbsp extra-virgin olive oil
- 1 onion, chopped
- 1 celery stalk, chopped
- 2 medium carrots, chopped
- 1 green bell pepper, diced
- 2 garlic cloves, minced
- 2 tomatoes, chopped
- 4 cups vegetable broth
- 1 can black beans

- 1 tsp dried thyme
- ¼ tsp cayenne pepper
- 1 tbsp minced cilantro

Directions:
1. Heat the oil in a pot over medium heat. Place in onion, celery, carrots, bell pepper, garlic, and tomatoes. Sauté for 5 minutes, stirring often. Stir in broth, beans, thyme, salt, and cayenne. Bring to a boil and simmer for 15 minutes. Transfer the soup to a food processor and pulse until smooth. Serve topped with cilantro.

Nutrition Info:
- Per Serving: Calories: 195;Fat: 8g;Protein: 2g;Carbs: 26g.

Chicken & Ginger Soup

Servings: 4 | Cooking Time: 20 Minutes

Ingredients:
- 2 cups skinless leftover roasted chicken, diced
- 4 cups no-salt-added chicken broth
- 1 carrot, chopped
- 2 tbsp extra-virgin olive oil
- 1 onion, chopped
- 1 red bell pepper, chopped
- 1 tbsp grated fresh ginger
- Sea salt and pepper to taste

Directions:
1. Warm the olive oil in a pot over medium heat and add the onion, red bell peppers, carrot, and ginger. Sauté for 5 minutes until the veggies are soft. Mix in chicken, chicken broth, salt, and pepper. Bring to a boil, reduce the heat, and simmer for 5 minutes. Serve immediately.

Nutrition Info:
- Per Serving: Calories: 340;Fat: 16g;Protein: 7g;Carbs: 12g.

Spinach Soup With Gnocchi

Servings: 4 | Cooking Time: 25 Minutes

Ingredients:
- 1 tsp olive oil
- 1 cup red bell peppers
- Sea salt and pepper to taste
- 2 garlic cloves, minced
- 2 carrots, chopped
- 3 cups vegetable broth
- 1 cup gnocchi
- ¾ cup non-dairy milk
- ¼ cup nutritional yeast
- 2 cups chopped spinach
- ¼ cup black olives, chopped
- Croutons, for topping

Directions:
1. Heat the oil in a pot over medium heat. Place in bell peppers, garlic, carrots, and salt and cook for 5 minutes. Stir in broth. Bring to a boil. Put in gnocchi, cook for 10 minutes. Add in spinach and cook for 5 minutes. Stir in milk, nutritional yeast, and olives. Top with croutons.

Nutrition Info:
- Per Serving: Calories: 205;Fat: 7g;Protein: 7g;Carbs: 28g.

Spinach & Mushroom Soup

Servings: 4 | Cooking Time: 15 Minutes

Ingredients:
- ½ tsp fish sauce
- 1 cup baby spinach
- 4 scallions, sliced
- 4 cups vegetable broth
- 1 cup mushrooms, sliced
- 3 tbsp miso paste

Directions:

1. Place the fish sauce, 3 cups of water, vegetable broth, and mushrooms in a saucepan over high heat and bring to a boil. Turn the heat off. In a bowl, whisk miso paste and 1/2 cup of vegetable broth until the miso dissolved. Pour it into the pan and combine. Mix in scallions and spinach before serving.

Nutrition Info:
- Per Serving: Calories: 45;Fat: 0g;Protein: 2g;Carbs: 9g.

Special Miso Soup

Servings: 4 | Cooking Time: 5 Minutes

Ingredients:
- 4 cups vegetable broth
- 2 slices ginger root, peeled
- 2 slices turmeric root, peeled
- 1 garlic clove, lightly crushed
- 3 to 4 tablespoons white miso
- ½ cup cubed firm tofu
- 1 scallion, thinly sliced

Directions:

1. Into a large pot, pour the vegetable broth and add the ginger root, turmeric root, and garlic. Bring to a boil over medium-high heat. Reduce to a simmer and simmer for 5 minutes.

2. Remove and discard the ginger root, turmeric root, and garlic using a slotted spoon.

3. Put the miso in a small bowl, add one ladleful of hot broth, and whisk until smooth. Stir the miso broth mixture back into the pot and mix well.

4. Divide the broth among four serving bowls.

5. Divide the tofu and scallion among the bowls, and serve.

Nutrition Info:
- Per Serving: Calories: 40 ;Fat: 1g ;Protein: 3g ;Carbs: 4g .

Celery & Sweet Potato Soup

Servings: 6 | Cooking Time: 55 Minutes

Ingredients:
- 2 tbsp extra-virgin olive oil
- 1 onion, chopped
- 1 carrot, chopped
- 1 celery stalk, chopped
- 2 garlic cloves, minced
- 1 golden beet, diced
- 1 red bell pepper, chopped
- 1 sweet potato, diced
- 6 cups vegetable broth
- 1 tsp dried thyme
- Sea salt and pepper to taste
- 1 tbsp lemon juice

Directions:

1. Heat the oil in a pot over medium heat. Place the onion, carrot, celery, and garlic. Cook for 5 minutes or until softened. Stir in beet, bell pepper, and sweet potato, cook uncovered for 1 minute. Pour in the broth and thyme. Season with salt and pepper. Cook

for 45 minutes until the vegetables are tender. Serve topped with lemon juice.

Nutrition Info:
- Per Serving: Calories: 100;Fat: 5g;Protein: 1g;Carbs: 14g.

Italian Bean Soup

Servings: 6 | Cooking Time: 1 Hour 25 Minutes

Ingredients:
- 3 tbsp extra-virgin olive oil
- 2 celery stalks, chopped
- 2 carrots, chopped
- 3 shallots, chopped
- 3 garlic cloves, minced
- ½ cup brown rice
- 6 cups vegetable broth
- 1 can diced tomatoes
- 2 bay leaves
- Sea salt and pepper to taste
- 2 cans white beans
- ¼ cup chopped basil

Directions:

1. Heat oil in a pot over medium heat. Place celery, carrots, shallots, and garlic and cook for 5 minutes. Add in brown rice, broth, tomatoes, bay leaves, salt, and pepper. Bring to a boil, then lower the heat and simmer uncovered for 20 minutes. Stir in beans and basil and cook for 5 minutes. Discard bay leaves. Sprinkle with basil and serve.

Nutrition Info:
- Per Serving: Calories: 180;Fat: 8g;Protein: 2g;Carbs: 25g.

Green Bean & Zucchini Velouté

Servings: 6 | Cooking Time: 30 Minutes

Ingredients:
- 2 tbsp minced jarred pimiento
- 3 tbsp extra-virgin olive oil
- 1 onion, chopped
- 1 garlic clove, minced
- 2 cups green beans
- 4 cups vegetable broth
- 3 medium zucchini, sliced
- ½ tsp dried marjoram
- ½ cup plain almond milk

Directions:

1. Heat oil in a pot and sauté onion and garlic for 5 minutes. Add in green beans and broth. Cook for 10 minutes. Stir in zucchini and cook for 10 minutes. Transfer to a food processor and pulse until smooth. Return to the pot and mix in almond milk; cook until hot. Top with pimiento.

Nutrition Info:
- Per Serving: Calories: 95;Fat: 7g;Protein: 2g;Carbs: 8g.

Beef Stew With Sweet Potato Noodles

Servings: 4 | Cooking Time: 40 Minutes

Ingredients:
- 2 tbsp extra-virgin olive oil
- 1 yellow onion, diced
- 2 garlic cloves
- 2 sweet potatoes, spiralized
- 1 lb beef stew meat, cubed
- 1 can diced tomatoes
- 1 tsp chili powder
- ½ tsp ground cumin

- Salt
- Sea salt and pepper to taste
- 2 cups beef broth
- ½ cup green beans, diced

Directions:
1. Warm the olive oil in the skillet over medium heat. Add the onion and garlic and sauté for 3 minutes until tender. Stir in the sweet potato noodles and sauté for 3-4 minutes or until fork-tender. Remove from the pot and set aside.
2. Add the cubed beef to the same pot and cook for 5 minutes, stirring often until browned. Add the broth and bring to a boil. Add the green beans, reduce the heat, and continue to cook for 5-10 more minutes. Return the sautéed vegetables and noodles to the pot and simmer for 10 more minutes. Serve immediately.

Nutrition Info:
- Per Serving: Calories: 575;Fat: 19g;Protein: 43g;Carbs: 57.9g.

Mushroom & Bean Stew

Servings: 4 | Cooking Time: 35 Minutes

Ingredients:
- 8 oz porcini mushrooms, sliced
- 1 can cannellini beans, drained
- 2 tbsp extra-virgin olive oil
- 1 onion, chopped
- 1 carrot, chopped
- 2 garlic cloves, minced
- 1 red bell pepper, chopped
- ½ cup capers
- 1 zucchini, chopped
- 1 can diced tomatoes
- 1 cup vegetable broth
- Sea salt and pepper to taste
- 3 cups fresh baby spinach
- ½ tsp dried basil

Directions:
1. Heat oil in a pot and sauté onion, carrot, garlic, mushrooms, and bell pepper for 5 minutes. Stir in capers, zucchini, tomatoes, broth, salt, and pepper. Bring to a boil, then lower the heat and simmer for 20 minutes. Add in beans and basil. Simmer for 2-3 minutes. Serve.

Nutrition Info:
- Per Serving: Calories: 300;Fat: 8g;Protein: 9g;Carbs: 58g.

Cold Cantaloupe Soup

Servings: 4 | Cooking Time: 5 Minutes

Ingredients:
- 2 tbsp matcha powder
- 2 cups cantaloupe, cubed
- 2 tbsp chopped mint
- 2 tbsp honey
- ¼ tsp ground cinnamon
- ½ cup non-fat greek yogurt

Directions:
1. Place the matcha powder, cantaloupe, honey, cinnamon ½ cup of water, and yogurt in your food processor or blender and pulse until smooth. Serve topped with mint.

Nutrition Info:
- Per Serving: Calories: 170;Fat: 1g;Protein: 4g;Carbs: 41g.

Habanero Bean Soup With Brown Rice

Servings: 6 | Cooking Time: 30 Minutes

Ingredients:
- ¼ cup sun-dried tomatoes, chopped
- 2 tbsp extra-virgin olive oil
- 3 garlic cloves, minced
- 1 tbsp chili powder
- 1 tsp dried oregano
- 1 can kidney beans
- 1 habanero pepper, chopped
- 6 cups vegetable broth
- Sea salt and pepper to taste
- ½ cup brown rice
- 1 tbsp chopped cilantro

Directions:
1. Heat the oil in a pot over medium heat. Place in garlic and sauté for 1 minute. Add in chili powder, oregano, beans, habanero, tomatoes, broth, rice, salt, and pepper. Cook for 20-30 minutes. Garnish with cilantro to serve.

Nutrition Info:
- Per Serving: Calories: 285;Fat: 6g;Protein: 5g;Carbs: 46g.

Cannellini Bean Soup

Servings: 4 | Cooking Time: 8 Hours 15 Minutes

Ingredients:
- 2 cans cannellini beans, rinsed and drained
- 4 cups vegetable broth
- 2 onions, thinly sliced
- ¼ cup extra-virgin olive oil
- Sea salt and pepper to taste
- ½ tsp garlic powder
- 1 bay leaf

Directions:
1. Add onions, oil, beans, broth, garlic powder, bay leaf, salt and pepper to your slow cooker. Cover and cook for 8 hours on "Low". Remove and discard the bay leaf. Serve.

Nutrition Info:
- Per Serving: Calories: 330;Fat: 15g;Protein: 10g;Carbs: 39g.

Parsley Tomato Soup

Servings: 4 | Cooking Time: 25 Minutes

Ingredients:
- 4 cups no-salt-added vegetable broth
- 2 tbsp parsley, chopped
- 2 tbsp extra-virgin olive oil
- 1 onion, finely chopped
- 2 garlic cloves, minced
- 2 cans diced tomatoes
- Sea salt and pepper to taste

Directions:
1. Warm the olive oil in a pot over medium heat and place the onion. Cook for 7 minutes until browned. Add in garlic and cook for another 30 seconds. Stir in tomatoes, vegetable broth, salt, and pepper and simmer for 5 minutes. Puree the mixture with an immersion blender until smooth. Serve warm topped with parsley.

Nutrition Info:
- Per Serving: Calories: 240;Fat: 8g;Protein: 11g;Carbs: 36g.

Sweet French Onion Soup With White Bean

Servings: 4 To 6

Cooking Time: 3 Hours To 4 Hours

Ingredients:
- 2 large onions, thinly sliced
- ¼ cup extra-virgin olive oil
- ¾ teaspoon sea salt
- 2 cans cannellini beans, 14 ounces, rinsed and drained well
- 4 cups vegetable broth
- ½ teaspoon garlic powder
- ½ teaspoon thyme leaves, dried
- 1 bay leaf
- Freshly ground black pepper

Directions:
1. Combine the onions, olive oil, and salt in your slow cooker.
2. Cover the cooker and set it to high. Cook for 3 hours to allow the onions to caramelize.
3. Stir the onions well and add the beans, broth, garlic powder, thyme, and bay leaf, and season with pepper.
4. Re-cover the cooker and set it to low. Cook for 4 hours.
5. Remove and discard the bay leaf before serving.

Nutrition Info:
- Per Serving: Calories: 328 ;Fat: 14g ;Protein: 11g ;Carbs: 39g .

Gingery Soup With Carrots & Celery

Servings: 6 | Cooking Time: 40 Minutes

Ingredients:
- 3 tbsp extra-virgin olive oil
- 2 celery stalks, chopped
- 2 carrots, chopped
- 2 onions, chopped
- ½-inch piece ginger, sliced
- Sea salt to taste
- 2 cups coconut milk
- 4 scallions, chopped

Directions:
1. Warm the olive oil in a large pot over medium heat and sauté the celery, carrots, onions, ginger, and salt for 5 minutes or until tender. Add 5 cups of water and bring to a boil. Reduce the heat and simmer for 20 minutes. Pour the soup into a blender and pulse until creamy and smooth. Stir in coconut milk. Top with scallions to serve.

Nutrition Info:
- Per Serving: Calories: 230;Fat: 20g;Protein: 3g;Carbs: 15g.

Chili Gazpacho

Servings: 4 | Cooking Time: 15 Minutes

Ingredients:
- 2 tbsp extra-virgin olive oil
- 1 red onion, chopped
- 6 tomatoes, chopped
- 1 red bell pepper, diced
- 2 garlic cloves, minced
- juice of 1 lemon
- 2 tbsp chopped fresh basil
- ½ tsp chili pepper

Directions:
1. Place the olive oil, half of the onion, half of the tomato, half of the bell pepper, garlic, lemon juice, basil, chili pepper, and 2 cups of water in your food processor. Season with salt and pepper. Blitz until smooth. Transfer to a bowl and add in the reserved onion, tomatoes, and bell pepper. Let chill in the fridge before serving.

Nutrition Info:
- Per Serving: Calories: 120;Fat: 7g;Protein: 3g;Carbs: 13g.

Mixed Mushroom Soup

Servings: 4 | Cooking Time: 40 Minutes

Ingredients:
- 5 oz button mushrooms, chopped
- ½ cup cremini mushrooms, chopped
- ½ cup shiitake mushrooms, chopped
- 1 vegetable stock cube, crushed
- 2 tbsp extra-virgin olive oil
- 1 onion, finely chopped
- 1 clove garlic, minced
- ½ lb celery root, chopped
- ½ tsp dried rosemary
- 1 tbsp plain vinegar
- 1 cup coconut cream
- 4 leaves basil, chopped

Directions:
1. Place a saucepan over medium heat, warm the olive oil, then sauté the onion, garlic, mushrooms, and celery root until golden brown and fragrant, about 6 minutes. Fetch out some mushrooms and reserve for garnishing. Add the rosemary, 3 cups of water, stock cube, and vinegar. Stir the mixture and bring it to a boil for 6 minutes. After, reduce the heat and simmer the soup for 15 minutes or until the celery is soft. Mix in the coconut cream and puree the ingredients using an immersion blender. Simmer for 2 minutes. Spoon the soup into serving bowls, garnish with the reserved mushrooms and basil. Serve.

Nutrition Info:
- Per Serving: Calories: 290;Fat: 28g;Protein: 7g;Carbs: 9g.

Fennel & Parsnip Bisque

Servings: 6 | Cooking Time: 30 Minutes

Ingredients:
- 1 tbsp extra-virgin olive oil
- 2 green onions, chopped
- ½ fennel bulb, sliced
- 2 large carrots, shredded
- 2 parsnips, shredded
- 1 turnip, chopped
- 2 garlic cloves, minced
- ½ tsp dried thyme
- ¼ tsp dried marjoram
- 6 cups vegetable broth
- 1 cup plain soy milk
- 1 tbsp minced fresh parsley

Directions:
1. Heat the oil in a pot over medium heat. Place in green onions, fennel, carrots, parsnips, turnip, and garlic. Sauté for 5 minutes until softened. Add in thyme, marjoram, and broth. Bring to a boil, lower the heat, and simmer for 20 minutes. Transfer to a blender and pulse the soup until smooth. Mix in soy milk. Top with parsley to serve.

Nutrition Info:
- Per Serving: Calories: 115;Fat: 3g;Protein: 2g;Carbs: 20g.

Tofu Miso Soup

Servings: 4 | Cooking Time: 15 Minutes

Ingredients:
- 1 tbsp extra-virgin olive oil
- 4 cups vegetable broth
- 1-inch peeled ginger root
- 2 peeled turmeric root slices
- 1 garlic clove, crushed
- 3 tbsp white miso
- ½ cup cubed firm tofu
- 1 red chili, sliced
- 1 scallion, thinly sliced

Directions:
1. Place the olive oil, vegetable broth, ginger root, turmeric root, and garlic in a pot over medium heat and bring to a boil. Low the heat and simmer for 5 minutes. Drain and reserve the cooking broth. Whisk 1 ladleful of the hot broth with miso in a bowl, then pour it in the remaining broth. Add the tofu and stir well to combine. Ladle into bowls and garnish with red chili and scallions. Serve.

Nutrition Info:
- Per Serving: Calories: 50;Fat: 2g;Protein: 3g;Carbs: 5g.

Homemade Succotash Stew

Servings: 4 | Cooking Time: 30 Minutes

Ingredients:
- 1 cup canned chickpeas
- 2 tbsp extra-virgin olive oil
- 1 onion, chopped
- 2 carrots, sliced
- 1 can diced tomatoes
- 16 oz frozen succotash
- 2 cups vegetable broth
- 2 tsp low-sodium soy sauce
- 1 tsp dry mustard
- ½ tsp dried thyme
- ½ tsp ground allspice
- ¼ tsp cayenne pepper
- Sea salt and pepper to taste

Directions:
1. Heat oil in a saucepan. Place in onion and sauté for 3 minutes. Stir in chickpeas, carrots, tomatoes, succotash, broth, soy sauce, mustard, sugar, thyme, allspice, and cayenne pepper. Sprinkle with salt and pepper. Bring to a boil and simmer for 20 minutes. Serve hot and enjoy!

Nutrition Info:
- Per Serving: Calories: 390;Fat: 12g;Protein: 16g;Carbs: 59g.

Mushroom & Tofu Soup

Servings: 4 | Cooking Time: 20 Minutes

Ingredients:
- 4 cups water
- 2 tsp low-sodium soy sauce
- 4 white mushrooms, sliced
- ¼ cup minced green onions
- 3 tbsp tahini
- 6 oz extra-firm tofu, diced

Directions:
1. Pour the water and soy sauce into a pot. Bring to a boil. Add in mushrooms and green onions. Lower the heat and simmer for 10 minutes. In a bowl, combine ½ cup of hot soup with tahini. Pour the mixture into the pot and simmer 2 minutes, but do not boil.

Stir in tofu. Serve.

Nutrition Info:
- Per Serving: Calories: 160;Fat: 11g;Protein: 7g;Carbs: 7g.

Vegetable Soup With Vermicelli

Servings: 6 | Cooking Time: 20 Minutes

Ingredients:
- 1 tbsp extra-virgin olive oil
- 1 onion, chopped
- 4 garlic cloves, minced
- 1 can diced tomatoes
- 6 cups vegetable broth
- 8 oz vermicelli
- 5 oz baby spinach

Directions:
1. Warm the oil in a pot over medium heat. Place in onion and garlic and cook for 3 minutes. Stir in tomatoes, broth, salt, and pepper. Bring to a boil, then lower the heat and simmer for 5 minutes. Pour in vermicelli and spinach and cook for another 5 minutes. Serve warm.

Nutrition Info:
- Per Serving: Calories: 180;Fat: 3g;Protein: 1g;Carbs: 39g.

Green Chili Bean Stew

Servings: 4 | Cooking Time: 40 Minutes

Ingredients:
- 1 can diced green chiles, drained
- 2 cups cooked kidney beans
- 2 tbsp extra-virgin olive oil
- 1 yellow onion, chopped
- 2 carrots, sliced
- 3 garlic cloves, minced
- 1 tsp grated fresh ginger
- ½ tsp ground cumin
- 1 tsp ras el hanout
- 1 can diced tomatoes
- 1 ½ cups vegetable broth
- Sea salt and pepper to taste
- 3 cups eggplants, chopped
- 2 tbsp chopped peanuts

Directions:
1. Heat the oil in a pot over medium heat. Place the onion, garlic, ginger, and carrots and sauté for 5 minutes until tender. Stir in cumin, ras el hanout, beans, tomatoes, chiles, and broth. Season with salt and pepper. Bring to a boil and simmer for 20 minutes. Add in eggplants and cook for 10 minutes. Serve garnished with peanuts.

Nutrition Info:
- Per Serving: Calories: 400;Fat: 17g;Protein: 12g;Carbs: 52g.

Gingered Broccoli Soup

Servings: 4 | Cooking Time: 50 Minutes

Ingredients:
- 1 onion, chopped
- 1 tbsp minced fresh ginger
- 2 tsp olive oil
- 2 carrots, chopped
- 10 oz broccoli florets
- 1 cup coconut milk
- 3 cups vegetable broth
- ½ tsp turmeric
- Sea salt and pepper to taste

Directions:

1. In a pot over medium heat, place the onion, ginger, and olive oil, cook for 4 minutes. Add in carrots, broccoli, broth, turmeric, pepper, and salt. Bring to a boil and cook for 15 minutes. Transfer the soup to a food processor and blend until smooth. Stir in coconut milk and serve.

Nutrition Info:
- Per Serving: Calories: 200;Fat: 17g;Protein: 3g;Carbs: 12g.

Cauliflower Dill Soup

Servings: 4 | Cooking Time: 30 Minutes

Ingredients:
- 2 tbsp coconut oil
- ½ lb celery root, trimmed
- 1 garlic clove, minced
- 1 white onion
- ¼ cup fresh dill, chopped
- 1 tsp cumin powder
- 10 oz cauliflower florets
- 4 cups vegetable stock
- Juice from 1 lemon
- ¼ cup coconut cream

Directions:

1. Set a pot over medium heat, add the coconut oil and allow heating until no longer shimmering. Add the celery root, garlic clove, and onion; sauté the vegetables until fragrant and soft, about 5 minutes. Stir in the dill and cumin and fry further for 1 minute. Mix in the cauliflower florets and vegetable stock. Cook the soup for 12-15 minutes or until the cauliflower is soft. Turn the heat off. Add the lemon juice. Puree the ingredients with an immersion blender until smooth. Mix in coconut cream and season the soup with salt and black pepper. Serve warm.

Nutrition Info:
- Per Serving: Calories: 125;Fat: 8g;Protein: 2g;Carbs: 12g.

Hearty Stew With Kasha And Squash

Servings: 4 | Cooking Time: 4 Hours

Ingredients:
- 1 tablespoon extra-virgin olive oil
- 2 pounds winter squash, peeled and cubed
- 1 fennel bulb, sliced thin
- 2 leeks, white part only, sliced thin
- 2 garlic cloves, chopped
- 1 cup kasha, rinsed
- 1 teaspoon salt
- ½ teaspoon black pepper, freshly ground
- 3 cups water, or vegetable broth
- 4 cups chopped kale, thoroughly washed and stemmed

Directions:

1. Combine the olive oil, squash, fennel, leeks, garlic, kasha, salt, pepper, and water in the slow cooker. For 4 hours, set the cooker on high.

2. Stir in the kale before serving. The heat from the stew will wilt it, making it easy to chew and digest.

Nutrition Info:
- Per Serving: Calories: 325 ;Fat: 6g ;Protein: 12g ;Carbs: 60g .

Spanish Gazpacho

Servings: 4 | Cooking Time: 15 Minutes

Ingredients:
- 3 tbsp extra-virgin olive oil
- 2 garlic cloves, crushed

- Sea salt and pepper to taste
- 2 cucumbers
- 2 tsp lemon juice
- 2 lb plum tomatoes, diced
- 1 can diced tomatoes
- 1 cup tomato juice
- 2 tbsp chopped dill

Directions:

1. Pulse the garlic, olive oil, and salt in a food processor until paste-like consistency forms. Add in 1 cucumber and lemon juice. Blitz until smooth. Put in tomatoes, tomato juice, salt, and pepper. Blend until smooth. Put in a bowl and let chill in the fridge before serving.

Nutrition Info:
- Per Serving: Calories: 200;Fat: 12g;Protein: 5g;Carbs: 24g.

Tomato Lentil Stew

Servings: 4 | Cooking Time: 25 Minutes

Ingredients:
- 2 tsp olive oil
- 4 carrots, chopped
- 1 onion, chopped
- ½ green bell pepper, diced
- 1 tbsp paprika
- 2 garlic cloves, sliced
- 4 cups vegetable broth
- 1 can diced tomatoes
- 2 cans lentils

Directions:

1. Heat the oil in a pot over medium heat. Place in carrots, onion, bell pepper, paprika, and garlic. Sauté for 5 minutes until tender. Stir in broth, tomatoes, and lentils. Bring to a boil, then lower the heat and simmer for 15 minutes. Sprinkle with salt and pepper. Serve warm.

Nutrition Info:
- Per Serving: Calories: 225;Fat: 4g;Protein: 9g;Carbs: 46g.

Vegetable Chili

Servings: 4 | Cooking Time: 30 Minutes

Ingredients:
- 1 onion, chopped
- 1 cup vegetable broth
- 2 garlic cloves, minced
- 1 turnip, cubed
- 1 carrot, chopped
- 2 tsp olive oil
- 1 can tomatoes
- 1 tbsp tomato paste
- 1 can chickpeas
- 1 tsp chili powder
- Sea salt and pepper to taste
- ¼ cup parsley, chopped

Directions:

1. Heat oil in a pot over medium heat. Place in onion and garlic and sauté for 3 minutes. Add in turnip, carrot, tomatoes, broth, tomato paste, chickpeas, and chili; season. Simmer for 20 minutes. Top with parsley. Serve.

Nutrition Info:
- Per Serving: Calories: 180;Fat: 5g;Protein: 7g;Carbs: 30g.

Lime Pumpkin Soup

Servings: 4 | Cooking Time: 30 Minutes

Ingredients:
- 2 tsp olive oil
- 3 cups pumpkin, chopped
- 1 onion, chopped
- 1 garlic clove, minced
- 2 cups water
- 1 can black-eyed peas
- 2 tbsp lime juice
- 1 tbsp pure date sugar
- 1 tsp paprika
- 1 tbsp red pepper flakes
- 3 cups shredded cabbage
- 1 cup mushrooms, chopped

Directions:
1. Warm the oil in a pot over medium heat. Place in pumpkin, onion, garlic, and salt. Cook for 5 minutes. Stir in water, peas, lime juice, sugar, paprika, and pepper flakes. Bring to a boil and cook for 15 minutes. Add in cabbage and mushrooms and cook for 5 minutes. Serve.

Nutrition Info:
- Per Serving: Calories: 195;Fat: 3g;Protein: 29g;Carbs: 36g.

Chipotle Pumpkin Soup

Servings: 4 | Cooking Time: 25 Minutes

Ingredients:
- 2 tbsp sage leaves, minced
- 2 garlic cloves, sliced
- 1 onion, chopped
- 1 can pumpkin purée
- 4 cups vegetable broth
- 2 tbsp extra-virgin olive oil
- 2 tsp chipotle powder
- Sea salt and pepper to taste

Directions:
1. Warm the olive oil in a pot over medium heat. Add the onion and garlic and stir-fry for 3 minutes or until the onion browns. Pour in the pumpkin pur é e and vegetable broth, then sprinkle with chipotle powder, salt, and ground black pepper. Stir. Bring to a boil and simmer for 5 minutes. Serve garnished with chopped sage leaves.

Nutrition Info:
- Per Serving: Calories: 385;Fat: 20g;Protein: 11g;Carbs: 45g.

Kabocha Squash Soup

Servings: 4 | Cooking Time: 30 Minutes

Ingredients:
- 2 tbsp extra-virgin olive oil
- 1 onion, chopped
- ½ lb kabocha squash, diced
- 1 red bell pepper, chopped
- 2 cups vegetable broth
- 1 can coconut milk
- Sea salt and pepper to taste
- 2 tbsp chopped fresh cilantro

Directions:
1. Heat the olive oil in a pot over medium heat. Place in onion, squash, and bell pepper and sauté for 5 minutes. Stir in broth, salt, and pepper. Bring to a boil and simmer for 20 minutes. Blend the soup using an immersion blender. Stir in coconut milk. Top with cilantro and serve.

Nutrition Info:
- Per Serving: Calories: 160;Fat: 11g;Protein: 3g;Carbs: 15g.

Beef & Mushroom Rice Soup

Servings: 6 | Cooking Time: 40 Minutes

Ingredients:
- 1 lb stew beef meat, cubed
- 3 tbsp extra-virgin olive oil
- 1 onion, chopped
- 1 carrot, chopped
- 1 celery stalk, chopped
- 1 cup wild mushrooms, sliced
- ½ cup brown rice
- 7 cups vegetable broth
- 1 tsp dried dill weed
- Sea salt and pepper to taste

Directions:
1. Heat the oil in a pot over medium heat. Add the beef, onion, carrot, and celery and sauté for 6-8 minutes. Add in mushrooms, rice, broth, dill weed, salt, and pepper. Bring to a boil, then lower the heat and simmer uncovered for 30 minutes. Serve and enjoy!

Nutrition Info:
- Per Serving: Calories: 330;Fat: 11g;Protein: 21g;Carbs: 39g.

One-pot Chunky Beef Stew

Servings: 6 | Cooking Time: 35 Minutes

Ingredients:
- 2 tbsp extra-virgin olive oil
- 1 ½ lb sirloin steak, cubed
- 3 chopped sweet potatoes
- 4 baby carrots, sliced
- 1 celery stalk, sliced
- 1 small onion, chopped
- 4 cups beef broth
- 2 garlic cloves, minced
- 1 cup green peas
- ½ tsp dried thyme
- Sea salt and pepper to taste
- 3 tablespoons arrowroot

Directions:
1. Warm the extra-virgin olive oil in a pot over medium heat. Add the beef, sweet potatoes, baby carrots, celery, garlic, and onion and sauté for 5-8 minutes until the beef is browned. Pour in the broth and thyme. Bring to a boil, lower the heat, and simmer for 15 minutes.
2. Mix the arrowroot with 1 soup ladle in a small bowl and pour the slurry gradually into the pot, whisking continuously. Add the green peas and cook for 2-4 more minutes. Taste and adjust seasoning. Serve warm.

Nutrition Info:
- Per Serving: Calories: 396;Fat: 13g;Protein: 41g;Carbs: 27.6g.

Super Simple Stew With Mango And Black Bean

Servings: 4 | Cooking Time: 10 Minutes

Ingredients:
- 2 tablespoons coconut oil
- 1 onion, chopped
- 2 pieces of 15 ounces cans black beans, drained and rinsed
- 1 tablespoon chili powder
- 1 teaspoon salt

- ¼ teaspoon black pepper, freshly ground
- 1 cup water
- 2 ripe mangos, sliced thin
- ¼ cup chopped fresh cilantro, divided
- ¼ cup sliced scallions, divided

Directions:
1. Melt the coconut oil in a large pot over high heat.
2. Add the onion and sauté for 5 minutes.
3. Add the black beans, chili powder, salt, pepper, and water. Bring to a boil. Reduce the heat to simmer and cook for 5 minutes.
4. Remove the pot from the heat; stir in the mangos just before serving. Garnish each serving with cilantro and scallions.

Nutrition Info:
- Per Serving: Calories: 431 ; Fat: 9g ;Protein: 20g ;Carbs: 72g .

Minestrone Soup With Quinoa

Servings: 6 | Cooking Time: 30 Minutes

Ingredients:
- 14 oz canned cannellini beans, drained
- 3 tbsp extra-virgin olive oil
- 2 garlic cloves, minced
- 1 white onion, diced
- 2 carrots, chopped
- 2 celery stalks, diced
- 1 small zucchini, diced
- ½ red bell pepper, diced
- 5 cups vegetable broth
- 14 oz canned diced tomatoes
- 1 cup kale
- ½ cup quinoa, rinsed well
- 1 tbsp lemon juice
- 2 tsp dried rosemary
- 2 tsp dried thyme
- 1 bay leaf
- Sea salt and pepper to taste

Directions:
1. Warm the olive oil in a large pot over medium heat and sauté the garlic, onion, carrots, and celery for 3 minutes. Add the zucchini and red bell pepper, and sauté for 2 minutes. Stir in the broth, tomatoes, beans, kale, quinoa, lemon juice, rosemary, thyme, bay leaf, and salt, and season with black pepper. Bring to a simmer, reduce the heat to low, cover, and cook for 15 minutes, or until the quinoa is cooked. Remove the bay leaf. Serve hot.

Nutrition Info:
- Per Serving: Calories: 320;Fat: 5g;Protein: 17g;Carbs: 43g.

Chili Cannellini Bean Stew

Servings: 4 | Cooking Time: 40 Minutes

Ingredients:
- 2 cans cannellini beans
- 1 can mild chopped green chilies
- 2 tbsp extra-virgin olive oil
- 1 onion, chopped
- 1 can diced tomatoes
- 2 tbsp tamarind paste
- 1 cup vegetable broth
- 2 tbsp chili powder
- 1 tsp ground coriander
- ½ tsp ground cumin
- Sea salt and pepper to taste
- 1 cup green peas

Directions:

1. Heat the oil in a pot over medium heat. Place in the onion and sauté for 3 minutes until translucent. Stir in beans, tomatoes, and chilies. Cook for 5 minutes more. In a bowl, whisk the tamarind paste with broth. Pour the mixture into the pot. Stir in chili powder, coriander, cumin, salt, and pepper. Bring to a boil, then lower the heat and simmer for 20 minutes. Add in peas and cook for another 5 minutes. Serve warm and enjoy!

Nutrition Info:
- Per Serving: Calories: 400;Fat: 10g;Protein: 7g;Carbs: 69g.

Lime Lentil Soup

Servings: 2 | Cooking Time: 35 Minutes

Ingredients:
- 1 tsp olive oil
- 1 onion, chopped
- 6 garlic cloves, minced
- 1 tsp chili powder
- ½ tsp ground cinnamon
- Sea salt to taste
- 1 cup yellow lentils
- 1 cup canned diced tomatoes
- 1 celery stalk, chopped
- 10 oz chopped collard greens

Directions:
1. Heat oil in a pot over medium heat. Place onion and garlic and cook for 5 minutes. Stir in chili powder, celery, cinnamon, and salt. Pour in lentils, tomatoes and juices, and 2 cups of water. Bring to a boil, then lower the heat and simmer for 15 minutes. Stir in collard greens. Cook for an additional 5 minutes. Serve in bowls and enjoy!

Nutrition Info:
- Per Serving: Calories: 155;Fat: 3g;Protein: 7g;Carbs: 29g.

Easy Sweet Potato Soup

Servings: 4 | Cooking Time: 25 Minutes

Ingredients:
- 8 cups no-salt-added vegetable broth
- 2 tbsp avocado oil
- 1 carrot, chopped
- 1 onion, chopped
- 1 garlic clove, minced
- 4 cups cubed sweet potatoes
- 1 tsp curry powder
- 1 tsp ground turmeric
- Sea salt and pepper to taste

Directions:
1. Warm the avocado oil in a pot over medium heat. Sauté the onion and garlic for 5 minutes until tender and translucent. Mix in sweet potatoes, carrot, vegetable broth, curry powder, turmeric, salt, and pepper and bring to a boil. Simmer for 10 minutes. Puree your soup using an immersion blender until smooth. Serve warm.

Nutrition Info:
- Per Serving: Calories: 260;Fat: 8g;Protein: 4g;Carbs: 46g.

Anti-Inflammatory Cookbook

Sharp-tasting Soup With Rice And Sweet Potato

Servings: 4 To 6

Cooking Time: 15 Minutes

Ingredients:
- 4 cups vegetable broth
- 1 large sweet potato, peeled and cut into 1-inch cubes
- 2 onions, coarsely chopped
- 2 garlic cloves, sliced thin
- 2 teaspoons fresh ginger, minced
- 1 bunch broccolini, cut into 1-inch pieces
- 1 cup cooked basmati rice
- ¼ cup cilantro leaves, fresh

Directions:
1. Add the broth and bring to a boil in a large Dutch oven over high heat.
2. Add the sweet potato, onion, garlic, and ginger. Simmer for 5 to 8 minutes, or until the sweet potato is cooked through.
3. Add the broccolini and simmer for 3 minutes more.
4. Remove the pan from the heat. Stir in the rice and cilantro.

Nutrition Info:
- Per Serving: Calories: 167 ;Fat: 2g ;Protein: 8g ;Carbs: 29g .s

Spicy Gazpacho

Servings: 4 | Cooking Time: 10 Minutes

Ingredients:
- 1 English cucumber, cubed
- 6 heirloom tomatoes, diced
- ¼ cup extra-virgin olive oil
- ¼ cup fresh basil leaves
- 2 garlic cloves, minced
- 1 lemon, zested and juiced
- ½ red bell pepper, chopped
- ½ tsp hot sauce

Directions:
1. Place the cucumber, tomatoes, olive oil, basil, garlic, lemon juice, lemon zest, bell pepper, and hot sauce in a food processor and blitz for 20 seconds until a smooth consistency is reached. Serve immediately.

Nutrition Info:
- Per Serving: Calories: 170;Fat: 14g;Protein: 4g;Carbs: 13g.

Beef & Tomato Chili

Servings: 4 | Cooking Time: 40 Minutes

Ingredients:
- 1 lb ground beef
- 1 onion, chopped
- 2 garlic cloves, minced
- 2 tbsp extra-virgin olive oil
- 1 tsp sea salt
- 1 ½ tsp chili powder
- 1 tsp Thai red curry paste
- ½ tsp ground cumin
- 3 tomatoes, diced
- 2 cups chicken broth

Directions:
1. Warm the olive oil in a pot oven over high heat. Place the ground beef and cook for 5 minutes until it browns. Add in garlic, cocoa, chili powder, salt, curry paste, cumin, and onion and cook for 1 more minute. Pour in tomato sauce and chicken broth and simmer covered for 20-25 minutes, stirring often. Serve immediately.

Nutrition Info:
- Per Serving: Calories: 372;Fat: 28g;Protein: 4g;Carbs: 10g.

Cold Soup With Coconut And Avocado

Servings: 6 | Cooking Time: 0 Minutes

Ingredients:
- 3 ripe avocados, peeled and pitted
- ¼ red onion, chopped, or about ¼ cup precut packaged onion
- 1 cup Herbed Chicken Bone Broth
- 1 tablespoon lemon juice, freshly squeezed
- 1 garlic clove, crushed
- 1 teaspoon fresh ginger, grated
- ½ teaspoon chopped fresh dill, plus fresh dill sprigs
- 2 cups canned coconut milk, full-fat
- Sea salt
- Freshly ground black pepper
- Sliced radishes

Directions:
1. Coarsely chop three of the four avocado halves. Dice the remaining half and set it aside for garnish.
2. Combine the chopped avocado, onion, chicken broth, lemon juice, garlic, ginger, and chopped dill in a food processor. Purée until very smooth. Transfer the avocado soup to a lidded container.
3. Whisk in the coconut milk.
4. Season with sea salt and pepper. Chill the soup for at least 1 hour.
5. Garnish with the diced avocado, radishes, and dill sprigs just before serving.

Nutrition Info:
- Per Serving: Calories: 395 ;Fat: 39g ;Protein: 4g;Carbs: 14g .

Lentil Soup

Servings: 4 | Cooking Time: 40 Minutes

Ingredients:
- 4 garlic cloves, minced
- 1 tsp cumin
- 4 cups veggie broth
- ½ onion, chopped
- 2 celery stalks, chopped
- 2 carrots, chopped
- 1 cup dry lentils
- 2 bay leaves
- 2 tbsp extra-virgin olive oil
- Sea salt and pepper to taste

Directions:
1. Heat the olive oil in your pressure cooker on "Sauté". Add onions, garlic, and carrots, and cook until they start to 'sweat'. Add celery and sauté for one more minute. Stir in the remaining ingredients. Seal the lid and set the Instant Pot on "Manual". Cook on High pressure for 25 minutes. When it is done, perform a quick pressure release. Remove the lid and serve warm.

Nutrition Info:
- Per Serving: Calories: 259;Fat: 8g;Protein: 13g;Carbs: 35g.

Cayenne Pumpkin Soup

Servings: 6 | Cooking Time: 55 Minutes

Ingredients:
- 1 pumpkin, sliced
- 3 tbsp extra-virgin olive oil
- 1 tsp sea salt
- 2 red bell peppers
- 1 onion, halved
- 1 head garlic
- ¼ tsp cayenne pepper
- ½ tsp ground coriander
- ½ tsp ground cumin
- Toasted pumpkin seeds

Directions:
1. Preheat your oven to 350ºF. Brush the pumpkin slices with oil and sprinkle with salt. Arrange them skin-side-down and on a greased baking dish; bake for 20 minutes. Brush the onion with oil. Cut the top of the garlic head and brush with oil. Add the bell peppers, onion, and garlic to the pumpkin. Bake for 10 minutes. Cool.
2. Take out the flesh from the pumpkin skin and transfer to a food processor. Cut the pepper roughly, peel and cut the onion, and remove the cloves from the garlic head. Transfer to the food processor and pour in 6 cups of water. Blend the soup until smooth. If it's very thick, add a bit of water to reach your desired consistency. Sprinkle with salt, cayenne pepper, coriander, and cumin. Serve.

Nutrition Info:
- Per Serving: Calories: 130;Fat: 8g;Protein: 1g;Carbs: 16g.

Proteinaceous Noodle Bowl With Vegetable

Servings: 4 | Cooking Time: 20 Minutes

Ingredients:
- 3 cups canned lite coconut milk
- 1 cup vegetable broth, low-sodium
- 1 tablespoon coconut aminos
- 1 tablespoon honey, raw
- 3 garlic cloves
- ¼ sweet onion or about ¼ cup precut packaged onion
- 1 piece fresh ginger, 2 inch and peeled
- Juice of 1 lime, 1 or 2 tablespoons
- 1 large carrot, julienned or spiralized
- 1 parsnip, julienned or spiralized
- 1 cup bok choy, shredded
- 1 cup bean sprouts
- 2 tablespoons fresh cilantro, chopped

Directions:
1. Combine the coconut milk, vegetable broth, coconut aminos, honey, garlic, onion, ginger, and lime zest in a blender. Pulse until puréed. Pour the mixture into a large saucepan and bring to a boil over high heat. Reduce the heat to low and simmer for 15 minutes.
2. Stir in the carrot, parsnip, bok choy, and bean sprouts. Simmer for 4 minutes or until the vegetables are tender.
3. Serve topped with the cilantro.

Nutrition Info:
- Per Serving: Calories: 183 ;Fat: 10g ;Protein: 6g;Carbs: 25g .

Rotini & Tomato Soup

Servings: 4 | Cooking Time: 25 Minutes

Ingredients:
- 1 tbsp extra-virgin olive oil
- 1 medium onion, chopped
- 1 celery rib, minced
- 3 garlic cloves, minced
- 1 can diced tomatoes
- 3 cups chopped tomatoes
- 2 tbsp tomato paste
- 3 cups vegetable broth
- 2 bay leaves
- 1 cup plain soy milk
- ½ cup whole-wheat rotini
- 2 tbsp chopped fresh basil

Directions:
1. Heat oil in a pot and sauté onion, celery, and garlic for 5 minutes. Add in tomatoes, tomato paste, broth, sugar, and bay leaves. Bring to a boil and add the rotini. Cook for 10 minutes. Discard bay leaves. Top with basil.

Nutrition Info:
- Per Serving: Calories: 230;Fat: 5g;Protein: 6g;Carbs: 41g.

Soothing Broth With Mushrooms

Servings: 4 | Cooking Time: 10 Minutes

Ingredients:
- 1 tablespoon extra-virgin olive oil
- 1 onion, halved and sliced thin
- 3 garlic cloves, sliced thin
- 1 celery stalk, finely chopped
- 1 pound mushrooms, sliced thin
- 1 teaspoon salt
- ½ teaspoon black pepper, freshly ground
- Pinch nutmeg
- 4 cups vegetable broth
- 2 tablespoon fresh tarragon, chopped

Directions:
1. Heat the olive oil in a large pot over high heat.
2. Add the onion, garlic, and celery. Sauté for 3 minutes.
3. Add the mushrooms, salt, pepper, and nutmeg. Sauté for 5 to 10 minutes more.
4. Add the vegetable broth and bring the soup to a boil. Reduce the heat to simmer. Cook for 5 minutes more.
5. Stir in the tarragon and serve.

Nutrition Info:
- Per Serving: Calories: 111 ;Fat: 5g ;Protein: 9g ;Carbs: 9g .

Gluten-free Tortellini Minestrone Soup

Servings: 6 | Cooking Time: 15 Minutes

Ingredients:
- 1 onion, diced
- 2 carrots, diced
- 1 tbsp minced garlic
- 2 tbsp extra-virgin olive oil
- 4 cups veggie broth
- 24 oz jarred spaghetti sauce
- 2 celery stalks, sliced
- ¼ tsp black pepper
- 1 ½ tsp Italian seasoning
- 14 oz canned diced tomatoes
- 8 oz whole wheat tortellini
- 4 tsp grated Parmesan cheese

Directions:
1. Add the olive oil to your Instant Pot and heat on "Sauté". Add the onions, garlic, celery, and carrots, and cook until they start to 'sweat'. Stir in the rest of the ingredients. Seal the lid and set the Instant Pot on "Manual" on High pressure for 4 minutes. Once cooking is complete, do a quick pressure release, then carefully open the lid. Serve topped with Parmesan cheese and basil.

Nutrition Info:
• Per Serving: Calories: 250;Fat: 9g;Protein: 7g;Carbs: 34g.

Tomato Chicken Soup

Servings: 6 | Cooking Time: 30 Minutes

Ingredients:
• 1 can diced green chiles
• 3 tbsp avocado oil
• 3 garlic cloves, minced
• 1 white onion, diced
• 1 jalapeño pepper, minced
• 6 cups chicken broth
• 1 lb shredded cooked chicken
• 1 can diced tomatoes
• 3 tbsp lime juice
• 1 tsp chili powder
• 1 tsp ground cumin
• Sea salt and pepper to taste
• ¼ tsp cayenne pepper
• 1 avocado, sliced
• 2 tbsp cilantro, chopped

Directions:
1. Warm the avocado oil in a large pot over medium heat and sauté the garlic, onion, and jalapeño pepper for 5 minutes. Stir in the broth, chicken, tomatoes, green chiles, lime juice, chili powder, cumin, salt, and cayenne pepper, and season with black pepper. Bring to a simmer and cook for 10 minutes. Serve hot topped with slices of avocado and garnished with cilantro.

Nutrition Info:
• Per Serving: Calories: 285;Fat: 9g;Protein: 28g;Carbs: 12g.

Coconut Artichoke Soup With Almonds

Servings: 4 | Cooking Time: 30 Minutes

Ingredients:
• 1 tbsp extra-virgin olive oil
• 2 medium shallots, chopped
• 10 oz artichoke hearts
• 3 cups vegetable broth
• 1 tsp fresh lemon juice
• Sea salt to taste
• 2 tbsp olive oil
• ⅛ tsp cayenne pepper
• 1 cup plain coconut cream
• 1 tbsp snipped fresh chives
• 2 tbsp toasted almond slices

Directions:
1. Heat the oil in a pot over medium heat. Place in shallots and sauté until softened, about 3 minutes. Add in artichokes, broth, lemon juice, and salt. Bring to a boil, lower the heat, and simmer for 10 minutes. Stir in cayenne pepper. Transfer to a food processor and blend until purée. Return to the pot. Mix in coconut cream and simmer for 5 minutes. Top with chives and almonds.

Nutrition Info:
• Per Serving: Calories: 450;Fat: 43g;Protein: 5g;Carbs: 17g.

Yellow Soup With Lentils

Servings: 4 | Cooking Time: 8 Hours 15 Minutes

Ingredients:
• 1 small onion, diced
• 1 carrot, diced
• 1 cup yellow lentils
• 4 cups vegetable broth
• 1 celery stalk, minced
• 2 tsp ground turmeric
• 1 tsp garlic powder
• Sea salt to taste
• ½ tsp ground ginger
• ½ tsp ground cumin
• ½ tsp dried thyme leaves
• ¼ tsp ground cinnamon

Directions:
1. Place the lentils, broth, onion, carrot, celery, turmeric, garlic, salt, ginger, cumin, thyme, and cinnamon in your slow cooker. Cover and cook for 8 hours on "Low".

Nutrition Info:
• Per Serving: Calories: 330;Fat: 20g;Protein: 13g;Carbs: 32g.

Low Maintenance Vegan Minestrone With Herb Oil

Servings: 8 | Cooking Time: 40 Minutes

Ingredients:
• 3 tablespoon olive oil
• 1 cup diced carrots, 140g
• ¾ cup [70 g] diced celery, 70g
• 1 yellow onion, sliced
• Kosher salt
• 2 garlic cloves, minced
• Pinch of red pepper flakes, crushed
• 4 zucchinis, diced
• 2 crookneck squash, diced
• 8 cups low-sodium vegetable broth, 2L
• Two 14 ½ ounces cans diced San Marzano tomatoes
• 1 bunch rainbow chard, stems removed, coarsely chopped
• Two 15 ounces cans cannellini beans, rinsed and drained
• Herb Oil:
• ¼ teaspoon kosher salt
• 2 garlic cloves, peeled
• ½ cup extra-virgin olive oil, 120ml
• ½ cup packed herbs

Directions:
1. Warm the olive oil in a large stockpot or Dutch oven over medium heat. Add the carrots, celery, onion, and ½ teaspoon salt and cook while stirring frequently until tender for 10 minutes. Add the tomato paste (if using), garlic, and red pepper flakes, and cook until the paste turns brick red for a minute. Add the zucchini and squash and cook for 1 minute. Stir in the broth and tomatoes, bring to a boil over high heat, then turn the heat to medium-low and simmer uncovered for 15 minutes. Stir in the chard and simmer for 5 minutes longer. For 3 minutes, stir in the beans and warm them. Season with salt.
2. Make the herb oil by placing the salt and garlic in a small food processor or blender and process until the garlic is minced for 20 seconds. Add the olive oil and herbs and blend until the oil is bright green for 20 seconds.
3. Fill each bowl with soup and drizzle with 2 teaspoons of herb oil to serve.

Nutrition Info:
• Per Serving: Calories: 186 ;Fat: 12g ;Protein: 4g ;Carbs: 18g .

Classic Minestrone Soup

Servings: 4 | Cooking Time: 20 Minutes

Ingredients:
- 2 tbsp extra-virgin olive oil
- 1 onion, chopped
- 1 carrot, chopped
- 1 stalk celery, chopped
- 2 garlic cloves, minced
- 4 cups vegetable stock
- 1 cup green peas
- ½ cup orzo
- 1 can diced tomatoes
- 2 tsp Italian seasoning
- Sea salt and pepper to taste

Directions:
1. Heat the oil in a pot over medium heat. Sauté the onion, garlic, carrot, and celery for 5 minutes until tender. Stir in vegetable stock, green peas, orzo, tomatoes, salt, pepper, and Italian seasoning. Cook for 10 minutes. Serve warm.

Nutrition Info:
- Per Serving: Calories: 170;Fat: 8g;Protein: 5g;Carbs: 22g.

Turnip & Rutabaga Soup

Servings: 5 | Cooking Time: 30 Minutes

Ingredients:
- 2 tbsp extra-virgin olive oil
- 1 onion, diced
- 3 garlic cloves, minced
- 1 carrot, chopped
- 1 rutabaga, chopped
- 1 turnip chopped
- 5 cups vegetable stock
- 2 tsp dried thyme

Directions:
1. Heat the oil in a pot over medium heat. Place the onion and garlic and sauté for 3 minutes until translucent. Stir in carrot, rutabaga, turnip, vegetable stock, salt, pepper, and thyme. Simmer for 10 minutes. In a food processor, put the soup and blend until purée. Serve warm.

Nutrition Info:
- Per Serving: Calories: 115;Fat: 6g;Protein: 1g;Carbs: 15g.

Curry Soup With Butternut Squash And Coconut

Servings: 4 To 6

Cooking Time: 4 Hours

Ingredients:
- 2 tablespoons coconut oil
- 1 pound butternut squash, peeled and cut into 1-inch cubes
- 1 small head cauliflower, cut into 1-inch pieces
- 1 onion, sliced
- 1 tablespoon curry powder
- ½ cup no-added-sugar apple juice
- 4 cups vegetable broth
- 1 can coconut milk, 13 ½ ounces
- 1 teaspoon salt
- ¼ teaspoon white pepper, freshly ground
- ¼ cup chopped fresh cilantro, divided

Directions:
1. Combine the coconut oil, butternut squash, cauliflower, onion, curry powder, apple juice, vegetable broth, coconut milk, salt, and white pepper in the slower cooker. Set on high for 4 hours.
2. Before serving, purée it in a blender.
3. Garnish with cilantro.

Nutrition Info:
- Per Serving: Calories: 416 ;Fat: 31g ;Protein: 10g ;Carbs: 30g .

Rustic Lamb Stew

Servings: 4 | Cooking Time: 30 Minutes

Ingredients:
- 2 tbsp mint leaves, minced
- 1 lb lamb stew meat, cubed
- 2 tbsp extra-virgin olive oil
- 1 onion, chopped
- Sea salt and pepper to taste
- 28 oz canned diced tomatoes
- 2 garlic cloves, minced
- 1 Bird's eye chili, minced

Directions:
1. Warm the olive oil in the skillet over medium heat. Add the onion, garlic, Bird's eye chili, salt, and pepper and sauté for 3 minutes until tender. Add the cubed lamb and cook for 5 minutes, stirring often. Add the tomatoes and 1 cup of water and continue to cook for 5 more minutes. Scatter with mint and serve immediately.

Nutrition Info:
- Per Serving: Calories: 290;Fat: 7g;Protein: 19g;Carbs: 33.7g.

Sudanese Veggie Stew

Servings: 6 | Cooking Time: 30 Minutes

Ingredients:
- 3 tbsp extra-virgin olive oil
- 2 carrots, sliced
- 4 shallots, chopped
- 2 garlic cloves, minced
- ½ cup brown rice
- 1 tbsp ground turmeric
- 1 tsp ground ginger
- 1 ½ cups vegetable broth
- 4 cups shredded spinach

Directions:
1. Heat the olive oil in a saucepan over medium heat. Place in carrots and shallots and cook for 5 minutes. Stir in garlic, turmeric, ginger, and salt. Cook for 1 minute more. Add in the broth and brown rice. Bring to a boil, then lower the heat, and simmer for 20-25 minutes. Stir in the spinach and cook for another 3 minutes. Serve.

Nutrition Info:
- Per Serving: Calories: 140;Fat: 7g;Protein: 1g;Carbs: 16g.

Comfortable Chicken Soup

Servings: 4 | Cooking Time: 20 Minutes

Ingredients:
- 3 cups shredded rotisserie chicken, skin removed
- 2 red bell peppers, chopped
- 1 onion, chopped
- 1 tbsp grated fresh ginger
- 8 cups chicken broth
- 2 tbsp extra-virgin olive oil
- Sea salt and pepper to taste

Directions:
1. Warm the olive oil in a large pot over medium heat and sauté

the red bell peppers, onion, and ginger for about 5 minutes, stirring occasionally, until the vegetables are soft. Stir in the chicken, chicken broth, salt, and pepper. Bring to a simmer. Simmer for 5 minutes. Serve warm.

Nutrition Info:
- Per Serving: Calories: 340;Fat: 16g;Protein: 39g;Carbs: 11g.

Veggie Thai Curry Soup

Servings: 4 To 6

Cooking Time: 6 To 8 Hours

Ingredients:
- 4 cups vegetable broth
- ½ cup mushrooms, sliced
- 3 carrots, diced
- 1 bunch baby bok choy
- 1 sweet potato, peeled and diced
- 1 small head broccoli, florets chopped
- 1 small onion, diced
- 1 lemongrass stalk, chopped into 1-inch segments
- 1 tablespoon lime juice, freshly squeezed
- 1 tablespoon curry paste
- 2 teaspoons fish sauce
- ¾ teaspoon sea salt
- ½ teaspoon ginger, ground
- ½ teaspoon garlic powder
- ¾ cup coconut milk, full-fat
- Fresh cilantro leaves

Directions:
1. Stir together the broth, mushrooms, carrots, bok choy, sweet potato, broccoli, onion, lemongrass, lime juice, curry paste, fish sauce, salt, ginger, and garlic powder in your slow cooker.
2. Cover the cooker and set it to low. Cook for 6 to 8 hours.
3. Stir in the coconut milk and garnish with the cilantro before serving.

Nutrition Info:
- Per Serving: Calories: 229 ;Fat: 9g ;Protein: 8g ;Carbs: 31g .

Ginger Squash Soup

Servings: 4 | Cooking Time: 30 Minutes

Ingredients:
- 3 tsp toasted pumpkin seeds
- 1 tbsp chopped ginger paste
- 1 tbsp extra-virgin olive oil
- 1 onion, chopped
- 1 celery stalk, chopped
- 4 cups vegetable broth
- 1 acorn squash, chopped
- 1 tsp low-sodium soy sauce
- ¼ tsp ground allspice
- Sea salt and pepper to taste
- 1 cup plain soy milk

Directions:
1. Heat the olive oil in a pot over medium heat. Place in onion and celery and sauté for 5 minutes until tender. Add in broth and squash, bring to a boil. Lower the heat and simmer for 20 minutes. Stir in soy sauce, ginger paste, allspice, salt, and pepper. Blend the soup in a food processor until smooth. Return to the pot. Mix in soy milk. Serve garnished with pumpkin seeds.

Nutrition Info:
- Per Serving: Calories: 195;Fat: 10g;Protein: 6g;Carbs: 23g.

Easy To Make Egg Drop Soup

Servings: 4 | Cooking Time: 25 Minutes

Ingredients:
- 2 tablespoons sesame oil, toasted
- 2-inch piece fresh ginger, peeled
- 4 cloves garlic, peeled
- 4 cups bone broth
- 1 tablespoon coconut aminos
- 1 tablespoon fish sauce
- Pinch of fine Himalayan salt
- 4 large eggs, whisked
- 2 green onions, sliced,
- 4 sprigs fresh cilantro, minced,

Directions:
1. Heat the sesame oil in a 6- or 8-quart pot over medium heat. Add the ginger and garlic and stir until lightly browned.
2. Add the broth, coconut aminos, fish sauce, and salt. Bring to a low simmer, reduce the heat to low, cover, and cook for 20 minutes.
3. Slowly drizzle in the eggs while stirring the soup so the eggs cook instantly in ribbons as they hit the broth.
4. Garnish with green onions and cilantro and serve hot. Store leftovers in an airtight container in the fridge for up to 5 days.

Nutrition Info:
- Per Serving: Calories: 185 ;Fat: 12g ;Protein: 16g;Carbs: 4g .

Homemade Warm And Chunky Chicken Soup

Servings: 4 | Cooking Time: 40 Minutes

Ingredients:
- 1 whole free-range chicken, cooked and no giblets
- 1 bay leaf
- 5 cups of homemade chicken broth/water
- 1 onion, chopped
- 2 stalks of celery, sliced
- 3 carrots, chopped and peeled
- 2 parsnips, chopped and peeled
- sprinkle of pepper

Directions:
1. Into a large pot, add all of the ingredients minus the pepper, and boil on high heat.
2. Lower the heat once boiling and allow to simmer for 30 minutes, or until the chicken is piping hot.
3. Remove the chicken and place it on a chopping board.
4. Slice as much meat as you can from the chicken and remove the skin and bones.
5. Add it back into the pot and either serve right away as a chunky soup or allow it to cool and whizz through the blender to serve.
6. Add black pepper to season and serve alone or with your choice of whole-grain bread, just pop it into the soup 20 minutes before the end to soak up all the delicious flavors.

Nutrition Info:
- Per Serving: Calories: 101 ;Fat: 1g ;Protein: 7g ;Carbs: 22g .

Green Bean & Rice Soup

Servings: 4 | Cooking Time: 50 Minutes

Ingredients:
- 2 tbsp extra-virgin olive oil
- 1 medium onion, minced
- 2 garlic cloves minced
- ½ cup brown rice
- 1 cup green beans, chopped
- 2 tbsp chopped parsley

Directions:
1. Heat oil in a pot over medium heat. Place in onion and garlic and sauté for 3 minutes. Add in rice, 4 cups water, salt, and pepper. Bring to a boil, lower the heat, and simmer for 15 minutes. Stir in beans and cook for 10 minutes. Top with parsley. Serve and enjoy!

Nutrition Info:
- Per Serving: Calories: 170;Fat: 8g;Protein: 1g;Carbs: 23g.

Native Asian Soup With Squash And Shitake

Servings: 2 | Cooking Time: 45 Minutes

Ingredients:
- 15 dried shiitake mushrooms, soaked in water
- 6 cups low salt vegetable stock
- ½ butternut squash, peeled and cubed
- 1 tablespoon sesame oil
- 1 onion, quartered and sliced into rings
- 1 large garlic clove, chopped
- 4 stems of pak choy or equivalent
- 1 sprig of thyme or 1 tablespoon dried thyme
- 1 teaspoon tabasco sauce

Directions:
1. Heat sesame on medium-high heat oil in a large pan before sweating the onions and garlic.
2. Add the vegetable stock and bring to a boil over a high heat before adding the squash.
3. Turn down the heat and allow to simmer for 25 to 30 minutes.
4. Soak the mushrooms in the water if not already done, and then press out the liquid and add to the stock into the pot.
5. Use the mushroom water in the stock for extra taste.
6. Except for the greens, add the rest of the ingredients and allow to simmer for 15 minutes more or until the squash is tender.
7. Before serving, add in the chopped greens and let them wilt. Serve with the tabasco sauce if you like it spicy.

Nutrition Info:
- Per Serving: Calories: 1191 ;Fat: 56g ;Protein: 19g ;Carbs: 158g .

Spicy Thai Soup

Servings: 6 | Cooking Time: 30 Minutes

Ingredients:
- ¾ cup toasted cashews
- 2 red chili peppers, diced
- 3 garlic cloves, minced
- 1 white onion, diced
- 2 tbsp coconut oil
- 1 ½ tbsp minced ginger
- 2 carrots, chopped
- 1 butternut squash, diced
- 1 small cabbage, shredded
- 1 lb trimmed green beans
- 3 cups vegetable broth
- 1 can coconut milk
- Sea salt and pepper to taste
- 1 cup mung bean sprouts
- 4 tbsp coconut shavings

Directions:
1. Warm the coconut oil in a large pot over medium heat and sauté the cashews and sauté for 2 minutes. Remove them from the pan and set aside. Add the peppers, garlic, and onion, and sauté for 6 minutes. Then add the ginger and carrots, and sauté for about 3 minutes, or until the carrots and squash begin to soften. Stir in the cabbage, green beans, broth, coconut milk, and salt. Season with pepper. Simmer for 15 minutes. Turn off the heat and stir in the bean sprouts and coconut shavings. Pour into soup bowls and serve immediately.

Nutrition Info:
- Per Serving: Calories: 340;Fat: 26g;Protein: 6g;Carbs: 24g.

Mediterranean Soup

Servings: 4 | Cooking Time: 20 Minutes

Ingredients:
- 2 tsp olive oil
- 1 leek, chopped
- 4 garlic cloves, minced
- 2 carrots, chopped
- 1 tbsp Mediterranean herbs
- 4 cups vegetable broth
- 2 cans white beans
- 2 tbsp lemon juice
- 1 lb green beans, chopped

Directions:
1. Heat the oil in a pot over medium heat. Place in leek, garlic, carrots, pepper, and salt. Cook for 5 minutes until fragrant. Season with dried herbs. Stir in broth, green beans, and white beans, reduce the heat and simmer for 10 minutes. Stir in lemon juice. Serve and enjoy!

Nutrition Info:
- Per Serving: Calories: 110;Fat: 3g;Protein: 3g;Carbs: 19g.

Sauces, Condiments, and Dressings

Sauces, Condiments, and Dressings

Buttery Slow Cooked Ghee

Servings: 2 | Cooking Time: 2 Hours

Ingredients:
• 1 pound unsalted butter, 4 sticks

Directions:
1. Add the butter in the slow cooker. Set the slow cooker to high and leave it uncovered.
2. White foam should appear in 45 minutes. Over time, from 1 to 2 hours, the foam will turn golden brown and give off a nutty smell.
3. Turn off the slow cooker once the foam has turned brown.
4. Line a strainer with a triple thickness of cheesecloth and place the strainer over a wide-mouth jar.
5. Skim off as much of the brown foam as possible using a large spoon or ladle and discard it. Carefully ladle the remaining ghee into the cheesecloth-lined strainer.
6. Discard the cheesecloth once all the ghee has been strained and let the ghee come to room temperature before covering the jar with an airtight lid and refrigerating it. It will last for three months.

Nutrition Info:
• Per Serving: Calories: 102 ;Fat: 12g ;Protein: 46g;Carbs: 4g.

Verde Chimichurri With Parsley

Servings: 1 | Cooking Time: 0 Minutes

Ingredients:
• 1 cup coarsely fresh parsley, chopped
• ½ cup fresh mint leaves
• ¼ cup olive oil
• 2 tablespoons lemon juice, freshly squeezed
• 2 teaspoons minced garlic, bottled
• Pinch sea salt

Directions:
1. Combine the parsley, mint, olive oil, lemon juice, garlic, and sea salt in a blender or food processor. Pulse until finely chopped and the ingredients are well mixed.
2. Refrigerate the mixture in a sealed container for up to 1 week.

Nutrition Info:
• Per Serving: Calories: 61 ;Fat: 6g ;Protein: 1g;Carbs: 1g .

Satisfying And Thick Dressing With Avocado

Servings: 2 | Cooking Time: 0 Minutes

Ingredients:
• 1 ripe avocado
• 1 cup coconut yogurt, plain
• ¼ cup lemon juice, freshly squeezed
• 1 scallion, chopped
• 1 tablespoon fresh cilantro, chopped

Directions:
1. Blend in a food processor the avocado, yogurt, lemon juice, scallion, and cilantro until smooth.
2. Refrigerate in an airtight container.

Nutrition Info:
• Per Serving: Calories: 33 ;Fat: 3g ;Protein: 8g;Carbs: 2g .

Fantastic On Hand Marinara Sauce

Servings: 6 | Cooking Time: 7 To 8 Hours

Ingredients:
• 2 cans diced tomatoes, 28 ounces
• 3 tablespoons tomato paste
• 1 yellow onion, diced
• 1 carrot, minced
• 1 celery stalk, minced
• 2 bay leaves
• 1 tablespoon basil leaves, dried
• 2 teaspoons oregano, dried
• 1½ teaspoons garlic powder
• 1 teaspoon sea salt
• Pinch red pepper flakes
• Freshly ground black pepper

Directions:
1. Combine in your slow cooker the tomatoes, tomato paste, onion, carrot, celery, bay leaves, basil, oregano, garlic powder, salt, and red pepper flakes, and season with black pepper.
2. Cover the cooker and set it to low. Cook for 7 to 8 hours.
3. Remove and discard the bay leaves. Blend using an immersion blender the sauce to your preferred consistency or leave it naturally chunky.

Nutrition Info:
• Per Serving: Calories: 71 ;Fat: 5g;Protein: 3g ;Carbs: 17g .

Excellent Tapenade With Green Olive

Servings: 1 | Cooking Time: 0 Minutes

Ingredients:
• 1 cup pitted green olives
• 2 garlic cloves
• ¼ cup extra-virgin olive oil
• ¼ cup lemon juice, freshly squeezed
• Pinch dried rosemary
• Salt
• Freshly ground black pepper

Directions:
1. Combine the olives, garlic, olive oil, lemon juice, and rosemary in a food processor. Season with salt and pepper. Process until the mixture is almost smooth and a little chunky is okay.
2. Refrigerate in an airtight container. The tapenade will keep for several weeks.

Nutrition Info:
• Per Serving: Calories: 73 ;Fat: 8g ;Protein: 6g;Carbs: 2g ;

Feels Like Summer Chutney With Mint

Servings: 2 | Cooking Time: 0 Minutes

Ingredients:
• One 10 ounces bag frozen no-added-sugar peach chunks, thawed, drained, coarsely chopped, juice reserved
• ½ medium red onion, diced
• ¼ cup dried cherries, coarsely chopped
• 2 tablespoons lemon juice, freshly squeezed
• 1 tablespoon raw honey or maple syrup
• 1 teaspoon apple cider vinegar
• ¼ teaspoon salt

- 1 tablespoon fresh mint leaves, chopped

Directions:
1. In a medium bowl, place the peach chunks.
2. Stir in the onion, cherries, lemon juice, honey, cider vinegar, and salt.
3. Let the mixture stand for 30 minutes before serving.
4. Stir in the mint when ready to serve.
5. Refrigerate in an airtight container for no more than three days.

Nutrition Info:
- Per Serving: Calories: 42 ;Fat: 2g ;Protein: 1g ;Carbs: 1g .

Decadent And Simple Alfredo With Cauliflower

Servings: 2 | Cooking Time: 12 Minutes

Ingredients:
- 3 cups cauliflower, florets
- 5 cloves garlic, peeled
- 1 cup coconut milk, full-fat
- 3 tablespoons salted butter, ghee, or lard
- 1 tablespoon fish sauce
- 1 tablespoon red wine vinegar
- 1 teaspoon Himalayan salt, fine
- 1 teaspoon black pepper, ground

Directions:
1. Fill a saucepan with about an inch of water and add the cauliflower and garlic. Heat the pan over medium-high heat and bring to a boil with the lid on. Cook for 8 minutes until the cauliflower is fork-tender. Remove from the heat and drain.
2. In a blender, place the cauliflower, garlic, and remaining ingredients. Purée until smooth.
3. Store in an airtight container in the fridge for up to 10 days. Bring to a simmer in a saucepan over medium heat to reheat.

Nutrition Info:
- Per Serving: Calories: 250 ;Fat: 24g ;Protein: 4g ;Carbs: 9g .

Herbaceous Spread With Avocado

Servings: 2 | Cooking Time: 0minutes

Ingredients:
- 1 avocado, peeled and pitted
- 2 tablespoons lemon juice, freshly squeezed
- 2 tablespoons fresh parsley, chopped
- 1 teaspoon fresh dill, chopped
- ½ teaspoon coriander, ground
- Sea salt
- Freshly ground black pepper

Directions:
1. Pulse the avocado in a blender until smoothly puréed.
2. Add the lemon juice, parsley, dill, and coriander. Pulse until well blended.
3. Season with sea salt and pepper.
4. Refrigerate the spread in a sealed container for up to 4 days.

Nutrition Info:
- Per Serving: Calories: 53 ;Fat: 5g ;Protein: 1g;Carbs: 2g .

Colourful And Sweet Spread With Carrot

Servings: 2 | Cooking Time: 0 Minutes

Ingredients:
- 3 carrots, peeled and cut into chunks
- ½ cup almonds
- 2 tablespoons lemon juice, freshly squeezed
- 1 tablespoon pure maple syrup

- ½ teaspoon cardamom, ground
- Sea salt

Directions:
1. Pulse the carrots until very finely chopped in a food processor.
2. Add the almonds, lemon juice, maple syrup, and cardamom then process until smooth.
3. Season the spread with sea salt and transfer to a lidded container. Refrigerate for up to 6 days.

Nutrition Info:
- Per Serving: Calories: 26 ;Fat: 2g ;Protein: 1g;Carbs: 3g ,

Great On Everything Ginger Sauce

Servings: 1 ½

Cooking Time: 0 Minutes

Ingredients:
- ½ cup full-fat coconut milk
- ¼ cup coconut aminos
- ¼ cup fresh ginger, peeled and minced
- 4 cloves garlic, peeled
- 2 tablespoons coconut vinegar or red wine vinegar
- 2 tablespoons sesame oil
- 1 tablespoon Dijon mustard
- 1 tablespoon fish sauce
- 1 teaspoon minced lemongrass or grated lemon zest

Directions:
1. Place all of the ingredients in a blender and blend on high until the mixture is smooth and light brown.
2. Store in an airtight container in the refrigerator for up to 10 days. Shake before using.

Nutrition Info:
- Per Serving: Calories: 113 ;Fat: 10g ;Protein: 1g;Carbs: 6g .

Herbaceous Dressing With Creamy Coconut

Servings: 1 | Cooking Time: 0 Minutes

Ingredients:
- 8 ounces coconut yogurt, plain
- 2 tablespoons lemon juice, freshly squeezed
- 2 tablespoons fresh parsley, chopped
- 1 tablespoon fresh chives, snipped
- ½ teaspoon salt
- Pinch freshly ground black pepper

Directions:
1. Whisk together the yogurt, lemon juice, parsley, chives, salt, and pepper in a medium bowl.
2. Refrigerate in an airtight container.

Nutrition Info:
- Per Serving: Calories: 14 ;Fat: 1g ;Protein: 6g;Carbs: 2g.

Vegan Sauce With Honey, Mustard, And Sesame

Servings: 1 | Cooking Time: 0 Minutes

Ingredients:
- ½ cup Dijon mustard
- ½ cup raw honey or maple syrup
- 1 garlic clove, minced
- 1 teaspoon sesame oil, toasted

Directions:
1. Whisk together the Dijon, honey, garlic, and sesame oil in a small bowl.
2. Refrigerate in an airtight container.

Nutrition Info:
- Per Serving: Calories: 67 ;Fat: 1g ;Protein: 1g ;Carbs: 14g .

Lemony Honey With Ginger

Servings: 1 | Cooking Time: 0 Minutes

Ingredients:
- 1 cup water
- ¼ cup lemon juice, fresh
- 2 tablespoons honey
- 2 teaspoons grated fresh ginger root

Directions:
1. In an airtight jar, combine all the ingredients and shake until the honey is dissolved.
2. Refrigerate for a day before using so the ginger can permeate the mixture.
3. Store in the refrigerator for up to a week.

Nutrition Info:
- Per Serving: Calories: 20 ;Fat: 15g;Protein: 46g;Carbs: 5g .

Creamy Dressing With Sesame

Servings: ¾
Cooking Time: 0 Minutes
Ingredients:
- ½ cup canned coconut milk, full-fat
- 2 tablespoons tahini
- 2 tablespoons lime juice, freshly squeezed
- 1 teaspoon minced garlic, bottled
- 1 teaspoon fresh chives, minced
- Pinch sea salt

Directions:
1. Whisk in a small bowl the coconut milk, tahini, lime juice, garlic, and chives until well blended. You can also prepare this in a blender.
2. Season with sea salt and transfer the dressing to a container with a lid. Refrigerate for up to 1 week.

Nutrition Info:
- Per Serving: Calories: 40 ;Fat: 4g ;Protein: 1g;Carbs: 2g .

Awesome Multi-purpose Cream Sauce

Servings: 3 ½

Cooking Time: 12 Minutes
Ingredients:
- 3 cups cubed butternut squash
- ½ cup cashews, soaked in water for 4 hours, drained
- ½ cup water, plus additional for cooking and thinning
- 1 teaspoon salt, plus additional as needed

Directions:
1. Fill a large pot with 2 inches of water and insert a steamer basket. Bring to a boil over high heat.
2. Add the butternut squash to the basket. Cover and steam for 10 to 12 minutes or until tender.
3. Remove from the heat and cool slightly.
4. Transfer the squash to a blender. Add the cashews, ½ cup of water, and salt. Blend until smooth and creamy. Add more water depending on the consistency to thin if necessary.
5. Taste and adjust the seasoning if needed.

Nutrition Info:
- Per Serving: Calories: 73 ;Fat: 5g ;Protein: 2g ;Carbs: 8g .

Goddess And Vibrant Green Dressing

Servings: 2 | Cooking Time: 0 Minutes

Ingredients:
- 4 cloves garlic, peeled
- ½ cup fresh chives or green onions, minced
- ¼ cup lemon juice
- 2 tablespoons coconut aminos
- 1 tablespoon Dijon mustard
- 1½ teaspoons Himalayan salt, fine
- 1 teaspoon chia seeds
- 1 teaspoon black pepper, ground
- 1 teaspoon poppy seeds
- 1 teaspoon hemp seeds, shelled
- 5 drops liquid stevia
- 1 cup avocado oil

Directions:
1. Place all of the ingredients except the oil in a blender and pulse to combine. Drizzle slowly in the avocado oil while the blender runs until the sauce comes creamy and smooth.
2. Store in an airtight container in the refrigerator for up to 10 days. Shake before using.

Nutrition Info:
- Per Serving: Calories: 128 ;Fat: 14g ;Protein: 4g;Carbs: 1g.

To Die For Homemade Mayonnaise

Servings: 1 | Cooking Time: 0 Minutes

Ingredients:
- 3 tablespoons coconut vinegar
- 1 teaspoon thyme leaves, dried
- ½ teaspoon garlic, granulated
- ½ teaspoon mustard, dry
- ½ teaspoon Himalayan salt, fine
- 3 large egg yolks
- 1 cup avocado oil

Directions:
1. Place the vinegar and seasonings in a 16 ounces measuring cup or quart-sized mason jar. Add gently the egg yolks and the avocado oil.
2. Insert the immersion blender into the mixture and turn it on high then move it up and down slightly until the mix is completely emulsified. Scrape all of the mayonnaise off of the blender by using a spatula and then transfer the mayonnaise to a jar or other container with a tight-fitting lid.
3. Store in the refrigerator for up to 10 days.

Nutrition Info:
- Per Serving: Calories: 262 ;Fat: 30g ;Protein: 1g;Carbs: 4g.

French Pistou

Servings: 1 ½

Cooking Time: 0 Minutes
Ingredients:
- 3 packed cups fresh basil leaves
- 6 cloves garlic, peeled
- ¾ cup avocado oil
- ½ cup hemp seeds, shelled
- 1 teaspoon Himalayan salt, fine
- 1 teaspoon garlic powder
- 1 teaspoon black pepper, ground

Directions:
1. Place all of the ingredients in a blender or food processor. Pulse until all of the basil and garlic is minced.
2. Blend on low for 20 to 30 seconds to smooth it out just a bit

and bring the texture of the sauce together. Use a spatula to scrape it all out into a glass jar with a lid. Store in the fridge for up to 10 days.

Nutrition Info:
• Per Serving: Calories: 490 ;Fat: 47g ;Protein: 14g;Carbs: 5g .

Full Of Spice And Zesty Rub

Servings: ½
Cooking Time: 0 Minutes
Ingredients:
• 1 tablespoon turmeric, ground
• 1 tablespoon ginger, ground
• 1 tablespoon fennel seed, ground
• 1 tablespoon coconut sugar
• 2 teaspoons salt
• 2 teaspoons onion powder
• 1 teaspoon garlic powder
• 1 teaspoon paprika
• ½ teaspoon black pepper, freshly ground

Directions:
1. Combine in a small bowl all the ingredients and mix well.
2. Store in an airtight container for up to 12 months.

Nutrition Info:
• Per Serving: Calories: 20 ;Fat: 15g;Protein: 1g ;Carbs: 5g .

Gluten Free Apple Chutney

Servings: 2 | Cooking Time: 10 Minutes
Ingredients:
• 1 tablespoon almond oil
• 4 apples, peeled, cored, and diced
• 1 small onion, diced
• ½ cup white raisins
• 1 tablespoon apple cider vinegar
• 1 tablespoon honey
• 1 teaspoon cinnamon, ground
• ½ teaspoon cardamom, ground
• ½ teaspoon ginger, ground
• ½ teaspoon salt

Directions:
1. Heat in a medium saucepan the oil over low heat.
2. Add the apples, onion, raisins6, vinegar, honey, cinnamon, cardamom, ginger, and salt. Cook briefly until the apples release their juices. Bring to a simmer, cover, and cook until the apples are tender for 5 to 10 minutes.
3. Allow to cool completely before serving.

Nutrition Info:
• Per Serving: Calories: 120 ;Fat: 2g ;Protein: 1g ;Carbs: 24g .

Smoothies

Smoothies

Delicate Smoothie With Green Tea And Pear

Servings: 2 | Cooking Time: 0 Minutes

Ingredients:
- 2 cups green tea, strongly brewed
- 2 pears, peeled, cored, and chopped
- 2 tablespoons honey
- One 1 inch piece fresh ginger, peeled and roughly chopped, or 1 teaspoon ground ginger
- 1 cup almond milk, unsweetened
- 1 cup ice, crushed

Directions:
1. Combine in a blender the green tea, pears, honey, ginger, almond milk, and ice. Blend until smooth.

Nutrition Info:
- Per Serving: Calories: 208 ;Fat: 2g ;Protein: 1g ;Carbs: 51g.

Combating Gingery Milkshake With Blackberry

Servings: 1 | Cooking Time: 0 Minutes

Ingredients:
- thumb sized piece of ginger, grated
- 2 cups blackberries, washed
- 2 cups chopped peaches
- 2 cups almond milk

Directions:
1. Add all the ingredients to a blender or juicer then blend together until smooth.
2. Serve with a scattering of fresh blackberries.

Nutrition Info:
- Per Serving: Calories: 1156| Fat: 17g ;Protein: 24g ;Carbs: 246g.

Pain Reliever Smoothie

Servings: 1 | Cooking Time: 0 Minutes

Ingredients:
- 1 stalk celery, chopped
- 1 cup cucumber, chopped
- ½ cup pineapple, chopped
- ½ lemon, zest juice
- 1 cup coconut water
- 1 apple, chopped

Directions:
1. Take all of the ingredients except the lemon zest and blend until smooth.
2. You can add ice cubes at this point if you want it chilled.
3. Serve with a sprinkling of lemon zest.

Nutrition Info:
- Per Serving: Calories: 237 ;Fat: 1g ;Protein: 4g ;Carbs: 58g .

Cheery Cherry Smoothie

Servings: 1 | Cooking Time: 0 Minutes

Ingredients:
- 1 cup frozen pitted cherries, no-added-sugar
- ¼ cup fresh, or frozen, raspberries
- ¾ cup coconut water
- 1 tablespoon raw honey or maple syrup
- 1 teaspoon chia seeds
- 1 teaspoon hemp seeds
- Drop vanilla extract
- Ice

Directions:
1. Combine in a blender the cherries, raspberries, coconut water, honey, chia seeds, hemp seeds, vanilla, and ice. Blend until smooth.

Nutrition Info:
- Per Serving: Calories: 266 ;Fat: 2g ;Protein: 3g ;Carbs: 52g.

Nut-free Green Smoothie Bowl

Servings: 2 | Cooking Time: 0 Minutes

Ingredients:
- 3 cups packed baby spinach
- 1 green apple, cored
- 1 small ripe banana
- ½ ripe avocado
- 1 tablespoon maple syrup
- ½ cup mixed berries
- ¼ cup slivered almonds, toasted
- 1 teaspoon sesame seeds

Directions:
1. Combine the spinach, apple, banana, avocado, and maple syrup in a blender and blend until smooth. The mixture should be thick.
2. Divide the mixture between two bowls. Top with the berries, almonds, and sesame seeds, then serve.

Nutrition Info:
- Per Serving: Calories: 280 ; Fat: 14g ;Protein: 6g ;Carbs: 38g .

Tropical Strong Green Smoothie

Servings: 2 | Cooking Time: 0 Minutes

Ingredients:
- 2½ cups spinach
- 1½ cups water
- 1 cup pineapple, frozen
- 1 cup mango, frozen
- ¼ cup hemp seeds
- 1 teaspoon fresh ginger, grated

Directions:
1. Combine the spinach, water, pineapple, mango, hemp seeds, and ginger in a blender. Blend until smooth.
2. Pour into two glasses and enjoy.

Nutrition Info:
- Per Serving: Calories: 196 ;Fat: 7g ;Protein: 7g ;Carbs: 29g .

Southern Smoothie With Sweet Potato

Servings: 2 | Cooking Time: 0 Minutes

Ingredients:
- ½ cup almond milk, unsweetened
- ½ cup orange juice, freshly squeezed
- 1 cup sweet potato, cooked
- 1 banana
- 2 tablespoons pumpkin seeds
- 1 tablespoon pure maple syrup
- ½ teaspoon pure vanilla extract
- ½ teaspoon cinnamon, ground
- 3 ice cubes

Directions:
1. In a blender, combine the almond milk, orange juice, sweet potato, banana, pumpkin seeds, maple syrup, vanilla, and cinnamon. Blend until smooth.
2. Add the ice and blend until thick.

Nutrition Info:
- Per Serving: Calories: 235 ;Fat: 4g ;Protein: 5g ;Carbs: 43g .

Delectable Multivitamin Smoothie

Servings: 1 | Cooking Time: 0 Minutes

Ingredients:
- 1 cup red or white grapes
- 1 cup peaches, sliced frozen or fresh
- 1 cup cabbage, chopped
- 1 carrot, peeled and sliced
- ½ cup ice cubes
- ½ cup water
- 1 sprig of fresh mint

Directions:
1. Toss all of the ingredients in a blender or juicer until smooth.
2. Serve immediately in a tall glass with fresh mint to garnish.

Nutrition Info:
- Per Serving: Calories: 472 ;Fat: 14g ;Protein: 5g ;Carbs: 86g .

Stomach Soothing Smoothie With Green Apple

Servings: 1 | Cooking Time: 0 Minutes

Ingredients:
- ½ cup coconut water
- 1 green apple, cored, seeded, and quartered
- 1 cup spinach
- ¼ lemon, seeded
- ½ cucumber, peeled and seeded
- 2 teaspoons raw honey, or maple syrup
- Ice

Directions:
1. Combine the coconut water, apple, spinach, lemon, cucumber, honey, and ice in a blender then blend until smooth.

Nutrition Info:
- Per Serving: Calories: 176 ;Fat: 1g ;Protein: 2g ;Carbs: 41g .

Smoothie That Can Soothe Inflammation

Servings: 1 | Cooking Time: 0 Minutes

Ingredients:
- 1 pear, cored and quartered
- ½ fennel bulb
- 1 thin slice ginger, fresh
- 1 cup packed spinach
- ½ cucumber, peeled if wax-coated or not organic
- ½ cup water
- Ice

Directions:
1. Combine the pear, fennel, ginger, spinach, cucumber, water, and ice in a blender. Blend until smooth.

Nutrition Info:
- Per Serving: Calories: 147 ;Fat: 1g ;Protein: 4g ;Carbs: 37g .

For Advanced Green Juice

Servings: ½
Cooking Time: 0 Minutes

Ingredients:
- 3 cups spinach, 120g
- 1 Granny Smith apple
- 1 cucumber
- 1 fennel bulb
- One 1 inch piece fresh ginger
- One 1 inch piece fresh turmeric
- Freshly ground black pepper
- 1 lemon

Directions:
1. Wash all the fruits and vegetables and pat dry. Juice the spinach, apple, cucumber, fennel, ginger, turmeric, and a pinch of pepper according to your juicer's instructions. Squeeze in the lemon juice and stir. Serve immediately then garnish with another pinch of pepper.

Nutrition Info:
- Per Serving: Calories: 225 ;Fat: 2g ;Protein: 225g ;Carbs: 51g.

For Beginners Juice With Granny Smith Apples

Servings: 4 ¼

Cooking Time: 0 Minutes

Ingredients:
- 2 celery stalks
- 2 Granny Smith apples
- 2 cucumbers
- 2 hearts romaine lettuce
- 1 bunch lacinato kale, stems removed
- ½ bunch parsley
- One 1 inch piece fresh ginger
- 1 lemon or lime

Directions:
1. Wash all the fruits and vegetables and pat dry. Juice the celery, apples, cucumbers, lettuce, kale, parsley, and ginger according to your juicer's instructions. Squeeze in the lemon juice and stir. Serve immediately.

Nutrition Info:
- Per Serving: Calories: 204 ;Fat: 12g;Protein: 1g ;Carbs: 15g .

Fresh Berry Smoothie With Ginger

Servings: 2 | Cooking Time: 0 Minutes

Ingredients:
- 2 cups blackberries, fresh
- 2 cups almond milk, unsweetened
- 1 to 2 packets stevia, or to taste
- One 1 inch piece fresh ginger, peeled and roughly chopped
- 2 cups ice, crushed

Directions:
1. Combine the blackberries, almond milk, stevia, ginger, and ice in a blender. Blend until smooth.

Nutrition Info:

Per Serving: Calories: 95 ;Fat: 3g ;Protein: 3g ;Carbs: 16g.

Crunchy And Creamy Pistachio Smoothie

Servings: 2 | Cooking Time: 0 Minutes

Ingredients:
- 1 cup almond milk, unsweetened
- 1 cup kale, shredded
- 2 frozen bananas
- ½ cup pistachios, shelled
- 2 tablespoons pure maple syrup
- 1 teaspoon pure vanilla extract

Directions:
1. Combine the milk, kale, bananas, pistachios, maple syrup, and vanilla in a blender. Blend until smooth and thick.

Nutrition Info:
- Per Serving: Calories: 275 ;Fat: 4g ;Protein: 6g;Carbs: 48g .

Delicious Proteinaceous Smoothie

Servings: 1 | Cooking Time: 0 Minutes

Ingredients:
- 1 cup packed kale leaves, thoroughly washed
- ¼ avocado
- 1 cup fresh grapes
- ¼ cup cashews
- 1 tablespoon hemp seed
- 1 or 2 mint leaves
- 1 cup coconut milk
- Ice

Directions:
1. Combine the kale, avocado, grapes, cashews, hemp seed, mint leaves, coconut milk, and ice in a blender. Blend until smooth.

Nutrition Info:
- Per Serving: Calories: 500 ;Fat: 32g ;Protein: 13g ;Carbs: 47g.

Delightful Smoothie With Apple And Honey

Servings: 2 | Cooking Time: 0 Minutes

Ingredients:
- 1 cup canned lite coconut milk
- 1 apple, cored and cut into chunks
- 1 banana
- ¼ cup almond butter
- 1 tablespoon raw honey
- ½ teaspoon cinnamon, ground
- 4 ice cubes

Directions:
1. Combine the coconut milk, apple, banana, almond butter, honey, and cinnamon in a blender. Blend until smooth.
2. Add the ice and blend until thick.

Nutrition Info:
- Per Serving: Calories: 434 ;Fat: 30g ;Protein: 4g;Carbs: 46g .

Minty Juice With Pineapple And Cucumber

Servings: 3 ½

Cooking Time: 0 Minutes

Ingredients:
- 1 large, ripe pineapple, skin removed and core intact
- ¼ cup mint leaves
- 1 cucumber

Directions:
1. Cut the pineapple in long strips that will fit through the juicer feed tube. Process the pineapple, adding the mint leaves in between pieces, on the proper setting of the juicer. Juice the cucumber, then stir. Serve immediately.

Nutrition Info:
- Per Serving: Calories: 9 ;Fat: 5g;Protein: 1g ;Carbs: 2g .

Vegetarian Mango Smoothie With Green Tea And Turmeric

Servings: 2 | Cooking Time: 0 Minutes

Ingredients:
- 2 cups mango, cubed
- 2 teaspoons turmeric powder
- 2 tablespoons matcha powder
- 2 cups almond milk
- 2 tablespoons honey
- 1 cup ice, crushed

Directions:
1. Combine in a blender the mango, turmeric, matcha, almond milk, honey, and ice. Blend until smooth.

Nutrition Info:
- Per Serving: Calories: 285 ;Fat: 3g ;Protein: 4g ;Carbs: 68g .

Distinctive Chai Smoothie

Servings: 1 | Cooking Time: 0 Minutes

Ingredients:
- 1 cup unsweetened almond milk
- 1 date, pitted and chopped
- ¼ teaspoon vanilla extract
- ½ teaspoon chai spice blend
- Pinch salt
- 1 banana, sliced into ¼-inch rounds
- Ice cubes

Directions:
1. Combine in a blender the almond milk, date, vanilla, chai spice blend, salt, banana, and ice then blend until smooth.

Nutrition Info:
- Per Serving: Calories: 171| Fat: 4g ;Protein: 3g ;Carbs: 35g.

Great Watermelon Smoothie

Servings: 1 | Cooking Time: 0 Minutes

Ingredients:
- 1 cup watermelon chunks
- 2 cups mixed berries, frozen
- 1 cup coconut water
- 2 tablespoons chia seeds
- ½ cup tart cherries

Directions:
1. Blend ingredients in a blender or juicer until puréed.
2. Serve immediately and enjoy.

Nutrition Info:
- Per Serving: Calories: 1134 ;Fat: 26g ;Protein: 16g ;Carbs: 218g.

Desserts

Desserts

Coconut Chocolate Barks

Servings: 4 | Cooking Time: 35 Minutes

Ingredients:
- 1/3 cup coconut oil, melted
- ¼ cup almond butter, melted
- 2 tbsp coconut flakes.
- 1 tsp pure maple syrup
- A pinch of sea salt
- ¼ cup cocoa nibs

Directions:
1. Line a baking tray with baking paper and set aside. In a medium bowl, mix the coconut oil, almond butter, coconut flakes, maple syrup, and fold in the rock salt and cocoa nibs. Pour and spread the mixture on the baking sheet, chill in the refrigerator for 20 minutes or until firm. Remove the dessert, break into shards, and enjoy. Preserve extras in the refrigerator.

Nutrition Info:
- Per Serving: Calories: 280;Fat: 28g;Protein: 4g;Carbs: 9g.

Easiest Pressure-cooked Raspberry Curd

Servings: 4 | Cooking Time: 25 Minutes + Chilling Time

Ingredients:
- 12 oz raspberries
- 2 tbsp almond butter
- Juice of ½ lemon
- 1 cup packed brown sugar
- 2 egg yolks

Directions:
1. Combine the raspberries, sugar, and lemon juice in your Instant Pot. Close the lid and cook for a 1 on "Manual". Release the pressure naturally for 5 minutes. Puree the raspberries and discard the seeds. Whisk the yolks in a bowl. Combine the yolks with the hot raspberry puree. Pour the mixture into your pot. Cook with the lid off for a minute on "Sauté". Stir in the butter and cook for a couple more minutes, until thick. Transfer to a container with a lid. Refrigerate for at least an hour before serving.

Nutrition Info:
- Per Serving: Calories: 250;Fat: 7g;Protein: 2g;Carbs: 50g.

Great Pudding With Chocolate And Avocado

Servings: 4 | Cooking Time: 0 Minutes

Ingredients:
- 12 Medjool dates, pitted
- 2 avocados, halved and pitted
- ½ cup cacao powder
- 1 cup coconut milk, divided

Directions:
1. Combine the dates, avocado flesh, cacao powder, and ¾ cup of coconut milk in a food processor. Blend until smooth. Add the remaining ¼ cup of coconut milk if the pudding is too thick and blend well.
2. Refrigerate for an hour before serving.

Nutrition Info:
- Per Serving: Calories: 488 ;Fat: 36g ;Protein: 6g ;Carbs: 48g .

Vanilla Berry Tarts

Servings: 4 | Cooking Time: 35 Minutes + Cooling Time

Ingredients:
- 4 eggs, beaten
- 1/3 cup whole-wheat flour
- ½ tsp salt
- ¼ cup almond butter
- 3 tbsp pure malt syrup
- 6 oz coconut cream
- 6 tbsp pure date sugar
- ¾ tsp vanilla extract
- 1 cup mixed frozen berries

Directions:
1. Preheat your oven to 350ºF. In a large bowl, combine flour and salt. Add almond butter and whisk until crumbly. Pour in the eggs and malt syrup and mix until smooth dough forms. Flatten the dough on a flat surface, cover with plastic wrap, and refrigerate for 1 hour.
2. Dust a working surface with some flour, remove the dough onto the surface, and using a rolling pin, flatten the dough into a 1-inch diameter circle. Use a large cookie cutter, cut out rounds of the dough and fit into the pie pans. Use a knife to trim the edges of the pan. Lay a parchment paper on the dough cups, pour on some baking beans, and bake in the oven until golden brown, 15-20 minutes. Remove the pans from the oven, pour out the baking beans, and allow cooling. In a bowl, mix coconut cream, date sugar, and vanilla extract. Divide the mixture into the tart cups and top with berries. Serve.

Nutrition Info:
- Per Serving: Calories: 590;Fat: 38g;Protein: 13g;Carbs: 56g.

Peanut Chocolate Brownies

Servings: 6 | Cooking Time: 40 Minutes

Ingredients:
- 1 ¾ cups whole-grain flour
- 1 tsp baking powder
- ½ tsp sea salt
- 1 tbsp ground nutmeg
- ½ tsp ground cinnamon
- 3 tbsp cocoa powder
- ½ cup dark chocolate chips
- ½ cup chopped peanuts
- ¼ cup canola oil
- ½ cup dark molasses
- 3 tbsp pure date sugar
- 2 tsp grated fresh ginger

Directions:
1. Preheat your oven to 360ºF. Combine the flour, baking powder, salt, nutmeg, cinnamon, and cocoa in a bowl. Add in chocolate chips and peanuts and stir. Set aside. In another bowl, mix the oil, molasses, ½ cup water, date sugar, and ginger. Pour into the flour mixture and stir to combine. Transfer to a greased baking pan and bake for 30-35 minutes. Let cool before slicing.

Nutrition Info:
- Per Serving: Calories: 430;Fat: 19g;Protein: 12g;Carbs: 58g.

Almond & Chia Bites With Cherries

Servings: 2 | Cooking Time: 20 Minutes

Ingredients:
- 1 cup cherries, pitted
- 1 cup shredded coconut
- ¼ cup chia seeds
- ¾ cup ground almonds
- ¼ cup cocoa nibs

Directions:
1. Blend cherries, coconut, chia seeds, almonds, and cocoa nibs in a food processor until crumbly. Shape the mixture into 24 balls and arrange on a lined baking sheet. Let sit in the fridge for 15 minutes. Serve and enjoy!

Nutrition Info:
- Per Serving: Calories: 95;Fat: 2g;Protein: 4g;Carbs: 22g.

Cinnamon Pumpkin Pie

Servings: 4 | Cooking Time:70 Minutes + Cooling Time

Ingredients:
- For the piecrust:
- 4 eggs, beaten
- 1/3 cup whole-wheat flour
- ½ tsp salt
- ¼ cup cold almond butter
- 3 tbsp pure malt syrup
- For the filling:
- ¼ cup pure maple syrup
- ¼ cup pure date sugar
- 1 tsp cinnamon powder
- ½ tsp ginger powder
- 1/8 tsp clove powder
- 1 can pumpkin purée
- 1 cup almond milk

Directions:
1. Preheat your oven to 350ºF. In a bowl, combine flour and salt. Add the almond butter and whisk until crumbly. Pour in crust's eggs, maple syrup, vanilla, and mix until smooth dough forms. Flatten, cover with plastic wrap, and refrigerate for 1 hour.
2. Dust a working surface with flour, remove the dough onto the surface and flatten it into a 1-inch diameter circle. Lay the dough on a greased pie pan and press to fit the shape of the pan. Use a knife to trim the edges of the pan. Lay a parchment paper on the dough, pour on some baking beans and bake for 15-20 minutes. Remove, pour out the baking beans, and allow cooling. In a bowl, whisk the maple syrup, date sugar, cinnamon powder, ginger powder, clove powder, pumpkin puree, and almond milk. Pour the mixture onto the piecrust and bake for 35-40 minutes. Let cool completely. Serve sliced.

Nutrition Info:
- Per Serving: Calories: 590;Fat: 36g;Protein: 12g;Carbs: 61g.

Lime Avocado Ic E Cream

Servings: 4 | Cooking Time: 10 Minutes

Ingredients:
- 2 large avocados, pitted
- Juice and zest of 3 limes
- 1/3 cup stevia
- 1 ¾ cups coconut cream
- ¼ tsp vanilla extract

Directions:
1. In a blender, combine the avocado pulp, lime juice and zest, stevia, coconut cream, and vanilla extract. Process until the mixture is smooth. Pour the mixture into your ice cream maker and freeze based on the manufacturer's instructions. When ready, remove and scoop the ice cream into bowls. Serve immediately.

Nutrition Info:
- Per Serving: Calories: 515;Fat: 51g;Protein: 6g;Carbs: 18g.

Berry Macedonia With Mint

Servings: 4 | Cooking Time: 20 Minutes

Ingredients:
- ¼ cup lemon juice
- 4 tsp maple syrup
- 2 cups chopped pears
- 2 cups chopped strawberries
- 3 cups mixed berries
- 8 fresh mint leaves

Directions:
1. Chop half of the mint leaves; reserve. In a large bowl, combine together pears, strawberries, raspberries, blackberries, and half of the mint leaves. Divide the mixture between 4 small cups. Top with lemon juice, maple syrup, and mint leaves and serve chilled.

Nutrition Info:
- Per Serving: Calories: 520;Fat: 10g;Protein: 5g;Carbs: 108g.

Apple & Cashew Quiche

Servings: 6 | Cooking Time: 55 Minutes

Ingredients:
- 5 apples, peeled and sliced
- ½ cup pure maple syrup
- 1 tbsp fresh orange juice
- 1 tsp ground cinnamon
- ½ cup whole-grain flour
- ½ cup old-fashioned oats
- ½ cup chopped cashew
- 2 tbsp pure date sugar
- ½ cup almond butter

Directions:
1. Preheat your oven to 360ºF. Place apples in a greased baking pan. Stir in maple syrup and orange juice. Sprinkle with ½ tsp of cinnamon. In a bowl, combine the flour, oats, cashew, sugar, and remaining cinnamon. Blend in the almond butter until the mixture crumbs. Pour over the apples and bake for 45 minutes. Serve and enjoy!

Nutrition Info:
- Per Serving: Calories: 820;Fat: 42g;Protein: 9g;Carbs: 115g.

Apple & Berry Parfait

Servings: 4 | Cooking Time: 15 Minutes

Ingredients:
- 2 tbsp pistachios, chopped
- 1 can coconut milk
- 2 tbsp honey
- 4 cups mixed berries
- 1 peeled apple, chopped

Directions:
1. Put the coconut milk in the refrigerator to chill overnight. The next day, open the tin and scoop the solids have collected on top into a mixing bowl. Set aside the water. Add the honey to the coconut milk and whisk well. Divide half of the mixture between 4 glasses. Top with half of the fruit. Spoon over the remaining coconut mixture and finish with the remaining fruit. Chill the parfaits until needed. Sprinkle with pistachios before serving.

Nutrition Info:
• Per Serving: Calories: 390;Fat: 22g;Protein: 10g;Carbs: 47g.

Delectable Honeyed Apple Cinnamon Compote

Servings: 4 | Cooking Time: 10 Minutes

Ingredients:
• 6 apples, peeled, cored, and chopped
• ¼ cup apple juice
• ¼ cup honey
• 1 teaspoon cinnamon, ground
• pinch sea salt

Directions:
1. Combine the apples, apple juice, honey, cinnamon, and salt in a large pot over medium-high heat. Simmer for 10 minutes while stirring occasionally until the apples are quite chunky and saucy.

Nutrition Info:
• Per Serving: Calories: 247 ;Protein: 1g ;Carbs: 66g .

Wonderful Whipped Goat Cheese With Dark Berries

Servings: 4 | Cooking Time: 0 Minutes

Ingredients:
• 5 oz goat cheese, at room temperature
• 1 ½ tablespoon honey, plus more for serving
• 1 tablespoon lemon juice
• ½ teaspoon orange zest, grated
• Kosher salt
• 2 cups blueberries, 240g
• 2 cups blackberries, 240g
• ¼ cup pistachios, chopped and 30g

Directions:
1. In a medium bowl, place the goat cheese, honey, lemon juice, orange zest, and a pinch of salt. Whisk until the goat cheese is fluffy and smooth.
2. Divide the goat cheese mixture among bowls or wine glasses, reserving four spoonsful. Top each portion with berries, pistachios, and a spoonful of the whipped goat cheese. Drizzle with additional honey. Serve immediately.

Nutrition Info:
• Per Serving: Calories: 523 ;Fat: 17g ;Protein: 15g ;Carbs: 85g .

Melon Chocolate Pudding

Servings: 4 | Cooking Time: 25 Minutes

Ingredients:
• 1 cup cubed melon
• 4 tbsp non-dairy milk
• 2 tbsp cocoa powder
• 2 tbsp pure date sugar
• ½ ripe avocado

Directions:
1. Blitz the milk, cocoa powder, sugar, and avocado in a blender until smooth. Mash the melon with a fork in a bowl. Mix in the cocoa mixture and serve.

Nutrition Info:
• Per Serving: Calories: 85;Fat: 5g;Protein: 2g;Carbs: 12g.

Vanilla Chocolate Pudding

Servings: 4 | Cooking Time: 20 Minutes + Cooling Time

Ingredients:
• 3 eggs
• 1 cup cream cheese
• 2 ½ cups almond milk
• ½ pure date sugar
• 1 tbsp vanilla extract
• 6 oz dark chocolate chips
• ½ cup coconut cream
• 1 sliced banana

Directions:
1. In a large bowl, whisk the eggs with cream cheese until smooth. Pour in the almond milk into a pot and date sugar whisk again. Cook over medium heat while frequently stirring until the sugar dissolves. Reduce the heat to low and simmer until steamy and bubbly around the edges. Pour half of the almond milk mixture into the egg mix, whisk well and pour this mixture into the remaining milk content in the pot. Whisk continuously until well combined. Bring the new mixture to a boil over medium heat while still frequently stirring and scraping all the pot's corners, 2 minutes.
2. Turn the heat off, stir in the vanilla extract, then the chocolate chips until melted. Spoon the mixture into a bowl, allow cooling for 2 minutes, cover with plastic wraps, making sure to press the plastic onto the surface of the pudding, and refrigerate for 4 hours. Remove the pudding from the fridge, take off the plastic wrap, and whip for about a minute. Spoon the dessert into serving cups, swirl some coconut whipping cream on top, and top with banana. Enjoy!

Nutrition Info:
• Per Serving: Calories: 720;Fat: 46g;Protein: 11g;Carbs: 71g.

Compote With Blueberries & Lemon Juice

Servings: 4 | Cooking Time: 2 Hours 50 Minutes

Ingredients:
• 2 cups frozen blueberries
• 2 tbsp arrowroot or starch
• ¾ cups coconut sugar
• Juice of ½ lemon

Directions:
1. Place the blueberries, lemon juice, and sugar in your Instant Pot. Close the lid and cook for 3 minutes on "Manual". Release the pressure naturally for 10 minutes. Combine the arrowroot and 2 tbsp of water. Stir the mixture into the cooked blueberries and cook until the mixture thickens. Transfer the compote to a bowl and let cool completely. Refrigerate for 2 hours.

Nutrition Info:
• Per Serving: Calories: 220;Fat: 0.3g;Protein: 1g;Carbs: 62g.

Sweet And Special Spiced Pecans

Servings: 4 | Cooking Time: 17 Minutes

Ingredients:
• 1 cup pecan halves
• ¼ cup brown sugar, packed
• 3 tablespoons unsalted butter, melted
• 1 teaspoon cinnamon, ground
• ½ teaspoon nutmeg, ground
• ¼ teaspoon sea salt

Directions:
1. Preheat the oven to 350°F.
2. Line a rimmed baking sheet with parchment paper.

3. Toss in a medium bowl together with the pecans, brown sugar, butter, cinnamon, nutmeg, and salt to combine. Spread the nuts in a single layer on the prepared sheet.
4. Bake for 15 to 17 minutes until the nuts are fragrant.

Nutrition Info:
• Per Serving: Calories: 323 ;Fat: 30g ;Protein: 3g ;Carbs: 14g .

Apple-cinnamon Compote
Servings: 4 | Cooking Time: 25 Minutes

Ingredients:
• 6 peeled apples, chopped
• 1 tsp fresh lemon juice
• ¼ cup orange juice
• ¼ cup honey
• 1 tsp ground cinnamon
• A pinch of sea salt

Directions:
1. Place the apples, orange juice, lemon juice, honey, cinnamon, and salt in a pot over medium heat and simmer for 10 minutes until the apples are tender. Let cool completely before serving.

Nutrition Info:
• Per Serving: Calories: 250;Fat: 1g;Protein: 8g;Carbs: 67g.

Chocolate Fudge With Nuts
Servings: 4 | Cooking Time: 10 Minutes + Cooling Time

Ingredients:
• 3 cups chocolate chips
• ¼ cup thick coconut milk
• 1 ½ tsp vanilla extract
• A pinch of sea salt
• 1 cup chopped mixed nuts

Directions:
1. Line a square pan with baking paper. Melt the chocolate chips, coconut milk, and vanilla in a medium pot over low heat. Mix in the salt and nuts until well distributed and pour the mixture into the square pan. Refrigerate for at least 2 hours. Cut into squares and serve.

Nutrition Info:
• Per Serving: Calories: 905;Fat: 32g;Protein: 8g;Carbs: 152g.

Wound Healer Warm Almond Milk With Cinnamon And Turmeric
Servings: 4 To 6

Cooking Time: 3 To 4 Hours
Ingredients:
• 4 cups unsweetened almond milk
• 4 cinnamon sticks
• 2 tablespoons coconut oil
• 1 (4 inch) piece turmeric root, roughly chopped
• 1 (2 inch) piece fresh ginger, roughly chopped
• 1 teaspoon raw honey, plus more to taste

Directions:
1. Combine the almond milk, cinnamon sticks, coconut oil, turmeric, and ginger in your slow cooker.
2. Cover the cooker and set to low. Cook for 3 to 4 hours.
3. Pour the contents of the cooker through a fine-mesh sieve into a clean container; discard the solids.
4. Starting with just 1 teaspoon, add raw honey to taste.

Nutrition Info:
• Per Serving: Calories: 133 ;Fat: 11g ;Protein: 1g ;Carbs: 10g .

Elegant Panna Cotta With Honey And Blackberry-lime Sauce
Servings: 6 | Cooking Time: 5 Minutes

Ingredients:
• 2 ½ cups canned unsweetened coconut milk, 600ml
• 2 teaspoons gelatin
• ¼ cup honey, 60ml
• 1 vanilla bean, split and seeds scraped
• Kosher salt
• Blackberry-Lime Sauce:
• 2 cups blackberries, 240g
• Finely grated zest of ½ lime, plus 2 teaspoons lime juice
• 1 teaspoon raw cane sugar

Directions:
1. In a small bowl, place ½ cup (120 ml) of coconut milk. Sprinkle the gelatin over the top and allow it to sit for 2 minutes.
2. Place the remaining 2 cups (480 ml) coconut milk, honey, vanilla bean with its seeds, and a pinch of salt in a medium saucepan. Warm over low heat while whisking until bubbles form around the edge of the pan. Remove from the heat and let the mixture steep for 5 minutes.
3. Pour the coconut milk mixture through a fine-mesh strainer into a large bowl. Discard the vanilla bean. Whisk slowly the gelatin mixture into the warm coconut mixture until there are no lumps of gelatin. Divide evenly among six ½ cup ramekins or wine glasses. Cover and refrigerate until set for 4 hours or overnight.
4. Make the blackberry-lime sauce. In a medium bowl, place the blackberries, lime zest, lime juice, and sugar. Gently mash using a fork or pastry blender the berries, leaving some large pieces of berry while allowing some of the juices to make a sauce. Set aside for 10 minutes, or cover and refrigerate up to overnight.
5. Spoon the sauce over each chilled panna cotta. Serve immediately.

Nutrition Info:
• Per Serving: Calories: 357 ;Fat: 24g ;Protein: 4g ;Carbs: 39g .

Lemony Lavender With Strawberry Compote
Servings: 4 | Cooking Time: 30 Minutes

Ingredients:
• 2 cups strawberries, halved
• juice and zest a lemon
• 2 tablespoons raw honey
• 1 tablespoon lavender extract

Directions:
1. Into a saucepan, put all of the ingredients together and then simmer on a very low heat until the honey has been dissolved for 15 to 20 minutes.
2. Add the strawberries when the sauce starts to thicken and simmer for 5 to 10 minutes.
3. Serve warm right away or allow to cool and drizzle over yogurt later on.

Nutrition Info:
• Per Serving: Calories: 67 ;Fat: 2g;Protein: 1g ;Carbs: 15g .

Mango Muffins With Chocolate Chips

Servings: 6 | Cooking Time: 40 Minutes

Ingredients:
- 2 mangoes, chopped
- 1 cup non-dairy milk
- 2 tbsp almond butter
- 1 tsp apple cider vinegar
- 1 tsp pure vanilla extract
- 1 ¼ cups whole-wheat flour
- ½ cup rolled oats
- ¼ cup coconut sugar
- 1 tsp baking powder
- ½ tsp baking soda
- ½ cup cocoa powder
- ¼ cup sesame seeds
- A pinch of salt
- ¼ cup dark chocolate chips

Directions:
1. Preheat your oven to 360ºF. In a food processor, put the mangoes, milk, almond butter, vinegar, and vanilla. Blend until smooth. In a bowl, combine the flour, oats, sugar, baking powder, baking soda, cocoa powder, sesame seeds, salt, and chocolate chips. Pour into the mango mixture and mix. Scoop into greased muffin cups and bake for 20-25 minutes. Let cool completely before removing it from the cups. Serve and enjoy!

Nutrition Info:
- Per Serving: Calories: 230;Fat: 11g;Protein: 8g;Carbs: 35g.

Non-dairy Butter Mousse With Chocolate And Almond

Servings: 4 | Cooking Time: 0 Minutes

Ingredients:
- 2 avocados, peeled and pitted
- ¼ cup almond butter
- ¼ cup lite coconut milk
- ¼ cup cocoa powder, unsweetened
- ¼ cup pure maple syrup
- pinch sea salt

Directions:
1. Combine the avocados, almond butter, coconut milk, cocoa powder, maple syrup, and salt in a blender or food processor then process until smooth.

Nutrition Info:
- Per Serving: Calories: 271 ;Fat: 21g ;Protein: 2g ;Carbs: 23g .

Delicious Nutmeg Muffins With Vanilla And Blueberries

Servings: 4 | Cooking Time: 20 Minutes

Ingredients:
- 3 free range egg whites
- 1/10 cup chickpea flour
- 1 tablespoon coconut flour
- 1 teaspoon baking powder
- 1 tablespoon nutmeg, grated
- 1 teaspoon vanilla extract
- 1 teaspoon stevia
- ½ cup fresh blueberries

Directions:
1. Preheat the oven to 325°F.
2. In a mixing bowl, mix all of the ingredients.
3. Divide the batter into 4 and spoon into a muffin tin.

4. Bake in the oven for 15 to 20 minutes or until cooked through.
5. Your knife should pull out clean from the middle of the muffins once done.
6. Allow to cool on a wire rack before serving.

Nutrition Info:
- Per Serving: Calories: 63 ;Fat: 1g ;Protein: 4g ;Carbs: 10g .

Oatmeal Cookies With Hazelnuts

Servings: 2 | Cooking Time: 15 Minutes

Ingredients:
- 1 ½ cups whole-grain flour
- 1 tsp baking powder
- 1 tsp ground cinnamon
- ¼ tsp ground nutmeg
- 1 ½ cups old-fashioned oats
- 1 cup chopped hazelnuts
- ½ cup almond butter, melted
- ½ cup pure maple syrup
- ¼ cup pure date sugar
- 2 tsp pure vanilla extract

Directions:
1. Preheat your oven to 360ºF. Combine the flour, baking powder, cinnamon, and nutmeg in a bowl. Add in oats and hazelnuts. In another bowl, whisk the almond butter, maple syrup, sugar, and vanilla. Pour over the flour mixture. Mix. Spoon a small ball of cookie dough on a baking sheet and press down with a fork. Bake for 10-12 minutes until browned. Let completely cool on a rack.

Nutrition Info:
- Per Serving: Calories: 1580;Fat: 95g;Protein: 35g;Carbs: 190g.

Cashew & Plum Cheesecake

Servings: 4 | Cooking Time: 20 Minutes + Cooling Time

Ingredients:
- 2/3 cup toasted rolled oats
- ¼ cup almond butter, melted
- 3 tbsp pure date sugar
- 6 oz coconut cream
- ¼ cup oat milk
- ¼ cup just-boiled water
- 3 tsp arrowroot
- 4 plums, cored and diced
- 2 tbsp cashew, chopped

Directions:
1. Process the oats, almond butter, and date sugar in a blender until smooth. Pour the mixture into a greased baking pan and press the mixture onto the bottom of the pan. Refrigerate for 30 minutes until firm while you make the filling. In a large bowl, beat the coconut cream until smooth. Mix in the oat milk. Ina small bowl, whisk 2 tbsp of warm water and arrowroot until dissolved and pour the slurry into the coconut mixture. Fold in the plums. Remove the cake pan from the fridge and pour it in the plum mixture. Shake the pan to ensure smooth layering on top. Refrigerate for at least 3 hours. Garnish the cake with cashew nuts. Serve sliced.

Nutrition Info:
- Per Serving: Calories: 380;Fat: 29g;Protein: 7g;Carbs: 29g.

Hazelnut Topped Caramelized Bananas

Servings: 4 | Cooking Time: 15 Minutes

Ingredients:
- 2 bananas, peeled, halved crosswise and then lengthwise
- 2 tbsp coconut oil
- 2 tbsp coconut sugar
- 2 tbsp spiced apple cider
- 2 chopped hazelnuts

Directions:
1. Warm the coconut oil in a skillet over medium heat. Fry the bananas for 4 minutes, turning once. Pour the sugar and cider around the bananas, cook for 2-3 minutes, until thickens and caramelize. Remove to a serving plate and pour the cooked sauce over. Serve topped with hazelnuts.

Nutrition Info:
- Per Serving: Calories: 315;Fat: 25g;Protein: 5g;Carbs: 24g.

Walnut Pears With Maple Glaze

Servings: 4 | Cooking Time: 30 Minutes

Ingredients:
- 4 pears, peeled, cored, and quartered lengthwise
- 1 cup apple juice
- ½ cup pure maple syrup
- 1 tbsp grated fresh ginger
- ¼ cup walnuts, chopped

Directions:
1. Place the pears and apple juice in a pot over medium heat and bring to a simmer. Then low the heat and cook covered for 15-20 minutes until tender. Place the maple syrup and ginger in a saucepan and bring to a simmer. Turn the heat off and let it rest. Transfer the pears to a plate and drizzle with maple syrup. Scatter with walnuts.

Nutrition Info:
- Per Serving: Calories: 290;Fat: 4g;Protein: 8g;Carbs: 68g.

Nutty Date Cake

Servings: 4 | Cooking Time:1 Hour 30 Minutes

Ingredients:
- ½ cup cold almond butter, cut into pieces
- 1 egg, beaten
- ½ cup whole-wheat flour
- ¼ cup chopped nuts
- 1 tsp baking powder
- 1 tsp baking soda
- 1 tsp cinnamon powder
- 1 tsp salt
- 1/3 cup dates, chopped
- ½ cup pure date sugar
- 1 tsp vanilla extract
- ¼ cup pure date syrup

Directions:
1. Preheat your oven to 350ºF. In a food processor, add the flour, nuts, baking powder, baking soda, cinnamon powder, and salt. Blend until well combined. Add 1/3 cup of water, almond butter, dates, date sugar, and vanilla. Process until smooth with tiny pieces of dates evident.
2. Pour the batter into a greased baking dish. Bake in the oven for 1 hour and 10 minutes or until a toothpick inserted comes out clean. Remove the dish from the oven, invert the cake onto a serving platter to cool, drizzle with the date syrup, slice, and serve.

Nutrition Info:
- Per Serving: Calories: 440;Fat: 28g;Protein: 8g;Carbs: 48g.

Fruitylicious Hot Milk

Servings: 2 | Cooking Time: 10 Minutes

Ingredients:
- 1 can low fat coconut milk
- 3 bananas, sliced
- 2½cup fresh raspberries

Directions:
1. Simmer ingredients for 10 minutes on a medium-low heat in a pan.
2. Whizz up in a blender until smooth.
3. Serve warm or allow to cool and add ice cubes to serve as a chilled milkshake.

Nutrition Info:
- Per Serving: Calories: 116 ;Fat: 5g;Protein: 1g ;Carbs: 30g .

Almond Berry Cream

Servings: 4 | Cooking Time: 10 Minutes

Ingredients:
- 3 cans almond milk
- 3 tbsp maple syrup
- ½ tsp almond extract
- 1 cup blueberries
- 1 cup raspberries
- 1 cup strawberries, sliced

Directions:
1. Place almond milk in the fridge overnight. Open the can and reserve the liquid. In a bowl, mix almond solids, maple syrup, and almond extract. Share berries into 4 bowls. Serve topped with almond cream.

Nutrition Info:
- Per Serving: Calories: 201;Fat: 160g;Protein: 69g;Carbs: 111g.

Perfect Thickness Blueberry Ambrosia

Servings: 4 | Cooking Time: 0 Minutes

Ingredients:
- One 14 ounces can full-fat coconut milk, chilled
- 2 tablespoons honey
- 1-pint fresh blueberries
- 1-pint fresh raspberries
- 1 apple, peeled, cored, and chopped

Directions:
1. Into a large bowl, open the chilled can of coconut milk and scoop the solids that have collected on top. Discard the water.
2. Whisk the coconut milk with the honey.
3. Stir gently the blueberries, raspberries, and apple to coat the fruit with the coconut milk.

Nutrition Info:
- Per Serving: Calories: 387 ;Fat: 21g ;Protein: 4g ;Carbs: 46g .

Coconut & Chocolate Brownies

Servings: 4 | Cooking Time: 40 Minutes

Ingredients:
- 1 cup whole-grain flour
- ½ cup cocoa powder
- 1 tsp baking powder
- ½ tsp salt
- 1 cup pure date sugar
- ½ cup canola oil
- ¾ cup almond milk
- 1 tsp pure vanilla extract
- 1 tsp coconut extract

- ½ cup dark chocolate chips
- ½ cup shredded coconut

Directions:
1. Preheat your oven to 360°F. In a bowl, combine the flour, cocoa, baking powder, and salt. In another bowl, whisk the date sugar and oil until creamy. Add in almond milk, vanilla, and coconut. Mix until smooth. Pour into the flour mixture and stir to combine. Fold in the coconut and chocolate chips. Pour the batter into a greased baking pan and bake for 35-40 minutes. Serve chilled.

Nutrition Info:
- Per Serving: Calories: 600;Fat: 31g;Protein: 7g;Carbs: 83g.

A Different Pumpkin Pie

Servings: 4 | Cooking Time: 30 Minutes

Ingredients:
- 1 lb butternut squash, diced
- 1 egg
- 2 tbsp honey
- ½ cup coconut milk
- ½ tsp cinnamon
- ½ tbsp arrowroot
- A pinch of sea salt

Directions:
1. Pour the water inside your Instant Pot and insert a trivet. Place the butternut squash in a steamer basket and put it on the trivet. Seal the lid and cook for 4 minutes on "Manual". Whisk all of the remaining ingredients in a bowl. Once the cooking is completed, perform a quick pressure release and drain the squash. Then, transfer to the milk mixture. Pour the batter into a greased baking dish. Place inside the Instant Pot. Seal the lid and cook for 10 minutes on "Manual". Once it goes off, let the pressure release naturally for 5 minutes. Then perform a quick pressure release. Very carefully remove the pan. Let it cool a few minutes before serving.

Nutrition Info:
- Per Serving: Calories: 170;Fat: 2g;Protein: 3g;Carbs: 40g.

Pressure Cooker Apple Cupcakes

Servings: 4 | Cooking Time: 25 Minutes + Cooling Time

Ingredients:
- 1 cup free-sugar applesauce
- 1 cup non-dairy milk
- 6 tbsp maple syrup
- ¼ cup spelt flour
- ½ tsp apple pie spice
- A pinch of sea salt

Directions:
1. In a bowl, combine the applesauce, milk, maple syrup, flour, apple pie spice, and salt. Scoop into 4 heat-proof ramekins. Drizzle with more syrup. Pour 1 cup of water into the pressure cooker and fit in a trivet. Place the ramekins on the trivet. Lock lid in place; set the time to 6 minutes on High. Once ready, perform a quick pressure release. Unlock the lid and let cool for a few minutes; take out the ramekins. Allow cooling and serve.

Nutrition Info:
- Per Serving: Calories: 170;Fat: 2g;Protein: 3g;Carbs: 38g.

Southern Apple Cobbler With Raspberries

Servings: 4 | Cooking Time: 50 Minutes

Ingredients:
- 3 apples, chopped
- 2 tbsp pure date sugar
- 1 cup fresh raspberries
- 2 tbsp almond butter
- ½ cup whole-wheat flour
- 1 cup toasted rolled oats
- 2 tbsp pure date sugar
- 1 tsp cinnamon powder

Directions:
1. Preheat your oven to 350°F and grease a baking dish with some almond butter. Add apples, date sugar, and 3 tbsp of water to a pot. Cook over low heat until the date sugar melts and then mix in the raspberries. Cook until the fruits soften, 10 minutes. Pour and spread the fruit mixture into the baking dish and set aside.
2. In a blender, add the almond butter, flour, oats, date sugar, and cinnamon powder. Pulse a few times until crumbly. Spoon and spread the mixture on the fruit mix until evenly layered. Bake in the oven for 25 to 30 minutes or until golden brown on top. Remove the dessert, allow cooling for 2 minutes, and serve.

Nutrition Info:
- Per Serving: Calories: 270;Fat: 5g;Protein: 5g;Carbs: 59g.

Almond & Chocolate Cookies

Servings: 6 | Cooking Time: 20 Minutes

Ingredients:
- ¼ cup cocoa powder
- ¾ cup almond butter, softened
- ½ cup coconut sugar
- 1 egg
- 1 egg yolk
- 2 tsp vanilla extract
- ½ cup dark chocolate chips,
- 1 tsp baking soda
- ¼ tsp salt

Directions:
1. Preheat the oven to 350°F. Line two baking sheets with parchment paper. Combine the cocoa powder, almond butter, vanilla extract, and coconut sugar in a bowl. In another bowl, beat the egg and egg yolk, pour it into the almond mixture, and stir. Mix in baking soda, salt, and chocolate chips. Shape 12 balls out of the mixture and place 6 of them on each sheet and bake for 9-10 minutes. Let rest for 5 minutes and sprinkle with salt. Serve cold.

Nutrition Info:
- Per Serving: Calories: 225;Fat: 7g;Protein: 6g;Carbs: 22g.

Pistachios & Chocolate Popsicles

Servings: 4 | Cooking Time: 5 Minutes + Cooling Time

Ingredients:
- 2 oz dark chocolate, melted
- 1 ½ cups oat milk
- 1 tbsp cocoa powder
- 3 tbsp pure date syrup
- 1 tsp vanilla extract
- 2 tbsp pistachios, chopped

Directions:
1. In a blender, add chocolate, oat milk, cocoa powder, date syrup, vanilla, pistachios, and process until smooth. Divide the mixture into popsicle molds and freeze for 3 hours. Dip the pop-

sicle molds in warm water to loosen the popsicles and pull out the popsicles.

Nutrition Info:
• Per Serving: Calories: 120;Fat: 3g;Protein: 6g;Carbs: 24g.

Chocolate Peppermint Mousse

Servings: 4 | Cooking Time: 10 Minutes + Chilling Time

Ingredients:
• ¼ cup stevia, divided
• 4 oz cream cheese, softened
• 3 tbsp cocoa powder
• ¾ tsp peppermint extract
• ½ tsp vanilla extract
• 1/3 cup coconut cream

Directions:
1. Put 2 tablespoons of stevia, cream cheese, and cocoa powder in a blender. Add the peppermint extract, ¼ cup of warm water, and process until smooth. In a bowl, whip vanilla extract, coconut cream, and the remaining stevia using a whisk. Fetch out 5-6 tablespoons for garnishing. Fold in the cocoa mixture until thoroughly combined. Spoon the mousse into serving cups and chill in the fridge for 30 minutes. Garnish with the reserved whipped cream and serve.

Nutrition Info:
• Per Serving: Calories: 315;Fat: 30g;Protein: 5g;Carbs: 14g.

Walnut Chocolate Squares

Servings: 6 | Cooking Time: 10 Minutes

Ingredients:
• 4 oz dark chocolate
• 4 tbsp peanut butter
• 1 pinch of sea salt
• ¼ cup walnut butter
• ½ tsp vanilla extract
• ¼ cup chopped walnuts

Directions:
1. Pour the chocolate and peanut butter into a safe microwave bowl and melt in the microwave for 1-2 minutes. Remove the bowl from the microwave and mix in salt, walnut butter, and vanilla. Pour the batter into a greased baking dish and use a spatula to spread out into a rectangle. Top with walnuts and chill in the refrigerator. Once set, cut into squares. Serve while firming.

Nutrition Info:
• Per Serving: Calories: 245;Fat: 26g;Protein: 2g;Carbs: 2g.

Hearty Gelato With Chocolate And Cinnamon

Servings: 4 To 6

Cooking Time: 0 Minutes

Ingredients:
• 2 teaspoon cornstarch
• 3 cups Almond Milk or whole milk, 720 ml
• ¼ cup raw cane sugar, 50 g
• ¼ teaspoon kosher salt
• 4 ounces dark chocolate (70 percent cacao), coarsely chopped
• 1 teaspoon cinnamon, ground
• ½ teaspoon vanilla extract
• Chocolate shavings, crushed walnuts, or crushed fresh raspberries

Directions:
1. In a small bowl, put the cornstarch, add 1 tablespoon of almond milk and stir with a fork to dissolve the cornstarch.

2. Into a medium saucepan, pour the rest of the almond milk. Bring to a simmer over medium heat, then turn lower the heat. Whisk in the cornstarch mixture, sugar, and salt to dissolve. Add the chocolate and cinnamon and whisk until the mixture is completely smooth. Cook while whisking until the mixture starts to thicken for 5 minutes.
3. Pour the milk mixture through a fine-mesh strainer into a large bowl. Stir in the vanilla. Refrigerate until chilled for 3 hours.
4. Whisk the chilled mixture. Freeze in an ice-cream maker according to the manufacturer's instructions. The gelato is ready when it has the consistency of soft-serve ice cream. Transfer to an airtight container and freeze for up to 1 week.
5. To serve, scoop into serving bowls and garnish as desired.

Nutrition Info:
• Per Serving: Calories: 354 ;Fat: 18g ;Protein: 8g ;Carbs: 42g .

Glazed Chili Chocolate Cake

Servings: 4 | Cooking Time: 45 Minutes

Ingredients:
• 1 ¾ cups whole-grain flour
• 1 cup pure date sugar
• ¼ cup cocoa powder
• 1 tsp baking soda
• ½ tsp baking powder
• 1 ½ tsp ground cinnamon
• ¼ tsp ground chili
• 3 tbsp olive oil
• 1 tbsp apple cider vinegar
• 1 ½ tsp pure vanilla extract
• 2 squares dark chocolate
• ¼ cup soy milk
• ½ cup pure date sugar
• 3 tbsp almond butter
• ½ tsp pure vanilla extract

Directions:
1. Preheat your oven to 360ºF. In a bowl, mix the whole-grain flour, date sugar, baking soda, baking powder, cinnamon, and chili. In another bowl, whisk the oil, vinegar, vanilla, and 1 cup cold water. Pour into the flour mixture, stir to combine. Pour the batter into a greased baking pan. Bake for 30 minutes. Let cool for 10-15 minutes. Take out the cake inverted onto a wire rack and allow to cool completely. Place the chocolate and soy milk in a pot. Cook until the chocolate is melted. Add in sugar, cook for 5 minutes. Turn the heat off and mix in almond butter and vanilla. Cover the cake with the glaze. Refrigerate until the glaze is set. Serve.

Nutrition Info:
• Per Serving: Calories: 680;Fat: 36g;Protein: 10g;Carbs: 85g.

Macedonia Salad With Coconut & Pecans

Servings: 4 | Cooking Time: 15 Minutes + Cooling Time

Ingredients:
• 1 cup pineapple tidbits, drained
• 1 can mandarin oranges
• 1 cup pure coconut cream
• ½ tsp vanilla extract
• 2 bananas, cut into chunks
• 1 ½ cups coconut flakes
• 4 tbsp toasted pecans, minced
• ¾ cup maraschino cherries

Directions:
1. In a medium bowl, mix the coconut cream and vanilla extract until well combined. In a larger bowl, combine the bananas, co-

conut flakes, pecans, pineapple, oranges, and cherries until evenly distributed. Pour on the coconut cream mixture and fold well into the salad. Chill in the refrigerator for 1 hour and serve afterward.

Nutrition Info:
- Per Serving: Calories: 530;Fat: 35g;Protein: 5g;Carbs: 55g.

Healthy Brownies With Cacao

Servings: 4 To 6

Cooking Time: 2 ½ To 3 Hours

Ingredients:
- 3 tablespoons coconut oil, divided
- 1 cup almond butter
- 1 cup cacao powder, unsweetened
- ½ cup coconut sugar
- 2 large eggs
- 2 ripe bananas
- 2 teaspoons vanilla extract
- 1 teaspoon baking soda
- ½ teaspoon sea salt

Directions:
1. Coat the bottom of the slow cooker with 1 tablespoon of coconut oil.
2. Combine in a medium bowl the almond butter, cacao powder, coconut sugar, eggs, bananas, vanilla, baking soda, and salt. Mash the bananas and stir well until the batter forms. Pour the batter into the slow cooker.
3. Cover the cooker and set to low. Cook for 2½ to 3 hours until firm to a light touch and gooey in the middle then serve.

Nutrition Info:
- Per Serving: Calories: 779 ;Fat: 51g ;Protein: 18g ;Carbs: 68g .

Raisin Oatmeal Biscuits

Servings: 6 | Cooking Time: 20 Minutes

Ingredients:
- ½ cup almond butter
- 1 cup date sugar
- ¼ cup pineapple juice
- 1 cup whole-grain flour
- 1 tsp baking powder
- ½ tsp salt
- 1 tsp vanilla extract
- 1 cup old-fashioned oats
- ½ cup dark chocolate chips
- ½ cup raisins

Directions:
1. Preheat your oven to 370ºF. Beat the almond butter and date sugar in a bowl until creamy and fluffy. Pour in the juice and blend. Mix in flour, baking powder, salt, and vanilla. Stir in oats, chocolate chips, and raisins. Spread the dough on a baking sheet and bake for 15 minutes. Let completely cool on a rack. Serve and enjoy!

Nutrition Info:
- Per Serving: Calories: 385;Fat: 17g;Protein: 6g;Carbs: 60g.

Tangy Yogurt With Coconut And Vanilla

Servings: 3 ½

Cooking Time: 1 To 2 Hours

Ingredients:
- 3 cans full-fat coconut milk, 13 ½ ounces
- 5 probiotic capsules
- 1 teaspoon raw honey
- ½ teaspoon vanilla extract

Directions:
1. Pour the coconut milk into the slow cooker.
2. Cover the cooker and set to high. Cook for 1 to 2 hours until the temperature of the milk reaches 180ºF measured with a candy thermometer.
3. Turn off the slow cooker and allow the temperature of the milk to come down close to 100ºF.
4. Open the probiotic capsules and pour in the contents along with the honey and vanilla. Stir well to combine.
5. Cover again the slow cooker, turn it off and unplug it, and wrap it in an insulating towel to keep warm overnight as it ferments.
6. Pour the yogurt into sterilized jars and refrigerate. The yogurt should thicken slightly in the refrigerator, where it will keep for up to 1 week.

Nutrition Info:
- Per Serving: Calories: 305 ;Fat: 30g ;Protein: 2g ;Carbs: 7g .

Mid Afternoon Grilled Banana And Homemade Nut Butter

Servings: 2 | Cooking Time: 5 Minutes

Ingredients:
- 2 bananas
- 1 cup almonds

Directions:
1. Peel bananas and cut lengthways with a knife down the center to form a banana split.
2. Blend the almonds until smooth to form your own nut butter.
3. Spread almond butter along the middle of the bananas and broil for 3 to 4 minutes on a medium heat until browned.
4. Serve immediately.

Nutrition Info:
- Per Serving: Calories: 3 ;Fat: 5g;Protein: 6g;Carbs: 2g

Pressure Cooked Cherry Pie

Servings: 6 | Cooking Time: 45 Minutes

Ingredients:
- 1 9-inch double pie crust
- ½ tsp vanilla extract
- 4 cups cherries, pitted
- ¼ tsp almond extract
- 4 tbsp quick tapioca
- 1 cup packed brown sugar
- A pinch of sea salt

Directions:
1. Add 1 cup of water to the Instant Pot and place the steam rack on top. Combine the cherries with tapioca, sugar, extracts, and salt. Place one pie crust on the bottom of a lined springform pan. Spread the filling over. Top with the other crust. Place the pan on the steam rack. Seal the lid and cook for 18 minutes on "Manual" on high pressure. Wait 10 minutes before releasing the pressure quickly. Carefully remove the top so that any condensation doesn't drip on the pie, then carefully remove the pan using oven mitts or tongs. Let it cool for at least 5 minutes before serving.

Nutrition Info:
- Per Serving: Calories: 395;Fat: 12g;Protein: 2g;Carbs: 70g.

Sherry-lime Mango Dessert

Servings: 4 | Cooking Time: 15 Minutes

Ingredients:
- 3 ripe mangoes, cubed
- ¼ cup pure date sugar
- 2 tbsp fresh lime juice
- ½ cup Sherry wine
- Fresh mint sprigs

Directions:
1. Arrange the mango cubes on a baking sheet. Sprinkle with some dates and let sit covered for 30 minutes. Sprinkle with lime juice and sherry wine. Refrigerate for 1 hour. Remove from the fridge and let sit for a few minutes at room temperature. Serve topped with mint.

Nutrition Info:
- Per Serving: Calories: 80;Fat: 1g;Protein: 1g;Carbs: 18g.

Spiced Supreme Orange

Servings: 2 | Cooking Time: 15 Minutes

Ingredients:
- ½ cup water
- 1 tablespoon raw honey
- 1 lemon
- 1 small cinnamon stick
- 1 clove
- 2 oranges, peeled and sectioned
- 1 sprig fresh mint

Directions:
1. Add all of the ingredients except the oranges to a saucepan.
2. Cook over a medium heat until thickened for 10 to 15 minutes.
3. Add the oranges, and then simmer for a minute.
4. Transfer all ingredients to a bowl or container and place in the fridge, marinate for 2 hours or preferably overnight.
5. Drain orange slices and garnish with a little fresher mint to serve.
6. Best served with low fat Greek yogurt for summer or warmed through in the winter.

Nutrition Info:
- Per Serving: Calories: 128 ;Fat: 3g ;Protein: 12g;Carbs: 27g .

Caribbean Pudding

Servings: 4 | Cooking Time: 10 Minutes + Chilling Time

Ingredients:
- 3 kiwis, divided
- 1 can coconut milk
- ¼ cup organic cane sugar
- 1 tbsp arrowroot
- 1 tsp vanilla extract
- 2 pinches of salt
- 1 tbsp turmeric
- Ground cinnamon

Directions:
1. In a blender, place the 2 kiwis, coconut milk, sugar, arrowroot, vanilla, and salt. Blitz until smooth. Stir in turmeric. Pour into a pot. Bring to a boil, lower the heat and simmer for 3 minutes until pudding consistency is achieved. Remove to a bowl and let cool. Refrigerate covered overnight to set. Before serving, cut the remaining kiwi into slices. In small glasses, put a layer of pudding, a layer of kiwi slices, a layer of pudding, and finish with kiwi slices. Serve sprinkled with cinnamon.

Nutrition Info:
- Per Serving: Calories: 225;Fat: 1g;Protein: 2g;Carbs: 27g.

Special Brownies With Chocolate And Coconut

Servings: 16 | Cooking Time: 30 To 35 Minutes

Ingredients:
- ½ cup gluten-free flour, 80g
- ¼ cup unsweetened alkalized cocoa powder. 30g
- ½ teaspoon sea salt
- 4 oz semisweet chocolate, coarsely chopped
- ¾ cup unrefined coconut oil, 120g
- 1 cup raw cane sugar, 200g
- 4 eggs
- 1 teaspoon vanilla
- 4 ounces semisweet chocolate chips

Directions:
1. Preheat the oven to 350°F. Grease a 9-by-9-inch baking pan and line with parchment paper.
2. In a medium bowl, combine the flour, cocoa powder, and salt. Set aside.
3. Melt in a double boiler or microwave the chopped chocolate and coconut oil. Slightly cool. Add the sugar, eggs, and vanilla, whisking until well combined. Whisk in the flour mixture. Fold in the chocolate chips. Pour into the prepared pan. Bake until a toothpick inserted in the center of the brownies comes out clean for 20 to 25 minutes. This will yield a somewhat gooey brownie. Continue to bake for 5 to 10 minutes if you desire a drier brownie.
4. Let the brownies cool completely, then cut into squares. Store in an airtight container at room temperature for up to 3 days.

Nutrition Info:
- Per Serving: Calories: 208 ;Fat: 15g ;Protein: 3g ;Carbs: 17g.

Mini Chocolate Fudge Squares

Servings: 6 | Cooking Time: 20 Minutes + Chilling Time

Ingredients:
- 2 cups coconut cream
- 1 tsp vanilla extract
- 3 oz almond butter
- 3 oz dark chocolate

Directions:
1. Pour coconut cream and vanilla into a saucepan and bring to a boil over medium heat, then simmer until reduced by half, 15 minutes. Stir in almond butter until the batter is smooth. Chop the dark chocolate into bits and stir in the cream until melted. Pour the mixture into a round baking sheet. Chill in the fridge for 3 hours. Serve sliced.

Nutrition Info:
- Per Serving: Calories: 445;Fat: 44g;Protein: 4g;Carbs: 14g.

Stunning Lemon Cake With Almond, Pistachio, Citrus Salad, And Coconut Whipped Cream

Servings: 6 To 8

Cooking Time: 40 To 45 Minutes

Ingredients:
- Cake:
- 1 ¼ cup raw almonds or almond meal, 240g
- ½ cup pistachios, 70g
- ½ teaspoon salt
- 6 eggs, separated
- 1 ¼ cup raw cane sugar, 250g
- 1 tablespoon lemon zest, grated
- 1 teaspoon orange zest, grated
- 1 teaspoon vanilla extract
- ¼ teaspoon almond extract

- Coconut Whipped Cream:
- One 13 ½ ounces can coconut milk, full-fat
- 1 tablespoon confectioner's sugar
- Citrus Salad:
- 2 oranges, sectioned
- 2 grapefruits, sectioned
- 1 tablespoon mint leaves, cut into strips
- 1 tablespoon honey, plus more as needed

Directions:

1. Make the cake. Preheat the oven to 350°F. Coat a 9-inch round springform pan with nonstick cooking spray.

2. Combine in a food processor the almonds, pistachios, and salt and pulse until finely ground. Combine the egg yolks and 1 cup (200 g) of the raw cane sugar in a large bowl. Beat until light and fluffy for 2 minutes. Add the lemon zest, orange zest, vanilla, and almond extract and beat until incorporated.

3. Beat the egg whites and the remaining ¼ cup (50 g) raw cane sugar on high speed until glossy in a clean bowl of a stand mixer fitted with the whisk attachment, stiff peaks form.

4. Alternate folding the egg whites and the almond mixture into the egg yolk mixture using a spatula, starting and ending with the egg whites. Pour into the prepared pan. Bake until a toothpick inserted into the center of the cake comes out clean and the top is golden brown for 40 to 45 minutes. Allow the cake to cool completely.

5. Make the coconut whipped cream. Chill the can of coconut milk, upside down, in the refrigerator overnight. Turn right-side up and open the can with a can opener. The water will be on the top. Pour carefully out the water and reserve for another use, only the coconut cream remains. Place the cream in a stand mixer fitted with the whisk attachment. Add the confectioner's sugar and whip on high speed until light and fluffy for 3 to 4 minutes.

6. Make the citrus salad. In a medium bowl, combine the orange and grapefruit sections with the mint and honey. Taste for sweetness and add more honey if necessary.

7. Remove the sides of the springform pan and transfer the cake to a serving platter. Spread the coconut cream into an even layer over the cake. Cut the cake into wedges, then top with the citrus salad and serve.

Nutrition Info:
- Per Serving: Calories: 334 ;Fat: 12g ;Protein: 12g ;Carbs: 43g .

Impressive Parfait With Yogurt, Berry, And Walnut

Servings: 2 | Cooking Time: 0 Minutes

Ingredients:
- 2 cups plain unsweetened yogurt, or plain unsweetened coconut yogurt or almond yogurt
- 2 tablespoons honey
- 1 cup blueberries, fresh
- 1 cup raspberries, fresh
- ½ cup walnut pieces

Directions:

1. Whisk the yogurt and honey in a medium bowl. Spoon into 2 serving bowls.

2. Top each with ½ cup blueberries, ½ cup raspberries, and ¼ cup walnut pieces.

Nutrition Info:
- Per Serving: Calories: 505 ;Fat: 22g ;Protein: 23g ;Carbs: 56g .

Oatmeal Chocolate Cookies

Servings: 2 | Cooking Time: 30 Minutes

Ingredients:
- ¼ cup whole wheat flour
- ¼ cup oats
- 1 tbsp olive oil
- 2 tbsp packed brown sugar
- ½ tsp vanilla extract
- 1 tbsp honey
- 2 tbsp coconut milk
- 2 tsp coconut oil
- ⅛ tsp sea salt
- 3 tbsp dark chocolate chips

Directions:

1. Combine all of the ingredients in a large bowl. Line a baking pan with parchment paper. Make lemon-sized cookies out of the mixture and flatten them onto the lined pan. Add some water to your Instant Pot and lower the trivet. Add the baking pan to your pot. Cook for 15 minutes on "Manual" on high pressure. Release the pressure quickly, carefully open the lid and serve warm.

Nutrition Info:
- Per Serving: Calories: 415;Fat: 20g;Protein: 6g;Carbs: 60g.

Mango & Coconut Rice Pudding

Servings: 4 | Cooking Time: 25 Minutes

Ingredients:
- 1 can coconut milk
- 1 mango, sliced
- ¼ cup caster sugar
- 1 tsp ground ginger
- A pinch of sea salt
- 2 cups cooked brown rice

Directions:

1. Place the sugar, ginger, and salt in a pot over medium heat and cook for 3-4 minutes until the sugar dissolves. Mix in brown rice and cook for another 3 minutes until the rice is heated through. Spoon into serving bowls and top with the sliced mango. Serve and enjoy!

Nutrition Info:
- Per Serving: Calories: 626;Fat: 21g;Protein: 9.4g;Carbs: 99g.

Blueberry Lime Granizado

Servings: 1 | Cooking Time: 15 Minutes

Ingredients:
- ½ cup pure date sugar
- 2 cups blueberries
- 2 tsp fresh lemon juice

Directions:

1. Place the sugar and ½ cup water in a pot. Cook for 3 minutes on low heat until the sugar is dissolved. Remove to a heatproof bowl and chill for 2 hours in the fridge. Blitz the blueberries and lemon juice in a blender until smooth. Add in cooled sugar and pulse until smooth. Place in an ice cream maker and follow the directions. Once ready, freeze another 1-2 hours for a firm texture.

Nutrition Info:
- Per Serving: Calories: 650;Fat: 2g;Protein: 3g;Carbs: 164g.

Flavourful Glazed Maple Pears And Hazelnuts

Servings: 4 | Cooking Time: 20 Minutes

Ingredients:
- 4 pears, peeled, cored, and quartered lengthwise
- 1 cup apple juice
- ½ cup pure maple syrup
- 1 tablespoon fresh ginger, grated
- ¼ cup hazelnuts, chopped

Directions:
1. Combine the pears and apple juice in a large pot over medium-high heat. Bring to a simmer and reduce the heat to medium-low. Cover and simmer for 15 to 20 minutes until the pears becomes soft.
2. Combine in a small saucepan over medium-high heat the maple syrup and ginger while the pears poach. Bring to a simmer while stirring. Remove the pan from the heat and let the syrup rest.
3. Remove the pears using a slotted spoon from the poaching liquid and brush with maple syrup. Serve topped with the hazelnuts.

Nutrition Info:
- Per Serving: Calories: 286 ;Fat: 3g ;Protein: 2g ;Carbs: 67g .

Savoury Spiced Pumpkin Pancakes

Servings: 4 | Cooking Time: 10 Minutes

Ingredients:
- flesh from ½ deseeded pumpkin
- 4 eggs, free range
- 3 egg whites, free range
- sprinkle black pepper
- ½ teaspoon baking soda, gluten-free
- 2 tablespoons coconut oil
- 1 tablespoon honey
- 1 handful pecan nuts

Directions:
1. Blend the pumpkin flesh together with some water to form a smooth pulp in a blender or food processor.
2. Add the eggs, freshly ground pepper, 1 tbsp of coconut oil, and a tiny pinch of baking soda to the pumpkin mix and blend until smooth.
3. Heat a large pan on a medium heat with the other 1 tablespoon of coconut oil.
4. Pour individual rounded pancakes into your pan.
5. Cook for 3 minutes then flip.
6. Plate and serve with pecan nuts and maple syrup.

Nutrition Info:
- Per Serving: Calories: 87 ;Fat: 7g ;Protein: 3g ;Carbs: 5g .

Comfort Cobbler With Blueberry And Peach

Servings: 4 To 6

Cooking Time: 2 Hours

Ingredients:
- 5 tablespoons coconut oil, divided
- 3 large peaches, peeled and sliced
- 2 cups blueberries, frozen
- 1 cup almond flour
- 1 cup rolled oats
- 1 tablespoon maple syrup
- 1 tablespoon coconut sugar
- 1 teaspoon cinnamon, ground
- ½ teaspoon vanilla extract
- Pinch ground nutmeg

Directions:

1. Coat the bottom of the slow cooker with 1 tablespoon of coconut oil.
2. Arrange the peaches and blueberries along the bottom of the slow cooker.
3. Stir together in a small bowl the almond flour, oats, remaining 4 tablespoons of coconut oil, maple syrup, coconut sugar, cinnamon, vanilla, and nutmeg until a coarse mixture form. Gently crumble the topping over the fruit in the slow cooker.
4. Cover the cooker and set to high. Cook for 2 hours and serve.

Nutrition Info:
- Per Serving: Calories: 516 ;Fat: 34g Protein: 10g ;;Carbs: 49g.

Interesting Snack Bars With Date And Pecan

Servings: 4 | Cooking Time: 40 Minutes

Ingredients:
- 4 cups of dates, pitted and chopped
- 3 cups pecans

Directions:
1. Preheat the oven to 350°F.
2. Put the dates in a bowl and cover them with water.
3. Leave for 20 minutes then blitz the pecans in a food processor until they form a breadcrumb texture.
4. Drain the water from the dates then add to the processor until the nuts and fruit create a dough that easily needs together with your hands.
5. Line a baking sheet with parchment paper and then spread the dough onto the pan into a layer 2 inches thick.
6. Bake for 35 to 40 minutes or until cooked through and crispy on the top.
7. Remove to cool and slice into bars to serve.

Nutrition Info:
- Per Serving: Calories: 928 ;Fat: 54g ;Protein: 10g ;Carbs: 121g

Avocado-chocolate Mousse

Servings: 4 | Cooking Time: 15 Minutes

Ingredients:
- 1 cup raspberries
- 2 peeled, pitted avocados
- ¼ cup almond butter
- ¼ cup lite coconut milk
- ¼ cup cocoa powder
- ¼ cup pure maple syrup
- A pinch of sea salt

Directions:
1. Place the avocados, almond butter, coconut milk, cocoa powder, maple syrup, and salt in a food processor and pulse until smooth. Spoon the mixture into individual serving glasses. Place in the refrigerator for at least 1 hour. Decorate with raspberries just before serving.

Nutrition Info:
- Per Serving: Calories: 270;Fat: 20g;Protein: 7g;Carbs: 24g.

Friendly Homemade Hot Cross Easter Buns

Servings: 8 | Cooking Time: 20 Minutes

Ingredients:
- 3 cups almonds
- 1 cup raisins
- 1 tablespoon raw honey
- zest and juice of 1 orange and 1 lemon
- 1 teaspoon cinnamon
- 1 teaspoon cloves

- 1 teaspoon nutmeg

Directions:
1. Lightly oil a muffin tray.
2. In a food processor, whizz up the almonds into a powder.
3. Add the honey, spices, lemon juice and orange juice and process until you have a dough.
4. You can then blend in the raisins and the fruit zest for 30 seconds.
5. Divide mixture into eight in the muffin tray and then cross the top of each bun with a sharp knife.
6. Add to the oven for 15 to 20 minutes or until risen and cooked through.
7. Serve immediately and enjoy with your favorite fresh fruit.

Nutrition Info:
- Per Serving: Calories: 14 ;Fat: 15g;Protein: 46g;Carbs: 3g .

Tasty Haystack Cookies From Missouri

Servings: 24 | Cooking Time: 1 ½ Hours

Ingredients:
- ½ cup coconut oil
- ½ cup almond milk, unsweetened
- 1 overripe banana, mashed well
- ½ cup coconut sugar
- ¼ cup cacao powder
- 1 teaspoon vanilla extract
- ¼ teaspoon sea salt
- 3 cups rolled oats
- ½ cup almond butter

Directions:
1. Stir together in a medium bowl the coconut oil, almond milk, mashed banana, coconut sugar, cacao powder, vanilla, and salt. Pour the mixture into the slow cooker.
2. Pour the oats on top without stirring.
3. Put the almond butter on top of the oats without stirring.
4. Cover the cooker and set to high. Cook for 1½ hours.
5. Stir the mixture well. Scoop tablespoon-size balls out as it cools and press onto a baking sheet to continue to cool. Serve when hardened. Keep leftovers refrigerated in an airtight container for up to 1 week.

Nutrition Info:
- Per Serving: Calories: 140 ;Fat: 9g ;Protein: 2g ;Carbs: 14g .

Cinnamon Tropical Cobbler

Servings: 6 | Cooking Time: 45 Minutes

Ingredients:
- 3 apples, shredded
- 2 ripe pineapples, chopped
- 2 tsp lemon juice
- ½ cup pure date sugar
- 2 tbsp arrowroot
- 1 tsp ground cinnamon
- ½ tsp ground allspice
- 1 cup whole-grain flour
- 1 ½ tsp baking powder
- ¼ tsp sea salt
- 2 tbsp peanut butter
- ½ cup soy milk

Directions:
1. Preheat your oven to 390ºF. Arrange apples and pineapples on a greased baking pan. Drizzle with lemon juice, arrowroot, cinnamon, and allspice. In a bowl, combine flour, date sugar, baking powder, and salt. Stir in the peanut butter with a fork until the batter resembles crumbs. Mix in soy milk. Spread the mixture over the fruit and bake for 30 minutes. Serve and enjoy!

Nutrition Info:
- Per Serving: Calories: 190;Fat: 2g;Protein: 4g;Carbs: 41g.

Honey Pears With Pecans

Servings: 4 | Cooking Time: 25 Minutes

Ingredients:
- 1 tbsp coconut oil
- 2 tbsp honey
- 1 tsp cinnamon
- 4 peeled pears, quartered
- 2 cups plain yogurt
- ¼ cup toasted pecans, chopped
- 1/8 tsp sea salt

Directions:
1. Melt the coconut oil in a skillet over medium heat. Place the honey, cinnamon, pears, and salt and cook for 4-5 minutes until the fruit is tender. Simmer for a few minutes until the sauce thickens. Divide yogurt between 4 dessert bowls and top them with pear and pecans.

Nutrition Info:
- Per Serving: Calories: 292;Fat: 10g;Protein: 12g;Carbs: 40g.

Nightshade Free Cinnamon Pecans

Servings: 3 ½

Cooking Time: 3 To 4 Hours

Ingredients:
- 1 tablespoon coconut oil
- 1 large egg white
- 2 tablespoons cinnamon, ground
- 2 teaspoons vanilla extract
- ¼ cup maple syrup
- 2 tablespoons coconut sugar
- ¼ teaspoon sea salt
- 3 cups pecan halves

Directions:
1. Coat the slow cooker with the coconut oil.
2. Whisk the egg white in a medium bowl.
3. Add the cinnamon, vanilla, maple syrup, coconut sugar, and salt. Whisk well to combine.
4. Add the pecans and stir to coat. Pour the pecans into the slow cooker.
5. Cover the cooker and set to low. Cook for 3 to 4 hours.
6. Remove the pecans from the slow cooker and spread them on a baking sheet or other cooling surface. Before serving, let cool for 5 to 10 minutes. Store in an airtight container at room temperature for up to 2 weeks.

Nutrition Info:
- Per Serving: Calories: 195 ;Fat: 18g ;Protein: 2g ;Carbs: 9g .

Blueberry & Almond Greek Yogurt

Servings: 4 | Cooking Time: 5 Minutes

Ingredients:
- 3 cups plain greek yogurt
- 1 ½ cups blueberries
- ¾ cup almonds, chopped
- ½ cup honey

Directions:
1. Divide the greek yogurt between four bowls and top each with blueberries, almonds, and honey. Serve and enjoy!

Nutrition Info:
- Per Serving: Calories: 460;Fat: 19g;Protein: 4g;Carbs: 63g.

Energy Boosting Thumbprint Cookies With Strawberry Jam

Servings: 4 To 6

Cooking Time: 15 Minutes

Ingredients:
- 1½ cups sunflower seeds
- 3 tablespoons coconut oil
- ¼ cup maple syrup
- ½ cup strawberry jam, divided

Directions:
1. Preheat the oven to 350°F.
2. Line a baking sheet with parchment paper.
3. Process the sunflower seeds in a blender, food processor, or spice grinder into a fine meal. Transfer to a large bowl.
4. Add the coconut oil, mashing it into the sunflower meal with a spoon as if you are crumbling butter into flour. Stir in the maple syrup. Mix well.
5. Scoop the dough using a tablespoon measure onto the prepared sheet and make 12 cookies. Gently press down on the cookies with the back of a wet spoon to flatten them.
6. Make imprints with your thumb in the center of each cookie. Fill each depression with 2 teaspoons of strawberry jam.
7. Place the sheet in the preheated oven and bake for 12 to 14 minutes.
8. Cool before eating.

Nutrition Info:
- Per Serving: Calories: 392 ;Fat: 19g ;Protein: 4g ;Carbs: 54g .

Easy Maple Rice Pudding

Servings: 4 | Cooking Time: 30 Minutes

Ingredients:
- 1 cup short-grain brown rice
- 1 ¾ cups non-dairy milk
- 4 tbsp pure maple syrup
- 1 tsp vanilla extract
- A pinch of salt
- ¼ cup dates, chopped

Directions:
1. In a pot over medium heat, place the rice, milk, 1 ½ cups of water, maple, vanilla, and salt. Bring to a boil, then reduce the heat. Cook for 20 minutes, stirring occasionally. Mix in dates and cook for another 5 minutes. Serve chilled in cups.

Nutrition Info:
- Per Serving: Calories: 1100;Fat: 96g;Protein: 4g;Carbs: 60g.

Vanilla Cranberry & Almond Balls

Servings: 6 | Cooking Time: 25 Minutes

Ingredients:
- 2 tbsp almond butter
- 2 tbsp maple syrup
- ¾ cup cooked millet
- ¼ cup sesame seeds
- 1 tbsp chia seeds
- ½ tsp almond extract
- Zest of 1 orange
- 1 tbsp dried cranberries
- ¼ cup ground almonds

Directions:
1. Whisk the almond butter and syrup in a bowl until creamy. Mix in millet, sesame seeds, chia seeds, almond extract, orange zest, cranberries, and almonds. Shape the mixture into balls and

arrange on a parchment paper-lined baking sheet. Let chill in the fridge for 15 minutes.

Nutrition Info:
- Per Serving: Calories: 120;Fat: 8g;Protein: 2g;Carbs: 11g.

Mixed Berry Yogurt Ice Pops

Servings: 6 | Cooking Time: 5 Minutes + Chilling Time

Ingredients:
- 2/3 cup avocado pulp
- 2/3 cup berries
- 1 cup dairy-free yogurt
- ½ cup coconut cream
- 1 tsp vanilla extract

Directions:
1. Pour the avocado pulp, berries, dairy-free yogurt, coconut cream, and vanilla extract. Process until smooth. Pour into ice pop sleeves and freeze for 8 or more hours. Enjoy the ice pops when ready.

Nutrition Info:
- Per Serving: Calories: 145;Fat: 12g;Protein: 3g;Carbs: 9g.

Grain Free And Versatile Fruit Crisp

Servings: 4 To 6

Cooking Time: 30 To 35 Minutes

Ingredients:
- 3 cups mixed fresh berries
- ½ cup sunflower seeds
- ¾ cup shredded coconut, unsweetened
- ¼ cup coconut sugar
- ¼ cup coconut oil

Directions:
1. Preheat the oven to 350°F.
2. Combine the fruit in a 9-by-9-inch baking dish.
3. Mix together in a small bowl the sunflower seeds, shredded coconut, and coconut sugar.
4. Stir in the coconut oil and incorporate it throughout by using your hands.
5. Crumble the topping over the fruit.
6. Place the dish in the preheated oven and bake for 30 to 35 minutes or until the topping is golden and the fruit is bubbling.

Nutrition Info:
- Per Serving: Calories: 379 ;Fat: 29g ;Protein: 4g ;Carbs: 29g.

Scrumptious Fruity Dark Chocolate Mousse

Servings: 2 | Cooking Time: 5 Minutes

Ingredients:
- 1 cup strawberries, sliced
- ¼ cup free range egg whites
- 4 squares dark cooking chocolate
- 1 small banana, sliced
- ½ cup blueberries
- 2 tablespoons water

Directions:
1. Melt the dark chocolate over a bowl of boiling water on a low heat on the stove.
2. Add the water and egg whites to the melted chocolate and mix well to reach a thick consistency.
3. Spoon the batter out onto a small plate.
4. Put in the freezer for 30 minutes.
5. Garnish with the strawberries, banana and blueberries to serve.

Nutrition Info:

• Per Serving: Calories: 95 ;Protein: 4g ;Carbs: 20g .

Balsamic-glazed Caramelized Quinces

Servings: 4 | Cooking Time: 20 Minutes

Ingredients:
• 1 cup balsamic vinegar
• 5 tbsp pure date sugar
• ¼ tsp grated nutmeg
• A pinch of salt
• ¼ cup coconut oil
• 2 cored quinces, sliced

Directions:
1. Heat a saucepan over medium heat and add in the balsamic vinegar, 2 tbsp of date sugar, nutmeg, and salt. Cook for 10-15 minutes, stirring occasionally until the liquid has reduced by half. Melt the coconut oil in a skillet over medium heat and in place in the quinces; cook for 5 minutes until golden. Stir in the remaining date sugar and cook for another 5 minutes until caramelized. Serve in a plate drizzled with the balsamic glaze.

Nutrition Info:
• Per Serving: Calories: 200;Fat: 14g;Protein: 1g;Carbs: 17g.

Coconut Peach Tart

Servings: 6 | Cooking Time: 10 Minutes

Ingredients:
• ½ cup rolled oats
• 1 cup cashews
• 1 cup soft pitted dates
• 1 cup canned coconut milk
• 2 large peaches, chopped
• ½ cup shredded coconut

Directions:
1. In a food processor, pulse the oats, cashews, and dates until a dough-like mixture forms. Press down into a greased baking pan. Pulse the coconut milk, ½ cup water, peaches, and shredded coconut in the food processor until smooth. Pour this mixture over the crust and spread evenly. Freeze for 30 minutes. Soften 15 minutes before serving. Top with whipped coconut cream and coconut.

Nutrition Info:
• Per Serving: Calories: 120;Fat: 2g;Protein: 3g;Carbs: 26g.

Summer Banana Pudding

Servings: 4 | Cooking Time: 25 Minutes + Cooling Time

Ingredients:
• 1 cup almond milk
• 2 cups coconut cream
• ¾ cup
• ¼ tsp salt
• 3 tbsp arrowroot
• 2 tbsp almond butter
• 1 tsp vanilla extract
• 2 bananas, sliced

Directions:
1. In a medium pot, mix almond milk, coconut cream, date sugar, and salt. Cook over medium heat until slightly thickened, 10-15 minutes. Stir in the arrowroot, almond butter, vanilla extract, and banana extract. Cook further for 1-2 minutes or until the pudding thickens. Dish the pudding into 4 serving bowls and chill in the refrigerator for at least 1 hour. To serve, top with the bananas.

Nutrition Info:
• Per Serving: Calories: 410;Fat: 43g;Protein: 5g;Carbs: 9g.

Milk Dumplings In Cardamom Sauce

Servings: 6 | Cooking Time: 30 Minutes

Ingredients:
• 2 ½ cups brown sugar
• 3 tbsp lime juice
• 6 cups almond milk
• 1 tsp ground cardamom

Directions:
1. Place the milk in a pot inside your Instant Pot and bring it to a boil. Stir in the lime juice. The solids should start to separate. Pour the milk through a cheesecloth-lined colander. Drain as much liquid as you possibly can. Place the paneer on a smooth surface. Form a ball and then divide it into 20 equal pieces. Pour 6 cups of water into your pressure cooker and bring it to a boil. Add the sugar and cardamom and cook until dissolved. Shape the dumplings into balls, and place them in the syrup. Close the lid and cook on "Manual" for about 4-5 minutes. Let cool and then refrigerate until ready to serve.

Nutrition Info:
• Per Serving: Calories: 135;Fat: 1.5g;Protein: 2g;Carbs: 12g.

Coconut & Chocolate Macaroons

Servings: 4 | Cooking Time: 25 Minutes

Ingredients:
• 1 cup shredded coconut
• 2 tbsp cocoa powder
• 1 tbsp vanilla extract
• 1 cup coconut milk
• ¼ cup maple syrup
• A pinch of salt

Directions:
1. Preheat your oven to 360ºF. Place the shredded coconut, cocoa powder, vanilla extract, coconut milk, maple syrup, and salt in a pot. Cook until a firm dough is formed. Shape balls out of the mixture. Arrange the balls on a lined with parchment paper baking sheet. Bake for 15 minutes. Allow cooling before serving.

Nutrition Info:
• Per Serving: Calories: 170;Fat: 10g;Protein: 2g;Carbs: 20g.

Tropical Baked Fruit With Nut Pudding

Servings: 4 | Cooking Time: 1 Hour

Ingredients:
• 15 apricots
• 10 prunes
• 6 free range eggs
• 3 cups water
• 1 cup raw pecans/walnuts
• 2 tablespoons pure vanilla extract
• 2 broken cinnamon sticks

Directions:
1. Preheat the oven to 350°F.
2. Boil the water on a high heat and then add the apricots, prunes, and cinnamon sticks before turning down the heat and simmering for 30 minutes in a large saucepan.
3. Allow to cool.
4. Remove the cinnamon sticks and blend mixture, add in the eggs and vanilla until smooth.
5. Add mixture to a glass oven dish and top with the nuts.
6. Oven bake for 30 minutes.
7. Cool and serve.

Nutrition Info:
• Per Serving: Calories: 195 ;Fat: 13g ;Protein: 3g ;Carbs: 16g .

Tofu & Almond Pancakes

Servings: 6 | Cooking Time: 15 Minutes

Ingredients:
- 1 ½ cups almond milk
- 1 cup almond flour
- 1 cup firm tofu, crumbled
- 3 tbsp almond butter, melted
- 2 tbsp pure date sugar
- 1 ½ tsp pure vanilla extract
- ½ tsp baking powder
- ⅛ tsp sea salt

Directions:
1. Blitz almond milk, tofu, almond butter, sugar, vanilla, baking powder, and salt in a blender until smooth. Heat a pan and coat with oil. Scoop a ladle of batter at the center and spread all over. Cook for 3-4 minutes until golden, turning once. Transfer to a plate and repeat the process until no batter is left. Serve and enjoy!

Nutrition Info:
- Per Serving: Calories: 170;Fat: 12g;Protein: 4g;Carbs: 13g.

Poached Pears With Green Tea

Servings: 4 | Cooking Time: 15 Minutes

Ingredients:
- 4 pears, peeled, cored, and quartered lengthwise
- 2 cups green tea, strongly brewed
- ¼ cup honey
- 1 tablespoon fresh ginger, grated

Directions:
1. Combine the pears, tea, honey, and ginger in a large pot over medium-high heat. Bring to a simmer. Lower the heat to medium-low, cover, and simmer for 15 minutes until the pears soften. Serve the pears with the poaching liquid spooned over the top.

Nutrition Info:
- Per Serving: Calories: 190 ;Fat: 6g;Protein: 23g;Carbs: 50g .

Chocolate Campanelle With Hazelnuts

Servings: 4 | Cooking Time: 10 Minutes

Ingredients:
- ½ cup chopped toasted hazelnuts
- ¼ cup dark chocolate chips
- 8 oz campanelle pasta
- 3 tbsp almond butter
- ¼ cup maple syrup

Directions:
1. Pulse the hazelnuts and chocolate pieces in a food processor until crumbly. Set aside. Place the campanelle pasta in a pot with boiling salted water. Cook for 8-10 minutes until al dente, stirring often. Drain and back to the pot. Stir in almond butter and maple syrup and stir until the butter is melted. Serve garnished with chocolate-hazelnut mixture.

Nutrition Info:
- Per Serving: Calories: 360;Fat: 20g;Protein: 4g;Carbs: 44g.

60 Day Meal Plan

	Breakfast	Lunch	Dinner
Day 1	Breakfast Pudding With Chia	Scrambled Tofu With Bell Pepper	Chinese-style Cabbage Salad
Day 2	Almond Yogurt With Berries & Walnuts	Spicy Quinoa Bowl With Black Beans	High-spirited Salmon Salad
Day 3	Cherry & Cashew Pudding	Classic And Minty Lamb Burgers	Porky Salad With Spinach
Day 4	Tropical French Toasts	Holiday Turkey	Apple & Arugula Salad With Walnuts
Day 5	Chocolate & Carrot Bread With Raisins	Cumin Lamb Meatballs With Aioli	Tomato Bean & Bulgur Salad
Day 6	Nutritious Chia And Berry Breakfast	Baked Basil Chicken	Cowboy Salad
Day 7	Sweet Potato, Tomato, & Onion Frittata	Harissa Chicken Drumsticks	Radish & Tomato Salad
Day 8	Banana & Pumpkin Smoothie	Marvellous Chocolate Chili	Oily Salad With Celery And Kipper
Day 9	Ginger Banana Smoothie	Chicken A La Tuscana	Quick Insalata Caprese
Day 10	Strawberry & Pecan Breakfast	Basic Poached Wrapped Chicken	Pantry Salad With White Bean And Tuna
Day 11	Healthy And Tasty Vanilla Crepes	Cherry Tomato & Basil Chicken Casserole	Lemony Spinach Salad
Day 12	Vanilla & Chia Yogurt With Berries	Korean Chicken Thighs	Broccoli & Mango Rice Salad
Day 13	Satisfying Eggs Benny	Creamy Beef Tenderloin Marsala	Italian Vegetable Relish
Day 14	Coconut Oat Bread	Hawaiian-style Turkey Burgers	Warm Cod & Zucchini Salad
Day 15	Chocolate-blueberry Smoothie	Dairy Free Chicken Alfredo	Spinach & Pomegranate Salad

	Breakfast	Lunch	Dinner
Day 16	Veggie Panini	Sweet Potato-kale Egg Casserole	Bean & Roasted Parsnip Salad
Day 17	Breakfast Ground Beef Skillet	Scotch Eggs With Pork Sausage And Hemp Seeds	Broccoli Salad With Tempeh & Cranberries
Day 18	Sweet Kiwi Oatmeal Bars	Sunday Pork Tacos	Radish & Fennel Salad With Eggs
Day 19	Hazelnut & Raspberry Quinoa	Thyme Pork Loin Bake	Radish & Cabbage Ginger Salad
Day 20	Terrific Pancakes With Coconut And Banana	Worcestershire Pork Chops	Carrot & Cabbage Salad With Avocado
Day 21	Morning Green Smoothie	Lamb Shanks Braised Under Pressure	Cucumber, Lettuce & Tomato Salad
Day 22	Appetizing Crepes With Berries	Creamy Turkey With Mushrooms	Lettuce & Tomato Salad With Quinoa
Day 23	Cherry & Coconut Oatmeal With Chia	Cute Tiny Chicken Burgers	Effortless Half-sour Pickled Salad
Day 24	Thyme Cremini Oats	Hot & Spicy Beef Chili	Spinach Salad With Blackberries & Pecans
Day 25	Blackberry Waffles	Chicken Stir-fry With Bell Pepper	Mediterranean Pasta Salad
Day 26	Coconut Blueberry Muffins	Mexican-style Chicken	Ready To Eat Taco Salad
Day 27	Fiery Quinoa	Sloppy Joes & Coleslaw	Mushroom And Green Bean Salad
Day 28	Omelette With Smoky Shrimp	Mustardy Beef Steaks	Hot Chickpea Salad
Day 29	Giant Coconut Pancake	Grilled Chicken Sandwiches	Tender Chicken Salad
Day 30	Baked Berry Millet With Applesauce	Italian Turkey Meatballs	Beetroot Salad With Mackerel

	Breakfast	**Lunch**	**Dinner**
Day 31	Blueberry Chia Pudding	Mustard Pork Chops With Collard Greens	Minty Eggplant Salad
Day 32	Cherry Quinoa	Tempting And Tender Beef Brisket	Colorful Salad
Day 33	Hearty Smoothie	Simple Cooked Whole Chicken	Zucchini & Bell Pepper Salad With Beans
Day 34	Pecan & Pumpkin Seed Oat Jars	Appealing Hot Turkey	Tropical Salad
Day 35	Orange-glazed Raspberry Muffins	The Best General Tso's Chicken	Avocado Salad With Mango & Almonds
Day 36	Pumpkin Cake With Pistachios	Baked Turkey Meatballs	Beet Tofu Salad
Day 37	Almond Oats With Cherries	Tangy Beef Ribs	Tempting Salad With Celery, Beet, And Sliced Apple
Day 38	Morning Pecan & Pear Farro	Spicy Lime Pork Tenderloins	Cashew & Raisin Salad
Day 39	Berry, Walnut & Almond Yogurt Parfait	Smoky Lamb Souvlaki	Pleasant And Tender Salad With Kale
Day 40	Cherry & Chocolate Oatmeal	Chicken Piccata	Hazelnut & Pear Salad
Day 41	Sautéed Cherry Tomatoes With Scrambled Herb	Aromatic Turkey With Mushrooms	Maple Walnut & Pear Salad
Day 42	Cinnamon Apple Muesli	Delightful Stuffed Lamb With Peppers	Enticing Japanese Salad With Avocado And Shrimp
Day 43	Cinnamon Buckwheat With Almonds	Slow Cooker Chicken Curry	Arugula Salad With Salmon
Day 44	No-bread Avocado Sandwich	Chopped Lambs With Rosemary	Beet Slaw With Apples
Day 45	Matcha Smoothie With Berries	Hot & Spicy Shredded Chicken	Fragrant Coconut Fruit Salad

Anti-Inflammatory Cookbook 144

	Breakfast	**Lunch**	**Dinner**
Day 46	Maple Coconut Pancakes	Paleo Turkey Thighs With Mushroom	Radicchio & Cabbage Coleslaw
Day 47	Classic Walnut Waffles With Maple Syrup	Lemon & Caper Turkey Scaloppine	Carrot Salad With Cherries & Pecans
Day 48	Fantastic Fruit Cereal	Cinnamon Pork Chops In Apple Sauce	Marinated Chicken Salad With Turmeric
Day 49	Cold Oatmeal With Apple And Cinnamon	Classic Pork Chops And Creamy Green Beans	Summer Time Sizzling Green Salad With Salmon
Day 50	Coconut Fruit Smoothie	Scallion & Broccoli Chicken Sauté	Summer Salad
Day 51	Cranberry Oat Cookies	Spicy Beef Fajitas	African Zucchini Salad
Day 52	Flaxseed & Fig Smoothie	Enjoyable Braised Turkey Legs And Wilted Greens	Mango Rice Salad With Lime Dressing
Day 53	Almond Waffles	Italian Spinach Chicken	Daikon Salad With Caramelized Onion
Day 54	Simple Apple Muffins	Lettuce-wrapped Beef Roast	Asparagus & Pasta Salad
Day 55	Cauliflower Bowl With Avocado And Kale	Turkey Stuffed Bell Peppers	Irresistible Pear And Walnut Salad
Day 56	Breakfast Naan Bread	Authentic Chicken Curry With Coconut	Orange & Kale Salad
Day 57	Coconut Porridge With Strawberries	Incredible Tacos With Pork	Quick Fresh Salad
Day 58	Dilly Vegetable Quinoa	Rosemary Pork Loin	Yummy Salad With Sweet Potato And Salmon
Day 59	Choco-berry Smoothie	Miso Chicken With Sesame	Mushroom & Wild Rice Salad
Day 60	Sweet Orange Crepes	Cheap Pork Sausage	Diverse Salad With Shredded Root Vegetable

Anti-Inflammatory Cookbook

APPENDIX : Recipes Index

A

Acorn Squash
Ginger Squash Soup 114

Almond
Stunning Lemon Cake With Almond, Pistachio, Citrus Salad, And Coconut Whipped Cream 135
Friendly Homemade Hot Cross Easter Buns 137
Vanilla Cranberry & Almond Balls 139

Almond Milk
Almond Yogurt With Berries & Walnuts 18
Cherry & Cashew Pudding 18
Cinnamon Buckwheat With Almonds 27
Flaxseed & Fig Smoothie 28
Almond Waffles 28
Combating Gingery Milkshake With Blackberry 122
Fresh Berry Smoothie With Ginger 123
Distinctive Chai Smoothie 124
Wound Healer Warm Almond Milk With Cinnamon And Turmeric 129
Almond Berry Cream 131
Milk Dumplings In Cardamom Sauce 140

Apple
Morning Green Smoothie 22
Cinnamon Apple Muesli 26
Simple Apple Muffins 29
Apple & Arugula Salad With Walnuts 52
Tempting Salad With Celery, Beet, And Sliced Apple 57
Beet Slaw With Apples 58
Gluten Free Apple Chutney 120
Pain Reliever Smoothie 122
Stomach Soothing Smoothie With Green Apple 123
For Beginners Juice With Granny Smith Apples 123
Delightful Smoothie With Apple And Honey 124
Apple & Cashew Quiche 127
Delectable Honeyed Apple Cinnamon Compote 128
Apple-cinnamon Compote 129
Southern Apple Cobbler With Raspberries 132
Cinnamon Tropical Cobbler 138

Artichoke
Low In Calories Salad With Artichoke And Almond 53
Coconut Artichoke Soup With Almonds 112

Asparagus
Bell Pepper & Tempeh Balls With Asparagus 39
Asparagus & Pasta Salad 60
Salmon & Asparagus Parcels 71
Satisfying Eggs Benny 20

Avocado
Avocado Salad With Mango & Almonds 56
Cold Soup With Coconut And Avocado 110
Satisfying And Thick Dressing With Avocado 117
Herbaceous Spread With Avocado 118
Great Pudding With Chocolate And Avocado 126
Lime Avocado Ic E Cream 127
Melon Chocolate Pudding 128
Non-dairy Butter Mousse With Chocolate And Almond 130
Avocado-chocolate Mousse 137
Mixed Berry Yogurt Ice Pops 139

B

Banana
Ginger Banana Smoothie 20
Terrific Pancakes With Coconut And Banana 22
Hearty Smoothie 25
Green Banana Smoothie 30
Crunchy And Creamy Pistachio Smoothie 124
Hazelnut Topped Caramelized Bananas 131
Fruitylicious Hot Milk 131
Macedonia Salad With Coconut & Pecans 133
Healthy Brownies With Cacao 134
Mid Afternoon Grilled Banana And Homemade Nut Butter 134
Summer Banana Pudding 140

Bean
Chickpea & Bean Patties 32
Bean & Spinach Casserole 34
Appetizing Casserole With Broccoli And Bean 36

Grilled Tempeh With Green Beans 36
Spicy Moong Beans 37
Bean Gyros 37
Baked Mustard Beans 40
Spicy Black Bean 40
Hot Coconut Beans With Vegetables 42
Mediterranean Chickpeas With Vegetables 42
Habanero Pinto Bean & Bell Pepper Pot 44
Chipotle Kidney Bean Chili 45
Awesome Barley Jambalaya 46
Bean & Roasted Parsnip Salad 48
Fragrant Coconut Fruit Salad 58
Bean & Farro Salad 61
Rosemary White Bean Soup 97
Arugula Coconut Soup 97
Vegetable Bean Soup 100
Vegetable & Black Bean Soup 102
Italian Bean Soup 103
Habanero Bean Soup With Brown Rice 104
Cannellini Bean Soup 104
Sweet French Onion Soup With White Bean 105
Green Chili Bean Stew 106
Super Simple Stew With Mango And Black Bean 108
Minestrone Soup With Quinoa 109
Chili Cannellini Bean Stew 109
Low Maintenance Vegan Minestrone With Herb Oil 112
Green Bean & Rice Soup 115
Spicy Thai Soup 115
Mediterranean Soup 115
Ultimate Burger With Hummus 43

Beef
Breakfast Ground Beef Skillet 21
Remarkable Korean Beef Wrapped In Lettuce 80
Marvellous Chocolate Chili 81
Creamy Beef Tenderloin Marsala 82
A Fresh Lean Beef Burger That You Can Truly Enjoy 83
Hot & Spicy Beef Chili 85
Sloppy Joes & Coleslaw 86
Mustardy Beef Steaks 86
Tempting And Tender Beef Brisket 87
Tangy Beef Ribs 88
Spicy Beef Fajitas 91
Lettuce-wrapped Beef Roast 92
Veggie & Beef Brisket 94
Spicy Beef & Sweet Potato Soup 96
Beef-farro Stew 98
Beef Stew With Sweet Potato Noodles 103

Beef & Mushroom Rice Soup 108
One-pot Chunky Beef Stew 108
Beef & Tomato Chili 110
Gingery Swordfish Kabobs 66

Beet
Colorful Salad 56
Beet Tofu Salad 56

Bell Pepper
Teriyaki Vegetable Stir-fry 39
Basil Coconut Soup 99

Berry
Vanilla & Chia Yogurt With Berries 20
Appetizing Crepes With Berries 23
Great Watermelon Smoothie 124
Vanilla Berry Tarts 126
Berry Macedonia With Mint 127
Apple & Berry Parfait 127
Grain Free And Versatile Fruit Crisp 139

Blackberry
Blackberry Waffles 23
Choco-berry Smoothie 29
Wonderful Whipped Goat Cheese With Dark Berries 128
Elegant Panna Cotta With Honey And Blackberry-lime Sauce 129

Blueberry
Nutritious Chia And Berry Breakfast 19
Chocolate-blueberry Smoothie 21
Coconut Blueberry Muffins 23
Baked Berry Millet With Applesauce 24
Blueberry Chia Pudding 25
Berry, Walnut & Almond Yogurt Parfait 26
Matcha Smoothie With Berries 27
Compote With Blueberries & Lemon Juice 128
Delicious Nutmeg Muffins With Vanilla And Blueberries 130
Perfect Thickness Blueberry Ambrosia 131
Blueberry Lime Granizado 136
Comfort Cobbler With Blueberry And Peach 137

Bread
Tropical French Toasts 18

Broccoli
Broccoli Salad With Tempeh & Cranberries 48
Broccoli & Mango Rice Salad 54
Healthy Soup With Turmeric And Broccoli 98
Creamy Soup With Broccoli 99
Broccoli Cream Soup With Peanuts 100
Broccoli Fennel Soup 101

Gingered Broccoli Soup 106
Sharp-tasting Soup With Rice And Sweet Potato 110

Butternut Squash
Indian Curried Stew With Lentil And Spinach 97
Coconut Butternut Squash Soup 99
Curry Soup With Butternut Squash And Coconut 113
Awesome Multi-purpose Cream Sauce 119
A Different Pumpkin Pie 132

C

Cabbage
Savoy Cabbage Rolls With Tofu 37
Amazing Toasted Cumin Crunch 38
Chinese-style Cabbage Salad 51
Cashew & Raisin Salad 57
Radicchio & Cabbage Coleslaw 58
Crunchylicious Colourful Asian Salad 61
Kale & Cabbage Stew 96
Vegetable & Rice Soup 99
Delectable Multivitamin Smoothie 123

Carrot
Chocolate & Carrot Bread With Raisins 19
Cucumber & Carrot Pizza With Pesto 35
Luxurious Creamy Carrot Marinara With Brown Rice Pasta 39
Hot Seitan With Rice 43
Vegetarian Sloppy Joes 45
Carrot & Cabbage Salad With Avocado 49
Carrot Salad With Cherries & Pecans 58
Quick Fresh Salad 60
Diverse Salad With Shredded Root Vegetable 61
Awesome Herbaceous Roasted Chuck And Scrummy Vegetable 83
Soulful Roasted Vegetable Soup 98
Classy Soup With Carrot And Ginger 101
Dairy-free Rice Soup With Mushrooms 102
Gingery Soup With Carrots & Celery 105
Fennel & Parsnip Bisque 105
Tomato Lentil Stew 107
Lentil Soup 110
Yellow Soup With Lentils 112
Veggie Thai Curry Soup 114
Colourful And Sweet Spread With Carrot 118

Cauliflower
Sweet Potato-kale Egg Casserole 22
Cauliflower Bowl With Avocado And Kale 29
Cheesy Cauliflower Casserole 32

Veggie Burger Patties 35
Meatless Shepherd's Pie 38
Colourful Roasted Cauliflower 39
Italian Vegetable Relish 55
Cauliflower Dill Soup 107
Decadent And Simple Alfredo With Cauliflower 118

Cheese
Quick Insalata Caprese 54

Cherry
Cherry & Coconut Oatmeal With Chia 23
Almond Oats With Cherries 26
Cheery Cherry Smoothie 122
Almond & Chia Bites With Cherries 127
Pressure Cooked Cherry Pie 134

Cherry Tomato
Sautéed Cherry Tomatoes With Scrambled Herb 26
Black Olive & Chickpea Lunch 38
Tofu Caprese Casserole 43
Tomato & Alfredo Penne 46

Chicken
Cute Tiny Chicken Burgers 85
Simple Cooked Whole Chicken 87
Herby Green Whole Chicken 94
Chicken & Ginger Soup 102
Tomato Chicken Soup 112
Comfortable Chicken Soup 113
Homemade Warm And Chunky Chicken Soup 114

Chicken Breast
Refreshingly Spicy Chicken Salad With Cumin And Mango 50
Ready To Eat Taco Salad 50
Tender Chicken Salad 51
Marinated Chicken Salad With Turmeric 59
Mexican-style Chicken With Butternut Squash 81
Chicken A La Tuscana 81
Basic Poached Wrapped Chicken 82
Fruity Chicken Breast With Cherry Sauce 82
Homemade Chicken & Pepper Cacciatore 85
Chicken Stir-fry With Bell Pepper 86
Mexican-style Chicken 86
Grilled Chicken Sandwiches 87
The Best General Tso's Chicken 88
Chicken Piccata 89
Hot & Spicy Shredded Chicken 90
Scallion & Broccoli Chicken Sauté 91
Italian Spinach Chicken 92
Refreshingly Spicy Chicken Salad With Cumin And Mango 50

Chicken Drumstick
Harissa Chicken Drumsticks 81

Chicken Thighs
Baked Basil Chicken 81
Cherry Tomato & Basil Chicken Casserole 82
Korean Chicken Thighs 82
Dairy Free Chicken Alfredo 83
Slow Cooker Chicken Curry 89
Authentic Chicken Curry With Coconut 92
Miso Chicken With Sesame 93
Turmeric Chicken & Chickpea Stew 93

Chickpea
Oat & Chickpea Patties With Avocado Dip 39
Cashew & Chickpea Curry 44
Mediterranean Pasta Salad 50
Hot Chickpea Salad 51
Chickpea & Vegetable Soup 100
Homemade Succotash Stew 106
Vegetable Chili 107

Chocolate
Peanut Chocolate Brownies 126
Vanilla Chocolate Pudding 128
Chocolate Fudge With Nuts 129
Coconut & Chocolate Brownies 131
Almond & Chocolate Cookies 132
Pistachios & Chocolate Popsicles 132
Walnut Chocolate Squares 133
Hearty Gelato With Chocolate And Cinnamon 133
Glazed Chili Chocolate Cake 133
Special Brownies With Chocolate And Coconut 135

Coconut Flake
Fantastic Fruit Cereal 27
Coconut Chocolate Barks 126

Coconut Flour
Hot Lentil Tacos With Guacamole 33

Coconut Milk
Strawberry & Pecan Breakfast 20
Giant Coconut Pancake 24
Maple Coconut Pancakes 27
Health Supportive Vegetable Curry 44
Distinctive Thai Soup With Potato 98
Proteinaceous Noodle Bowl With Vegetable 111
Great On Everything Ginger Sauce 118
Creamy Dressing With Sesame 119
Delicious Proteinaceous Smoothie 124
Tangy Yogurt With Coconut And Vanilla 134

Cod
Warm Cod & Zucchini Salad 55
Golden, Crispy, Buttery Pan-seared Cod 64
Mushroom & Olive Cod Fillets 65
Cod In Tomato Sauce 70
Dense Oven Roasted Cod And Shiitake Mushrooms 71
Shanghai Cod With Udon Noodles 72
Fancy Cod Stew With Cauliflower 74
Tropical-style Cod 77

Corn Tortilla
Soft Vegetarian Tacos 45

Crab Meat
Old Bay Crab Cakes 67
Creamy Crabmeat 74

Cranberry
Coconut Fruit Smoothie 28

Cream
Tempeh Garam Masala Bake 43
Spinach & Kale Soup With Fried Collards 101
Chocolate Peppermint Mousse 133

Cucumber
Smoothie That Can Soothe Inflammation 123

D

Daikon
Daikon Salad With Caramelized Onion 60
Daikon & Sweet Potato Soup 101

Date
Nutty Date Cake 131
Interesting Snack Bars With Date And Pecan 137

E

Egg
Healthy And Tasty Vanilla Crepes 20
Unforgettable Tasty Calamari 72
Easy To Make Egg Drop Soup 114
To Die For Homemade Mayonnaise 119

Eggplant
Minty Eggplant Salad 55

F

Firm Tofu
Scrambled Tofu With Bell Pepper 18
Hot And Spicy Scrambled Tofu And Spinach 35
Brussels Sprouts & Tofu Soup 96
Special Miso Soup 103
Tofu Miso Soup 106
Mushroom & Tofu Soup 106
Tofu & Almond Pancakes 141

Fish
Yummy Fish Curry 66
Minimalist Chowder With Whitefish 66
Simple Tacos With Fish And Pineapple Salsa 71
Fish Stew 73
Aromatic Curried Whitefish 74
Baked Swordfish With Cilantro And Pineapple 78

Fillet
Impressive Super Salad With Beetroot And Mackerel 48
Wonderful Baked Sea Bass With Tomatoes, Olives, And Capers 68
Fried Haddock With Roasted Beets 72
Greek-style Sea Bass 73
A Must-try Spicy Sea Bass Fillets With Ginger 74
Smoky Boneless Haddock With Pea Risotto 64
Pineapple Mahi-mahi 65

G

Greek Yogurt
Baked Tofu With Roasted Peppers 45
Gratifying Healthy Sweet Potato Salad With Mustard And Tarragon 52
Oily Salad With Celery And Kipper 53
Cold Cantaloupe Soup 104
Blueberry & Almond Greek Yogurt 138

Green Olive
Excellent Tapenade With Green Olive 117

Ground Turkey
Hawaiian-style Turkey Burgers 83
Italian Turkey Meatballs 87
Baked Turkey Meatballs 88
Turkey Stuffed Bell Peppers 92

H

Halibut Fillet
Saucy Tropical Halibut 63
Baked Garlicky Halibut With Lemon 63
Halibut Al Ajillo 66
Mango Halibut Curry 76

Hazelnut
Chocolate Campanelle With Hazelnuts 141

J

Jumbo Shrimp
Love At First Bite Shrimp Linguine 70

K

Kale
Frittata With Kale & Seeds 41
Sweet Potato & Kale Salad With Pine Nuts 55
Pleasant And Tender Salad With Kale 57
Summer Salad 59
Orange & Kale Salad 60

Kiwi
Sweet Kiwi Oatmeal Bars 21
Caribbean Pudding 135

L

Lamb
Classic And Minty Lamb Burgers 80
Cumin Lamb Meatballs With Aioli 80
Smoky Lamb Souvlaki 89
Delightful Stuffed Lamb With Peppers 89
Nutritious Apricot And Zucchini Mash With Lamb Shoulder 91
Rustic Lamb Stew 113

Lamb Chop
Chopped Lambs With Rosemary 90

Lamb Leg
Lamb Shanks Braised Under Pressure 84

Lemon
Lemony Honey With Ginger 119

Lettuce
No-bread Avocado Sandwich 27
Light And Excellent Salad With Mango And Avocado 48
Cucumber, Lettuce & Tomato Salad 49
Lettuce & Tomato Salad With Quinoa 49

Lobster Tail
Lobster & Parmesan Pasta 77

M

Mackerel
Beetroot Salad With Mackerel 51

Mango
Mango Rice Salad With Lime Dressing 59
Vegetarian Mango Smoothie With Green Tea And Turmeric 124
Mango Muffins With Chocolate Chips 130
Sherry-lime Mango Dessert 135
Mango & Coconut Rice Pudding 136

Mushroom
Veggie Panini 21
Thyme Cremini Oats 23
Mushroom Crepes 24
Full Of Flavour Braised Bok Choy With Shiitake Mushrooms 33
Festive Pesto-mushroom Burgers 33
Mushroom & Green Bean Biryani 41
Mushroom And Green Bean Salad 51
Mushroom & Wild Rice Salad 60
Tuna & Pea Cheesy Noodles 76
Carrot & Mushroom Broth 96
Shiitake Mushroom Soup 99
Spinach & Mushroom Soup 103
Mushroom & Bean Stew 104
Mixed Mushroom Soup 105
Soothing Broth With Mushrooms 111
Native Asian Soup With Squash And Shitake 115

N

Napa Cabbage
Radish & Cabbage Ginger Salad 49

O

Oat
Coconut Oat Bread 21
Pecan & Pumpkin Seed Oat Jars 25
Cherry & Chocolate Oatmeal 26
Cold Oatmeal With Apple And Cinnamon 27
Granola Dish With Buckwheat, Berries, Apples, Pumpkin Seeds And Sunflower Seeds 28
Cranberry Oat Cookies 28
Oatmeal Cookies With Hazelnuts 130
Raisin Oatmeal Biscuits 134
Oatmeal Chocolate Cookies 136
Tasty Haystack Cookies From Missouri 138

Olive
Quinoa A La Puttanesca 42

Orange
Orange-glazed Raspberry Muffins 25
Sweet Orange Crepes 30
Orange-bran Cups With Dates 30
Fruity Salad With Spinach, Orange, And Cranberry 55
Spiced Supreme Orange 135

P

Pea
Pea & Basil Fettuccine 41
Black-eyed Pea Soup 96
Dairy-free Split Pea Soup 99
Spinach, Rice & Bean Soup 102
Classic Minestrone Soup 113

Peach
Feels Like Summer Chutney With Mint 117
Coconut Peach Tart 140

Peanut
Breakfast Naan Bread 29

Pear
Morning Pecan & Pear Farro 26
Hazelnut & Pear Salad 57
Maple Walnut & Pear Salad 57
Irresistible Pear And Walnut Salad 60
Delicate Smoothie With Green Tea And Pear 122
Walnut Pears With Maple Glaze 131
Flavourful Glazed Maple Pears And Hazelnuts 137
Honey Pears With Pecans 138
Poached Pears With Green Tea 141

Pecan
Sweet And Special Spiced Pecans 128
Nightshade Free Cinnamon Pecans 138

Pineapple
Minty Juice With Pineapple And Cucumber 124

Plum
Cashew & Plum Cheesecake 130

Pork
Cheap Pork Sausage 93
Magnificent Herbaceous Pork Meatballs 94

Pork Chop
Worcestershire Pork Chops 84
Mustard Pork Chops With Collard Greens 87
Cinnamon Pork Chops In Apple Sauce 90
Classic Pork Chops And Creamy Green Beans 91

Pork Loin Chop
Thyme Pork Loin Bake 84
Rosemary Pork Loin 93
Easy Thai Pork Stew 98
Porky Salad With Spinach 52

Pork Sausage
Scotch Eggs With Pork Sausage And Hemp Seeds 30

Pork Shoulder
Sunday Pork Tacos 84
Korean Vegetable Salad With Smoky Crispy Kalua Pork 84
Incredible Tacos With Pork 93

Pork Tenderloin
Pecan-dusted Pork Tenderloin Slices 80
Spicy Lime Pork Tenderloins 88

Potato
Sweet Potato, Tomato, & Onion Frittata 19
Balanced Sweet Potatoes And Buckwheat 33
Yummy Spiced Soup With Almond And Sweet Potato 101
Celery & Sweet Potato Soup 103
Easy Sweet Potato Soup 109

Prawn
Crispy Coconut Prawns 77

Prosciutto
Egg Tart With Cheesy Yellow Sauce Or Cauliflower Alfredo 19

Pumpkin
Banana & Pumpkin Smoothie 19
Pumpkin Cake With Pistachios 25

Marinated Tempah And Spaghetti Squash 35
Lime Pumpkin Soup 108
Cayenne Pumpkin Soup 111
Savoury Spiced Pumpkin Pancakes 137

Pumpkin Puree
Chipotle Pumpkin Soup 108
Cinnamon Pumpkin Pie 127

Pumpkin Seed
Southern Smoothie With Sweet Potato 123

Q

Quinoa
Spicy Quinoa Bowl With Black Beans 21
Hazelnut & Raspberry Quinoa 22
Fiery Quinoa 24
Cherry Quinoa 25
Dilly Vegetable Quinoa 29
Quinoa & Chickpea Pot 37
Hot Quinoa Florentine 42
Herby Quinoa With Walnuts 44

R

Radish
Traditional Middle Eastern Chopped Salad 48
Radish & Fennel Salad With Eggs 49
Coleslaw & Spinach Salad With Grapefruit 52
Radish & Tomato Salad 53

Raspberry
Easiest Pressure-cooked Raspberry Curd 126

Rice
Lovely Spring Roll Wraps With Vegetable 34
Easy Maple Rice Pudding 139

S

Salmon
Smoked Salmon And Cucumber Wrap With Lettuce 22
High-spirited Salmon Salad 52
Cowboy Salad 53
Luscious Salad Niçoise 54
Arugula Salad With Salmon 58

Summer Time Sizzling Green Salad With Salmon 59
Yummy Salad With Sweet Potato And Salmon 60
Wild Salmon With Toasted Coconut 63
Sheet Pan Baked Salmon With Asparagus 64
Japanese Salmon Cakes 64
Pan-seared Salmon Au Pistou 65
Seared Salmon With Gremolata 65
Glazed And Curried Salmon With Quinoa 68
Cumin Salmon With Daikon Relish 69
Lime Salmon Burgers 69
Olive & Salmon Quinoa 69
Beautifully Glazed Salmon With Honey Mustard 70
Beneficial Baked Salmon Patties With Vegetables 73
Asian-inspired Salmon 74
Rich Grandma's Salmon Chowder 75
Fennel & Shallot Salmon Casserole 75
Mustardy Salmon Patties 76
Autenthic Salmon Ceviche 76
Rosemary Salmon With Orange Glaze 77
Skinless Salmon And Arugula With Lime 77

Sardine
Tasty Sardine Donburi 69
Sardine & Butter Bean Meal 75

Scallop
Tarragon Scallops 63
Extraordinary Scallops With Lime And Cilantro 66

Shrimp
Omelette With Smoky Shrimp 24
Enticing Japanese Salad With Avocado And Shrimp 57
Flavourful Shrimp And Grits 67
Battered Bite Size Shrimp With Gluten-free Coconut 68
Shrimp & Egg Risotto 68
Hot Shrimp Paella 69
Spicy Shrimp Scampi 72
One-skillet Shrimp With Sriracha Pak Choy 75
Lemony Spanish Shrimp With Parsley 76

Snow Pea
Tropical Salad 56

Spinach
Sneaky Fiery Veggie Burgers 34
Challenging Grain-free Fritters 40
Delicious Creamy Polenta With Buckwheat And Vegetable 41
Spinach & Cheese Sauté 43
Spinach Salad With Blackberries & Pecans 50
Balanced Salad With Avocado And Grapefruit 53

Lemony Spinach Salad 54
Spinach & Pomegranate Salad 55
Ruby Salad With Avocado Dressing 56
Chipotle Trout With Spinach 77
Power Green Cream Soup 97
Shallot Lontil Soup With Walnuts 100
Spinach Soup With Gnocchi 102
Vegetable Soup With Vermicelli 106
Sudanese Veggie Stew 113
Nut-free Green Smoothie Bowl 122
Tropical Strong Green Smoothie 122
For Advanced Green Juice 123

Squash
Hearty Stew With Kasha And Squash 107
Kabocha Squash Soup 108

Strawberry
Coconut Porridge With Strawberries 29
Lemony Lavender With Strawberry Compote 129
Energy Boosting Thumbprint Cookies With Strawberry Jam 139

T

Tilapia Fillet
Baked Tilapia With Chili Kale 63
Parsnip & Tilapia Bake 73

Tofu
Vegan Sloppy Joes 42
Tofu Cabbage Stir-fry 44

Tomato
Vegetarian Spaghetti Bolognese 32
Scrumptious Lentils With Tomatoes And Turmeric 32
Celery & Turmeric Lentils 38
Seitan & Lentil Chili 40
Sweet Potato Chili 41
Out Of This World Salad With Basil And Tomato 50
Tomato Bean & Bulgur Salad 52
Homemade Pizza With Lean Meat, Jalapeno, And Tapioca Starch 86
Tomato Lentil Dahl 97
Parsley Tomato Soup 104
Chili Gazpacho 105
Spanish Gazpacho 107
Lime Lentil Soup 109
Spicy Gazpacho 110
Rotini & Tomato Soup 111
Gluten-free Tortellini Minestrone Soup 111

Fantastic On Hand Marinara Sauce 117

Trout
Southern Trout With Crusty Pecan 67
Trout Fillets With Almond Crust 68
Mediterranean Trout 71
Seared Trout With Greek Yogurt Sauce 71
Chard Trout Fillets 78

Tuna
Pantry Salad With White Bean And Tuna 54
Fresh, Delicate And Meaty Tuna Steak With Fennel
Salad 64
Avocado & Tuna Toast 65
Hawaiian Tuna 67
Elegant Sesame Tuna With Asparagus 70
Briny Flavoured Herbed Tuna Cakes 75
Satisfying Peperonata With Seared Ahi Tuna 75

Turkey
Effortless Half-sour Pickled Salad 49
Appealing Hot Turkey 88
Enjoyable Braised Turkey Legs And Wilted Greens 92

Turkey Breast
Holiday Turkey 80
Creamy Turkey With Mushrooms 85
Lemon & Caper Turkey Scaloppine 90

Turkey Thighs
Aromatic Turkey With Mushrooms 89
Paleo Turkey Thighs With Mushroom 90

Turnip
Turnip & Rutabaga Soup 113

W

Walnut
Classic Walnut Waffles With Maple Syrup 27
Tropical Baked Fruit With Nut Pudding 140

Y

Yogurt
Herbaceous Dressing With Creamy Coconut 118
Impressive Parfait With Yogurt, Berry, And Walnut 136

Z

Zucchini
Pressure Cooked Ratatouille 32
Versatile Zucchini Patties 34
Zucchini & Chickpea Casserole 34
Stuffed Zucchini Rolls With Tempeh & Tofu 35
Soft Zucchini With White Beans And Olives Stuffing
36
Energy Boosting Bright Red Lentil Stew 44
Traditional Buckwheat Noodle Pad Thai 46
Zucchini & Bell Pepper Salad With Beans 56
African Zucchini Salad 59
Green Bean & Zucchini Velouté 103

Printed in Great Britain
by Amazon

20099178R00088